THE LIVING LIGHT DIALOGUE

Volume 14

THE LIVING LIGHT DIALOGUE

Volume 14

Through the mediumship of
Richard P. Goodwin

Living Light Books

The Living Light Dialogue Volume 14
Copyright © 2021 Serenity Association

Through the mediumship of Richard P. Goodwin.

All rights reserved. No portion of this book may be reproduced—electronically, mechanically, or via internet transmission—without advance, express written permission of the publisher except in the case of brief quotations embodied in critical articles and reviews. No derivative work—games, supplemental material, video—may be created without advance, express written permission of the publisher. For information address Living Light Books, P.O. Box 4187, San Rafael, CA 94913-4187.

Cover design copyright © 2021 by Serenity Association
Cover photograph by Serenity Association, 2021; copyright © 2021 by Serenity Association.

www.livinglight.org

Library of Congress Control Number 2007929762
ISBN: 978-1-947199-20-0

FIRST EDITION

This volume of teachings is dedicated to the spirit friends who brought to Earth the Living Light Philosophy. With eternal gratitude, we pray that we may demonstrate these principles and continue to bring to publication these teachings.

CONTENTS

Acknowledgment ix
Preface xi
Introduction xvii
A/V Class Private 1 3
A/V Class Private 2 31
A/V Class Private 3 55
A/V Class Private 4 83
A/V Class Private 5 105
A/V Class Private 6 141
A/V Class Private 7 171
A/V Class Private 8 199
A/V Class Private 9 233
A/V Class Private 10 265
A/V Class Private 11 299
A/V Class Private 12 339
A/V Class Private 13 365
A/V Class Private 14 401
A/V Class Private 15 443
Appendix 487

ACKNOWLEDGMENT

Grateful acknowledgement is made to the many friends and associates for invaluable aid in compiling this book, for their helpful suggestions, for their loyal interest and encouragement.

Special acknowledgement is due to those who painstakingly and selflessly transcribed and proofread the text.

PREFACE

It was through the mediumship of the Serenity Association founder, Mr. Richard P. Goodwin, that a philosophy known as the Living Light was given in more than 700 classes over a twenty-five-year period.

To be specific, the philosophy was imparted through Mr. Goodwin by a magistrate who had lived on Earth some 8,000 years ago. The former magistrate is known to Living Light students as "the Wise One," and he narrated the journey of his soul on the other side of life, the experiences—especially the difficulties—he encountered in having to face himself, as well as the teachings he earned to help himself through the realms in which he traveled. It was his decision to share the teachings with souls on both sides of "the curtain."

Prior to the advent of the Wise One, Mr. Goodwin had prayed for a teacher from the realms of light. Mr. Goodwin, since age fourteen, had been the instrument through which spirit was able to communicate with those seeking help. But he saw that his mediumship brought only temporary solace, because the people he was trying to help soon became fascinated with the phenomena and ignored the help that spirit was imparting. He prayed for someone who would bring forth teachings that would benefit any soul seeking a path to a greater awareness of himself and of God.

His prayers were answered in 1964 when the Wise One came through for the first time. Mr. Goodwin, at first apprehensive about what this new teacher would impart, was taken into deep trance and not able to control what was being revealed through him. Upon hearing the recorded classes afterward, however, he became convinced of the goodness of the teacher and of the value of the simple, beautiful teachings. This, then, was the beginning of the Living Light Philosophy given to Earth through the mediumship of Richard P. Goodwin.

In carrying out the request of the Wise One and Mr. Goodwin, students of the Serenity Association transcribed from audiotape the classes that had been brought through. Because most are in the form of teacher-student interaction, the classes became known as *The Living Light Dialogue*; and the students were instructed to publish the classes as a multi-volume set of the Living Light Philosophy. *Volume 1* was published in the autumn of 2007.

The present book, *Volume 14,* begins a new series of classes, the A/V Class Private series. As their name suggests, these classes were originally given as private classes and were to be shared and discussed only with those who were in attendance. The guidance Mr. Goodwin gave to his students requested that all classes be published after he had passed on to the higher life; and so, these private classes are now becoming more widely available. In many ways, these classes are of a more personal nature. The teacher frequently addressed the students by name and the students would often interact with each other. Many of the teacher's responses include references to the individual experiences of the questioner, and although this helps the student to better relate to the teaching, his responses also reveal the principle involved. Thus, in this series the names of the students are included, but have been replaced with more generic terms of identification to respect their privacy.

These teachings include guidance on the cleansing breath, which does not use audio tones, as well as the rhythmic cleansing breath, which uses tones. In total, six of the classes included the tones, specifically A/V Class Private 3 through 8. The audio cassettes of these classes included approximately three minutes of tones. However, the videotapes had the full spiritual exercise, which is almost eighteen minutes. The role of the tones in the rhythmic cleansing breath spiritual exercise is to guide the student on when to inhale and when to exhale. In addition to the tones, the videotapes included a sunrise, which was videotaped from the balcony of the Serenity Temple at the time these classes were given. For those students who are interested, the sunrise video (including the tones) may be found at a few of the more popular online video-sharing websites.

These classes began when the Serenity Spiritualist Church services ended and were held Sunday mornings at the Serenity Temple. Typically, a new semester or series of classes was announced frequently at various Serenity gatherings and well in advance of their commencement date. However, these classes began somewhat differently. The previous evening Serenity held a dinner social at the American Legion log cabin in San Anselmo, California. As that social was coming to a close, Mr. Goodwin announced to all who were present that the church services, which had been scheduled for the following morning, had ended and that all who were in attendance were welcomed to apply for a new series of classes that would begin the following morning. Although not everyone chose to attend these classes, a few new students did request to participate. Of course, many continuing students also applied. This particular volume includes fifteen classes, from A/V Class Private 1 through A/V Class Private 15, and cover the period of time from June 16, 1985, until September 22, 1985.

The foundation of the classes—the foundation of the Living Light Philosophy itself—is the Law of Personal Responsibility which states, in part, that we are responsible for all our experiences, and that our experiences are the return of the laws that we have established with our thoughts, acts, and deeds. Through greater awareness of our thoughts and by exercising our divine right of choice, we may choose to establish laws of greater harmony and goodness.

The Living Light Dialogue teaches that we have come to Earth to learn the lessons that are necessary to free us from the dictates and limits of our own thoughts and judgments, which are the mental patterns that we follow through our own lack of awareness and are so very potent, forceful, and limiting. These teachings guide us in making the necessary changes in our thinking in order to free ourselves from those patterns and to express our soul consciousness.

The choice of guiding the direction of our life, as stated by the Wise One when he speaks of being with a person, place, or thing, is, in essence, of being in this world and not a part of this world. He further explains that no matter what experiences we encounter, no matter what we do or do not do, we—our spirit—may view the experience in objectivity from a soul level of consciousness where peace reigns supreme.

The teachings of this volume help us to restore harmony or balance in our life by flooding the consciousness with spiritual affirmations and prayers, a few of which can be found in the appendix. When reason is restored, by balancing our sense functions with our soul faculties, we will consciously experience peace. Without annihilating our ego or our sense functions, we will find a pathway of expression for our soul. Where there was once disturbance, now there is acceptance. Where there was disease, now there is poise. And where there was hopelessness and despair, now there is reason, divine neutrality; and peace shows the way.

If you make the effort to apply these laws, such as, "If man is a law unto himself, what are you doing with the law that you are?", and demonstrate the wisdom of patience, the truth of this philosophy will be your living demonstration.

As the teacher states in CC 130, "My journey of many centuries and much experience has brought me here to Earth to share with you these simple teachings that have come as the effect of a long, long, long journey. Let not *your* journey be so long in the realms of illusion. For it is not necessary for you. For in your evolution, you have earned an awakening. But it is up to you to do something that is constructive and worthwhile."

INTRODUCTION

[This introduction was written by Mr. Goodwin and originally appeared in *The Living Light*, which were the first teachings of the Living Light Philosophy published in book form. The entire text of *The Living Light* was republished in *The Living Light Dialogue,* Volume 1.]

"Think, children. Think more often and think more deeply."

The teachings in this book were given as a progressive series of lessons to a group of four students who were sitting for spiritual unfoldment with me beginning in January of 1964. The communications were regular until October of that year, when nearly a seven-year silence ensued, and resumed in 1971 to the present. They were received in three ways by me as a channel. The main text was taped from a direct control of my voice in deep trance at special sittings of our group, during which I had no experience of the voice or what was being transmitted. A few scattered verses were given independently when I was privileged to see and hear our teacher clairvoyantly. I have also been a channel for this communicant when speaking from the podium at church and in answering difficult questions at our public seminars.

Nearly all we know about our teacher is contained in the lectures. He reports that he had tried for sixteen years to break through an interference barrier that the channel had to deep trance. When our conditions were in resonance with his patient wisdom, he came through ready to teach his understanding. I have seen him as an old man dressed in white with long flowing white hair. He has blue eyes, slightly smiling and deeply compassionate. I have always called him the Old Man. The students liked to call him the Wise One. He is surely one of those often called a Teacher of Light. I do not know his country, although he indicated at one time that he was from 6000 B.C., and a form of a judge in his time.

The text is often difficult, but it is complete, having been transcribed word for word from the original tapes recording the trance voice. It is presented with a minimum of punctuation to be freer for the individual interpretation of each reader. The lessons given before the long silence are phrased with many allegories often paradoxical. There are repetitions and renewals of theme, but it is explained that if an understanding is not perceived, compassion dictates that it be said again. Some of the topics have but a simple mention with little development but all are revealed, we are told, according to merit.

The Old Man is a fine teacher. He has in a hundred ways intertwined his allegory, progressive explanations, unfolding exercises, and timely references to reach a multitude of levels of individual understanding. A notable change is his more direct style of presentation beginning in 1971.

There is an endearing intimacy of person that can be felt through his lectures, a meaningful and loving encounter with a wise friend. Like an old man, he makes a mistake and conscientiously corrects himself a few paragraphs later. He listens often and carefully to our earnest discussions of his words. He consults with a group of experts on evolution and cites their learning in his lesson. His use of the direct address "children" or "my children" is not patronizing but infinitely loving and supportive.

A word must be said about the teachings. The Old Man makes clear that his lessons are not dogma, a creed or a narrow way, but simply his own understanding offered to us as a form of instruction to aid us in our own individual progression. When he speaks of Laws, he does not refer to man-made rules or moral traditions but to the cosmic and atomic way-things-are, the natural world of what-is, the universal laws of life, part of the original creative design and through which creation is fulfilled. These laws are beyond the possibility of being changed, suspended, transcended, or destroyed but they are ever a tool of mankind, not his master. First, through our awareness of the universal laws and then slowly through our developed understanding, the powers of creation are accessible to us. Not power over men's minds or circumstances, but power over whatever is selfish and imperfect in ourselves is the way up the eternal ladder of progression. When the Old Man cautions us concerning the Law of Responsibility or gives us a thinking exercise to explore the Law of Identity in a dynamic manner, he prepares us to take another step. And all move in accordance with the Law of What Can Be Borne.

Our teacher shows us how the two worlds are drawn together. In his realm, he describes, there is a great diversity of thought, many schools of understanding; but the Light is always known by the Light. Because of the interdependence of the two realms, listening to our discussions helped to clarify his teaching to others on his side of the curtain. His love and gratitude he humbly equates with ours.

The lessons to be perceived are not new, they are very old, but they are new to certain levels of our being. I would personally advise the reader, after reading this volume of discourses in full, to make a daily habit (or when there is a feeling or need) to sit quietly with the book. Open it at random and be guided to the Light by the passage that is there for the day. This technique is still used by the original students who were given the lessons and by many students after them who have studied in unfolding classes with me through these teachings.

Go beyond the words into feeling, into the immediate meanings for you. Touch into the inspiration that flows into the form of this book. It is from the Divine.

RICHARD P. GOODWIN
San Geronimo, California
June, 1972

A/V Class Private

A/V Class Private 1

Good morning, students. Welcome to our special Sunday morning classes.

And this morning we are going to discuss varied approaches in experiencing the goodness of life. We know from the many teachings that we have already received that it is through our efforts of controlling our mind that we experience the goodness of life. And so to those of you who find such difficulty and struggle in that effort, slow steps are sure steps when they're under the guidance of the light of reason.

And this morning I would like to share with you the slower steps of your ever-evolving being. Take a few moments each day to be consciously aware of what your mind tells you that you need. Take a few moments each day and write down these various things that your minds tell you that you are without. Then be aware, consciously, of what those things are, and one thing at a time you work with until you convince your mind that you have it. That is one of the many ways of working oneself through these realms of creation. By convincing yourself that you have what you judge that you need, you therefore satisfy the form that's in control, and in so satisfying that form, you permit your mind to allow your little soul to rise. For example, it is ever conviction, how convincing you are. If you have really convinced yourself that you need a certain thing and then you really believe that that in your mind that tells you you need it is you, you have established the Law of Mental Conviction. You must therefore use the same mind to convince yourself in consciousness that you do have it. That is one of the many ways of working through these realms of bondage. And you have that ability to do that, for you have already demonstrated that ability by believing that you need what your mind tells you that you need.

Now, for example, all judgments made by the mind are dependent upon experiences in your life that you have encountered that you believe are you. So therefore, in convincing yourself that you have what the form in your mind tells you that you need, you free yourself from the obstruction to the light of goodness that is within you. Say, for example, you have convinced yourself that you need more money, and you have further justified that conviction by declaring that you don't have it, you must use the same mental substance that you used to establish that form to establish the form that will neutralize it.

Now many people say to themselves, "I am very tired. I have worked very hard. I need a vacation." You don't have to move your physical body to have a vacation. You have to move your physical body to have a vacation if you have established within consciousness that a vacation to you is only the movement of your physical body to some other physical place. Try to understand this is established, these needs, by your mind; they are neutralized by your mind so that you can experience the goodness of life.

Now we've taught you this in many different ways: to place your attention upon the way and not upon the obstruction. For example, when you permit your mind to tell yourself something is difficult for you, you believe that you are what your mind is telling you; you therefore establish the Law of Conviction for you, and you experience the difficulty and the struggle that is necessary that you may (your mind) prove to you and, in so doing, convince you that you are right. Now you know that is not you. And it is only you as long as you believe that it is you. That is one of the many ways of working through those realms of consciousness. Try it with your small needs. Slowly but surely. And once you have had success, which is guaranteed through your own efforts, once you have had success in the small things your mind tells you that you need, you will have established the Law of Success and, slowly but surely, move to the bigger things in your life that you believe are you, that you believe are real. Reality is ever dependent upon your own view. What is real to you is dependent upon your conviction by your mind based upon what has been, never based upon what is.

And so our reality in life changes moment by moment. One moment our reality is a joyous and a happy experience; the next moment our reality is the direct opposite. That only reveals to us and demonstrates to us that reality is subject to what we do with our mind and our own thoughts. I'm sharing with you a little way to work your way through those realms of bondage and belief.

Without, you see, accepting the possibility of a change, without that acceptance you guarantee the continuity of a level of consciousness that you desire to be freed from. Only in accepting the possibility do you permit the human mind to begin to create new experiences in your life. Those experiences are dependent on the wisdom that you use in the creating processes.

You see, my friends, long ago I stated—and state once again—God is not a creator. Man is the creator. God, Goodness is the sustainer.

And so here today, this new dawn, this new day, this new moment and this new beginning, you are experiencing the new Serenity in reference to the philosophy that you have come here to experience.

Now on our last class I spoke to you on the many things of the shadows, the obstructions, and that down below. *[The teacher may be referring to class A/V Seminar 3, which was given on June 13, 1985.]* Let us look with a clear eye at what life truly has to offer. Let us change our own reality, for that is our right to change. We change our reality through our own effort to bring about a change within our consciousness. That is not only our right to do, it is our duty in keeping with our return within consciousness to what we are and not what we ofttimes think that we are. Whoever sees the obstruction in life to what they judge is their needs cannot be freed from what they judge is their need. Only by accepting the possibility, only, in so doing, by believing that it is happening, that it *is* taking place can the changes within your reality take place for you; only in the effort to declare each day and every day your right to the abundant good, your birthright. For that's what you are: the abundant good.

If you do not experience that, it is because you are not declaring your right. And when you do not declare your right within consciousness to the abundant goodness that you are, something else declares a right to it. That something else that declares a right to it is the error of ignorance. It is the demands of shallow forms to continue to survive. For all forms created by the mind are of mental substance and have no life, only that which you give them. You give form and thought and feeling life in your reality. Those who are in tune with your reality experience what you have created. They experience ever in keeping with the law that like shall attract like. Whoever enters your reality is subject to, within their own consciousness, whatever reality you insist on believing that you are.

So in these stages of evolution, while so much time and effort is spent in the realms of believing, use the realms of believing, those realms you create, to your benefit, not to your detriment. Use them wisely. If you must believe, then believe in the possibility of something without need. Believe in the possibility of your right to the experience of fulfillment. That is how the realms of belief offer their bondage. It is a realm we all must pass through. There is no way around it. We all experience, my students, I assure you. Some of us take long. And some of us seemingly short.

To those who receive the way and use it not must pay a greater price. To those who know not the way, therefore, have yet to earn their right to the way. There is a vast difference in creation between the two. For whoever knows the way and uses it not must pay a greater price when the day comes that they inspire themselves to use it.

Now it's time to pause for a few moments, for there are so many questions of your mind. It's time for you, in your thinking, to ask the questions in reference to that realm [with] which minds are so familiar. And so I will, as you raise your hands, share with you what I have, in my many centuries of experience, earned a little. *[After a short pause, the teacher continues.]* Fear not, for fear is only an expression of the possibility that whatever you believe you are may be threatened. *[After another pause, the teacher again continues.]* And I know you will not appreciate such a long pause on your video class. Yes, the lady there, please.

This is on a different subject, but it's a question that I have. Could you speak on how fear and procrastination work together?

Yes, indeed. Whatever in life we choose to put off or to procrastinate, we do not have to face. Therefore, we do not have to experience the fear that we judge the experience will offer us. For example, we ofttimes in life know that we should make a change. Would you not agree?

Yes.

A change within our mind. And when we think about making that change, we put it off and we procrastinate. Would you not agree?

Yes.

We do that because we believe those thoughts in our mind that rise up, that know if you are permitted to make a change within consciousness, they will no longer have the vitality, the substance of energy, that you are providing them. And therefore, whenever, *whenever* they [the forms] are in control of the mind and a person believes that they are them, then they [the people] do not do what they [the people] want to do. And they fear even the thought of doing it.

Now to control those things when you consciously choose to make a change, it is necessary to bring about not only a change in the mental world but a change of the chemistry of the human body to which the mental world is subject. For example, the physical world is subject to the mental world; and the mental world is subject in creation to the physical world. And so the physical, chemical changes must be brought about at the time of one's choice to make the necessary changes.

Now I have spoken before, and to some of my students I have given, what is known as the cleansing breath. I will demonstrate that for you, whereas these classes are restricted to the students in attendance, if you wish.

Please.

First of all, the spine must be kept comfortably and erect for the energy flows from the base of the spine up over the human brain. The palms must be upturned. In a state of complete relaxation and an erect spine, you inhale through the mouth. It's known as a cleansing breath. As you do so, you inhale that which you have chosen to do. Do you understand? You inhale that, then you hold the breath, and then you exhale it through the nostrils. Now the longer you hold the breath comfortably, you solidify the chemistry; you solidify within consciousness the form that you are creating in a mental world. You understand? *[The teacher demonstrates the cleansing breath. Each step in the cleansing breath (the inhale, the holding, and the exhale) was approximately eighteen seconds.]*

Now if you do that properly, *properly*, you will experience the Living Light known as, the fluid known as *prana* in the physical body. You will experience it in each and every part of your little temple of God, your human body. You will especially experience it in the very tips of your toes. And in so doing, you will begin to establish the solidification of the change you wish to make.

One thing it's time to reveal to you, in reference to that cleansing process, is that as you are holding the breath and as you are exhaling the breath, the tip of your tongue at that particular time should be touching the roof, the roof of your mouth, lightly. You should not attempt to overdo the cleansing breath. It should be done daily. It should be done in an ever-increasing and strengthening way. You actually solidify within the consciousness that change.

Now when you desire, through conscious choice, a particular change, be rest assured that you should make that change within mental thought as short as possible. Now when that breath is being held at that time, there is a complete solidification within the consciousness for the chemistry of the physical body has been brought about and changed at that moment. Do you understand? Do you have any further questions on that particular cleansing process?

For each thing that you want to change—

Speak right up, please.

For each thing that you want to change, you should have a separate process of the cleansing breath?

For each thing you want to change is one step at a time. The cleansing breath is indispensable to that change. Now when 51 percent of this private class body demonstrate their ability in your world to bringing about those changes, at that time I will share with you the breath of power. You only require (to bring about the change in mental consciousness) the cleansing breath and not the other. Does that help with your question?

Thank you.

You're welcome. The gentleman—I'm sorry, the lady there is waiting. Yes.

I was wondering what the difference between belief and fulfillment of life is and acceptance of fulfillment of life.

Yes, that is a wonderful question in the difference in the mental realms between the belief in the fulfillment of life and the acceptance of the fulfillment of life. When one no longer is convinced by mental substance that they are the thought, they are then, at that time, qualified and demonstrate the acceptance of the fulfillment of life for they are what they are. They no longer believe they are the thought that passes through their consciousness. And that is the difference between the acceptance—what you are is the acceptance; what you are not is subject to belief. Does that help with that question? That's very important to understand. What you are is the will of Goodness, the will of God; that is total acceptance. What you are not is the belief in the thoughts—so varied they are—that are passing through your consciousness. Yes. Does that help you?

Yes. Thank you.

Certainly. The gentleman here, please.

Yes. During, during our state of, when we're doing the cleansing breath and we're holding it, should we be trying to image the change that we [are] trying to make?

That is not necessary for in the, in reference to imaging, you won't have to; this is another process that even is simpler to do for you. For example, when you inhale, you inhale the change itself, you understand? Say that you want a change in your life; you want to feel good. So as you are inhaling, you are feeling good. Do you understand the importance of that? You see, you must learn to be what you choose to be while you are identified with the realms of belief.

And, like the lady here just asked, the difference between accepting the fulfillment of life and believing you have the fulfillment of life. Believing you have the fulfillment of life is working and neutralizing what you already believe that you needed because you don't have it. That's working with belief. Accepting the fulfillment of life, there is no need, there is no belief, for you are. Does that help with your question?

Yes.

Now, for example—Not quite. It doesn't quite help with your question. So we'll go on with that. You believe you have a need. Is that correct?

Yes, sir.

At times. Because you believe you have a need, you demonstrate at those moments of belief what you are not.

Yes, sir.

And being convinced that you are what you are not, you must use the processes to neutralize the believing what you are not and experiencing need to believing what you are not and experiencing fulfillment. Does that help with your question?

Yes, sir.

The truth of the matter is you don't need either, but as long as you believe you are your thought, then you must work with that realm of belief. You see, when a person identifies with what they are not, we identify with the limited, physical body. That is not what we are. We, however, believe that we are a limited, physical body. Is that not correct?

Yes, sir.

Because we have convinced our self and we believe that we are separate and we believe that we are different and we believe that we are unique and we believe that we are red hair; we believe that we are black hair; we believe we have this; we believe we do not have that because we have convinced our self through the realms of belief, the process of the cleansing breath to establish fulfillment of the needs by believing that you are what you are not is what we are discussing. Does that help with your question?

Yes, sir. It does.

Yes. So as you do your cleansing breath, which—you see, my friends, the cleansing breath cleans the forms, permits you to solidify within consciousness what it is that you want that is subject to your divine right. Remember, what it is that you want can only be for you in your realm of conscious right, not the rights of another in those realms of belief. For to tempt to desire something that you declare you need that is under the control of another individualized soul is to tempt absolute disaster from below. Did that help with your question?

Yes, sir.

Now, I have tried—and will continue in my efforts with you—to show you the wisdom of accepting that which you are, instead of the other process of believing what you are not and neutralizing the beliefs of needs. You see, my friends, it's an evolutionary process. But let us work with what we are in at the moment. Show me, one student please rise, who no longer believes they are the physical form that they believe that they are. To that student I will move to the power breath. The power breath is the right and domain of the world of spirit. You are spirit; so it is your right. But only your right when you demonstrate and identify with it. Does that help with your question?

It does. Thank you.

Yes, you're more than welcome. Anyone else have any questions in experiencing the good of life while identified to believing that they are the limit in which they believe they are? Yes.

Could you—is there such a thing as an addictive personality? Is there truth to that, that some have addicting addictions?

Addicted personality?

Right.

Yes. When a person has to do a certain thing and they believe that what they have to do is them and they are not able to set it aside for five minutes, they have to do it and have to do it now, that is, in your world, what you could call an addiction. It is completely and totally controlling what you are. And it is doing so by your belief that you are the thought in mental substance at any moment. Does that help with your question?

Yes.

Very important. Yes. Yes, the lady here, please.

At the time of the cleansing breath, while you're holding it, does that put you in neutrality at that time so that you become the true I, if you're doing it correctly?

What is being given to you is the cleansing breath so that you may place within your consciousness the solidification of what it is that you desire that is in your right, in your world, in your domain, not transgressing the rights of another individualized soul. So the neutralizing process in that realm of belief is solidifying a form opposite and contrary to the form that is within the consciousness that you believe that you are and, from that belief, experience the need that it tells you you are.

I see.

[Does] that help with your question?

Yes.

You are bringing about a neutralization in the process. Now when that form is solidified to the point that you believe you are the new form that you have created, that neutralizes (energy-wise) out the form that you have been believing that you are, and that's when you go to work and create this new form.

Thank you.

Yes. For the creation of it, you understand, is the battle between the new form you have created in the realms of belief with the old form that is long created. It has much energy that you have already directed to it (the old form), through your identification with it, your belief and conviction that you are it. And the cleansing breath will permit the solidification, chemical-wise, within your being. Yes.

Thank you.

You're welcome. Yes, the lady there, please.

Is it correct that we have been advised to be careful in doing the cleansing breath around another person? Is that correct?

Absolutely. Because I can assure you that I thought well and long before this moment and doing the cleansing breath simply as a demonstration. For forms exist in realms your physical sight does not see. And so one must choose wisely, should have fresh air, and should have control of their mind when they're doing their cleansing breath.

Thank you.

Of course, you can only accept the forms that would be in harmony with the level that may be in control at the moment of your own consciousness. However, because there are eighty-one levels of consciousness and it is rare that a person is aware which level they're on at any moment, it would behoove a person, of course, to choose the tree to inhale [a] form. You know, such a neutral thing. It just is, you see. Happy as can be. Expressing itself. Especially if it's watered and cared for. You wouldn't want to stand under a tree that hadn't been cared for, that wasn't happy. Does that help with your question?

Yes. Thank you.

The lady in back of you, please. Yes, the lady there.

I'm, I'm sorry. It's gone.

It will return, for once something rises within the consciousness and knowing how we believe we are our mind nothing is ever lost to us. Someday it shall return. I'll come back to you. Yes. *[After a short pause, the teacher continues.]* Now don't you think you students deserve a few answers to a few questions? I haven't come to make you cripples, you know. That's not my purpose. And I know you won't appreciate too long an audio silence. We may have to put some music in that area. Hmm. Yes.

I'd like to ask the most advisable position to do our resting in, like in the evening.

First of all, prior to all rest, I would advise the cleansing breath. Prior to all rest. And once the cleansing breath has been completed, to recline in a reclining position, not to exceed a 45-degree reclining angle. That's the best position that you can have for true rest. The head should never be permitted to be lower than the feet for a proper reclining position for rest. Does that help with your question? Yes.

And I'd also like to ask, Is it necessary to have the head straight rather than turned or does it matter?

Because of the physical position of the spine and because of the fluids that rise and because those fluids are ofttimes obstructed in certain centers—unfortunately so often in the earth center, usually, however, in the water center—it is advisable, of course, to keep the head and neck relaxed and in alignment with the spinal column. You see, my friends, it is very important that through these cleansing breaths, that these fluids may, this life force that is within your physical body, that it may be risen by the power of your will [and] pass the water center, that it may rise, through your conscious effort, to the air center where the faculty of reason rules supreme. So it is in the air center that you will bring about a balance in your life and be freed from these forms that convince you, you are them. Yes.

I'd also like to ask, Does having a light on during the resting period interfere in any way? And from where does the desire come to want the light on?

Fear. It is a mental thing. And, you see, the light within is the light of our life. And when we turn the light on within our consciousness, there is no dependence on something outside for the right that is our duty to the light within. And so a person, especially a child, should learn very early in the formative months that the light gets turned on in their consciousness. Do not permit them or be so unkind to a child as to addict them to dependence on light without when it is at the sacrifice of turning the light on within. Does that help with your question?

Thank you.

You're welcome. Yes.

Do we do the cleansing breath nine times or is once enough?

Well, nine times is totality. And that law applies beautifully to the cleansing breath. One should be sure that their physical position and their spine, especially at the area of what you call the lower back, is erect. That is very, very important in the cleansing breath and to rest in a reclining position. Does that help with your question? You see, long ago so much of this was given to my students and then once again because, you see, the lessons are learned only through experiences and repetition.

Their benefits and their value reveal themselves when the price in old creation is well paid.

[Thank you.]

You're welcome. Yes, the lady there, please.

What is the length of the rest period after the cleansing—

Not to exceed twenty minutes. Not to exceed twenty minutes. And when you are doing it properly, twenty minutes will be more refreshing than any twenty hours you've ever slept in your life. Twenty minutes will completely restore and rejuvenate your being. Twenty minutes.

Thank you.

You're welcome. Yes.

Should this cleansing breath be used only for forms, self-forms or can it be used for universal problems?

No, no. It should be used only for one's own universe, for self-forms because you are working in a realm of belief and you are responsible personally for your realm of belief. Working in universal consciousness is the next step. When you demonstrate what you are and not what you believe you are, belief no longer exists; need no longer exists; fulfillment *is*. And that is the next step where, in working with universal situations, the power breath would be used following the cleansing breath. Yes.

You spoke about solidifying a form of change of your choice. And the other form, which is battling with it.

Correct.

Now you had spoken before to us about speaking to the form that you want to go and telling it to go to sleep.

That is correct. That takes great use of the power of will. When that doesn't work, you use the other method.

The other method?

The one that I've just given you.

The cleansing breath.

You see, my friends, there are many ways to accomplish the same good. And because people and their minds are on various levels of consciousness, one should wisely use that which works for them. And I have shared with you many, many ways and will continue to share with you in different methods to gain control over that realm, which is not only your divine right to control, it is your duty to control.

Some people, in different stages of evolution, are more apt to be able to create new forms rather than to put the other ones to sleep. To put an existing form to sleep that you believe that you are takes great power of your will. To create another form does not take as much and the battle is not as strong; it's only a skirmish. Hmm? Yes.

Yes, the gentleman here, please.

Yes. In, in preparation of, to do the cleansing breath, like, all right, most of us wake up out of sleep, we'd be asleep. Or off somewhere and, I mean, is it all right for us to take a shower and sit down for a minute and then do the cleansing breath?

Nine times. It would be in your best interest—you know, so many people think that they awake in the morning and believe they're still half asleep. And they have a great difficulty. Those forms are in control. And so upon awakening in the morning, as long as you're upright, your spine is erect, it would be advisable to do the cleansing breath immediately. Then take your shower and do all your other things of creation, then come back and do your cleansing breath again.

Thank you.

Yes. You're welcome. Yes.

Are the nine times meant to be consecutively?

Yes.

I see. Thank you.

Do not overdo it by trying to inhale more oxygen than you have trained yourself to do. Slow steps are sure steps. And especially to those who are talented in singing, how extremely beneficial for them, especially it will be, though it's extremely beneficial for everyone. Proper effort of placing the correct image in consciousness through inhaling it and solidifying it, they will, of course, experience all those other benefits. You cannot experience the benefits until you start doing it. And whoever experienced the benefit from any effort in life by trying for one or two times? Hmm?

Yes.

Yes.

Thank you.

Yes, the gentleman there, please.

When I have . . .

Speak right up.

When I believe that I am a judgment that I do not have—

Well, I'm sorry I'm going to say I can't hear you. My special technician over here tells me that he can't hear you. *[The teacher refers to the technician recording the class.]* I can hear you, but you're the ones that are going to be getting the tape. So you start over again, and let's hear how you sound when you talk to a lady that you're trying to correct. *[Some students laugh.]*

When I have a belief and that belief is a denial and it tells me that it's something that I do not have, in consciousness I, when I say that I do have it, the original belief that says that I do not have it has a field day.

May I say one thing at this time?

Yes, sir.

Why, certainly, because justification, justifications are the defenses of all judgments. And so when you tell yourself that you do have it, it has a field day in justifying how foolish you are. Is that not correct?

That's correct!

All right. Now this is why I have given you the cleansing breath. You see, when you inhale that you do have it, in the process of inhaling and especially at the time you are holding your breath, you solidify you do have it. No new thought can enter your mind. It is physically, chemically, and mentally impossible. And so that's where you have a chance, so to speak, to get it established. Give it birth and solidify it. Now once you exhale your breath, they'll have a great field day. Do another cleansing breath. And every time it rises do another cleansing breath. Don't you understand, you see, that's the way that realm works? And so when that starts all of its defense mechanisms, because it uses justifications to defend itself, then you just take another cleansing breath. And at the time you're holding it, you make your new form even more solidified.

You see, all of your experiences in life are effects of the forms that you've created in consciousness and continue to create. You see, the physical manifestations, which [are] your so-called experiences in life, are nothing more than the solidification of mental substance in what you call [the] physical world returning to you. That's all that they are. You see?

So if you want new experiences, this is a new dawn, a new life, a new reality, then solidify what it is that you want that's within your own domain and right and divine right. And keep it solidified. Work on it. You know, there's no limit to the cleansing breath. You can do it—do it in sessions at nine times. And so you rest a little bit; those other old forms rise up; do the cleansing breath again. And again. And again. And again. And again. And soon you will experience a temporary state of what you judge is exhaustion, and you will feel good. *[Several students laugh.]* Does that help with your question?

Yes. Thank you.

Thank you. Hmm. It is best in your world, and I'm sure you will agree, to be exhausted if the effect of the exhaustion is feeling good. And I'm sure you've all had experiences that you only felt good when you were totally exhausted.

And my new student here is in the wrong position for registering what's going on. And I think it's a terrible waste not only of his money, [but] of his effort. And I'm sure he won't do that again, for if he feels tired, then it is only an expression of a judgment. And you have my permission while I'm working here to sit straight, with your spine, your hands aside, and do your cleansing breath of what a beautiful day and how wide awake you are. Now, please. The secretary here is permitted to help him. Please. Now.

Now the rest of you have any questions?

Go right ahead. You step right over there. Do your cleansing breath, young man. I have eyes in more than one world.

Now we'll continue on with our questions, as my student is doing his cleansing breath. In fact, I'll demonstrate it once again for him as a new student. *[The teacher demonstrates the cleansing breath. The inhale, holding, and exhale portions of the cleansing breath are each approximately eleven seconds.]* Don't forget, my student, to touch the roof of your mouth with the tip of your tongue. Fine.

Now we'll go on with our questions, please. All of my students, four-legged and two-legged—here now, just let him be. *[The teacher refers to one of his four-legged students.]* My, oh my. It is very important for most of you do not have the rhythm breath. You do not have the other various breaths that are in your best interest.

And I want my new student to know, for his soul, that a wise man does not share what he worked so hard to attain in life with the uninitiated. Hmm? You'll be fine. Do your cleansing breath again; you're just beginning to get a new form in there. Do your cleansing breath again! And again! And again! Such a beautiful day.

Now any more questions here? I would have plenty of questions if I were sitting where you are. I would be so filled with questions I don't know if I would ever stop. I remember those centuries long ago. Yes?

You advised no longer than a twenty-minute rest after the cleansing breath and I'd like to ask, in the evening instead of doing our so-called rest or sleep, which we do for an extended period, would it be advisable to wake up every twenty minutes and rest in intervals?

As long as you awaken from within and don't set out some outside crutch to depend upon. It is not in your best interest to depend upon an alarm clock that is outside. Your own inner light, if it awakens you in an hour, do your cleansing breath and go back to rest. If it awakens you again, do your cleansing breath and go back to rest. For rest is far more valuable than sleep: the forms are not feeding off of your vitality when you are resting. That help with your question?

Yes. Thank you.

You're welcome. Yes, the lady here, please.

If a person wanted to quit a habit or, or change a habit or just not do it anymore, what new form would they, would they have when they were doing the cleansing breath or—

Why, the new habit they want to create. Why, in that realm, it's all habit. It's all serving patterns established. So you're—try to understand you're working with a realm, identified with a realm where habit is the king of kings. And so habit is habit. "That's the realm I'm working with. I don't like that habit. God guide me to a new habit, because this is a realm of habits." That particular realm. Hmm? So there are many habits that you would find most beneficial. And when you're tired of the habit controlling you, you create a new habit. And you demonstrate your ability in that realm to change habits by creating new ones.

You see, my friends, it's like people, you know, they say, "Oh, they have that habit of drinking." Well, they no longer drink anymore. Or they have that habit of smoking. "Why, they're so wonderful; they've grown so spiritual and awakened they no longer smoke anymore." Well, I can assure you that each and every habit only changes for another one. Now, for example, I have witnessed in your world many people who have decided they're going to be free from the habit of smoking. And I have witnessed, yes, they no longer physically smoke; they're now smoking in another way. They're smoking in the glory of their superiority and their special ability that everyone else is so pathetic. So they have a new habit, you see. Tell me, if you must make choices and see differences, which habit would you prefer?

Smoking. [The student laughs.]

You know what you got, and if you have not made the judgment it's killing you off, then be grateful you got it. And when you choose, choose something that you consciously, intelligently want to choose. Hmm? Does that help with your question on habits?

Yes, very much.

Yes. Such a lovely day. I prefer my classes this way in your world. *[This class was held outdoors in the backyard garden of the temple.]* More informal. And I expect from you more questions, for it reveals, on your part, more interest. It reveals, on your part, your willingness to find out what you want to find out. To be informed is a wise policy, especially in the realms you believe that you are. Hmm? Yes.

Would, would changing a habit include—is an allergy a habit, like an allergy to an animal? Could you overcome that by this cleansing breath?

Well, may I say this, first of all, the judgment has to be made by the human consciousness that you have a certain susceptibility to something and by having that susceptibility you are the victim of it. Now if you want to call that an allergy, that is fine. Because what you do—as I said earlier, the human mind and mental substance affects the physical body. The physical body in turn has its reaction upon the mental body. So you have action and reaction, you see, just like a yo-yo, up and down, between the mental body and the physical body. Now if a person has decided through errors of ignorance that *[The teacher sniffs several times.]* there's something there that they're the victim of, then they are in service to it. Because it is a chemical within the physical body and because mental substance the physical body is subject to, by working with the physical chemical and a change in the mental consciousness, yes, you may create a new belief that you are no longer the victim of that *[The teacher again sniffs several times.]* for you now have a new established form. But you have to take slow steps and sure steps.

You see, how long it takes in the solidification of a new form for you to experience the reality of it is ever dependent upon your absolute conviction that you are your mind. Now if you are as convinced that you are still your mind as you were convinced that you were at the time you created the other habit, then you shall neutralize the other habit.

You see, the mind is a very interesting, intricate, and delicate thing. You can convince it of anything, through a little effort. But you must remember, in convincing yourself of anything, the judgment is ever dependent upon all your senses. For example, say that you have convinced yourself you don't have any money. Then you work to convince yourself that you do. Well, your form that you're trying to neutralize to bring about this new form has all this defense mechanism: "Well, there's nothing physical in my hand. I haven't seen it in my bank account." Isn't that right, my good student over there? And it starts its whole justification or defense process. It is defending itself. Do you understand?

Yes.

And it's using all of your senses to justify and to convince you that that's foolish. You must learn through wisdom, through effort. And you have a very good chance when you have the new form solidified. Now at the process of solidification (when the breath is held), you will have no battle. Oh, everything will be just beautiful. That thought is solidified. It is when you exhale that the other one will come in. And it is when you [are] inhaling [that] it is trying to get it. But at the moment of holding your breath, that form you wish to be and believe you are must be absolutely solidified in your consciousness, absolutely convinced, you see. Nothing will disturb it when you hold your breath. But everything will come after it when you breathe again. Does that help with your question? Yes.

May I ask as someone going through that—

Certainly.

—is that, like if you want an animal very much and you've had this other judgment, it's like giving that form a carrot and that'll help make it a little stronger, won't it? I mean, my desire form.

Well, what you, what—yes, it will appear to you. You see, it will appear in keeping with the solidification within the consciousness. Then, you see, the physical substance moves in to fit the mold. Do you understand? That's what actually happens, you see. You see, right now you are experiencing physical substance moving in to fill the mold that you have created of want.

Uh-huh.

Now that's well solidified, and you have the experience in the physical world. Now you want to have—you want the experience of an animal in your life. All right. So that has to be solidified in consciousness so that it neutralizes out the other form you already believe that you have. Then, after that neutralization takes place, this new form, this experience you have, this lovely little dog is solidified within your consciousness. And when it is properly solidified, this dog will fit into it. Do you understand?

Yes.

That's what happens in all experiences, my dear. That's just exactly the way that realm, that you believe you are, that's how it works and always did. Yes, there [is] another question. The lady there, please.

When you're working with someone—when one is working with someone and you're—and conflict arises where you both feel you're in the right, what is the best—and that keeps happening— what is the best course to take? What would be the best . . .

To create, in reference to the conflict, to create a form within your consciousness that is the opposite of conflict: that of harmony. And whenever your senses in any way register the other person, you are in the belief that you are your thought and you experience your new form you have created and for you there is only harmony, no matter what they think or do. Do you understand?

Yes.

Yes.

Thank you.

That's how that realm works. Yes, the gentleman there, please.

You made reference earlier to certain centers.

Yes?

Could you speak more on those centers? [The student who was previously encouraged to speak more loudly asks another question.]

What was that you said?

You made reference to certain centers earlier in this class.

Yes.

Could you speak more on those centers?

Well, we have a little time. You know we have class every Sunday now, or didn't you know that?

Yes, sir.

All right. Earth. Fire. Water. Air. How many do you have?

Four.

Earth. Fire. Water. Air. You have four?

Yes, sir.

Do you understand those four?

No.

You can relate to earth, can't you?

Yes.

Fire?

Yes.

I know you can relate to fire. Those are the realms of lust. Water? *[After a short pause, the teacher continues.]* You certainly can relate to emotion, can't you.

Yes, I can.

Oh, very good for you. Don't worry, you're not alone in relating to the fire center. Air? *[After another short pause, the teacher again continues.]* Thinking. Reason. Hmm? You can relate to that, can't you?

Yes.

Hmm. Electric. You are electric, aren't you?

Yes.

Magnetic.

Yes.

Hmm. How many do you have?

Six.

You do? I think that's enough for this class. We have class every Sunday. Hope that's helped you.

Thank you.

The lady there's waiting for . . .

Yes. Is my understanding—the less we believe we are our minds, is, that you said, the harder it is to create new forms because that's of the mental realms. Was that my understanding?

The less you believe that you are your mind, the more you accept what you are and not what you believe that you are. I am speaking today on using methods in the realms where it is so difficult because people still believe they are their physical form. Now you do not believe you are the form of the little fellow lying next to you, do you? *[Lying beside the student was her infant and a dog.]*

Oh, yes, I have. [The student may be referring to her child.]

That four-legged one?

This one?

That's the one I'm speaking of. You don't believe that you're that form, do you? There's the difficulty, see? So you believe you are *your* form.

Right.

That's you.

Right.

You are not my four-legged student that's next to you.

Right.

I see. You really believe that?

Yes.

Therefore, it is best for you to work with the realm of belief. So [when] you believe that you do not have something, then work with the cleansing breath and establish the new form and experience that you do have [it]. And therefore, the other form will die from lack of energy, from lack of attention in your consciousness. Did that help you?

Yes.

Yes. Because, you see, no one's going to push a light in your consciousness that you may say and really know, not believe or disbelieve, "I am not this suit. I do not feel this suit. I do not experience this suit. I use this suit." So they have a little ways to go there. So we're working today in sharing with you methods to use while still over-identified and, therefore, believing and in bondage and in limit to a physical piece of clay.

Thank you.

That help with your question?

It does.

Now when in evolution there is no longer thought, there's no longer difference, then you will know beyond a shadow of any and all doubt you are the Light, and that Light is inside the little four-legged student that's lying beside you there.

Yes.

Yes. Yes. Thank you.

This, the cleansing breath, it's freeing us of something. Would you tell us what it's freeing us from?

What is the cleansing breath freeing one from?

Yes.

It's freeing one from, in the realms to which they over-identify, it is freeing them from forms that bring them experiences that they judge are not beneficial and they don't like them.

Only ones that we judge that are not beneficial.

Why, certainly. That's the only ones you would be even tempted to work on. The other ones wouldn't even get your attention. They're just fine. *[A few students laugh.]* You see, you see, my friends, try to understand that you are neutralizing these seeming experiences which are only filling the vacuum of these created forms, you see. You see, they are coming into your world in keeping with your creating them within consciousness. And so while you still believe you are that physical suit, then you work with that realm who has control of that physical suit, you see. Because you believe that you are your thought, you believe you are what you are not. You do believe you are that form you're in, don't you?

Yes, sir.

What happens when you leave it? What are we going to do with that form when it's down, put down below? When they come with a shovel and they put it there to fertilize the lawn, what are we going to do with that then?

This form?

Yes, the one you believe you are. What are you going to do if I get the shovel and put it down there to fertilize the tree over there? Hmm? What are you going to do then? What are you going to do? Are you going to be angry with me if I do that?

Well, if I'm still—

You have no—you won't be able to use it. You know, you know, it's like one of those throw away thrift shops. You won't be able to use it. You won't be able to move it. You won't be able to see through it. You won't be able to hear through it. Are you going to be angry if I take a shovel and plant it there so I can get some use out of it for that lovely tree?

I hope not.

Ah, my dear student, then start working on these things. For it came from there, it shall return to there, for that is the law that is demonstrable. From there it came, down below (the form) and to down below it is destined to return. So a wise man makes effort to stop believing so much that he is what belongs to that down there. Now the wise use of it, instead of just throwing it over there, is to simply fertilize, you know. Turn it to fertilizer because there's a lot of chemicals there that'll help the flowers and the plants to grow beautifully. Hmm?

And another thing, you see, cremation, before we conclude today's class, is a fine purifying process. We all are very familiar with the fire center. And therefore, we can easily relate when the old shoe is ready for down below to send it through the center which we are most familiar with.

And thank you so much and good day, my good students. 'Til next time.

JUNE 16, 1985

A/V Class Private 2

Good morning, class, and welcome to this beautiful day, this new dawn, this new beginning.

If any one of you cannot hear me, please raise your hand. I see that you can, and we'll begin today's private class with the enjoyment of sleep. Considering so many still believe that they enjoy sleeping, I felt that it would be a good discussion to begin our class with today.

Now a person says to themselves, "Oh, I enjoy sleeping so much." And yet a person does not and is not aware of joy or sadness while they are sleeping. They are not consciously aware of what is happening, let alone to declare that it is joyful or its opposite. They are, however, aware of a judgment that justifies itself in the mind that says, "I feel very good for I slept twelve hours." However, the judgment reveals itself to indeed be fallible for many times a person, upon awakening from a twelve- or fourteen-hour sleep, tells themselves they feel miserable. And so we find that it is not sleep that we enjoy or do not enjoy. It is, however, in truth a judgment that has been satisfied while you have been unconscious and, in its own satisfaction, justifies what it has taken from your vital body and tells you, upon awakening to a conscious awareness, that you feel good, which means "know God," because you slept a certain length of time. And yet there are times when you awaken that you have slept that same amount of time and another judgment tells you that you feel miserable. So let us investigate this phenomenon that our mind calls the enjoyment of sleep.

During the unconscious process, which you know as sleep, there are various forms ever battling for your attention through your direction of energy to them. Those which win the battle and are still with you upon the moment of awakening, if they are still with you, they tell you how good you feel because you had such a long sleep. Now if those particular forms are not still in control of your mind upon awakening to a conscious awareness and another judgment form is in control of you that is not satisfied because it did not get the amount of energy that it demanded, that judgment tells you what a miserable morning it is and what a struggle you have to face for the day.

Now we're all susceptible to the faculty of reason. So let us be a little bit more aware, awake, and alert. And let us be honest with our self, and let us clearly see if in sleeping, a state of conscious unawareness, we feel the same every morning upon awakening and set our self a little clock and see if the same judgment remains in control of our mind. I assure you and I can guarantee you that through an honest investigation you will find, beyond a shadow of any doubt, that the judgment that tells you how much you enjoy sleeping will not always be in control of you each morning upon your awakening, and there will be times, even though you have slept the same number of hours, that a judgment will tell you how tired you are, how exhausted you are, how miserable you feel, and you need to sleep another hour or two.

Some time ago I shared with you the importance of flooding your consciousness, the importance of solidifying within the consciousness a form, whereas you and you alone by your conscious choice would remain in control during your so-called sleep time. By so doing, you will awaken feeling, thinking, and believing, if you honestly do your part, the way that you alone have established the vibration before giving, for a time, your most valuable asset: your faculty of reason.

So I look here over this past week. I see that a few, a very few of you have applied the cleansing breath in order that you may gain more control over all your experiences.

Now also I stated to you, in one of our little classes, that outward manifestations were nothing more nor less than revelations of inner attitudes of mind, forms created, forms in control of the mental substance of which we are responsible for.

I also granted permission to my little student, only for a short time, that he, because of his twenty-three months of earthly form, may have a nap, if necessary, during these classes. I also shared with my students that he and he alone, for a limited time, would be the only one allowed that little nap during any class that I have come to you to give. Any other student so tempted by getting what a little twenty-three-month-old child appears to be getting shall be excused and expelled from my private classes.

I have come here to your world over these number of years to share with you the Light, the truth that frees you. The time has now come, as time, an effect of the illusion of your world, when it meets the Light, the truth. You call that in your world the time has come. I shall now not only continue with your philosophy classes, I, from this moment on, shall be more active and participate in the application of what you receive here in this temple and these temple gardens. Therefore, I am not dependent on what you tell me about your efforts. I know each of my students, and I know how many times, if at all, you have applied the cleansing breath in these past seven days and so-called nights.

Part of the requirement of continuing on in these private classes shall be the demonstration and application of what I have come to this world here to share with you. That begins with the cleansing breath. If I find that you are polluted and contaminated and have not been applying the cleansing breath, I shall be quick to act and not to justify. I have come to share with you. I have not come to support the freeloading of any mind. And now that the law has so guided me to be more active within the organization that brings the Light to your world—I am known for a long time as a strict disciplinarian. I was known before that as a very tough magistrate. So, my good students, if you are tempted to play, play in the playpen of creation. Do not be tempted to play with me.

Now we'll continue on with our class. And try to understand, now that the law has fulfilled itself, when I become active in anything—and I am now active in your efforts here to apply what you are receiving, for your golden calves cannot buy it, cannot steal it. So awaken, my children, your souls, for I shall not play games with my students at any time.

Now: sleep. Make your effort to understand what is truly going on by the application of the laws you have received. Emotional upsets: apply the cleansing breath you have received. Lack of control of your life: apply the cleansing breath you have received. I shall monitor you, as my private students, daily. I expect results. Without results, my students guarantee change.

We know what we have. Let's not be tempted to get something that we don't have without thorough investigation of the cost.

Now I'm going to pause a few moments here, for I see so many forms arise from the deep in reference to sleep. And I also note that in your world deep and sleep are hardly distinguishable.

Raise your hands for your questions. Yes.

My understanding of the cleansing breath is to be sitting upright. Always sitting. And then I think I got a different feeling when you said as soon as you are emotional or whatever, do it right away. Do it all the time until it exhausts you, if that happens to be what's going on with you. Are we to sit each time or can we do it standing up as we're doing our work or walking or in whatever circumstance we find our self upset in?

Most interesting question. In the students that I am looking at, I have yet to find one who has [a] problem sitting, no matter where they go in creation. *[A few students laugh.]* Therefore, there is no justification that in any way will benefit the human being by changing the demonstrable law that is. Did that help with your question?

Yes.

You're welcome.

Thank you.

The lady there, please.

Other than the cleansing breath, is there something else you can say to your mind that what it's going, what it's about to do before you go to rest or . . . well, I guess the question is, What's the best thing to say to your—what is the best thing to do with your mind before you lie down?

No problem at all: control it. You cannot control what you believe you are. That's demonstrable. I look at my students who believe they're in need; therefore, they are not able to experience fulfillment until they no longer believe that they are the thought and the emotion that they are serving.

Now first you will have to make the effort to separate truth from creation. To understand beyond a shadow of any doubt that you have formed what you call a thought. You alone have created it. Your choice is you continue on with the law that you created it to serve a certain purpose [or] you now intelligently decide it's not serving the purpose for which you have originally created it. If you do not make the effort, through your cleansing breath, to bring about a change in the solidification of that thought form, which becomes a judgment once thoroughly solidified, through belief, you service it; it no longer serves the true purpose of its design. Whoever believes they are a judgment of their mind is serving the form they have created. The form they have created in no way is serving them. Does that help with your question?

Use your cleansing breath. Stop permitting the judgment to tell you it's not working. For I have watched each of you these seven days. That is a part of the process of being in private class. I'm with you seven days a week, as long as you are in private class. And you have the opportunity to be in private class until you decide that you will not apply what you are being given. Does that help with your question?

Yes.

You're welcome. Yes, the gentleman there, please.

Is it advisable and recommended to do the cleansing breath every night prior to going to bed, sir?

Yes, indeed. In reference to your question, absolutely and positively. Because you have—at that time and through that effort you are solidifying that of your conscious choice. Therefore, though the battle will rage within the consciousness, that which is used to being fed that you have, in [an] intelligent decision, decided is no longer serving you, you will neutralize that through that neutralization process. As soon as that is neutralized, you solidify the form in the mental world that you, through conscious choice, wish solidified.

Now all of life's experiences are direct efforts of the forms in the mental world that are being fed. So if a person wants to know what kind of forms they are feeding, what kind of forms are still in control through years of error of ignorance, all they have to do is to look at their experiences. And by looking at our experiences in life, we—you see, let me explain how the forms receive more energy from your body. The form's created. It feeds on you while you sleep. It feeds on many students while they are supposedly awake. It gets its full feeding through what is known as the Law of Return. Those forms go out into the atmosphere, pull in like kind and come to you for a harvest. Did that help with your question?

Yes, sir. Thank you very much.

Yes. The lady here, please.

It's my understanding that what you're going to solidify during the holding of the breath—on the way, as you're inhaling, is there a thought of some kind, like harmony or peace that you're solidifying, if you wish to?

Yes, may I say something? Of course, it is beneficial for one to have a thought of peace. The only sadness with that: until we strengthen our self and no longer over-identify with limit, with form, with self, the only problem with that is that a person in thinking of peace does not sufficiently identify with it. And because they do not sufficiently identify with it, the forms they are trying to neutralize do not get neutralized in mental substance. Does that help with your question?

What—

For example, a person believes that they are in need. Would you not agree?

Yes.

That belief is very solidified to the point that a person says to themselves, "That is me. That is exactly my experiences." Wouldn't you agree with that?

Yes.

Now listen carefully, please. Your experiences are the effect of the form created: the judgment that you are in need; it goes out into the atmosphere. It returns unto you. Your mind looks at your experiences and says, "I am still in need." That is how the form becomes more in control of your life. For you to then take that great mental force and to think of peace and to expect the form of peace within your mental world to have sufficient energy and strength to neutralize out a form that is constantly bringing back unto you the justifications known as experiences [is not effective].

Now would you like to know what experiences are known, to our world, what they are known as? Experiences are in truth the justification and defenses of the judgments we believe that we are. That's all experiences really are. Investigate experiences through the honest light of your soul, and you will see clearly that experiences in your life support the judgments you believe that you are to the extent and to the degree that you believe you are those judgments. Does that help with your question?

Yes. May I?

Yes, you may.

Well, then, I understand exactly what you said about peace not being strong enough in my identification.

I didn't say yours. I said anyone's.

Excuse me. In one's identification. However, if you, if you do the opposite, like abundance, considering abundance and possibility, is that a strong . . .

Oh, it couldn't possibly be as strong because you have to create the experiences to give it the strength necessary. Now, for example, whoever sees the good in all things can only experience the good therefrom because that is established within mental consciousness. Do you understand that? Now we're not talking about the peace that is the power of God. We've got to grow to a higher level of consciousness, called a spiritual realm, for that.

Now when you want to make a change and you're using the cleansing breath, you must use your faculty of reason to search out for support for that which you are trying to create. Say that you want to declare and to experience abundance, that you want to have more money, then you must look and each time you see a penny, you must accept that is ever growing and ever increasing. Because you must, because of belief that you are the limit and the form, you must justify your new judgment. Do you understand that?

I do.

You see, my children, we are working with bondage because we are so identified we believe we're it. So we're taking the kindergarten approach in these private classes. The kindergarten approach, you understand, through our own awakening that, first of all, we still make judgments. We still compare. We still believe. Therefore, we must work with what we're doing. This is a private class of application. So let us apply.

So all of us would like to say, "Thank you, God, I'm freed from judgment." My dear children, that is at the cost and the expense of limit called self. Now when you enter that state of consciousness, I'll be happy to work along those other lines. But let's first work with what we absolutely are convinced that we are, for your conviction is necessary for you in a mental world that you believe that you are. Do you understand?

So, you see, the teaching is, "Be grateful for the crumb; you guarantee the loaf." Well, now stop and think about that demonstrable truth. You have a little crumb, perhaps five cents. And you look at that and you work with your mind and how grateful you are and how good you feel. Now listen carefully. Through that you send a new form out into the universe. Now it's got to battle against all those other forms you've created: that you're in need and you don't have this and don't have that. So you've got to work diligently, perhaps even hourly, moment by moment. "Oh, thank you, God. That's getting better. Oh, my gosh, yes. I'm so grateful. I know it is coming to me." You see, you must work in the realm that you believe that you are, for that is the cement of your own identification with limit. Does that help with your question?

Thank you.

All right. Yes, the lady there, please.

I have a question about the twenty minutes we're supposed to spend after we do the cleansing breath. Now, during the day, even if I go through changes, I have a time limit on my work schedule so that twenty minutes, if I went through two changes in one job, I would, you know, be very much beyond my limit.

Yes, my dear, I understand your justification completely. And I'll be happy to share with you—

Oh, thank you.

—a way through the jungle, known in some realms as the concentration camps of creation. Now we must not, *you* must not interfere with the solidified judgments that you believe that you are. So you can still get through the concentration camp of creation by not even thinking about your jobs and all you have to do about that by doing your twenty minutes in the morning—you understand?

Yes.

And therefore, whenever you feel yourself slipping into the service to those judgments of need and all those judgments of limit, in the particular work I see you in, there's always a chair present. You can take a few moments and do your cleansing breath and go right up back to work. Does that help you?

Yes. Thank you.

Certainly. So, you see, we don't have to battle the solidified forms, isn't that lovely? And we'll still find a way. Thank you. Yes, the gentleman over there, please.

What stands in the way of our establishing the continuity of our efforts to apply this cleansing—

The judgments that you believe that you are. That's what stands in the way of the continuity of effort. If you—well, first of all, you already have continuity of effort in servicing the judgments that you believe that you are. That you've already established. Now to bring about a change, you see, that's where the battle begins. So an intelligent person does it daily, never once loses hope to move on through those concentration camp realms of creation, knows inside, talks with it. You see, you see, there's a judgment within the human ego, when it's uneducated, that says, "I'm not going to make a fool of myself and talk to myself." That tells you a person who is absolutely controlled by the judgments that are not about to give up their feeding. And they'll use every defense mechanism. Remember, all justifications are defenses of the judgments that we believe that we are. And they work through the function of what? Do any of my students know? Surely, surely—

Resentment. [A student speaks very quietly.]

Pardon?

Resentment.

No. Yes. *[The teacher addresses another student.]*

Belief.
No. The thing we seem to believe beyond question that we are. What is it?
Mind.
No.
Ego.
It's a function. No. It's a function of our mental world.
Self—
It is the throne of thrones for the mental world.
Self?
No. It's a particular function. Yes.
Pride?
Pride. I knew somewhere that that would come from one of my students. *[Many students laugh.]* Pride is the great throne. Pride. We believe we are that function, and by believing that we are, they work beautifully in that throne of consciousness. Hmm? Now what is the other functions of that triune function? Yes, my student that knows pride. Yes, the lady there that raised her hand.
Ego.
Well, they service what we call ego, uneducated ego. Indeed, they do. Let us pause and think and think and think. Now when does our pride rise? Does it rise when our judgments tell us they've been offended? They have been threatened. Do they rise at any other time, this, this thing called pride? Does it rise up and tell us that we've been offended and tell us that someone else has done us in? And does it not tell us, when our judgments are threatened, that it's not our fault at all, that that person over there is stupid, selfish, greedy, trying to get something for nothing? Would you not agree? Pardon?
Um.
Hmm? So what does pride service?
Self.
Judgment.

Why, yes, it services judgment. And if you believe that you are the judgments passing through your mind and you believe you are the thoughts, then you've got a problem. And that problem is called self, separation from truth, believing you are that which is separated, not accepting that which you truly are. Does that help with your question? Yes.

Perhaps you may think I spend much time on that function that traps the soul called judgment. I want to share with you I am well qualified, considering the time I spent as a judge.

And so Truth, the Principle of Goodness, God, the Light That Is, there are no judgments. They do not exist, for all judgments are limits, and limit is not what you are. Limit is only what you believe that you are; it is not what you are. Did that help with your question? Yes. The lady there, please.

Yes, I'd like to know about the correlation between the cleansing breath and the creative principle.

As soon as 51 percent of this private class begins applying daily the cleansing breath that is given, the law shall be fulfilled, and we will begin to consider more advanced teachings. Thank you. The gentleman there, please.

Could you please speak on the relationship between our judgments and our emotions? [The student speaks very quietly.]

I think perhaps you're on the downwind side. Would you speak up, please?

Yes, sir. Could you please speak on the relationship between our emotions and our judgments?

Our emotions, my dear friend, that is the realm through which the defense soldiers, called justifications, work to protect the judgments that we have made and believe that we are, as we are servicing that which we have created instead of that which we have created servicing us. Does that help you with your question?

Yes.

Now how would you like to take a shovel to dig a hole to plant a plant where you want it planted and the shovel says no and moves over to another place that you don't want it planted? How would you feel? How would you feel?

A little upset that that—

A little upset. That's how you truly feel when you permit a judgment of your mind to make you service it instead of it servicing you. Does that help with your question?

Thank you.

You're welcome. Yes, the lady there, please.

With the cleansing breath, you're teaching us, then, to work on our beliefs. Our judgments, then, we can't work on those? Are they just solid, unchangeable?

Oh no, no, no, no, no! No. You see, in the teaching of your cleansing breath, you see, you cannot take and make a leap from a mental world of identification into a universal consciousness without disastrous results to the world of creation that you believe that you are. Therefore, a slow process of gaining control through the use of form or judgment is the wisest path at this stage of evolution. Once gaining that degree of control, you are, in that process, slowly but surely separating truth from creation for you are weakening the very substance that solidifies the judgments. You are no longer controlled to such an extent by belief in what you are not, and you gradually are moving in an acceptance of what you are.

And so faith isn't something that we can study from a book. It isn't something that's a talent that can be learned. It is an evolutionary process. It is a movement of your true being rising up, not only psychologically within the consciousness but rising up physiologically with the movement of the very life energy that is being siphoned off in the various centers and is causing you to be dissipated of the vitality of what you truly are. Does that help with your question?

Yes. Thank you.

So, you see, through working with that, it, to the mind identified with limit, it is struggle enough because the judgments that we all have in mental substance have made it so. Therefore, we work wisely by using creation, for it has spent a long time using us. And so what we are moving with is the use of creation, which is our responsibility, and not being used by creation. So as we move in using creation wisely and no longer allowing creation (that which we are not) to use us, our life, our being, our energy, then we grow onward in a more harmonious way. Does that help with your question there?

Thank you.

You're welcome. You see, my friends, look, judgment is not bad or good in the world of which it exists. Man makes judgment good or bad by believing he's the judgment that he has created. Does that help with your question?

Yes.

You see, judgments belong to a world of limit. Now a person using those judgments and gradually, through understanding, transform[s] them to decisions—you understand?—then a person using that, you see—you see, the difference between judgment and decision is the soul faculty of total consideration. That's the difference. So by slowly but surely—not just trying to annihilate what you believe you are. For if someone comes along and hands you an ax, and tells you to cut off your left foot, you know how you're going to think and feel. Is that not correct? So you don't want to try doing that. Do not annihilate the human ego. Educate it. This process will help you to educate and to encourage yourself so that you may grow harmoniously.

Try to understand: when we permit anything, *anything* in creation to so gain control of us that we believe we are it, then it's not good for us. When we maintain control of the reins of form—you understand?—we create the child and we hold on to the reins, because if we don't, the reins will turn around and they'll hold on to us. And that we do not want. It's contrary to the law. Did that help with your question?

Yes. Thank you.

So [it] doesn't matter what judgments you make. Remember, you made it, and it's not you. And if you move to the next step, you will make decisions. For when a judgment rises, based upon the ribbon, of course, of comparison, you'll say, "Now just a moment," and you'll start considering as much as possible. And then you'll make a decision, and you'll say, "I have made this decision. I am ever ready and willing to change. So, thought form that I have created, don't get it into your little brain, for you are made of the substance of my mind, don't get it into your little mind that you're going to run me around." That, my dear, is a degree of freedom in a world of creation. Did that help with your question?

Thank you.

You're welcome. The gentleman there, please.

Yes, thank you. When we are working to free ourselves from the temptation to quit before the victory, at what point in our endeavors would it be most beneficial to use the cleansing breath?

The moment that the judgment rises for you to service it and tempts you, through its defense mechanisms of justification, to quit before the victory, in the instant of your conscious awareness of that or the feeling of it, you go to work with your cleansing breath, specifically on that solidified form. Because, you see, my friends, it is created, as we well know, by our own mental substance.

The grave danger and the great struggle in creation is that we are so clever and so cunning. It is our child. It is so clever and so cunning it convinces us that we are it, so that it can be greater than its father, than its mother. Do you understand that?

Yes.

I, personally, in all these years and centuries, going through those realms and those many forms, of course, and my own creations, I was indeed grateful to have spent my time on your planet as a judge. For in looking through what I call hindsight, I gained a little more insight. Those forms at a time in my evolution that I believed that I was were indeed very unhappy with me. And because I was never a person with what I would consider a weak mind, those forms created by my mind were extremely strong and most convincing, as most judges to this day in your world are convincing. That help with your question?

Thank you.

Yes. Yes, the lady there, please.

Would you please speak to us on the magnetic principle of our being, known as love?

To those with great capacity of love, as I said so long ago, indeed do they have, through that magnetic attraction, a great struggle in a world of creation. Therefore, a person must use wisely the cleansing breath. Use it daily. You see, what the mind calls love is the filling of need. Would you not agree?

Yes.

Well, that's not love. Lust, yes. Love, no. First of all, if love is expressing itself in your consciousness, you couldn't possibly deny God, the Principle of Good, and experience need. So it's lust that deceives us, for it is born of the denial of God. It is born of the denial of goodness. It is born of the denial of what truly is and the absolute conviction of believing what we are not.

And so when a person says, "I love you very much," and you don't do what their judgments dictate, you'll soon find out what you thought they said was love was, in truth, lust. For when you do not do what they judge you should be doing, they experience, once again, need. And by experiencing need, you couldn't possibly love them because they are not servicing your judgments that you believe that you are. That's not the love of which I speak. But that is the love of which many in a world of creation know.

So true love respects the rights of difference. True love is freed from need, want, and desire. That's love. Anything else that we choose to call love shall rise in honesty, as truth crushed to earth shall rise again, and, like it or not, we'll see, "Oh, oh, that was lust. And I thought that was love." Yes. Did that help with your question?

Thank you.

The gentleman here has a question.

Yes. Why is it that sometime we are aware after this deep sleep of some of the dreams or so-called dreams that we have or experiences that we have?

Yes, that's a most interesting question. First, I would like to ask you a question. How do we know it's a deep sleep? [It] could have been a shallow one. I'm trying to help you, you see.

OK.

How do we know what kind of sleep it was? Our judgments tell us: "That was a great sleep. I feel good." "That was a horrible sleep. I didn't get to sleep at all. I feel terrible." "Oh, I [have] got to go to work this morning." "No, it's just—I didn't have enough sleep. I've got to go—I [have] got to have another half hour." Then a half hour turns into an hour; the hour turns into two hours; two hours turn into three. And the next thing you know we're walking around in what you call spaced-out.

Now, take control of your mind before something else does. That specifically and especially means before you lose conscious awareness. Now [if] you take control of your mind and you do your cleansing breath, and you go to what you call sleep and the last thought upon your mind is the one you have consciously chose[n], the last feeling upon your mind is the one you have consciously chose[n], [then] you [have] got a chance. And you won't have to worry about sleep. Did that help with your question?

Yes. That helps a lot.

That's what you must learn to do to gain control and experience better experiences in your life. Did you have another question?

Yes. I, I say, why, why, why are we consciously aware of some of the experiences that we have and, and why we're not consciously aware of some of the experiences we have when we go to sleep?

Yes, thank you very much. Well, it's quite simple and it's time to reveal it. It depends on what judgments you are servicing upon awakening. Some judgments are so designed and created by your mind: they're not interested in you having a little bit of conscious recall of what went on while sleeping, because you don't threaten them. Other judgments are totally threatened. And if those other judgments are in control upon your awakening, you won't even know what you dreamed if those judgments judge that it's a threat to them. Does that help with your question?

Yes, sir.

Does anyone not understand how important it is about what you do with your mind as you're going off to sleep? And especially what you do with your mind when you awaken? So many people, they awaken, you know, and they're so exhausted; they're so tired. And they are what they call slow awakeners. Well, fast [or] slow, depends on which judgment they're servicing, you see. Depends on which judgment you are servicing upon the time of awakening. Yes.

If, if a person—you hear of people passing on in their sleep to the other side. If they are in, in a dream servicing a judgment, will they go to the realms of that judgment during that time?

The soul is taken to the realms of the predominant vibration during a person's incarnation.

Oh.

Does that help with your question?

Thank you. Yes.

You're welcome. Yes, the lady there, please.

If you awaken and you're in a judgment, how do you get ahold of your space from that judgment so that you don't feel that way?

Very good question. That's why you have the cleansing breath, and you must learn to become proficient in it, if you want freedom from those conditions.

[Thank you.]

You're welcome. Yes, the lady there, please.

Could you please advise us on how to choose the replacement form that's to be created and held during the cleansing breath that we can identify with?

Rather than reveal the multitudes of forms publicly or privately to my students, they know what they really believe. So using what they really believe that is not dependent on anything they cannot control would be a wise path at that state of evolution. Does that help with your question?

Thank you.

Remember, there is nothing like what we judge is our own thought. We hear many things. But only the echoes here, *[The teacher points to his head.]* do we listen to in a world of creation. That help with your question?

Yes. Thank you.

And because we diligently work, our little beings, to prove how right we are, and so if someone tells you to paint the fence pink, be rest assured it's usually red. Rarely green. Often brown. Does that help with your question? Yes. We have time left [for more questions]. Yes.

In the exercise, what's the purpose of placing the tongue on the roof of the mouth?

To solidify the new judgment.

Thank you.

Without the tongue, life-giving energy does not exist in your world of creation. I gave that to you long ago. The spoken word is life-giving energy. And therefore, the spoken word is subject to the tongue. Without the tongue, it does not exist in your world of creation. And someday, in keeping with the laws of application of these classes, we will go into more [and] further detail in reference to how that spoken word works and why, using that which is critical to the spoken word, you close the door, so to speak. I do hope that's helped with your question, until a future time when the application of this truth is applied. Yes.

The lady right there, please. And I'll be with you in a moment, child.

The twenty minutes that we take after the cleansing breath . . .

Yes?

When the mental realms start to rise, what can we do to stay in a better space during that twenty minutes?

Should you have done your cleansing breath proficiently and accurately, you may be rest assured in your world of time, through application daily, you will have no concern about any disturbance during your meditation. It will not exist.

Yes. Now the gentleman there, please.

May I have a recommendation on how much rest is required for the body?

Rest? Yes. Frequent rest. Nine minutes. Ten minutes. Twenty minutes is far, far superior in benefit than 8, 10, or 12 hours of sleep, for you are being drained while you sleep; rejuvenated while you are resting, should you do it properly. Hmm?

Now in reference to [sleep], you must have some sleep, because if you don't, the expression of the forms—you understand, they express while you are sleeping. Because they express, they use your energy. Some people call it nightmares, and some people call it dreams. And some people it's astral projection and all kinds of things are taking place. And therefore, without doing that and suddenly moving from any sleep at all to rest, you would not long be in that little form that you're in. Does that help with your question?

Yes.

Yes.

Trying to make—

You see, you see, you should take note that when the forms that you have created are active and using up your energy, there is a rapid fluttering movement of your eyelashes, because, you see, your eyes represent awareness and they're determined to get everything they can get and they want to see and know and have everything. Does that help with your question? It's called greed of the forms.

Yes, the gentleman here, please.

During one's meditation process, which would include the, the cleansing breath, and one has several exercises that they're doing prior to going into their twenty-minute meditative state, should the cleansing breath be the last exercise they do just entering into the meditative state?

I would definitely. Definitely. Just before the actual entering because you clean up everything.

Ah.

You clean up everything. Especially you, a student of so many years. You actually clean up your aura, your atmosphere, and your universe. And you should easily be able to hold that for fifteen to twenty minutes.

Yes, sir.

Easily be able to hold that. Now after, there's another factor. But try to understand that the forms we have created, they express the energy from our vital body while we are unaware, what you call sleep. And the flickering of the eyes, the movement of the eyes, the rapid eye movement is—they use that part of our form as they are sense creators, you see. They create and they thrive and live on energy, which is received through their senses in keeping with that which you have created. Tell me, who will create in consciousness peace when it cannot compare with the forms of other creations that we really believe we are when we believe we are in need. Hmm? Does that help? I was answering all the questions, my student there. But it is very, very important.

It's a lovely day. If you have any more questions, we'll continue on. Otherwise, class has progressed. Time passes quickly. The lady here, please.

If we have a meditation stool that we use, at another time during the day when we find ourselves upset and using the cleansing breath, is it advisable to use that stool if it's available or not contaminate it for our meditation?

It is advisable as long as we keep control so we don't go off into a secondary and third and fourth meditation because the dangers of meditation, as I've spoken before, are always the dangers of the forms creating a type of self-hypnosis. This is why I've always used a certain type of meditation and have recommended it to all my students in years past and now present that one meditation a day will keep you aware, awake, and alert. More than that, you may soon find out you not only don't know what you are, you don't know who you are, you don't know what you're doing or where you're going.

And, you see, there are chemical processes that are taking place. They are not just mental processes. They are physical processes. There are chemical changes that are taking place. Now you all are familiar with chemical changes taking place within your mind, your physical brain, and your body when you take certain types of narcotics. But you are yet to accept the demonstrable truth that through certain attitudes of mind and certain states and conditions of mind, you are releasing within your physical body certain chemicals. Some of them beneficial. Ofttimes they are of a narcotic state. In other words, the chemicals are there; it is you who release them through errors of ignorance. Now the purpose of these classes in gaining control is so that you will release the chemicals that are beneficial to your body and to your mind.

And now I think it's time to say good day to all of you. And I know you will have a good week. And I know you won't be afraid—sorry, I'm putting this down on you. *[The teacher refers to his lapel microphone.]* Well, I better put it back up there. And I know you won't be afraid to see me next Sunday. And try to think about the goodness of life a little more often because when you're not doing that, something else is doing you.

And thank you and good day.

JUNE 23, 1985

A/V Class Private 3

Good morning, students, and welcome to a new dawn.

Whenever we permit our mind to create a thought and, in creating that thought, believe that we are that thought, through that belief we solidify that thought form into a judgment. The effect thereof are the experiences that we have in life. We already know from years of experiences that we are disturbed and controlled by them, for that is a transgression of what is and what you are. That transgression is made possible by a lack of understanding and a lack of application of the Law of Freedom, known as personal responsibility.

For example, I spoke to you at our last class and informed you at that time that a part of the requirement of being permitted in my private classes was your application of the law to free yourself from the effects of your own transgressions, and through that application, you gain objectivity in your life. You were instructed to apply the cleansing breath. You were informed that those of you who do not apply it as part of the requirement of being in these classes would be expelled from these classes.

For me to permit myself to be tempted to do it for you, by being the buffer of the return of those transgressions into your life, would reveal to me that I must first deny that which I am, the good and the joy of life without dependence on anything. For example, whenever you permit yourself to experience what you call need, you are in truth only experiencing the effect of denying what you are and believing a thought form you have created, establishing the judgment, which in turn permits you that experience of need. And in those experiences of need, you, in your mind, judge who has what you need and you diligently work to get it. Because in so doing, in taking that path in life, you not only become dependent on the one that you judge has what you need, you are destined to service them as long as your judgment, which you believe that you are, remains in control of your mind.

These classes, designed to free you from servicing that which is not in your divine right to control, reveal to you that your freedom, your truth cannot be experienced within your consciousness until you refrain from denying what you are, creating a thought of what you need, solidifying it into a judgment, and servicing forms of creation beyond your sphere of divine right. That is known as dependence. That offers to you a continuity of past experiences. Many a teacher has taught that the past repeats itself. To those who believe the thoughts of the now, to those who so solidify the forms to their judgments, guarantee the continuity in principle of all of the experience, distasteful and otherwise, that they have already had. For to continue a law only supports and sustains the law that you have already serviced in creating the experiences of yesterday.

And so you're here to experience the way to free yourself from the entrapment that tempts you by your own lack of effort. The cleansing breath, as already given to you, does the job necessary for you in the moment that the return of your own creations come back to you through experiences.

And so there is good in all things, including the ones that disturb us and, therefore, control us; for [in] the repetition of them over a period of time, usually numbered in your world of time as centuries, you are never left without hope and you are never without encouragement.

So whenever you think that you are the effect of a form that you created—for that's the next step. When the experience comes into your life, to accept that it is an effect of your own ignorance, to accept that it is not in truth you, to accept it is in truth what you alone have created by your own ignorance, by accepting that it is what you have made or created, that it is not you, you gradually, slowly but surely, will separate yourself, which is truth, from creation, which is changing and false.

Now to those with strong wills directed to what they believe is their ego, a wiser path would be to look at the experience of return. You will have not much problem in your mind if the experience you judge to be distasteful is not you at all. It is something that you have created, for that's what it is. And that's moving from the step of supporting someone you can't control by permitting your mind to think and to judge that that person out there has done it to you. There's no way you can control that person out there. That person out there is the instrument through which your laws are returning. That's what that person out there truly is. However, you insist on believing that person out there has robbed you of your tranquility. You insist on believing it's that person out there, for by insisting in your mind on believing that it's that person out there, that which controls you does not have to make the change and does not have to bow to your divine right and respect that it is a child that you have created; it is not the master.

And so the first step, of course, is to stop supporting that deception of your mind by first refrain[ing] from blaming something beyond your control for your experience. For by blaming them, you only solidify that form and your belief that it is you in your own mind. So we start by refraining from blaming that which is beyond our control by divine law, that which is beyond our control as the cause of our problems and disturbances in life. By refraining from doing that, we start [on] the path of growing up and applying the law which frees us that we may experience intelligent, harmonious experiences in our life.

So first we stop blaming that which we cannot control for the cause of our experience. Then we move from refraining [from blaming] that which we cannot control, which is manifested to our senses by physical, gross form, we move to the next step of accepting, "This experience is a return of the law that I alone have established. That is not me. It has been created by me in my depths of ignorance and darkness." So move to those two steps. And when you do that, you will be ready and you will be prepared to move to the next step. When you start to create a thought in your mental substance—for you are responsible for its creation regardless of whether you are ignorant of it or not. You are still responsible for it. Ignorance of law is no excuse from the law. That is the law of the Divine.

And so it is your responsibility to be awake, aware, and alert of what your mind is doing. Are you consciously aware of the forms it is creating? Are the forms that your mind is creating by your conscious, intelligent choice under the guidance of your faculty of reason or are the forms created and, being created by your mind, effects of your laziness to be awake and alert in your own mental substance? Now if they are—and I'm sure that many of you, in fact, all of you will agree, for you all have experiences that you judge are not to your liking—if they are created and you are not consciously aware of them, be rest assured, the judgments you believe that you are, are doing a wonderful, wonderful job of diligently working on their defense mechanisms. And that is known as soldiers of justification.

Without that process and without your daily effort to your cleansing breath, which is a requirement for the privilege of being in my classes, without that, you cannot, by the very law of personal demonstration, remain in these particular classes for very long.

Now I do not have a need to be tempted to listen to the soldiers of defense of old creation, known as justification. I am not tempted to service what I used to service for centuries: judgments. The solidification, the solidification of a form and to believe that it is us is a glorification of what is called the throne of the human uneducated ego. It serves no other purpose. It does, however, serve the purpose of the delusion of your belief, when sitting upon that throne, known as the crown of pride, that you are perfect and always right.

Now whenever you ask a person if they believe that they are perfect and you ask a person if they believe they are always right, you will immediately get the answer, "Why, of course not." Because, you see, the human mind knows that for you to say that you are would reveal to another your own stupidity. And because you do believe you are perfect when you sit upon that throne, crowned with the crown of pride, your mind and its intelligence knows beyond a shadow of any doubt, depending on who you are talking to and what the subject matter is, that you would not say that you are perfect. However, your mind and experiences reveal to you, when you are in certain other experiences with an individual, when you believe beyond a shadow of any doubt how great your need is and that the person you are with has what you need so you may be fulfilled, you would be amazed how much you can speak and how many justifications you have to convince them of your perfection so they will bow to the temptation to service you. Now there are no adults in my classes that don't understand what I'm talking about. And if there are, then you've never had the experiences of what is commonly known as intercourse.

So let's stop and think. There are many moments in your life when you allow your mind to tell yourself you are the greatest there ever was. It depends on what you judge that another person has that you judge that you need and that you judge, through whatever you say, that you can convince them and, therefore, tempt and entrap them [determines] how perfect you're going to tell them that you are.

Now your responsibility here is not only your cleansing breath, which I'm not going to do for you—I'm not even tempted to do for you. Your responsibility here is to be prepared. And part of your preparation is to have intelligent questions. And intelligent questions and your judgment of what is intelligence helps you to know, personally, for yourself right where you are when you form the thought and the question. For your responsibility is to put something in, and in so doing, get something back. So it's easy enough to put in a piece of paper. It's most difficult to put in the direct energy because to do so you must take control of whatever obstructs you from doing so.

If you believe, so greatly, that you are the judgments of your mind, then you fear to ask me the questions that you want to ask, because by believing you are your judgments, you cannot offer me anything but your belief that I, too, am judging what you're about to say. Now that's the great censorship.

Just the other day I spoke to some of my students on the beauty here that surrounds you. You do not see the flower as it truly is. The closest you come to seeing the flower as it truly is, is when you view it on a film. Now you see it more accurately, the way it really is, when you view it on a film. Now how many of you have asked yourself the question, "Why do I not see these gardens as beautiful as I see them on films that are taken of them? I'm there. I'm looking at the same flowers. I'm looking at the same trees, but they're not as beautiful. They're not as vibrant in color. They're not—the depths and dimensions are not there. They're more flat. Why don't I see them the way the camera sees them?" Well, it's quite simple: your view is absolutely clouded. It is like looking out through a London fog. And the fog is created by the amount of judgments that are standing in front of you in your mental realm of consciousness as you're looking at the flower.

Now when you look at the same flower on film and you relax and you say, "My, that flower never looked to me so beautiful! And I'm looking at it all the time." How could it? When you're sitting in your chairs and relaxed and your senses are satisfied, your judgments have gone to sleep. And now you're able to see. You now are experiencing the light of reason. And so when your senses, your judgments are satisfied, they do not stand in front of your awareness; therefore, you are able to see clearly what is and not be dimmed by this mass, like a fog, that you have to peer through.

We all know and have experienced how good we feel at times. And yet those times seem to be, for so many, so very rare. And take that little angel and let it go on its way. *[The teacher gently removes an insect that had landed on his hand and lets it go.]* They seem to be so very rare. They are rare because, my dear children, you are not satisfying your multitudes of judgments and filling the needs you have created by denial and, therefore, do not feel good most of the time, when the law is clear: feeling good is a necessity and your responsibility *all* of the time.

Now for a person to go into creation with the untold hundreds of thousands of judgments that they have, dictating how their senses will be satisfied, that person will not long be allowed to survive in creation, for there are too many others rising to annihilate them for interfering with what they judge are their own needs. So that's not the wisest path to follow: the blatant license of fulfilling every single judgment that you have created by your denial of what you are.

The wisest path is to follow the one that is given to you: separating truth from creation. Experiencing the thought in your mind and being alert to what the thought is. Making the [un]intelligent choice to believe that it is you, guaranteeing the solidification of it into a judgment, guaranteeing the return of it through experience, guaranteeing to be disturbed, for whatever controls us in life indeed disturbs us. For whatever controls us disturbs us of the tranquility which is our right and our freedom. So you only guarantee experiences in your life daily, moment by moment, of the return of your unwillingness and laziness to nip it in the bud, to be alert and aware of what your mind is doing.

And when your mind is doing its many things, look clearly at them and see, "This form is being created here. I see. Do I want to believe this creation in my mind? Did I sit down and pause and intelligently decide that I wanted to create this form?" For that's what thoughts are, are forms. "Now if I did that, do I want to intelligently solidify it by believing that I am it? For if I do, I must pay the price." And so should you choose, "Yes, I want to believe this thought form that I have created, this child, I want to believe that it's me," you have at that moment absolutely solidified it. You absolutely guarantee the return, through what you call experience, of energy you have given to it. The child is created. He is now king in your consciousness for *you* have given him the kingdom by your belief that you are him, that which you have created.

Now we'll pause for a few moments and questions on that particular subject that we have been discussing here this morning. Yes, the lady there, please.

Yes. Are some of these forms that we're trying to, to work with or working with, in clearing up, are they, some of them, from before this earth life or are they all from this earth life?

In reference to your question, Are they all from this particular earth experience or ones we have brought with us from other experiences, other times, and other places? First of all, I answered that some time ago in: What benefit would it be for us to recall an experience or a form of 2,000 years ago if we were not able and willing and ready to work on the form that we created five minutes ago?

So, you see, what is important to you is to work on what you are aware of, of what you are doing. Now the law is very clear: whatever you permit yourself, through whatever justification you give yourself, to believe that you are a form, a thought of your mind, whatever you do with that, look at it clearly, and I guarantee you it is associated with a pattern which will repeat for you experiences you have already had in your earth life, not even considering the ones prior. Does that help with your question?

The gentleman here, please.

On one level I can say to myself that I know I am not this thought. Yet when my emotions, when something seems to threaten what I believe I am, I have great difficulty at that point separating them.

Yes. And so what is—your question is you have difficulty in separating?

Yeah, why is, why is it so much more difficult at some times than at other times when I can say, "Ah, yes, I am not this thought"?

Well, sometimes you're emotional and sometimes you are not. Is that correct?

That's correct.

Well, then you have to understand that forms, that which is created, creation, is controlled by a water center where the emotions live. The faculty of reason exists in an air center. And so whenever you permit yourself the luxury of being emotional, then you must pay the price of that transgression. For when you enter the water center and you believe you are what is offered there, then you must pay the payment of denying the air center where the faculty of reason exists. And so we find that through the emotions, what you call emotions, all the soldiers of defense do their number in our life. When you are not emotional, you are able to separate and talk to the thought form, is that not correct?

That is correct.

But if you permit the same thought form, if you allow yourself the luxury with the thought form to enter the realms of emotion, where truth, needing no defense, does not exist— truth, you understand, is not expressed in the water centers of emotion. That's where limit is expressed. You understand that, don't you? You see, you cannot ever experience emotion without experiencing need because you cannot experience the water centers of emotion, where there is no light of reason, without first denying what you are. So when you want to enter the realms of the water center of creation, which is the reign and the rule of the king of creation, then you want to choose intelligently, prior to entering that realm, "I'm going down there into the emotional realm where justification reigns supreme, which is, in truth, the defense mechanisms of any judgments that I have," and maintain the lamp of honesty, that little light to light your way through those realms. And don't stay too long, because if you do, you'll end up believing, in no time at all, that you are the judgment, the form that you have created. So you can't go down there without a lamp of honesty, a light of sincerity, and you cannot stay too long or you can't come back up. Do you understand that?

Yes.

Now many people—it seems to be rather a talent for them. They can get emotional and go down quickly and come back quickly. And then there are others who are slow to become emotional and seem to take forever to get back up. So the thing to do is to make an intelligent decision. "I have these forms. Through my own transgressions I am being tempted by the law I have established to service them. I don't like it." And move out of it.

You see, if it wasn't your own creation, you couldn't do anything about it. You see, you can do everything about your life. You can do everything you want about your life. In fact, you really are ever in keeping [with the saying,] "We always get what we really want." The question is knowing what it is that we really want and what we have really wanted. You see, we're not at home. You see, we're not aware. And when we become aware, we will soon find out, "Yes. Thank you. I'm getting exactly what I really wanted. And I know what I really want, and that's exactly what's happening in my life." But you have to apply the law.

You're applying the Law of Ignorance, and it's working for you beautifully. Now's the time to apply the Law of Intelligence, and see how beautiful it works for you by your conscious guidance.

You see, everything that happens to us is caused by us, and because you don't want to accept that it's caused by you only shows you how much you still believe that someone else controls your life. Because, you see, when you don't control your life, there's all kinds of people waiting to do [so] for you because there's all kinds of people filled with need by denying what they are. So anyone who doesn't make the effort to control their own life, there's a lot of mothers in the universe waiting to control your life for you. There's a lot of fathers waiting to control the lives of you young ladies. Did that help with your question?

Yes, sir.

And you'll never be without someone just waiting and panting like a puppy dog to control what you are too lazy to make the effort to do.

Yes, the lady here with her arms crossed has been waiting for a question and she almost missed out as three other arms rose up. Yes.

What causes a person to go to nod out, so to speak, during class or when they should be paying attention?

Oh, yes. Well, they don't nod out during my classes because I have the—I wouldn't want to put it in those particular words—but I have all the tools necessary to help them help themselves. Now what causes them to do that? The forms that they believe that they are. Now, of course, if a person is interested in a particular subject and they're not getting to participate or to perform the particular subject that they're interested in, quite often they will nod off into what they call sleep and can't help themselves. But they could help themselves the minute they were honest with themselves and start doing their cleansing breath and take control of those things that they are tempted to believe that they are through need, which is a denial of the goodness, to glorify that thing called pride and self-glory. Does that help with your question?

Thank you.

Yes. Because, you see, everything that anyone could ever judge that they need for their greater good already exists inside of themselves. When they stop denying that truth, then they will experience it. Does that help with your question?

Yes. Now the lady here, and then the gentleman over there. Yes.

Is it—so my question is, when you look at the flower and you're in a state, a clear state, and you see it in its, its total beauty, is it possible to reach that state in form? Is it possible to maintain that if you—or do you have to go into those centers, like the—

I understand. Yes, now in reference to that question, how long—I accept that's the question you're asking—you maintain that state of consciousness where you see things as they are and not through the deception of the forms you have created and believe that you are. As long as you can hold your breath, you can see clearly. Those are the moments that you have while still identified with limit.

And so your cleansing breath is the most important thing that you have to do. It is so important to the atmosphere and to the health and well-being of my own channel, who is exposed to your atmosphere here in these classes, it is so important that unless your cleansing breath is done, 51 percent and more, the class will get smaller as it gets spiritually greater. Thank you. Does that help with your question?

Yes.

Yes. The gentleman there is waiting.

When, when we're having an experience and we accept personal responsibility for that experience, I mean, how important is it for us to trace back, because when, when I start tracing back on this experience, my mind, I, evidently, I'm doing it in my mind because I want to see the, the experience of the, that I had to create this on a personal level rather than principle. Is it important for us to trace it back to, to the actual experience of, of the actual creation? Or, or what can we do just to accept it in principle and move on?

Thank you. In reference to your question, it is not beneficial at all to trace the cause of any experience until we have, through our own effort, gained control over all our experiences, for to tempt our self to trace an experience back to the cause inside of our self is only to tempt all of those other temptresses in our consciousness that ever existed in our own eternity.

So the first thing that we have to do and the wisest thing to do is to declare the truth: "Thank you, God. This experience, I didn't appreciate it. I don't like it. However, I'm going to make great effort. First, I accept that it's an effect of what I've done. I don't need to play with my mind and tempt all those temptresses down there and become entrapped." And so acceptance is the will of God. Acceptance is the way of goodness. Do you understand that? So stop at that point and declare the truth: "Acceptance is the will or movement of the Principle of Goodness. I accept. I accept the possibility of growing up. I accept the possibility of waking up. I accept personal responsibility. Therefore, by my acceptance, which is the will of God, the movement of the Principle of Goodness, I am no longer controlled by something outside for I am no longer disturbed by it." Do, do you understand?

Yes.

Do that and you won't have no problem. Start with that little short thing right there in your consciousness. "Here it is. I don't like it. I'm going to stop liking or disliking it for I accept the demonstrable truth of personal responsibility. I accept the Principle of Goodness in my life. I declare that truth." That's called the will of God. Thank you. The lady here, please.

Thank you.

You're welcome. Yes? Yes.

Ah—

You're still a lady, young lady.

I have two questions about the cleansing breath.
Yes.
When we're lying down, should our eyes be open or closed or does it matter? And should our palms be—
Lying down?
Yes, for the twenty minutes after we do the breath.
Did someone hear—perhaps I'm getting senile in my old age—but did someone hear me tell a person to lie down for twenty minutes after? Please raise your hand if anyone heard that. All right. Now in reference to your question, I'm going to help you greatly. The secretary of our organization here is going to explain to you in microscopic detail exactly what you do and don't do. And I shall be watching closely her universe when she does so. And you can just stay over the necessary time for her to tell you; so we can move on to the many questions that have yet to be covered that have not yet been covered. All right? For that does not have to do with a question that was asked [and] can it be answered; it has to do with an interpretation of the answer that was already given. All right?
Thank you.
Yes. Now the secretary, be sure that that's taken care of. And the lady here is waiting, please.
In our philosophy it is said exposure frees the soul. And it does. And the cleansing breath, is that something to free us before we even get so polluted?
Well, it is designed to help you control the forms of your own creation, to control your own children that you are responsible for. You see, when you permit your mind to say, "There's my child," you have no problem with that. "There's my child. My child is disturbing the atmosphere and robbing everyone of the peace and tranquility of the moment." For you ever to permit your mind to say, "What can I do?" reveals that you can do nothing, for it's no longer your child: you are his toy. Don't you understand that, my dear?

Yes, I do.

So if you want to be the toy for someone, if your need is that great, then you must graciously pay the price and say, "Thank you, God. I have this great need by denying the truth to be someone's toy to be played with." Whenever you permit the dark side of your mind, known as ignorance, to declare, "What can I do with my child?" when it's your child—and so your thoughts are your children. Your judgments are how they do what they do to you. Hmm? Did that help with your question?

Yes.

Well, if it doesn't, I can be much more specific.

Yes.

First, accept it's your child.

Yes.

Have you done that?

Yes, I have.

You have created your child for a certain purpose.

Yes.

Have you done that?

Yes.

You had the control to create them, right?

Right.

For you to declare what can you do when they don't do what you want them to do is blatant, blatant darkness. Would you not agree?

I would agree.

Then take corrective steps. Thank you very much for your lovely question. The lady over here, please. Yes.

What happens to these neutralized forms after we've used the cleansing breath and worked on them?

Thank you so much. What happens to the neutralized forms? They do exactly what your flesh does: it returns to the source from whence it came to rise once again in another form. You see, it is created of mental substance. That which is created from a thing returns unto the thing. And so that which is neutralized is like the decaying body of the flesh, the decaying process. You see, it is returning to the very substance from which it rose. It returns and rises again.

You see, all creation, all limit returns to the very source from whence it came forth. This is why that which you are returns unto its true Source. That true Source is within you. Your awakening of it is subject to your absolute acceptance, which is freedom from all limit, freedom from all judgments, freedom from all creation. Then you awaken, "Oh, yes, the lemon is feeling so happy. There's a little sunlight on it." Or "There's too much," or "It's chilly." *[This class was given in the garden of the Serenity temple, which had a lemon tree.]* You will experience that, for that is what you *are*. You *are* the very Essence, Energy, Intelligence, and Light that is expressing through all form. You are inseparably a part of it. To be over-identified with limit, with form, to believe you are the flesh limits you. And therefore, in that limit you cannot experience that true being that you are, that is everywhere and never absent or away.

You see, when the statement is made, "You are God. Therefore, you are good," you must not permit your mind to say, "Oh, I'm God!" because, you see, you believe limit. Well, that's not what God is. God's expressing through limit. So that which you are, good, God, is expressing through this limited form. And when you stop believing you are the limited form, you will start experiencing what you are and by so doing, slowly and gradually—because you'll experience many things. You will experience the Intelligence that you are expressing through another person, and at the moment that you are aware of that which you are expressing through them, you probably will not like the experience of what their mind is telling them that they are by their own belief. Do you understand that?

And so in keeping with this wonderful truth, that what we cannot and will not permit our self to tolerate in another is still waiting to be educated within our self. This is why we cannot tolerate certain things in other people, because we are waiting to educate them within ourselves. Do you understand?

So, you see, any forms that rise up—forms, thought forms solidified into judgments—they return to their source the instant that they are neutralized. In other words, from good they came and to good they shall return, you see. See, neutral, neutralization, perfect balance is what goodness is. That's what God is. This is why God cannot deny and God cannot judge. This is why God is not a doer. That is why God, Good, the Principle is a sustainer.

Creation, this substance that creates, that's where judgment exists, for that's where limit exists. God cannot be a judge and be God, the Principle of Good, and have judgment, for judgment is limit, and limit is not the Principle of Good. Does that help with your question?

Yes. Thank you.

You're welcome. Someone else here—the gentleman there, please.

If a person is expressing their seeming problems to you, is there any way we can help our self by helping them?

Why, certainly. God helps those who help themselves by helping others. First of all, in your efforts to help another with their problems, you first must qualify yourself by helping yourself with your own problems. So if you want to experience the goodness that is, you first work on your own problems and get them out of the way that you may be an instrument of the Principle of Good and, therefore, help another to help themselves to the same level of consciousness. Yes?

If you feel that you, that you aren't having problems yourself, can you express yourself to them to help them?

Well, first of all, if a person is not experiencing problems, that means a person who is totally resigned to whatever creation has to offer and is not making the effort to control their lives. Now, nothing exists in form or limit, [including] a person, through identification that they are form or limit, that doesn't have discord or disturbance because it is the principle of limit. Now, do you believe that you are the form that you are expressing through? *[After a short pause, the teacher continues.]* Question, please.

Ah, to a, to a—yeah, partly.

Partly. So you only have partly problems. And I'm sure you can help. You think about that, and this lady here is waiting, please. Yes. The lady right there, and I'll be right with you.

I had a question in an earlier—

Yes, you speak right up so that you may receive an answer.

Yes. I had a question in an earlier class, but I was told that 51 percent of the class had to be using the cleansing breath. May I ask it at this time?

Yes. How long ago was that class? And did I say here that 51 percent were now doing their cleansing breath daily? Hmm? Was that not a question about a class or two ago?

Yes.

Oh, my, patience, how beautiful you are. How beautiful. You know, I know that you appreciate beauty. Hmm?

Yes.

Call upon the principle of patience, she is so beautiful. Fifty-one percent—we've got a ways to go. And they best not take too long.

Thank you.

But you, you hold on to your question. It'll help you grow and appreciate the beauty of patience. Hmm? Yes. The gentleman there, please.

Yes. What state of conscious[ness], if we're in a state of conscious[ness], are we in when we're holding our cleansing breath?

Is it important to it working for you?

Is it important—I, I can't say that it's important for it—

Then it's not necessary to entertain you at this time. First, the demonstration of it working for you is the number one thing you should direct all your energy and attention to: that it works for you. How many times has it worked for you? And how many times have you done it this past seven days, my friend?

I don't know how many times I did it. I know—

Is it more than—Pardon?

I know I did it at least twice each day.

Twice a day.

For sure.

Now, has it worked for you twice a day?

Has it worked? I know, I—to my mind I know a couple times it has worked.

Out of twice a day times 7 is 14 times and a couple of times it has worked. Now you start practicing it 20 times a day. All right?

Yes, sir.

Because, you see, the more you practice it, the better it works. You see, now this is the reason why my students—or anyone—are tempted not to make the effort to do the cleansing breath. When a student of mine is not doing their cleansing breath, by recommendation of the demonstrable law, which is very clear—it works—that reveals to me that that student believes they are those forms that they have created and solidified. And those forms know that it works, and that's why they won't allow you to do it. And so that's just the way that it is. Understand what's in control and when you know that it would benefit you to do your cleansing breath—and there's never a day that passes that you don't have at least a few dozen times that you could use it and be benefited by it—and when you know that you should do it and you find that you're not doing it, well, just say, "Thank you, God. I have a need to service these things by believing they're me." Because that's who's in control of you. That's not you at all, but it is indeed what you're servicing.

Now, you ask any man that likes to pride himself on a little independence and tell him he's servicing this woman or that woman. He gets very upset. Wouldn't you agree?

Oh, yes.

Well, any woman that disturbs a man, that man is servicing her; he's servicing her in his own mind, you know. You don't have to move the physical body to be a servant. There's slavery of mental substance. There's slavery of the mind. Many people are in human bondage in slavery of their mind by the lack of initiative thought and the lack of the experience of freedom and independence. Now usually a man will say, "Now, yes, I want to go into bondage. I have denied the truth that I am, and I have permitted my mind to convince me, by my believing I am the thought I have created, that I'm only half there." Now men who believe they are half there demand and believe that they must have someone else in order to experience the goodness of life, which would put them all there (in their mind). Now no human being wants to believe that they're half there, but when they demonstrate that they are half there by insistence on believing they need someone else to make them whole and complete, the demonstration, of course, is the revelation.

So if we find in our life that some lovely person, we believe, is an instrument of robbing us of the tranquility and serenity of our day, then be rest assured we are in service to that particular person. Does that help with your question? Yes, I see your hand.

We are constantly creating thoughts that are controlling our lives, aren't we?

Yes. So why not consciously? We're not consciously creating them. We are creating them all the time. There are few moments when we're conscious. There're a few moments when we're at home, and we said, "Yes, this is what I'm going to make. Oh, that's what's going to happen from that, and that's what it's going to do, and that's what I'm going to experience down the road." Now that's conscious, intelligent reasoning, you see. But creating forms every day, all the time, most of them we're not conscious of, but we're always conscious of their return. Yes. Go ahead with your question.

Yes, but I'll have to . . .

You just woke up. I understand.

Well, I was speaking about so-called accidents.

There aren't any.

Yeah, that's what I was—OK, there aren't any. Well, incidents that happen in our lives that we, that we don't want to happen, I mean, after they happen, but yet still they, yet still they do happen while we find our self in that situation.

Yes, of course they happen because we at the time we say we don't want these experiences to happen to us, yet in our own lack of effort we continue to create them. We alone create them. Do you understand that?

Yes, sir.

And, you see, we create them and don't know we have created them by not making the effort to be aware of what our own mind is doing. And we are responsible to guide that vehicle, called our mind. That's our responsibility. And when we don't do it, something else is always waiting to do it for us. Do you like someone to think for you?

No, I don't.

When you don't make the effort to think for yourself, there's all kinds of things thinking for you. Do you understand that?

I'm experiencing that.

You are experiencing that. That's wonderful! I'm very happy for you because I know that experiences a person really dislikes soon get to change by their own effort in acceptance of the demonstrable law. No one likes to be in service to something that creates in their mind a disturbance. Would you not agree?

I–yes.

Pardon?

I agree.

So where we have to root it out is where we've—we have the right to control it, and that's in our mind. You see, it's our mind. It's our thought. We created it, and it's our judgment we solidified and, therefore, believe that we are. But we did it, and we can change it any moment we want to change it. It's up to us. Hmm? You don't like to be in service to someone else, do you?

No. No, sir, I don't.

Fine. Therefore, if you don't like to service someone else—whoever does not care to service someone else starts to enjoy servicing themselves by taking conscious choice in their mind and being aware of what their mind is doing. Hmm? I hope that's helped with your question. Now there's a lady here, please, waiting for a question. Yes.

In using the cleansing breath and in creating the new form, I'm having difficulty knowing how to go about that. Is it—do you think about it or do you use—

Oh, your problem is an intellectual one, and the secretary of our organization will be very happy to discuss the intellectual merry-go-round with you, although she's very busy working and will not have time to play with the intellect too much. I have already given the demonstrable truth. It's up to you to apply it. Any intellectual difficulties you have with it—that's why we have a secretary for our school. And she will be more than happy to guide your soul to take control of what you call an intellect. Thank you. The lady back there, please.

Yes. You spoke of contaminating the wild animals by, by approaching them and touching them.

You mean my channel spoke to you yesterday about it.

Yes.

I see.

I'm wondering whether feeding wild birds with a bowl of wild birdseed causes a contamination.

Do you have the need to pet them?

No!

What is your motive for feeding them when the Divine Principle has supplied more than enough for all of them?

I guess it's just to have them near me.

So, you see, we are in truth servicing our need, not theirs, aren't we?

Yes.

They just happen to be the ones that are there that help us with our delusion that we believe that their God is not providing for them. Is that not true? Is that charity or is that self-glory? You think of the difference in your mind and whether that's charity or whether it's self-glory and then I'll return to you. And another lady here had a question. Yes, the lady here, please.

Yes. Some time ago you said that at a future time you would discuss the significance of the wedding ring.

Well, I'll be more than happy to discuss advance teachings, further advanced teachings when you, as a student, are encouraged to help the others to get moving on what the requirement is. And that's their cleansing breath. I do hope that that's helped with your question.

Now we'll go back to the lady here on servicing her needs. To look out at creation and to deny the just law that whatever happens to us is caused by us, including a bird or an ant, reveals unto us that we do not accept the just law for our own life.

Now what is the difference, [which] I have already discussed with some of my students, between charity and self-glory? Does the bird come to you and tell you that it is hungry? Or does— and does the bird come to you and tell you there is no food left for them to work and to therefore survive? Or does the bird come to you and tell you, "I am too lazy to do like my brothers and sisters and go out into the world and make the effort to find something to eat so I can survive. Therefore, I come to you in keeping with the law that like attracts like and becomes the Law of Attachment and expect from you to feed me without me making the effort." Now, I'm telling you the bird's side of this story. Do you understand? And not you personally, but anyone. And so the little bird, like so many other creatures in the world, comes and appeals to what it senses is your need, the effect of your own denials.

Now there's a fine line of distinction between being charitable and servicing the glory of self. There's a fine, fine, fine line.

If we, in our denial of the Principle of Good, deny the law, and we look out and we say, "Without me, that being cannot survive." Hmm? "Without me." Without pausing and being honest with oneself and asking oneself the truth, "This being I have pulled into my universe and I am having this experience. What does the light of reason within me reveal that I should do in reference to the appeal that I am judging his or her eyes are revealing to me? Where am I in consciousness?" And you pause and you think. Now if [in] your light of reason within you, that you at that moment are capable of rising to, you take a look and you say, "Well, this will require on my part, this will require on my part making the effort to feed you two or three times a day. This will require on my part seeing that you, if you're going to live in my house, [are] taken out into the woods to have your daily constitution. This will require on my part the effort to be made to exercise you, etc., etc., etc., etc."—now that's intelligent thinking. And then you look at the little creature and you say, "Now listen, this is what I know I have to do for your benefit and for mine, if I judge that I need you. I am willing to take on that responsibility and to make the effort never to consider that it is a burden for me. Now this is what *you* are going to have to do in doing your share, for I'm not supporting freeloaders for the glory of my ego." Does that help with your question?

Yes. Thank you.

You're more than welcome. Now that's not limited to two-legged creatures. That includes the winged creatures and the little cats and the dogs. You have a responsibility to communicate with them so that they may, in the limits of their forms, do their part. Their part is not just to lie around and snore. Their part is not to be a lounge lizard. Otherwise, what you call the wild animals would all be lying down, like lounge lizards, twenty-four hours a day, and the two-legged animals would be racing back and forth stuffing food in their mouth[s]. That's contrary to demonstrable law. So let's not be tempted by the glory of self, and let's remind all forms, the Intelligence within them, that they have a responsibility.

If it's a bird, what is a bird supposed to do? Not to fight with another bird. The bird is supposed to chirp, and do whatever it does to express its happiness and its harmony for that's why you allow him around. Now if it's one of these four-legged creatures, they're supposed to pay attention to the spiritual classes. They are supposed to listen. They're not supposed to interrupt and be tempted to bark and to disturb the atmosphere and the tranquility of the class. You have to make an effort to communicate with them: to tell them in no uncertain terms, "That's the way it is. You're not going to be here freeloading." Now I hope that's helped with your question.

Yes, I see you have a question. The lady right there. Yes.

Ah, I was—

Considering your experiences, I see you have a lot of questions. You go right ahead.

Earlier you mentioned that when you're not home that someone is creating for you. And I was wonder—

Why, of course.

—I was wondering how that law or principle or what that is to establish that?

Yes, I'm very happy that you made that question. It's very important. And again—and I'm happy to reveal it because you have paid the price of what it's like not to make the effort to do your cleansing breath when you know that you should be doing it. Is that not correct?

Right.

Uh-huh. Now when you are not making the effort to be conscious aware, conscious and aware of your mind and the thoughts that are being created by it—in other words, you, your reason, your intelligence that you are aware of is not saying, "I choose this thought to be solidified and become a judgment by my believing that I am it. God, the Principle of Good, help me never to forget what I have done. So when the price comes, the payment of this judgment that I choose to believe that I am, I will have a little light to wrench myself free."

Now when you're not making that little bit of effort, your mind, designed to create—for that *is* the creator. The mental substance is the creator. That's [the] creator. When you're not there, patterns, judgments created that you believe that you are, long ago established in your consciousness, rise up, creating their own kind and creating all kinds of little wild children; [so] that when you go back home, that is when you once again be aware of where you are, you and what your mind is doing, you're not going to be happy at all. They'll have your house all torn up.

Take control of your mind before confusion sets in, for that which you do not, with the faculty of reason, consciously take control of, confusion is the payment you must make. Does that help with your question?

Yes, it does. Thank you.

Yes. Time is passing quickly. So move your questions in, if you have any. Yes, the lady there, please.

What is the difference between intellect—that's not . . .

What is the difference between what?

Is intellect the thinking of something and reason the expression?

Oh, yes! You were the one that the secretary was going to help with your intellect. Please be sure to spend a few moments after the class. And the gentleman back there. Thank you so much there. That's a secretarial question. The gentleman back there, please.

The thoughts that, that I seem to be entertaining for many years have come from you.

From me?!

Well, through you, be—

Oh, really.

—because of your—

Those are the only thoughts that you entertain within your consciousness? You are my most illumined student in all of the eons of my work. Yes, go right ahead, young man. I feel—I know you feel so good, but I want you to feel good without that kind of payment. Yes, go ahead.

How can I express through them without, without being attached to them?

Well, I haven't found anyone attached to me, and I'm grateful for that, especially my channel.

Not to you, but to the thoughts that come through you.

Well, this is a rather interesting statement that you're making. I think we best spend a little time on that. Are you telling me that I am responsible for your attachment to a form that you have within in your consciousness? Because if you are doing so, you are tempting me to greatness which I will not accept.

No, I'm not, I'm not accusing you of, of, of—

But, don't you see, if you credit me with the only thoughts that you have within your consciousness are the ones from me, then that can only tell me that I'm responsible for any experience in your life that you don't like. And I happen to know you've just got through having an experience that you don't like, just as recent as two months ago. So if the experience that you didn't like that you had just two months ago was a thought of mine, then it's quite alien to me, and I cannot in honesty accept responsibility therefore. Hmm?

Now, you see, I think we should broaden our horizon a little bit. I think, perhaps, we have a communication problem. I have yet to experience a student, throughout my service to the Light, that had only thoughts that had passed through me. Ofttimes I wish it might be true they'd have an increasing amount of thoughts that I've been happy to share with you. But I have, I have never had an experience of having a student, their only thoughts they ever entertained in their life were the ones that came from me. And I want to be honest with all of you—and perhaps we'll have a shower. *[The teacher looks toward the sky.]* Yes, it would be nice. Who knows? No, I doubt it. But anyway—that's not my business, that job—anyway, even if it were true, which it is not, I still think that we ought to pause before we speak that some of the things you do which are effects of your thoughts are so foreign to my experiences I cannot in all honesty take credit for them.

Thank you so much, class. And we'll see you. Good day. Thank you.

JUNE 30, 1985

A/V Class Private 4

I am very encouraged, as I know some of you are, that the majority of this class has found sufficient value to establish the law and do your daily cleansing breath. And in keeping with that established law, we are now able to move on to even more advanced instruction and application of what you are receiving. And to begin with, let us pause for a moment and declare what we are that we may refrain from believing what we have been. For what we have been is what we have spent our life believing.

And now we have evolved to that step in evolution of being. So let us start with our practice each day of being by declaring what we are. You pause in your activities in the course of your day and declare the truth: "I am the goodness that I know for I am the one that makes it so." Declare that great truth. Pause. And listen carefully to what you think your mind is answering to that declaration of truth. For it is guaranteed that it will have something to say to you, and it will not be in harmony nor in keeping with the declaration that you have just made. That in turn will reveal to you how you are trapped, by what form, and what to do about it.

Now you have received the cleansing breath. You have received it and are using it to bring about a neutralization of those thought forms that you have created that you are tempted to believe, at times, that you are.

Now it is time in the use of that cleansing breath to rise in consciousness beyond thought, beyond the mental realms. And so, effective with this class, those of you receiving video audiotapes will benefit from the aid that is placed upon them by my orders to my channel. You will receive the exact notes of harmony that bring about a perfect balance within your consciousness that you may rise above, for you shall rise above, in application of what you see and what you hear. To those of you who are not benefiting from video audio magnetic tape, you will receive the audio portion only, of course, on what you call an audiotape. *[Students in these classes were permitted to purchase video or audiotapes. Many students purchased both.]*

I hereby instruct you explicitly not to move, drive, or do anything that would require your mental attention while listening to what we call a twenty-minute contemplation time that you will hear on your audiotape class effective this day. Contemplation means exactly what it says: to contemplate. You will not create a form in mental consciousness for that will be contrary to the very purpose of this contemplation time. You will, however, be receptive. Be not concerned, for being concerned you are creating a form. It is simply a sound. It is *the* sound. It is perfect balance in the spheres of harmony. Your receptivity is all that is necessary. Your visual will reveal to you, as a visual aid, the benefits of that perfect harmony. It will be an instrument to assist you in freeing yourself, for that time of contemplation, from forms in mental substance that, through error of ignorance, you have created and are no longer serving you in a beneficial way.

Many times I hear what you believe are questions, only to have it proven to yourself that the question was never a question. It was a statement of a form seeking support and justification to do what it desired to do with your vital life energy. That is a part, of course, of the slow but sure process of awakening.

Apply this simple truth that declares truth needs no defense. For truth can never be truth and contain what you know as need. Truth *is*. Light *is*. Energy *is*. What we do with it is ofttimes a very different story. Remember, when you believe that you need to defend anything, be rest assured that is a revelation unto you that that belief, your belief, is not you. It is something you have created. Never forget you alone have created it. Never forget you are a law unto yourself. Never forget the question you should daily ask yourself: "I am a law unto myself. I demonstrate it moment by moment. I am indeed successful for I have and continue to succeed in whatever I permit, by being a law unto myself, whatever form I permit to serve in my mental world at any time."

Everyone is successful. We are at this moment and all moments past and moments yet to be successful. We are indeed successful for we are a law that does not fail. This day, be it what you consider a joyous or a sad one, is your success. You have succeeded in making it what you make it. Enjoy the fruits, if you wish to. No matter what your mind says your day is, it is the revelation of how successful you are. And so if it is your desire to believe what has passed, to believe the things you have created, then so be it: you are indeed successful with it.

These classes, designed to help you to see what you are doing and to help you to inspire yourself to do something that you feel would be more beneficial to you, do not guarantee success. You already have success. They only guide you to show you a better way. That this great success that you all are may be guided by the light of reason and that you may benefit from the harmony and the goodness that you are.

Do not concern yourself with what you believe, at times, are your failures, what you believe at times you cannot do without. That is not you who is speaking. You are responsible, for it is your mouth. It is not you who believe what you are seeing. You are responsible for your eyes as surely as you are responsible for the ears of your temple. Your temple, your body is the temple of God, which is the Principle of Goodness. You are successful with whatever you choose to do with it. Do not cry over your success. Rejoice in its seeming disasters and struggles for in all disaster there is Divinity, for it takes the Light, the Energy, the Infinite Intelligence to sustain the forms of disaster as well as it takes the Infinite Light and Eternal Energy to sustain what you call happiness, fulfillment, and joy. You are that power. You are successful in your use of it. Direction is what should be your interest. Directing it intelligently to bring about for you the goodness that you seek, for you seek in keeping with what you have denied. And therefore, from your denials of mental substance you experience the need, for you know beyond a shadow of any doubt that what you are is not struggle and strife, that what you are is not lack and limitation, that what you are is the joy of being. Inside of you, you know that.

And so I will now discuss for a few moments your new video and new audio, so-called, tapes. Twenty minutes, approximately, have been set aside at the beginning of each class as it's recorded. Those twenty minutes contain a perfect sound of balance. That perfect sound, for those of you who do not yet know, happens to be, on your so-called keyboards, middle C. Your responsibility to receive the benefit of this contemplation time is for you to remain still, and in that stillness, you become receptive. You can only be receptive in keeping with that audio-video aid, you can only be receptive to that which is beyond the control of your limited mind and thought forms.

Some of you, when you return from that awakening within yourself and once again reidentify with the limit you call yourselves and believe that you are temporarily, will come up with many justifications in order to protect the realm of consciousness that, at times, you believe that you are. That's the realm of consciousness known as duality, discord, disaster, and disease. You will find that your minds, some of you, will justify that you've been hypnotized, I think is the word you use. But you must ask yourself intelligently what is it that's doing it to you. And in an honest and sincere answer, you must answer, "Whatever it was, I did it to myself." And that will help you to discern what is you and what is the things you believe that you are.

The greatest difficulty that some of you have had here in these classes, these last few classes, is that when you think of your cleansing breath, something happens inside of your mind and you don't do it. Should you do it, you don't do it correctly. Now you must ask yourself what is it inside of you, with such a simple exercise, that you find yourself unable to do, and if you are able to do, you do it incorrectly. You are not so unintelligent. So the only answer can possibly be, even to your minds of logic, is quite simple: that simple truth presents to the forms of the mental world that you believe that you are, it presents a great threat. Not to you, but to the things that you temporarily believe that you are. And so you wait until the so-called last gun is fired and you say, "Oh, I must do my cleansing breath." By waiting so long those forms have so convinced you that you are them that you either don't do your cleansing breath at all or you do it incorrectly.

Now, like with all truth that frees the eternal being that you are, mental substance presents its cloud before you and demands its dictates to do it just a bit different than you have received it. They know, as mental substance is intelligent, that if they can do it just a bit different, that will make it theirs. But who is *they*? Who are they? At times you believe they are you. And when you believe that they are you, then you feel satisfied, "Fine. I'm doing this cleansing breath. I'm doing it my way." Well, my friends, doing it what you believe is your way only feeds the forms so they may protect themselves and not be annihilated by the eternal Light of truth.

Demons cannot walk a straight line. It is in the realm of impossibility. Demons cannot walk a straight line. All prophets have taught you that simple truth. The path to the Light is straight and narrow. It's not a freeway upon which old creation can have its heyday.

You are not going to be without. How could you possibly be without the goodness of life when you demonstrate how successful you are with anything you permit your mind to entertain and demand? You are extremely successful. When you permit those forms to use your mouth that tell you, you don't have this and you don't have that, when you permit those forms to use your mouth and to tell you that life is such a struggle and such a strife, you receive from the listening ears that you are able to pollute the energy necessary to keep the forms active using your own mouth. I've taught you that truth over these many years: the simple declaration that misery does not only love company, it is indispensable to its own existence. And so when you, in your great success, activate the forms that guarantee misery in your life, you know very well from your own experiences you ever seek out in your world of creation listening ears to share with you the great suffering and struggle that you have. You do that so that you may receive from others the necessary energy that the demons you are serving may receive more energy for they never ever get enough. Therefore, you are often blinded to how successful you are because when they control your mind, they're ever hungry and they never get enough.

And so pause in these thoughts that you believe that you are at times and declare this great truth of who and what you are, and see what it takes for you to take control of your mind and your children that you have created and who you have permitted to convince you, from use and abuse of your mental consciousness, to believe that you are now the child that you have created.

Now let us look at your physical world. A parent is an instrument through which a soul enters your Earth planet. [It] goes through its process and it's born. Now physical and mental substance. When the child doesn't do what you want, when you want, and how you want, you see clearly how you in those moments, by your own upset, by your own disturbance in your own mind, you see how much you believe that you are the child that you were an instrument in its creation; you see clearly.

And you don't have to reserve that great demonstration to a physical child. To those of you who temporarily, at times, believe you're in love with someone and they don't do what you want when you want, you experience this great disturbance. That is ever in keeping with your belief, with your own belief that they are you. That is what those things offer to you.

Say that you're in business, and business goes the way that the forms tell you that it should be going. And you believe that you are the forms of your mind. And when business seems to be going in an opposite direction than what those forms you believe that you are, are telling you that it should, see whether or not you are disturbed. Have you lost the tranquility of your day? Are you still the person you believed you were when things that you believe are you don't go your way?

You are successful each and every moment that you breathe. You are successful in doing your number. I said that long ago in stating that we always get what we really want. How sad at times that we forget what it is we wanted when we established the law and proved how successful that we are.

Now I'm going to give you, in a few moments, [an opportunity] to see if you've done your homework for your question time. Your question time is very important. That reveals to your co-students what homework you have been doing. You know, I stated here last Sunday to you: I have not come for you to freeload off of me. I'm not about to let you come and freeload off of my channel. So don't get it into your little pea consciousness that I am just here to feed you all of the energy of my channel and leave him flat as a so-called flounder while you lap up all of the benefits. These classes of mine are participating classes. And if you don't have enough vitality to participate, that tells all the co-students that you've been lapping up the energy feeding more forms who do their number for you to do what we might call the Irish jig each day. Well, there's no jigging here. So let's see these hands and let's see this participation. Yes, the lady there, please. That lady.

I'd like to know the correlation—[The student speaks very quietly.]

Oh, no, my dear, you'll have to give forth more energy than that. Yes, go right ahead.

I'd like to know the correlation between the cleansing breath and the creative principle. [The student speaks slightly louder, but not loud.]

Well, now you just pause a moment, and speak just a little bit louder. I've never considered that I had a hearing impairment nor [that] my channel has one. He's out and I'm in, and I hear very clearly. But I know that many cannot hear. You may state your question one more time. Speak like you would speak to what you might consider a husband long gone. Yes, thank you.

I'd like to know the correlation between the cleansing breath and the creative principle. [The student speaks loudly and very clearly.]

Wonderful! Now I hear you as clear as a crystal bell. Thank you. The lady would like to know the correlation, if any, between the cleansing breath and the creative principle. Because in this here private class, so many that I am looking at have not received the creative principle—you hear?—and this is not the day or the class in which you should explain the creative principle; we will reserve your question 'til next Sunday. And that will give you time to review the cleansing—the creative principle that you have been given so long ago, you understand? And you will be able to share in class your understanding of the creative principle. When you have finished, I will then state, for your benefits, the correlation between the cleansing breath and the creative principle, if any exists. Does that help you? So you have seven whole days to refresh your memory on the creative principle that is of such interest to you. All right? Because you will be sharing with the uninitiated present who have never received the creative principle. Do you understand? *[After a short pause, the teacher continues.]* Pardon? Hello?

Yes.

That's wonderful. Thank you. The lady here has a question.

Yes. I was wondering when you're setting new laws into motion, mental laws, or new forms for your life, and you appear to be getting the opposite of what you consciously feel you are setting forth, I'm wondering what is the . . .

Problem?

Yes.

Well, in reference to that beautiful question that one is doing what they understand is right and their results are wrong, they are not in harmony, we must look at the law itself. The one I just discussed: we're all successful. So our thought and our act must be first united. For the law is revealing they are not, and a house divided cannot stand. Now this is very important. One personally believes, beyond a shadow of any doubt, that they are doing what is right with their efforts, and the results are not showing what they should in harmony with their motivation. Hmm?

Right.

Therefore, one must become aware of what they're really setting in motion for their results, in keeping with the law that like attracts like, is bringing them opposite of what they believe they're setting into motion. Does that help with your question?

Yes.

So our thought must be united with our true motive, for there is a discrepancy between what we are thinking and what we are truly doing. Do you understand?

Yes.

You see, a person may say, "Well, I want my child to love me and to be a good person and to demonstrate that. I am doing all that is necessary for that to come about. And that is not the experience that I am having." Does that help with your question?

Right. Right.

Yes. So where is the change required? The change is required within the consciousness that is divided. The mouth is speaking forth one thing, and the Law of Motivation is doing the direct opposite. And the Law of Motivation is far greater than the spoken word. So one must unite their spoken word with their true motive by being honest with themselves and facing what their true motive is and, in so doing, uniting it with their spoken word, which is life-giving energy, which guarantees the return of experiences in keeping with the unity of motivation and spoken word. Does that help with your question?

Thank you very much. Yes, it does.

Yes. Now to be a little bit more specific with that. Ofttimes we truly believe that we are making great effort, and that is what we really desire. But we are not being honest with our self in looking at our true motivation. Now the experiences help us to see what our real motivation is. And so we can say in the experience, "Now what is this experience revealing to me? Outside of a form that I am creating that I don't believe that I have created it, but I have created it. Am I receiving attention? Am I receiving energy? Am I receiving pity for my plight?" And on down the list of self-interest. Does that help with your question?

Yes.

You're more than welcome.

Thank you.

Yes. The gentleman there, please.

Is . . .

Yes?

. . . the only purpose of sleep the expression of the forms that we have created? Is that the sole purpose of sleep? [The student speaks quietly. The teacher puts his hand to his ear as the student speaks.]

There's nothing particularly interesting I have with my ear, except my effort to hear you more clearly.

Is the only purpose of sleep the expression of forms which we have created? [The student speaks more loudly.]

My, I see you're starting to do a little homework. That's most encouraging for all of us. The only purpose for sleep in creation—and that's the only place sleep exists—is for the energy of your vital body to be drained by the forms that you have created in your mental substance and that you believe that you are. Without that so-called safety valve of the human mind, you would lose the balance of the human mind and would not be able to function in the world of creation. Yes, your answer is affirmative. Yes.

Why, then, must they express and consume that energy?

If they do not express and consume the energy from your vital body while you are unconscious, then the demands upon your mind while in a conscious state is known to some of you, the early stages of that, is known to you as time-pressure. Now time-pressure, I revealed to you some time ago, was the bombardment of desire forms upon your consciousness, and you experience a frustration and a breaking down of your nervous system. Now some people call that in your world (the final stages) a nervous breakdown. And so the law reveals clearly that through your unconscious state, where the forms are able to drain the vitality to express themselves, you have some degree of balance in your conscious state.

Now I have also, over these many years, shared with you the benefit of working on these forms: of placing within your consciousness a form sufficiently strong that it may be the one receiving your energy while you are sleeping. And therefore, that form [is] to be called forth to your conscious mind immediately upon awakening, and that is the guardian of the portal to keep those other forms from creating what you know in your waking state as frustration, time-pressure, and a final breakdown of your nervous system. Does that help with your question?

Yes. Thank you.

But, you see, you cannot benefit from it until you start applying it, anyone. Yes. And the lady there had a question. You had a question? Yes.

I would like to—

Speak right up, please.

Yes. Could you explain what it means to be qualified?
Qualified?
Yes.
Do you feel qualified in anything? Anything? Anything at all?
Yes.
Wonderful. How does it feel to feel qualified in something?
Understand, to understand it, to . . .
To your satisfaction.
To have a degree of confidence.
You have a degree of confidence. Do you have a degree of self-assurance when you feel qualified?
Yes.
Do you have any fear or any hesitation in your expression in the areas in which you feel qualified?
No.
Therefore, you reveal that in being qualified you are freed from forms of fear—correct?—you are freed from forms of self-concern. Is that correct?
Yes.
You are freed from the negative forms that would disturb you when you choose to do what you feel you are qualified in. Is that correct?
Yes.
Now what does that do for you? Do you experience encouragement within your consciousness?
Yes.
Do you experience a degree of dedication in your expression? Do you experience a freedom from disturbing factors and distractions at that time?
Yes.
So it reveals to you and to everyone present that when you have qualified yourself in anything, you are freed from all negative factions when you choose to do what you are qualified in, would you not agree?

Yes.

Therefore, let us make more effort in qualifying our self to something that is beneficial, that can only bring back unto us the goodness of life, that which we are, freed from depending on anyone else. Now when you feel qualified in something, you do not feel dependent on someone to express your qualifications, do you?

No.

Well, there you are. Aren't you grateful that you can, in your consciousness, look to something in which you feel, beyond a shadow of any doubt, qualified?

Yes.

That is a part of what it all means. That help with your question?

Yes. Thank you.

Yes. The gentleman here, please.

Yes. In reference to last week's class in which you were discussing stopping blaming outward and then declaring the truth that you are the creator of your experiences, could you please discuss how this would benefit persons who continue to go around feeling inferior to others?

Well, in reference to blaming outside for the experiences that you are encountering inside, let us first pause and look at the truth. You do not, nor does anyone, blame outside only when they are dependent for their life on something outside. People who depend on something outside for their life have no problem blaming outside for their problems. The blaming of outside or blaming something beyond your control or what you judge is your control reveals to the world your dependence on something outside. And so people who blame outside depend on outside for their life, for their goodness that they experience.

So one simply says, "Now I don't like depending on something or someone that there's no possible way that I can have control over. Therefore, how do I start the process of return to personal responsibility, the effect of which is my freedom?" Well, it's quite simple: stop blaming outside, and you'll stop depending outside. Was there a further question on that now?

I'm beginning to see how that can work on a person who, who feels inferior or who is identified with his own judgment—

Oh, you want to know why some people feel inferior?

Yes, I would.

Why, they're people who have taken great pleasure, great pleasure in being so perfect that their judgments are like hailstorms. You see, people who feel inferior spend most of their conscious time and so much of the unconscious time in comparing themselves with everyone and everything outside. And the more that they compare, the more inferior they feel for they constantly see in others what they demand that they lack in themselves. And so it's one old happy merry-go-round, one real merry-go-round of feeding the glory of self, known as self-pity. People over-identified with the uneducated ego not only have a flood of self-pity in their consciousness, they have a phenomenal amount of judgments and justifications, excuses and blaming outside for their plight in life. Does that help with your question?

Thank you very much.

You're welcome. *[After a short pause, the teacher continues.]* Who's doing their homework here? Yes, the lady there, please. Speak right up.

Desire, which is God—

It is the expression, my dear, of God. Yes.

Thank you.

Yes.

Focused by the human mind. Is that focused desire the same as need?

First of all, in reference to the divine expression known as desire and is the forming or focusing of the divine expression known as need? Now let us go to the steps. First of all, by denying what we are, we believe what we are not. We start by identifying, believing: we place a dent in the consciousness. It's known as identification. Most of us are quite familiar with denting our self to this limited piece of clay here of my channel—and yours, too. So you place a dent in the consciousness; you call that identification. In that instant you have denied what you are and now believe that which you are not. All right? Do you follow me so far? When you believe what you are not (the limit), you then use this divine expression, known as desire, through the only way that you can use it: through limit; you form it. Now when you form that, you understand, you now have it under the control of the mental substance—you understand, because that's where you have formed it, in mental substance—of judgment and justification. Do you understand? Fine.

Now, the desire itself *is*. You have formed it because you believe you have identified with your limit. And [when] you identify with your limit, all things you create are, therefore and thereafter, limit. As long as you identify with what you call self, you are governed and controlled by the Law of Payment and Attainment; you are governed and controlled by limit; you are governed and controlled by joy and sadness; you are governed and controlled by dual law. You are no longer—no longer do you walk a straight line. You are now walking a crooked mile in consciousness.

So if you accept that demonstrable truth and when you take and form by your mind the limits of the divine expression and in the formation of that you look at it and you give it back to the Source that has the just domain over the divine expression—and that is known as God, the Divinity—then, in keeping with laws of evolution, it will enter into your consciousness in the divine way, in the divine time, and you are freed from these so-called payments and attainments and all the suffering that they have to offer. Does that help with your question?

Yes. Thank you.

Yes. You're welcome. Yes, the lady there, please.

Um.

This lady here that didn't raise her hand has a question.

How can you—

Do you have the energy to raise your hand now?

Yes, I do.

Yes, fine.

How can you stay—how can you express initiative, but stay in divine will?

Well, first of all, how can you express initiative and stay in divine will? It takes initiative to enter divine will. That takes initiative. You see, divine will—you know what divine will is, don't you?

Total acceptance.

Total acceptance. You don't think that total acceptance takes a little initiative on your part? Or anyone's part?

Conscious effort.

Would anyone disagree that conscious effort is initiative? Does initiative not take conscious effort? I ask this young lady here. *[The teacher asks a different student.]*

Yes, it does.

All right. Now first of all, you have agreed that it takes conscious effort to enter divine will. Correct? *[The teacher returns to the student who asked the question.]*

Right.

It takes conscious effort to remain in divine will.

Uh-huh.

Do you agree that's initiative?

Yes, I do.

Therefore, you have answered your question. Now let's hear your question again, for your benefit.

OK.

[After a short pause, the teacher continues.]

How do you stay in divine will and express initiative? Wasn't that your question?

Right.

How do you feel now about your question?

Make conscious effort.

Conscious effort *is* initiative.

Right.

In other words, you see, ofttimes we get our self confused with words. You see, in all our getting, get understanding; in all our giving, give wisdom.

Let us stop here a moment. Communication is an avenue through which understanding expresses itself. So without communication, forget understanding. Now communication, clearly, is a problem that many, many, many people have, and certainly our little class is not without that seeming problem: communication.

Now, to one mind the question, How do you enter divine will and still express initiative?—well, we're not talking about the true meaning of the word *initiative*. No, no, no. We are looking at the word *initiative* and we're looking at the word *divine will*, which is total acceptance; we're looking at total acceptance [as], "That's fine. That's *your* way. Now initiative, this is my way." So we're looking at a battle. What does that have to do with the true meaning of the word *initiative*? What does that have to do with the true meaning of the words *divine will* or *total acceptance*? It reveals to us that we look at what is God's as something God has a right to. "But I don't agree with that right all the time; therefore, I want to know how to get what is God's and get what I judge is me." Now this is the separation here, you see: to believe one thing [and] to manifest its opposite is an absolute guarantee of failure. And failure is indeed an expression of success.

You see, there are many people that are so successful. And some of the forms at times rise up and say, "Oh, what a failure I am." And yet the truth of the matter is they are very successful for the other forms have succeeded in their mind, through directed energy by their own attention, the avenue through which it is flowing, they have succeeded in the battle within the consciousness of succeeding over the other ones. Now [when] the other army rises up, there's [the] time [they] take a look and they say, "What a failure I am." It means they lost the battle. All right.

Now so here we are with your question on initiative and total acceptance. That tells all of us, including yourself, that what you mean by the word of *initiative* is doing something your way. Would you not agree?

Right.

And your way is not in keeping with the demonstrable Law of Total Acceptance. Is that not correct?

That's right.

So you find a battle in the understanding and the communicating of the truth that you are. You look at total acceptance and you look at initiative, and you judge initiative is doing what you want when you want to do it. And yet you want that and you want the divine will of God. Lucifer, my dear, wanted the same thing. We all make our choices moment by moment. In your world you cannot have your cake and eat it, too. You have to give to gain. And the giving that you have to do is the delusion and deception of the forms that convince you that you are them to such an extent and degree that they not only use your mind, they use your mouth, your eyes, your ears, and all your senses. For whatever form enters supreme in the consciousness controls the temple of goodness, what you call your human body.

The battle is never won. It's one or the other. The choice is ever before us. There is no possible way that you can mix oil with water. You may have this or you may have that. A wise person takes a look and says clearly, "I shall enjoy the night and never forget it is not me. That in not forgetting, I may enter the Light of eternal goodness and I shall not try nor be tempted to mix the two for they are opposing armies in the universe, and I am a universe, a microcosm of a macrocosm." Does that help with your question?

Yeah. Thank you.

Set aside your time to let them control you. Use intelligence, and don't forget who is doing what and be deceived that that is you. Then you will never again be interested in communicating the word *initiative* as your way and *divine will* as someone else's way. Does that help with your question?

Yeah. Thank you.

You're welcome. Yes, the lady there, please.

In develop—in, in working on development of a new form to replace those that are, through the cleansing breath, to replace those that have been, is it a natural response to have what, you might call it, the hissing hounds afterwards for a while?

As long as you identify and believe that you are your form and the limit, you must forever pay the price: the price of payment and attainment. Now this day, this very day I spoke to you on the next step, which you will be receiving from this class, which is the sound to free you from all of those mental realms, at least for a time. So in creation, identified with limits and forms, to entertain within the consciousness, "Oh, I'm going to have to pay for this. I've experienced this goodness, well, I pay," well, you pay in advance in creation as long as you're identified to it. To over-identify with the payment is of no benefit. Would you say?

Not at all.

I think that's answered your question, hasn't it? Yes. *[After a short pause, the teacher continues.]* You have another question, miss.

It hasn't quite come up yet.

You hadn't quite formed it yet. Well, we'll wait until you get it formed. I'll ask this lady here. Yes.

How often should we watch our videotape and do the concentration?

Daily. Daily. I cannot stress the great importance in your ever-evolving steps throughout the universes. Now is the strongest you're going to be for you have the gross form that does not register the forms as they actually are because of the density of physical flesh. You see, when we believe that we are physical flesh, we build a wall between what we are. And therefore, we cannot see clearly. And so in that respect, through the belief that we are physical flesh, material substance, we are in that respect, in a sense, temporarily buffered from the full impact of the forms that we alone create.

Now, you're going to find, I would recommend, myself, looking into your various activities, I would recommend a minimum of twice a day, a minimum. It is not wise to overdo anything because as long as you identify with limit, as long as you believe you're physical substance, then you will have to, of course, in keeping with those laws, experience the forms trying to convince you that you are them for this is the one thing they absolutely—you see, demons, you understand, when exposed to the Light, if you believe that you are them, the Light blinds them and you believe you're in darkness. And so you want to prepare yourself. Not with fear, for that's another demon. That fear—fear reveals simply that you are over-identified with material substance. However, you will have experiences in keeping with your belief that you are limit and that you are form. You will have the experiences of whatever justifications and judgments they build in your consciousness to prevent you from the benefits of the Light within you, as they do all the time. Would you not agree? Not as much as they used to, would you not agree?

Hmm.

But they're still there and we're all still aware of them. Correct?

Right.

And so the step that you have the opportunity, all of you this day, to make is a step that is inevitable for all evolving beings. And you have the benefits of understanding demonstrable law to assist you, to strengthen, and to encourage you. And so twice a day is certainly not too much for I don't find any wimps in will power as students of mine in these private classes. I find great strength of will to do whatever it is that you decide you want to do or judge is necessary. And so the benefits here are to guide this *great* will that you have no absence of at all to intelligent benefits. Does that help with your question?

Yes. Thank you.

Yes, indeed. They'll tell you all kinds of things. Perhaps when I'm gone you might ask my channel; they [have tried] to do a royal number on him for forty-some years. They haven't succeeded, but he has a lot of will, too, you know. Yes. Yes, the lady there, please.

When you said that the forms cannot walk a straight line, I'm—what—why and how are we to walk the straight line?

Well, my dear, have you ever consumed that beverage called alcohol?

Yes.

Did you try to walk a straight line after?

No.

You don't even have to consume alcohol to—try to walk a straight and narrow line. You know, we're not going to paint a line on the driveway for you. However, I can assure you that whenever you believe you are the forms of your mind, it is physically impossible for you to walk a straight line. Why so? All forms, all birth is subject to and dependent upon what you call the water center. Each thought that you create, each one that you sustain utilizes moisture, the water center in your physical being. All right.

Now a straight line is in truth a complete circle. It is the living demonstration in your world of personal responsibility. A straight line, as you see a straight line, is only a portion of a circle. That is the law of the universes. And so demons who deny the Truth, the Light, cannot walk a straight line for a straight line, the perfect circle, returns unto itself and, therefore, demonstrates personal responsibility.

Now I think we've said enough on that. We have many future classes to discuss these things. Thank you for your question. Yes, the lady there, please.

Could that be the symbolic reason for the wedding band in a marriage?

I don't think you heard me. I said we had discussed enough on that.

Oh, excuse me.

And time is running along on us this day. And so I will say good day and look forward to our next class. And don't forget my student over there who is going to share with us her understanding of one of the teachings brought so long ago that some of you have never received, called the creative principle. Have a very good day. I know that you will as soon as you apply what little you have received, which is sufficient unto what you could call need.

Thank you. And good day. I keep forgetting that little thing. *[The teacher refers to his microphone, which he had removed before he had stopped speaking.]*

JULY 7, 1985

[Regarding the rhythmic cleansing breath, the video of the sunrise and the tones that are referred to may be found at a few of the more popular online video-sharing websites.]

A/V Class Private 5

Good morning, students, and welcome to this beautiful day here at the temple of Serenity.

We were discussing this wonderful life, this Living Light, this fluid that you are. Formless and free is this fluid flowing in your physical body. And your identification with any of the nine centers through which this river of life passes is, of course, where your little ship of destiny is. Your ship of destiny is the form, the form that you believe that you are. Therefore, through your own identification and through your attention upon anything in so-called creation do you place your little ship on that part of the river.

When you, in passing along on this river of life, this stream of consciousness, looking around at all of the things along the shore, you permit yourself to be fascinated and attracted to any of the forms upon the shore, you temporarily forget your responsibility as captain of your ship of destiny, and you find yourself aground in the mud for a time.

Now I had discussed a little earlier that the faculty of reason, which is between the edge of the air center and the edge of the electric center—the electric center being the will; this power of will for you to move this little ship of destiny that you believe you are. You see, if you do not identify, if you do not have a little ship of destiny to move upon this wonderful river of life, then you are no longer in the physical form that you are presently aware of. Therefore, of course, it is your responsibility to identify; however, it is not your responsibility for you to believe that you are that which you identify with. The problem is in believing you are that which you identify with, as your little ship moves along through these various centers of consciousness.

We also discussed the virgin births. The creation of forms in the purity of the light of reason. We discussed that the proper place to create a form is in the odic center of consciousness for ideas flow from the celestial realms, through the ethereal, into the odic. Now there in the odic center of consciousness is where you have virgin birth or immaculate conception. And that is the only place in consciousness that a virgin birth takes place.

Now at our last class here on Thursday evening, there was a discussion of the virgin and the immaculate conception. *[The teacher refers to class A/V Seminar 4, which was published in Volume 12.]* When you have two people on your planet of opposite sex (one of the positive, one of the negative, electric and magnetic, you understand), and these negative and positive poles come together, and both beings are in the odic center of consciousness, then you have manifested into a physical world what is known as a virgin birth.

Now don't misunderstand. This form that is brought into being is not subject to the lower centers of consciousness. Therefore, there is no physical contact. All the chemicals, all chemicals are available in the air center. And so forms created in the odic center, moving on into the air center and finally into the earth center are virgin births; they are immaculate conceptions. They have absolutely nothing to do with your understanding of physical birth through the need of physical contact.

Now your world is already moving at a rapid speed, scientifically, in its advancement and its technology. So that an imitation of what is known as immaculate conception or virgin birth is being made possible. For example, in the physical world, what you know as cloning is already taking place. You are little familiar with it. Because the human form contains all the necessary chemicals for birth, for formation in physical substance, cloning is possible and is the future wave in your physical world.

However, we should place most of our interest and attention upon this Living Light, this fluid that is within us and how we are creating this with our spoken word, for each time that you speak forth anything, you release a physical substance from your being. That physical substance forms. It forms what is your true motive. Not just what your words your mouth is speaking, but what your motivation is. And so when your motive is harmoniously united with the spoken word, this form that takes place, that your physical eyes do not yet see, actually does exactly what you form it to do. And so when your motive is pure, the manifestation is not only inevitable but it is right. And your motivation should be from the odic center of consciousness, which is wisely guided by the light of reason. The form that you have then conceived and created will do what it is told to do in keeping with its original formation or creation.

Now I'm going to take a few moments for you to ask the questions that you have.

And also, I feel that some of you have noted that that which you are now receiving is not only a direct threat to that which binds you, but be observant and see the various things that take place. One does not enter the higher realms of consciousness of truth and freedom by some kind of a ticket that you can buy at the store. One enters in keeping with the forms already created and their screaming to convince you that they are you and you are them. That is the price that everyone must pay to free themselves from the bondage of the functions. That does not mean you do without the functions, but you carry the light of reason into the lower realms of consciousness, and by so doing, you use creation in the lower centers of consciousness ever, ever alert, awake, and mindful that you are not them; that they are what you have created; and that they owe their allegiance and their duty to you. You in that respect are their god. And if you ever forget your responsibility, then you soon find out that they are your god for they have convinced you so easily. Because when you don't make the effort to be aware of what your mind is doing, then be rest assured something else is doing what it wants to do with it.

Now we'll take these few moments for your questions, and you please raise your hands. Yes, the gentleman there, please.

I have two brief questions, sir, regarding our cleansing breath.

Yes.

During—while we're, during the mantra portion, watching the TV—

Yes.

—listening to the, to the organ. First question is, on the exhale portion, If a person has difficulty in holding their breath in the exhale position for the period of time indicated on the tape, is it permissible to breathe one time prior to inhaling again or should we try to educate that and force our self to hold it on the exhale position?

No. Thank you for your question. You should not try to force anything because it uses a lower center. Force is always the servant of the lower four centers of being; and therefore, you do not want to use that, especially in your spiritual efforts. You should go ahead and take a breath. Over a period of time you will find that you will be able to refrain from inhaling until the proper time. Now though that may take weeks or months, be not concerned. It is in your own best interest to be patient with yourself. They are obstructions created over a period of time. They are not you. And therefore, you will live to see the day they are not you by conquering them. All right. Yes.

My second brief question, sir, is, Can we or should we do this mantra cleansing breath with our eyes closed or is it necessary, mandatory to watch that sunrise?

No. No. You may do it with your eyes closed. The purpose of the sunrise is to help you to control the visual aspects of your mind so that other forms of limit would not enter. It is specifically chosen to help your mind, the visual portion of your mind to remain ever open and ever expanding. You see, anything that you permit your mind to think about, to concentrate upon that has a boundary is controlled by the four lower spheres of consciousness. Those things that are of the limitless, of the free spirit, of that which you are do not have boundaries and are of the higher four centers of consciousness. Does that help with your question?

Yes, sir. Thank you very much.

Certainly. Now the gentleman there has a question and we'll go to the lady first, if you don't mind. Yes.

This has to do with the questions he just asked. If we had the audio [cassette] portion, is there an image that we can use that is expanding with our eyes closed?

Indeed, there is. Indeed, there is. Now the expansion, you understand, is what you call the sky. You see, you look at the sky and you see it; there is no limit. And also, [when] you look at the sky, you see a constant changing process. Though the sky may be blue, all you have to do is look at it for a moment and you will see various things in the blue that you are looking at. Because there's atmosphere there. There's electrons, atoms, and molecules that you are viewing the reflection of. And so they're in a constant panorama or patterns and changes. Sometimes some of you experience them as: "Well, there's some black spots appearing there." No, no, no, no. That's not what it is at all. There're other things that are changing and appearing. So you always want to select something that is moving, changing, and something that is constantly expanding. And in your earth world the only thing that you have, the element that is wise to use would be the sky, the air. Does that help with your question?

Yes. Thank you.

Yes. Now I'll be with you in a moment. This gentleman here has been waiting.

I'm not aware of the question that I . . .

Yes. Well, you best get re-aware of the question, if that's a proper word in your world, because you had the question earlier. So I'll give you a moment while I go—yes, you have the question now?

Yes.

You see, nothing is ever lost. We only temporarily step off the cliff and can't find it. Go ahead with your question.

How do we recognize the forms [of] the odic level, formed in the odic level that we are discussing?

Oh, yes. You'll have no problem recognizing them in the respect that you can't control them. *[After a short pause, the teacher continues.]* Now that should help with your question. Now that really causes a bewilderment in your mind. You cannot control by the dictates of the uneducated ego the forms of conception in the odic spheres and realms of consciousness. Does that help with your question?

Yes.

For example, the odic realm of consciousness is not subject to what you believe is need. Does that clarify it for you?

Yes.

Now need only exists in an uneducated ego. Uneducated in the sense that it believes the shadows and the forms that it has already created in the lower realms of consciousness. You cannot conceive and, therefore, control—you see, what you desire to control reveals to you what precedes it. And what precedes it is need. And what precedes the need is the judgment. And what precedes the judgment is the denial. Do you understand that? Does anyone have any problem with that? Pardon?

No. I understand that.

Yes, yes, I thought that you would. And so, you see, when you rise up into those realms, those beautiful realms of the high realms of consciousness, you don't experience frustration; you don't experience need because you have entered up into those limitless realms of consciousness. Now there you have the light of reason to conceive, you understand: what it is in the odic realms where you perceive, that perception becomes conception as it enters in the formation in the odic form, you see. This, what we call odic, what you know as odic, this is an actual physical substance. It is of a higher rate of vibration than the substance that is governed and controlled by earth, fire, water, and air centers of consciousness. Does that help you?

Yes.

Fine. Any other question on that?

Physical substance has a motion known as Brownian motion. It's the vibration—

Yes.

Is that, when you say it's on a higher rate of vibration, is that the motion that determines the rate of vibration?

[*The teacher sweeps his hand through the air.*] Have I moved my hand through physical substance?

Yes.

You are correct. Now, can you take with those hands of yours and control that substance that I've just moved my hand through?

No.

Well, there's the difference that we are speaking about, you see. You see, the substance is there. You are using it, and without it, you would not be in the physical form that you are. But you are not able to control that until you rise to other realms of consciousness that are within you that may change the temperature, that may change the environment around and about you. That is, it is within your domain to do so, but it is not within the domain of the uneducated ego, which is an effect of the denial of the truth, which, in turn, offers to you what you know as need. Does that help with your question?

Yes. Thank you.

Fine. Now we'll go to the lady here, please.

When you spoke of creating a form that will stay with you and keep you in the light of reason during the night before you go to sleep so that you wake up with it the next morning and it's the first thought you have, is the sky a way of doing that?

Well, the thing is, I think that we have discussed in reference to the perception in the odic realms of consciousness and the odic force, you see, first of all, you must make the effort through moving your little ship along the river, you see, the river of life that is within you. You must, through your identity, which is subject to your attention, the direction of your energy, you must first move that ship up into the higher realms of consciousness and into the odic, what we know as the odic center of consciousness. There you are in the domain of the soul faculties. Do you understand?

So that is where you have perception. You have the light of reason. There is where you have available to you this physical substance known as odic, odic force. That's what it is, you see. In your language it would be known as the odic; you call that odic force. All right. It is just as physical as this physical substance I am moving this physical hand of my channel's through. *[The teacher sweeps his hand through the air again.]* Therefore, that is where you create, you understand, in the sense, through your perception, guided by your light of reason. And then as you descend, you experience the formation to a lower, gross level of consciousness.

For example, when you permit yourself to identify with the fire center—of all the lower centers, the fire center is the most potent for in the fire centers you are absolutely convinced that you are the forms that control your mind and you believe you are the need that they tell you that you are. Now why is, of all of the centers of consciousness and the four centers of consciousness of the lower or gross realms of consciousness, why is the fire center the most potent? Yes.

I think it's a magnetic field, but, but I think it's because it has lust in it and it's, it's drawing . . . I never really thought about it.

Well, the fire center, what is known as the fire center of consciousness, is the only center through which that which you are, the Living Light, the light force, the vital energy, the *prana*, is physically released from your physical body. Therefore, the fire center is the most forceful and the most powerful center that you can experience while you identify with the four lower centers of consciousness. You see, you throw away—you see, the casting of pearls before the swine is the releasing of this actual fluid that is necessary for the goodness of your life. You see, that fluid is being released when you speak a word, but you do not see the form that it creates because you first must unite your motivation with your spoken word. Does that help with your question? Yes.

And, you see, all of your philosophies that have any worth have always taught, in various ways, why you do not cast your pearls before the swine and so graciously throw away the very substance that is necessary to bring into your life the things that you desire in life. Do you understand? All right. Yes, the gentleman there, please.

Yes. I would like to ask if the final note of the contemplation is an ascending one?

Which note?

The final one.

Well, final—beginning and final [are] notes, of course, that are subject to one's own awakening. Now, for example, when you hear the note of the mantra and the nine steps, you have, at that time, the opportunity through proper breath control, known in this philosophy as the cleansing breath, you have available to you the opportunity to step in consciousness from the earth center of which you are presently identifying, from the earth, to the fire, to the water, to the air, the electric, the magnetic, the odic, the ethereal, and the final, the celestial, that which you truly are. Now that is the opportunity that you have each time that you apply that simple truth. Those are the nine gates to heaven, you see. Those are the nine steps that you must ascend.

Now you want to know if you are descending or ascending on what you call the final note, is that correct?

Yes, sir.

Heaven on earth is stepping from the celestial to the earthly realm through the centers of consciousness and not being distracted and going aground with your little ship in the muds of the shore, fascinated with some form that is not you. Do you understand? So, you see, you are ascending, and you are descending. What will happen to your little form, to which you are personally responsible, if you are left off there in celestial realms? Who's going to feed that physical form of yours? You have a whole country that lies around, their physical bodies, denying the demonstrable truth of personal responsibility. It is one thing to step into the celestial realms; you have a responsibility to bring heaven on earth. Your responsibility is to ascend to the celestial realms and to descend once again to personal responsibility for the physical form that you have. Does that help with your question?

Yes, sir.

Yes. You know where you are at any moment whether you've ascended or descended. My purpose is not [to] come here to be an instrument for you to descend into the depths. You come to me; I show you the way to ascend and descend, and your responsibility is to make an intelligent choice. You understand?

Now you've spent a lot of time identifying with the earth center; that's where what you call money is offered. I gave it to you, I gave those centers—money, ego, and sex, you see. That's all one thing. We're now in our advanced teachings, teaching you the actual physical substance that you are using. Each time you have a thought, you use so much of this, this fluid that's in your body, you understand.

Now don't anyone be so ridiculous to think that that only applies to the male species. God forbid. I do hope that the women aren't so, so foolish. That energy, you see, each time you have a thought, you utilize some of that energy. Now each time you have an emotion, you utilize a great more of it, you see. And each time you are so stupid—excuse me for being so blunt—and so, so wasteful as to physically let it leave your body without your conscious choice and benefit therefrom—you see, oh, let's say, I don't want to be too blunt, but just say just a bit of it leaves your body physically; it would probably, energy-wise, bring into your world about $100,000 that you ofttimes seek on the earth realm of consciousness. Did that help with your question?

It's a very expensive luxury, the fire center, physically wasted as it is. Yes.

It is.

Yes. It's time that you see it for what it really is and understand it. Then perhaps you will understand why it's always been restricted for only one purpose: the purpose of procreation. Then you look around and you see, "Oh, there's a little bundle of flesh. Yes, I did expend that much of this valuable me that I am." Hmm? That help with the question?

Yes.

Fine. Yes, the lady there, please.

When the celestial forms are manifested in the odic—

Let's clarify one thing. Celestial is the Godhead, that which you truly are, formless and free Spirit. Now as there is a descent of that, it goes into the ethereal realm. Go ahead.

Well, my first question is, What happens to it in the ethereal?

That's where—you see, an idea is formless and free, all encompassing. That's what an idea is, all right? You think of an idea; you have an idea and instantaneously it has form; I mean, the idea itself has form. The idea is not form. The idea is that principle of good. That's all encompassing, total consideration; everything is considered, you understand? And therefore, it in and of itself is not limit, you see, for nothing is left out. You see, anything that is limit leaves out something. Do you understand it that way?

Right.

Anything that is limit is a boundary. There's always something outside of the boundary. Therefore, idea is not limit, has no boundary. That's the celestial realms of consciousness. Now that enters into the ethereal; that's where the idea begins its manifestation process. And from the ethereal realms it enters on into—there's my little friend over there *[The teacher may be referring to the church's dog or some other animal in the garden.]*—enters on into the odic realm of consciousness. And from that it goes down through into its magnetic, electric, its water centers, and its fire centers, air centers and etc. Yes.

I'd also like to ask, Does it take on a primary charge, either electric or magnetic, or is it always dual?

Well, my friends, you see, take a look at the descent of Jacob's ladder. You see, you can also, the centers of consciousness, the nine steps, is also Jacob's ladder in another one of the teachings of your world. You see, what does it take on? Well, what is the movement downward? The movement downward into gross form, you understand, first touches the magnetic, doesn't it? First you receive, you see. You see, that's the pull; the magnet that pulls it into you, for you, therefore, to use this electric power that is within you and to motivate it, you see. You see, that which is formed is brought into you within you, is it not? Yes. Go ahead with your question.

And I'd also like to ask, Is it necessary, once one of these forms are created by us, to nurture it with attention to keep it an active form?

Well, in reference, of course, you see, the thing is, if you permit one of the lower centers of consciousness and you believe that is placing attention or nurturing a form—you must remember that earth, fire, water, and air offer what is called concern: the dictates of mental substance of when is it going to happen. Now the instant that you do that, you are controlled by the realm of consciousness known as need. Do you understand? So, you see, there's one thing to direct intelligent energy or this life force, this Living Light, to direct it on to a form you've created, but you must be rest assured that it is done from a realm of consciousness within you that is not governed and controlled by need. Because if it's governed and controlled by need, then you must pay the price of the Law of Duality and ofttimes it's not worth it. I mean, after you get it, you said, "Oh, my, [it] never met up to my"—what did they say?—"expectations." Isn't that what some of my students have told my channel over the years? Yes.

In regard to the odic forms, a higher form—
Yes.

—my question is, Would it be necessary to use it, like, does it apply lack of use is abuse, so that it would go away, this good, higher form that we've created if we don't use it working in our universe?

Well, you use it working in your universe when you enter higher than the fourth center of consciousness, you see. You see, you cannot mix oil with water, and you cannot take the creation of what you know as angelic forms of goodness or the Principle of Good and try to get them to be the servants of the lower four centers of consciousness. It doesn't work. Does that help with your question?

Yes.

Yes. And now I had a lady here waiting. Yes.

We're told to use our will and I'm wondering, Is it synonymous with directing our attention?

Is the use of the will synonymous to directing the attention? Well, let's put it this way: first of all, you are instructed to use your will, and you are instructed to be awake, aware, and alert on what center of conscious[ness] you are when you choose to use it. Now, for example, already forms on the lower four realms of consciousness are using your will all the time. And they're using your will so successfully that you actually at times believe that you are those forms that you have created. So they are very good at manipulating and using this power within you. And they are so good at it that they actually convince you at times that you are them. Is that not correct?

That's correct.

So in directing one's attention to something, of course, it takes the power of will that is within you. Now many times a person says, "Well, I try to put my attention upon that but I have difficulty doing so." Many times a student will say, "I have great difficulty in concentrating. I have difficulty in remembering. I have difficulty in doing what I know I should be doing." Why, of course, you have difficulty doing what you know you should be doing because something else that you have created is using so much of your will power that it has convinced you that it is you and you are it. And that's where all the difficulty comes [from]. Does that help with your question?

Yes. Thank you.

Yes. But you don't have to continue to allow those forms you have created to use your will power. Your will power is yours.

Right.

And you must reclaim it, you see. You must reclaim it. That's your birthright. Yes. Now the lady here has a question.

The, the thought of the spirit of spontaneity came to me as you were talking about leaving the forms in the odic, when you were speaking to the former student about that.

Ah—

It seems to me that spirit of spontaneity could be a way, if you're in the right levels, of getting into the odic realm. Is that correct?

Well, the spirit of spontaneity reveals ofttimes that a soul has identified, seemingly without conscious effort, in the higher realms of consciousness. That's called the spirit of spontaneity. Not the letter of the law, which killeth, but the spirit of the law, which giveth life. However, the awakening into the higher realms of consciousness is rarely recognized by the lower realms of consciousness as something desirable or joyful or something to be done because it's always at their sacrifice. So if a person believes that they are the forms they've created in the fire center and they have a moment of spontaneity called spiritual, then they find that they have just instantaneously left the fire center. And tell me when they return how happy they are in the fire center by believing that they are the forms that they have created in the fire center while serving it. Does that help with your question?

Thank you.

And the lady over here has a question. Yes. The lady in back of you, please.

I had a question about the cleansing, the cleansing breath and the creative principle.

Yes. You're getting all of the answers. Did you have a little discourse to share with us from our last class? *[After a short pause, the teacher continues.]* Then share it. You have a few moments.

Well, the, the five steps of the creative principle are—

Yes. What is it governed by?

It's governed by five.

What does five mean to you?

Faith.

Yes. And how many centers are—name the centers you are going through in the creative principle.

Love—

No, no. Is that a center of consciousness? The centers of consciousness that we are discussing right here.

Oh. Fire—

No. You don't want to start with fire, do you? Without any earth?

Earth.

Let's start with earth, shall we?

All right.
Yes.
Earth.
Earth.
Water.
No, no, no. Let's start again. You know very well that—you see, I can tell where a person is, all I [have] got to do is ask them to name the centers and they tell me right away where they are. Now, now, my good student, let's start again. Earth.
Earth. Water.
No. Let's start all over again. Earth, fire.
Fire.
Water.
Water. Air.
Air. What's the next one?
Odic.
Well, I think you ought to call that electric, don't you?
The electric.
If you're—I noticed that. Let's go through that again now, you see, because you're on this five. Earth, fire, water . . .
Air.
Air. And the next one?
Electric.
Fine. Now we have these five steps, you understand, this higher teaching, of the creative principle, don't we? What do we have available to us in this great electric power? What is below it? What is below it? We've got as far in our evolution, at the moment, to the electric center of consciousness, right? Where the will and the power is used to bring unto you what? Whatever the earth offers, the fire offers, the water offers, and the air offers. Is that not correct?
Yes.
That's creation, isn't it?

Yes.

All right. Now what's your question, outside of getting stuck in the water center, temporarily? *[After a short pause, the teacher continues.]* Well, I'm happy you didn't get stuck in the fire center. *[The student being addressed laughs.]* Yes. Would you just speak right up? Because our producer over here is giving me a signal that he can't hear.

I was wondering about the—

Yes, speak right up.

—the creative principle and the cleansing breath.

What are you wondering about?

Well, what was the correlation between the two?

What did you just find as I just spoke to you? *[After another short pause, the teacher continues.]* Let's come to the lady in front of you and let's see—

All right.

—if she found out something in my discussion. Otherwise, I think I'm having, I must be having difficulty in communicating this morning. Yes, this lady right here. Now I want you to speak in reference to the question the lady asked. I just got through explaining earth, fire, water, air, and the fifth one, the electric, where the power is. But the power of what? The power of earth, fire, water, and air only. [It] has nothing to do with ethereal, does it? Has nothing to do with the odic. Has nothing to do with the higher realms of consciousness. Yes.

You're talking about will.

I'm talking about will, the power of will. So if you only move through the five centers, you have available to you the will to create anything you want in the fire center, anything you want in the earth center, anything you want in the air center, and anything you want in the water center. Is that what you really want in life?

Is that what I really want in life?

Yes. *[After a pause, the teacher continues.]* Wouldn't you like to have some angelic forms that don't demand that you pay the debt you owe them?

Yes.

Ah! Then we must move on to the magnetic. We must move on up through the odic and the ethereal and into the celestial realms of consciousness. Does that help with your question?

Yes.

Wonderful. Now the lady next to you was waiting and then the lady here in front. Yes, go right ahead.

So throughout the day, you move through these levels that you're speaking of.

Moment by moment I see students moving through them. Yes.

Moment by moment. So you—

Ofttimes stuck for many moments. Thank you. *[Many students laugh.]*

So you pause and that—and in pausing, then the power of reason . . .

You have the opportunity in the pause to, number one, be aware and to be awake whether or not you're on the muddy shore taking time to play and not really being aware of where you are while your ship is grounded. Perhaps a storm is coming up along the river. One should be on guard and take care of their ship because it's the only ship you're going to have in your present incarnation on earth. There's no other ship there for you to transfer over to. Yes.

OK. So I'm, I'm just trying to clarify my understanding.

Certainly.

So then the cleansing breath is what brings forth the power of reason? Is that . . .

The cleansing breath, the mantra, offers to you the opportunity to move your ship of destiny, which is stuck along the muddy shores of creation in one of the four lower centers of consciousness. Now as you are doing your cleansing breath, what happens is your identity, your identity is this little sailboat that's on the river. Do you understand that now? That *is* your identity. All right? That's what you believe that you are in order to have a form, a limited form. All right. Now the mantra cleansing breath offers to you—it doesn't do it for you—it offers to you the opportunity to, through your identification, that ship that's on that river of life inside of you, it offers, through your effort, a movement on the river. You see, the river is a rhythmic flow. Your little ship is stuck in the mud. When you do your cleansing mantra properly, what happens is your identification, your ship moves from the muddy shore—do you understand?—back onto the flow of the river of life that is within you. And you have the opportunity at that moment to sail up north into cooler regions, you see.

You know in your world you say, "Well, keep a cool head." Where do you think all those truths come from? You see, as you move your ship of destiny up north along the river, you find yourself cooling off, you understand. You're not all heated up with emotion. You're no longer stuck in the water center. Does that help with your question?

Yes.

You're welcome. Now I want to go [to] this lady [who has been] waiting. I'll come back to the gentleman, but before I come to this lady, I [have to] go to this lady back here.

And try to understand that love is something that you don't need. Love is something that you *are*. Do you hear me? Therefore, I am sure now you will feel better in reference to your multitude of questions concerning the creative principle—you hear?—for love is so important, isn't it? Without it, there is no life. Is that correct?

That's right.

So you don't need love. How can you need something that you are? You cannot possibly need what you already are, could you?

That's right.

All right. So you are Love. You are Life. You are Light. And when you permit yourself to be what you are, you cannot experience need for what you are already experiencing because you already are Love. How is it possible? It's not possible, is it? The only place you can experience what you say is a need for love is while you are stuck in the mud along the shore of the fire center. Pardon?

Thank you.

You're welcome. Now this lady here, then I want to get to the gentleman. Yes.

We've had the teaching that when we experience desire, that if we don't put a form to it but just give it back to God—

Correct.

—then it will be manifest in God's time.

That is correct. You know what happens at that process?

No.

When you experience the divine expression, known as desire, depending on the center of consciousness in which you are on at that moment, your little ship along the river, you form, you take, and you limit that experience, you see, that that you are receiving, the divine expression. Now you put a limit on it. If you are in the fire center, the only way it can be fulfilled for you is through that fire center of consciousness. Now that doesn't necessarily mean what you call sex or procreation. For example, if you permit yourself to experience the divine expression while you are identified with the fire center, then you will experience the impatient and the absolute lust for the fulfillment of what it is you desire. Do you understand that?

Now if you are in the earth center, you will have other experiences in reference to the limiting or the forming of the divine expression. And if you are in the water center, you'll have nothing but emotion, an emotional upheaval as you're waiting for the fulfillment of the form you have placed and created over the divine expression. Now if you're in the air center, you'll go through all kinds of mental gymnastics, analytical, and facts and this and that to experience what you have created in the air center. All right?

Now, so, say that you are, your little ship, through your identification, you are now on the fire center. And it begins to form. Well, in that instant you move you, your identification, your little ship, right on up the river, up into the odic realm of consciousness. Even better, if possible, right up on into the celestial realms. Now what happens at that time? You take this little form with you, aboard your little ship, and you sail right along. The more breeze there is, the faster you're going to go. Now, you see, the winds of reason, let them flow. And move your little ship with that little bundle that you've just created, you understand, that you have just then formed, right on up into the higher realms of consciousness, right up to the north pole. There, you see, you unload it. You unload your cargo.

You see, what happens, you know, say that we have, you know, our little ship and we're in the southern hemisphere there, in the earth center, you see. And we've loaded all this cargo onboard. Well, the more cargo that you load on a little sailing ship, the lower it sails in the water. Your chances, then, of being grounded on a sandbar as you're going on up the river are greatly increased. So the wisest thing to do is to unload the cargo. You don't need to carry all that cargo. Make an intelligent choice of what cargo you want to carry as you go to sail up the river to unload it in these higher realms of consciousness. And then sail on back, you see. You'll feel just wonderful until you allow yourself, as you're coming south once more, headed south-bound—you look over to the shore and say, "Oh, I'd like to have that onboard. And I'd like that onboard. And that and that." And you load your little ship down. And sometimes you don't even get back on the ship and you're grounded for some time. Does that help with your question?

Yes.

You see, you are a ship of destiny by the very Law of Individualization. For individualization is a limiting, and whatever is limited is individualized. So you, by identifying, you are form, you are limit, you are that ship of destiny. That's the price that everyone must pay. It is a denial of what you are and a belief in what you are not. Does that help with your question?

Yes.

But by believing in what you are not, you have the sensation, you have the experiences offered by the functions of being in the first four planes of consciousness, you see? And there you have these nine spheres of action to each plane of consciousness. So you have thirty-six avenues through which the forms you may create have their little heydays. Do you understand that?

It's a very simple and practical thing. If you will just, in your consciousness, see what you are: a little ship, a little, small sailing ship on a river of life. That is when you believe you are form, that is what you are. And if you understand that you alone are the one who tempts yourself to put all this cargo onboard—and the more cargo you have onboard, the more difficulty you have in entering the higher spheres of consciousness in those higher realms.

See, many people have a great deal of cargo that they've picked up in the air center. Others have a phenomenal amount of cargo they've picked up in the fire center or the earth center or the water center, you see. And, you know, it is through understanding—through communication one gains understanding. And it is through understanding that one becomes receptive to the winds of reason, you see, which move their little ship on up the river.

So if you will take time with yourself, for each one owes it to themselves, to use a little communication inside and gain understanding inside, within one's own self, then one becomes more receptive to the winds of reason to move their little ship.

Now ofttimes my students will say, "Well, now I've had enough." And they really meant it. And when they meant it, their little ship, I have witnessed it just move right on past that center and on up into another one. And they just feel wonderful, for a time. And then they turn their ship around, and they come on back, and they're tempted again. And they go aground, and they load all this cargo onboard, and get stuck in the mud all over again, you see.

You see, it is not—you know, some time ago I spoke to you—it is not what you have to put into the mind that will free you. It is what you must take out! You see, it is what you must unload off your ship. It's not the cargo you must put on. You have plenty of provisions for your life and, oh, what a beautiful life. You see, the thing is, you have too much. There's too much onboard. You see, you [have] got to dump it overboard. Throw it overboard, you see. You throw it overboard and your little ship will start sailing. Does that help with your question? Yes, go ahead.

I have one more.

Certainly.

In the lower five centers then, is it self-will that moves our little ship?

That is corr—well, it is will directed to what one believes is self. And, you see, in that sense it's known as self-will. You see, will is will. It's all divine. When one believes they are the limit, then it's called self-will or uneducated ego, yes. Then it is forms that they believe that they are that's doing the moving.

Isn't that trying—well, is only—then divine will moves the ship, too?

Divine will moves the ship at all times. You see, it is divine will. You are the one that makes the choice to believe you are the forms that you have created; and therefore, in service to the forms that you have created, that's called self-will. Does that help with your question?

Yes.

You see, you see, the will is divine. The will is still good. The will is God. What you do with the will is the payment that you have to make, you see. That's still God's will. God's will moves through you. That's what it is, this divine river, you see. The flow of the divine river is the divine will. That is what you are. Now when you use the will in the lower four centers of consciousness, that is being used by what you believe you are, not by what you are. Does that help with your question? So if you believe—now in the four centers of consciousness what you are subject to is the Law of Need. Do you understand that?

Yes.

For that is an effect of denial of what you are. So if you're in the earth, fire, water, and air centers of consciousness, then you are subject to and a victim of what you call need. For that is the price that all form pays by believing they are the forms that they have created. Does that help with your question?

Yes. Thank you.

You're welcome. Yes, the gentleman back there.

Is our ship of destiny moved only when we do the cleansing breath during the mantra or any time that we do the cleansing breath?

Yes. Your little ship is moving at many times, and it's usually moving through the lower centers of consciousness by the forms that you have created that you believe that you are. In the movement of the ship, through the cleansing mantra, you therefore have the opportunity to consciously choose the center of consciousness you wish to go to. Does that help with your question? Pardon?

Yes, sir.

Yes. Because then you can say, "All right. I consciously chose to rise into another sphere of experience in my life. I'm grounded on this one to such a point I believe that I'm it. And I don't want to be it anymore. I'm tired of serving this thing here." So what happens, you see, through your cleansing mantra, what happens is your identification, your little ship then starts to move through this, on to this rhythmic flow of what you naturally are, you see. "Rhythm, harmony, balance, peace. Thank you, God, I am at peace." You see? "Rhythm, harmony, balance, peace." Remember, I gave that to you many, many years ago. In fact, I brought it through for a little, small child a number of years ago. But that is what I was talking about at that time, and I'm talking about it again at this time. Did that help with your question?

Yes, sir.

You see, you see, you can consciously choose at that time. Your ship may be grounded in the earth center; it may be grounded in the air center. And in that grounding, which is an effect of your believing that you are the forms that you're loading on to your ship or you're sitting on shore playing. Do you understand? And so that's what's actually happening, you know. You want to—if you find that your ship is extremely low in the water, you know—and everyone knows how low their ship is in the water on the river of life because they know how they feel and what they experience—so if you find that your ship is low in the water, well, just get right onboard and get to work, because you'll be the only stevedore there. It's your ship. Nobody else is going to come and unload it for you. And you say, "That's it! I don't want that, that, that, that, that, and that!" And dump it all overboard! And sail right on. See? Does that help with your question?

Yes, it helps.

Very important. Yes, you can do that at any time. [If] you find yourself low in the water, dump that cargo overboard. It's too much. Yes.

And we don't need to play that tape, then, in order to move the ship of destiny.

Well, your ship of destiny is moving all the time. The playing of your tape is—what it does is offer you the opportunity to consciously get your ship into the flow of the river. That's what it does. Because the river flows at a certain beat. Do you understand? The rhythmic movement of the river itself, that which you are, has a certain rhythmic, repetitive beat. By your listening to that beat, you identify with that beat. When you identify with that beat, through your cleansing breath, which is moving the river, my friend—this is why you do your cleansing breath. You're actually, you, your identification, which is your ship, is now moving on that river in the river's natural flow. And that which flows naturally has no experiences of need or lack, because it naturally flows, you see. And you don't lose yourself. You sell out nothing. You yourself choose what you're going to dump overboard, you see. You have plenty of cargo. Loads of provisions to get you where you want to really go.

So your cleansing mantra is very important for your identification—remember, your ident, your identification is your ship. That is what it is. And so what you are doing with your identification is getting your ship into the flow of the river itself, that which you are, contrary to that which you believe you are. In other words, you are bringing about a marriage of what you believe you are, the limited form, into the natural flow of what you are. That's what's actually taking place. Does that help with your question?

Yes, sir. Thank you.

Yes. Someone else. The lady here has a question.

And that's what needs to happen for the balance?

That *is* balance.

That—

That's what balance is. When your ship flows on the river's natural flow, that is balance. And you are free. Yes.

And you're still, but you're still identified with form to some degree.

Yes, but you know you're not form.

OK.

You see, you see, I gave it to you in another way: be in creation, not a part of it. Separate truth from creation, you see. You see, you are still you, but you know who you are. And so you have an experience at one moment—my friends are all coming in here today. *[The teacher looks upward into the branches of the oak under which he is seated. He may be referring to some birds that had just landed in that oak.]* You have an experience. You say, "Oh, I am experiencing this. This is not me. I added this on to my ship. I don't like this on my ship." It's cargo. It's cargo you can do without. Dump it overboard. Do your cleansing breath; you get right back in. You see, in consciousness you will once again reidentify. And that makes you captain of the ship to move it off the sandbar, to move it out of the mud. Don't you understand that? Yes. Yes, go ahead.

Also, when you're inspired divi—well, if you get inspiration to put something together, do you just let it go then or does it have to come down into the, into the four centers to create it on this plane?

Well, for you to experience it on those centers, it would have to come into those centers, you see. Do you understand that?

But it . . .

But that isn't where you bring it in. You have the perception of it in the higher realms of consciousness.

And it doesn't necessarily have to come down to those, to the lower—

Why, no.

Oh, OK.

No, it doesn't have to. You can go up there every time you want to experience it. You see, for example, it's like taking a vacation. As long as you believe that you must move your physical body, then for you, you do not have a vacation until your physical body moves. Because, you see, your physical body is governed and controlled by those four centers of consciousness, what you call your physical. Do you understand? But you don't have to have the experience there, unless you choose to. Does that help with your question?

Except for when you're, when you're trying to, like, create something with your—in other words, if you're trying to create something on this level, it always has to come down to the four—

So you can experience it on that level. It doesn't have to, but if you want to experience it in the fire center, you must bring it into the fire center. You see, see what a vast benefit it [is] to make that little effort with your mantra, your cleansing mantra and to rise and to have control of your little ship and move it to where you desire to move it. Look at the benefit. You see, for example, so often you create things in the fire center, and you believe that you are the thing you have created when you identify with that center. Is that not correct?

That's true.

Well, you create that in the higher realms of consciousness. You bring it down to the fire center, you say, "Well now, here it is. I'm experiencing this, but this is not me. But I am responsible for it." You see, there's the difference. Then you are not so controlled and possessed by it. You know that it is something you have created. You are now in the fire center and you have brought your cargo with you to the fire center. But at least you know it isn't you.

There's no attachment there then.

Well, there can't be an attachment because you know it's not you. It's like, are you attached to the fork you use to eat your food?

Correct.

Does the food taste better if you have no fork? Does it taste better if you do have a fork? Food is food, isn't it?

Right.

Does that help with your question?

Yes.

All right. Fine. Yes, the lady there, please.

Are you saying, then, that the, each center—

Speak right up. Yes.

Are you saying, then, that each center on this river has a different beat?

No.

A different rhythm? Or is it—

No, no, no, no, no, no, no, no. No. The river itself, the river itself has a rhythmic beat which is given to you in your cleansing mantra. That is the river.

Right.

Now that is what you are, all right? Now your little ship, your little sailing ship, your identification, that—you believe you're form, correct?

Right.

That's your ship. That is your ship. Your little sailing ship. Now on these waters of life, that which you are, you're moving this identification, known as your little sailing ship. You're passing through these various centers of consciousness, earth, fire, etc., etc., right on up the river, going north. You understand that, don't you?

I, I guess I understand it as the, the centers are part of the river.

No, no, no, no. The centers are the shore on both sides. The river is an absolute rhythmic beat, a perfect flow of absolute balance. That is what you are. You look and you see the shores. Those are the centers of consciousness. Do you understand? Without you, of course they don't exist for you. So, you see, you, identifying on being the ship—the ship is moving along the river. You're the captain on that ship, right? You're the captain of your ship. You look and you see those forms on the shore. You see on your left and on your right.

Now the closest thing I—that you, you should study—I mentioned to you students, some of you, long, long ago, is one of the many fables. Specifically, I think you call it, one of the ancient fables, *Jason and the Argonauts*, I think. You see, you could gain much understanding of your ship of destiny. You see, it's been revealed throughout the ages in various stories and fables. You should study them and understand them. That's what he was going through. Now I think you'll find in that one particular story that he was sent for the golden fleece, you see. Well, the golden fleece is the celestial realms of consciousness, your experience thereof, you see. That's what it is, you see. And yours, of course, like everyone's, waits for them. But you must take control of your little ship. Did that help with your question?

Yes. Thank you.

Yes, the lady here, please.

In The Living Light *[in Discourse 31] you speak of middle C.*

Correct.

And advise each of us to find our note.

That's right.

I'd like to know if and how our note corresponds to the beat of the river.

Yes. You were advised to find your note. Now your note is ever the note that you believe that you are at any moment. So when you find your note, you will know what center of consciousness you are in and the mud you've got to pull yourself off of. Does that help with your question? You see, because you are what you believe you are through your process of identification and limit. Therefore, find your note, for your note varies in your own beliefs. Does that help with your question?

Yes. I'd—

You want to know what you really are: you are the river of consciousness; you are the perfect flow. That's what you are. What you are and what you believe you are, are two different things. You believe you are the note of the fire center when you identify with that center. Do you understand that? Yes, go ahead.

So should our effort be to change our note and our belief to get it as close as it can to middle C?

Well, I would certainly make great effort in changing my note if I believed I was a note that was stuck on any of those muddy shores along the lower four centers of consciousness. Absolutely. And, you see, what happens, you see, you're constantly attracted, as all people, minds are—you move to the air center and you say, "Oh, this is me. It just feels heavenly, you see." And for a time, you believe you're that note. And then you move to another center and—you know what heaven is like? Heaven is when you have an experience you wish would end—at the moment it ends, they call that heaven. *[A few students laugh.]* Does that help with your question?

Thank you.

Yes, you're more than welcome. Such a lovely day. Yes, the lady here, please.

During your cleansing breath, meditation, and contemplation, is there a proper direction to face in to do those things?

North.

Thank you.

North. You face east and have north where north should be. Now do you understand that? North? Put your head to the north. There's a lot leaving there. North. The gentleman back there has a question in reference to your question.

Face north or put our back?

Face east and have your head north. You know how to do that?

I don't.

You don't know how to face east and let your head be north?! Do you know how to do that? *[The teacher asks a different student. After a short pause, the teacher continues.]* Well, you know, if I wanted to face east and have my head north—let's ask our cameraman over there. What position would you put your body in? *[After another short pause, he again continues.]* Rather a 45-degree angle, wouldn't you say? Now perhaps you can understand why I have recommended a reclining position of a 45-degree angle. I do think that's taken care of your question, hasn't it?

Thank you.

Yes, you're more than welcome. Yes. And, you see, I don't think any of us have any problem reclining, do we? I see many lounge lizards having no problem to recline. All right? Yes, are there any more questions? I think we're running a little on our time here. Yes, he says he has loads of time. I'm interested in the tape. Yes, go right ahead. No more questions? That's fine. *[After a short pause, the teacher continues.]* The lady here, please.

Does your note carry with it a real sound, if we searched for it?

It most certainly does. I just got through explaining: your note is whatever you believe you are when you're looking at the shore. That's the note that you create. Now if you believe that you are satisfied with the note that you believe that you are, then pay the price of whatever center of consciousness in those realms of the functions that you are on. Because I guarantee you the law does not fail: you will always experience need in keeping with your belief. Hmm? Did that help with your question?

Thank you.

You see, there'll never be enough because it's contrary to the law for there to be enough. There cannot be enough in the four realms of consciousness (earth, fire, water, and air). There can never be enough. Why can there never be enough? Because those centers know beyond a shadow of any doubt that there is something that sustains them; and therefore, they're always filled with that feeling and that experience, and there's never enough. Not in those realms of consciousness.

Those are the realms of consciousness of temptation. Look, temptation is an experience that we have in our belief that we will get what we believe and judge we need. And so we look and we are tempted by a judgment that says that's where it is. We end up finding it was never enough. Don't we? It never quite met up to our expectations. And it never can. Not in the earth, fire, water, and air centers of consciousness. It is not possible.

As I explained to one student here a few moments ago in reference to love: How could you possibly need what you are? You can't need what you are! And so if you deny that you are love, then therefore you can experience a need for it. If you deny what you are, then you must pay the price of your denial. Your note is believing that you are the forms on the shore where you have grounded your own little ship. But try to understand, and to remember, and to accept, *you* are the one who grounded your ship; you are the one who can move it. You see? You see, a wise person doesn't overload their sailing ship when they start off. No, no, no, they don't do that at all. Because they know the more cargo they put onboard, the lower in the water their ship is going to be; and they never know where there's going to be a sandbar along that river. And there's quite a few in the lower four centers of consciousness. I can assure you of that. Does that help with your question? Yes.

Are there any other questions? Yes, the lady here, please.

Is there any worthwhile cargo? And if so, what would it be? Or is it advisable to sail the ship empty so it's more maneuverable?

Well, survival cargo. You know, when a person is passing through the four centers of consciousness, they'd like to have a little food to eat; they'd like to have, especially, a little water to drink. And so a wise person takes what they call [a] survival kit with them. I wouldn't take anything more than that myself.

You know, if you would only study some of these so-called fables that have already been in your world for thousands of years. I spoke to my channel and I've spoken to a couple of you students on the meaning of the flute. And these things that are seeming magic: there's nothing magical about them. They're in keeping with natural laws. Your responsibility in life is to understand yourself. So that you can understand these natural laws, you see.

It's like this morning in our wonderful experience, you see, through an opportunity to have the experience, you had no problems in making a choice. Had you not had the experience, then it is highly questionable that you would have made the choice to sit here in the light of this lovely sunshine. Do you understand? So to be forearmed [forewarned], as one might say, is to be forearmed. So perhaps the next time we have class, the ladies may have some of those little—what do they call those little things?—parasols or something. Or something, you know, a proper hat or something so that—who knows where we're going to be in the temple gardens, you see? And even though my channel wasn't particularly fond of the change that was made because, you know, he has his own sensing, and his mother knew beyond a shadow of any doubt, as I did, what was going to take place, but he doesn't interfere when it comes to the spiritual work and the teachings.

You see, you must realize and grant that to others; you do not make an intelligent choice without reference. Your reference is known as what you've already experienced. And so your shadows rise up and say, "Oh, no, I'm not going to go through that again." And you make an intelligent choice, you see. Does that help with any of your questions about being up here today? Hmm?

[The previous classes in this series were held in the backyard garden of the temple, where students sat in the shade of the trees. This class began in the backyard, but was interrupted. Class was reconvened a short time later and relocated to the front of the temple, where students sat on the driveway in the sunshine.]

Was it not better to have the experience for your ears so you can make an intelligent choice? And you shouldn't feel badly that I had the cameraman go all the way back to the beginning to remove any of those forms, you see. We just erased them, you see.

All right, are there any more questions, because I'm going to conclude for today. There's so much studying. Although you've had a few minutes left, you've had a nice class. Any questions before class ends today? No questions? Then I will say good day to you and look forward to seeing you here next Sunday morning, of course.

And don't be attached to where you're going to sit in the garden because you never know where you're going to sit. And if you do know where you're going to sit, then you may have another experience like you had this morning and I don't think you would appreciate it, would you? And don't forget now, that I only had one student who was unable [to attend], evidently was working—were you?—Thursday. But the secretary will take care of that today and see that he has his audiotape [of that class], of course. You see, that's separate, you know, the audiotape, on Thursday night. Because there's so much there that he's lost out and he should have.

All right, if [there are] no more questions, then I will see you next Sunday and good day.

JULY 14, 1985

A/V Class Private 6

Good morning, class. And welcome to a beautiful day here at Serenity.

And today we will continue on with our discussion of the Living Light. This pure Light made manifest in your physical world as a virgin substance from which all forms, in creation in the universes, are created. Now we discussed at one of our other classes what is known as the lower centers of consciousness: earth, fire, water, and air. We also discussed the lord of your universe: the fifth center, which is the electric center. We discussed also the higher centers of consciousness: magnetic, odic, ethereal, and celestial.

Now each thought that you form within your mind is dependent for its formation, its creation, its activation upon this life force that in truth is what you are: the virgin river of life itself.

Now the lower centers of consciousness (earth, fire, water, and air) are not only dependent [upon] but do not exist without belief. For example, you enter the lower centers of consciousness by permitting yourself to entertain within your consciousness the thought of I. Separation, individualization is totally dependent upon the thought of I, which offers to you belief and bondage.

These experiences that you have in what you call your world of creation in those centers are the effect of directing this river of consciousness to those centers. That is done by what is known as the lord of your universe or the power of will. Now it is this same power of will that you have available to you at all times to direct to higher centers of consciousness, and there create forms which are dependent upon you, this river within you, for their formation and for their continuity.

The law of this river is a harmonious flow. And when it is obstructed, when you, by direction of your will, utilizing the power that you are, create an obstruction to the natural flow of this river of life, you experience everything necessary for that transgression to motivate you to make the necessary changes within your mental world in order that you may once again experience the truth and the freedom that you are.

Now the river flows harmoniously from its source at the northern pole of consciousness to the south and returns. Its natural duration time in your world would be known as seventy-two hours. Now this river in its flow, in its natural flow, if it does not maintain by your will its natural flow, you experience conditions within your mind that are not healthy for they are not harmonious. Those who believe and who permit themselves to entertain in their consciousness the thought of I, commonly known as self-orientation or over-identification with belief, are bound and, so to speak, trapped in the lower centers of consciousness. Therefore, the natural flow of the river, which must be released within (in your time) every seventy-two hours, goes to feed and to create forms on those lower centers of consciousness.

Through direction of this power by this lord of your universe, known as will, you guide identity, your little ship of destiny, along this river in its natural flow to its source at the northern pole. There you experience harmonious, healthy, and abundant good, for you no longer are bound in the lower centers, which are dependent upon belief from your own direction in the belief in the thought or the formation of what you call I. When you understand and you apply that you are the I of eternity, you will no longer, through a weakness and lack of effort, continue to believe that you are the form of the I of eternity which you are, but you will know that you are the I and not the limit or form thereof.

Because it is the natural law that the release of the river must take place every seventy-two hours, it is understandable, when you study and apply, that seemingly beyond your ability to control your experiences these forms that you have created in the lower centers of consciousness are controlling you.

Now when the river is not released, it floods the banks along the shore. On the shore, as your little ship is passing, there are many, many forms of creation that you have created. And multitudes of forms [are] attracted to the shores through the laws of association and like attracts like. Consequently, as your little ship is passing and the river has not been brought into balance, these forms are flooded along the shore. And so they cry out, and they scream because they are being drowned by the river, which they know that you are.

Intelligent use of this pure energy, that which you are, is to release energy in constructive ways for the good of the whole, for that which is done for your good is for the good of the whole. It is only in the delusion and the deception that you are a form or thought of the I of eternity that you believe otherwise and, consequently, must pay the price of that error of ignorance.

Now all of you have had in your lifetime many, many experiences when you thought that you were doing something that you enjoyed. And while you were in the process of doing that, you experienced a feeling of good. Now this is what is taking place physically and mentally within you: you, at those times, direct and, therefore, release the river and bring this balance once again for a time into your life. The danger of doing what you believe you want to do is a momentary experience of a feeling of good at a very, very great cost to your life. And so one must first become conscious and aware of what center of consciousness that you are on before you permit the movement of your mind and body to do what you believe will make you feel good.

You can easily tell whether or not your consciousness, your little ship is stuck in the mud in the earth center, the fire center, the water center, or the air center. You know very well that if your consciousness is over-identified through the thought of I, bound by its bondage, known as belief, in the earth center of consciousness, then you are experiencing discord, the opposite of harmony and balance, and disease in your material and financial experiences in life.

If, however, you are compelled to fill a desire of the flesh to the extent that you are possessed and compelled to do it, then you know beyond a shadow of any doubt that you are over-identified with the thought of I which is temporarily low in the water or grounded in the fire center.

If, however, your experiences at any time are those of emotional upheaval, of upset, discord, and disturbance because you believe you are unjustly treated, you believe that the world owes you a living, or you believe that you are not being treated the way that you should be treated, and you find yourself exploding without the ability, seemingly, for a time to control yourself, then you know beyond a shadow of any doubt that you are over-identified and that you are low in the water or grounded in the water center.

If, however, you find that, in honesty, you have all the answers to everything that you experience in life, that you are never left without an excuse, a justification, or a judgment of how things are, that your analytical abilities have reached a state of perfection and that nothing really exists that is beyond your intellect to investigate and to solve, be rest assured you're not low in the water in the air center, you're totally stuck in the mud.

And so it is that all of you know at any moment exactly what center of lower consciousness that you are in. Now the lower centers of consciousness are much easier for you to perceive and to understand. For anyone who spends their lifetimes in the lower centers of consciousness cannot but qualify themselves to what the centers have to offer. And so your ability to understand where you are in consciousness in reference to these four lower planes and spheres of consciousness is not a problem for any of my students. For all of you, I am happy to say, are extremely well qualified. And because you are so well qualified in the lower four planes of consciousness, you are therefore potentially a greater servant to the Light of eternal truth. For you therefore, being so very well qualified, are potential instruments for awakening within your consciousness the faculty of reason, which offers to all awakened minds personal responsibility.

And so speaking on personal responsibility, [it] is not just something that we think about. It is something that we do something about, like staying awake. *[After a short pause, the teacher repeats himself and speaks more loudly.]* Like staying awake! That's known as personal responsibility: the application of truth.

You have so many experiences in your daily activities, and yet so seldom pause and speak to those realms of consciousness that temporarily you believe that you are. And so it is certainly time to pause and to demonstrate, "I have experienced an emotional upheaval, a disease, and discord in my experiences this moment. That reveals to me in honesty, through the law that is demonstrable, known as personal responsibility, that I have, through an error of ignorance of my own mind, called forth into my universe experiences that I, by my own will power, have chosen to identify with the lower center known as the water center. This has been my choice for this is my experience. This experience that I am experiencing is taking place within my own mind. I have a personal responsibility to my mind to tell my mind what it will do and to tell my mind what it will not do. And I have a further responsibility to see that my mind obeys my order." That is personal responsibility; the effect of that is freedom for only freedom could be the effect of personal responsibility, whereas personal responsibility is an application of demonstrable truth.

Now as long as you permit yourself to be upset, to demonstrate the disease of discord, you are only going deeper and lower in the water for the ship that is sailing is your identity. That's what the ship is. Now it's up to you to take control of what is yours; and what is yours, to use and not abuse, is your mind. That is yours.

It is understandable, through this creation process of belief, being limited by belief to the lower four centers of consciousness, that whenever a person releases a part of themselves—and in the lower four centers one believes "That river is me, and therefore that river, whatever it is released to create, is my right to control." Now that is the spoken word of truth. It *is* you. You release that river and you create a form. That form is yours. Your will, the power of your own will, has created it from this very substance, this Living Light that you are. Now you alone have created that. Its duty, its obedience, and its loyalty is to you, for you are the creator of it. It is in that sense a part of you. When that form or forms that you have created by your very life substance—for, you see, when you think it, you release some of that river to form it in a mental world. And as you continue to identify with it, through the use of the power of your will, you solidify it, and you gather the very substance out of your own being, and it materializes in what you call a physical, material world. It is yours. You have created it.

When it no longer serves you well, you have a responsibility to annihilate it. That is your responsibility. So when you demonstrate a lack of staying awake! When you come to these private classes and what you believe is the satisfaction of sleep is more important to you than the truth you are privileged to receive, you establish a law and you guarantee to go on your way. And if one more of my students, through a belief in the lower centers of consciousness, blinks their eyes into the darkness of satisfaction while in class, class shall come to an end on that day. And if those students who are awake do not demonstrate sufficient value for what is offered by helping their co-students to stay awake while in class, then they, too, shall graciously accept a five-minute class or a ten-minute class. For they are demonstrating their value is limited, and it is not what they believe that it is.

Now we will pause, and these students who seem to have such a need to sleep may ask their questions. *[After a pause, the teacher continues.]* And so if you have no interest in asking questions, then we will conclude this class. Yes, the lady there, please.

While we're doing our contemplation—

Speak right up, please.

While we're doing our contemplation, I wanted to ask if the, if the different sounds of the notes, are they, the timing, is it equal?

It is indeed balanced and equal. Yes. The gentleman there, please.

You talk about annihilating forms that we, that are not in our best interest, that we created through ignorance. How do we annihilate those forms?

Yes. The annihilation of any form is the absolute and total absence of identification with it. It only survives and is activated by the very life force that you are. And that life force is directed by the power of your will to the shadow or form of the past. So whenever it tempts to enter your consciousness, do your rhythmic cleansing breath. And I guarantee you, it shall disappear into the nothingness.

Now remember this, a form created by the mind is not only subject to the mind, it is dependent upon the river of life that you are. Do you understand?

Yes, sir.

Now each time it rises up—and it has proven to you beyond a shadow of any doubt it no longer obeys your wishes—you immediately use your cleansing rhythmic breath. It will dissipate before your very eyes. Each time that it rises up, you continue that practice. Now what you must understand, it takes energy for the form to rise. It rises up to be fed and to be activated. Do you understand that? So if you do not identify with it, if you use what you have been given, each time it rises, it uses energy. It's not getting any more energy from you, you understand that? So it will be weaker and weaker each time. It will not be as strong bombarding your consciousness for it does not have the energy.

Now what will happen to that form? That form has the intelligence of your mind. You understand that? It is getting weaker and weaker. You are not feeding it anymore. It faces annihilation and it knows it. What will it do? Before it will commit suicide—because self-preservation is its basic instinct, do you understand that? It is created in the animal instinct world of the four lower centers, you hear? So what it will do, it will look at the bridges that you have created. It will look and see, "Oh, now he knows that person over there. Now let's see, do we have—does he have a thread of rapport with that person?" If there is something that will establish the law that like attracts like in the person that you know or have known, that form will crawl across that bridge and go to that other person for feeding. Do you understand that?

Yes, sir.

And this is what happens here in this type of school of higher teachings of the Living Light. You see, these forms come in with my students. They're not making their effort on their cleansing breath, their rhythmic cleansing breath to annihilate those forms. Do you understand? They're not doing their homework. Now very soon in order for you students to continue to have these private higher teachings, you will be given homework, and I will give you tests until you grow up out of those centers of consciousness.

So what you will find—and I think you'll find this most interesting—people in your life that you've known years ago and, that is, some time in your life you had a rapport in certain areas of consciousness, you understand that? That's where there's a bridge, and the forms go back and forth, you understand. Yes, they call—I think you call that in your world a relationship. All right? Now years may pass, you see, and you pass them on the street perhaps. And you take a look and you cannot help but think they're worse than they were before in that particular area that you used to be in. You can see it very, very clearly. Well, it's most understandable. You've made the effort to grow up out of that level; they were in rapport with you at some time—a bridge, there's a connection there—and they all swarmed across and now they're in her universe (or his). Do you understand that?

Yes, sir.

You see, you see, when you leave the Light within your consciousness, you understand, whenever that happens to a student, they all swarm in after him. And the ones who are still left in the Light, as they continue to make the effort, because they knew the, what you would call, an ex-student, they all go that way, you see. Do you understand that? Did that help with your question?

Then by the same token, if we're in rapport with somebody, we can pick up their negative forms—

Oh, absolutely!

—through that level of rapport.

Oh, absolutely and definitely. Positively. You see, a wise man does not associate with those who choose the darkness. Especially if they have awakened to the Light. That's the one thing a wise man never does. Because a wise man cannot long bear the Light if he makes such an ignorant choice. Yes. And so we've stated it in many ways: if you are interested in learning something for your self-improvement, for the good of your own life, then you make the effort to associate, you see, with those—though you may or may not agree with them—who are making similar effort, at least a little effort, you see.

Now this type of school has never been permitted in the midst of a public arena. The reason being rather obvious, you see. Those who awaken in the Light have a greater potential of a source of supply of what you call energy. That river, you see, is really filled and flowing because as they awaken they do not cast their pearls so foolishly to the swine. And therefore, their pearls—they have more pearls available and use them more wisely. And they're known to, no matter whatever happens, they're able to rise again with the necessary vitality to do their job, you see.

And so some of you over these years, I'm sure, in fact, I know, have experienced speaking to someone on the telephone, or seeing someone, you know, and after you were through talking for a few minutes, perhaps, half an hour, you were so exhausted you could hardly crawl out of bed for hours. Do you understand what takes place? You see? And so you will find, especially minds who have chosen, after awakening a bit to the Light, who have chosen the darkness, they're ever seeking, like a moth in the night seeks the light. They always want to talk to you. They always want to call you. They always want to see you, whenever possible, you see. You see, their forms require energy, and they're so depleted themselves. Do you understand that? So one chooses very carefully.

Now out there in that arena, you see, you're not in some secluded mountaintop. This is the only type of schools there are: [those] in absolute seclusion. There is no possibility, you understand, of any of those forms coming in. See, they only have to work with their own forms. And they don't have—their teachers and students don't have all the forms coming in from the jungles of creation, you see.

And the only way that these private lessons can continue for you people is for the effort of what you call absolute discipline beyond a shadow of any doubt. You see, it's either in or out. There's no in-between. Either one makes the effort—you see, what happens is one goes for days and just lets those forms have their heyday, you see, on their vitality out there in that jungle. And then they say, "Oh, well, I'm coming to the temple. I better clean up my act." But, you see, it's definitely insufficient.

They're not able to clean up their act because there's no practice of cleaning up the act through the cleansing rhythmic breath and the changes in attitude, which is changes of forms, you see. They're not able to because they're not practicing during the week. This is why homework will be coming for you students very, very soon. And you will be getting your tests right here in front of everyone else. And then there will be no question in any of my students' mind for the students who are not making the effort will reveal themselves to all of my students. And so there will be no problem and no question when they go their way. Hmm? And I know we'll understand. Does that help with your question?

Thank you, sir.

You're welcome. Yes, the gentleman here, please.

The self-defense of the forms is our own lack of awareness of them.

The self-defense—may I clarify something with you?

Yes.

The defense of the forms is known in your world as excuses or justifications. You see, a form defends itself by justifying, by giving excuses, you see.

Yes, sir.

And by giving an emotional expression. You see, it uses—say that you have a form created in the fire center or perhaps say the earth center, either one, and you're permitting that form to control you by your belief that you are the thought of I. That's all you have to do is believe that you are the thought. All you have to do is *think* of the thought of I. The instant you think of the thought of I, you now believe in self. And when you believe in self, you are forms. You are all those forms you have created. That's what you do.

Now ofttimes, you see, the earth center forms or the fire center forms, they will use the water center forms to defend and to protect themselves, you see. [People often say,] "Oh, I didn't know," and they get all emotional. You see, they use the water center. They use each other, you see. Oh, they share tremendously. They're so greedy in selfishness. They use each other without the blinking of an eye, those forms of creation. Now go ahead with your question. I wanted to clarify that.

Thank you.

In fact, they use, they use your river, that which you are, that virgin consciousness which you truly are, they use that all the time, and they don't have any qualms about it at all. And try to do you in, in the process. They have one philosophy: do everything and everyone before everyone and everything does you. That's their philosophy. Go ahead. That's called creation. Yes.

When we are not aware of the form that we believe we are for a time . . .

Yes?

. . . how can we grow in awareness?

Well, that's quite simple. You see, the thing that blinds us to the forms controlling our mind is the thought of I. Now when we believe we are the self, when we take such pride in our perfection of how good and how great we are, you see, and that type of thinking—now it's very few people [who] will say that they're perfect, but most people believe that they are. Show me a person who truly believes in self, show me a person who is constantly entertaining the thought of I, and I will show you a person, if they would only be honest, would tell you that they are absolutely perfect: the greatest gift that God ever gave to your world. Yes. To say it is one thing, and they know it will make a fool out of them; so they won't say it. But I'm telling you what they believe.

That's the blindness. The more you believe in self, the more you think that you are the thought of I, the more you do that with yourself, then the more blindness you're going to have to the forms that control you.

You see, the intensity of density is measured by acceptance. Now I gave that to one of my students many years ago. The intensity of density, you know, the blindness, you see, not being aware, is measured by acceptance. [If] you have a little acceptance of the divine will, then you have a great density. You understand that?

Yes.

You see, the more you think of the thought of I, smaller and smaller becomes your acceptance of the divine will, total acceptance. You see, you see, so you narrow it down to what's called, commonly, the peashooter consciousness, and you're not even aware that those forms are controlling you. That's why I gave that to my student there a number of years ago. The intensity of density is measured by acceptance.

If you only want to accept the thought form of I, then everything else you are blind to, including your own forms. Does that help with your question?

Yes. Thank you.

Yes. The lady there, please.

Yes, as you—

Speak right up, please.

As you spoke to the other student a while ago, to take the cleansing breath immediately when you feel a form rising, do you try to create another form in its place at that time or just use the cleansing breath itself?

No. No. You use the cleansing rhythmic breath. That's all that is necessary. That's all that is necessary. And if you are truly doing it, the form will disappear right before your mind's eye. That help with your question?

Yes, very much.

Yes. The lady here, please.

If you have—I know you've spoken on this before, of habit. But if one has a habit that they're having great difficulty in breaking, and it just, it seems to be automatic, an automatic response where you're just not even aware that it's happening.

Yes, that takes place through the intensity of density, measured by acceptance. Go right ahead, please.

OK. Thank you.

You're welcome.

So the, would the, the rhythmic breath, then—my question is, then it would be good to use the rhythmic breath at that time when you perceive it, when the habit again reoccurs.

I see. Well, first of all, I have never experienced a moment when I didn't feel that good would benefit me. Number one: I've never experienced a moment when I didn't think that good would not be of benefit to me. Yes.

Now it doesn't matter whether you have a solidified judgment or just a little thought form being born. It doesn't matter whether you have what you call a habit pattern or something else. The rhythmic cleansing breath is moving your ship on the river, which we have already covered at one of our other classes, to higher centers of consciousness. Therefore, if you feel that something just compels you, well, before it takes control of you to the point you don't do your rhythmic cleansing breath, you understand, you move up to other centers and realms of consciousness. Of course, it is waiting for you when, once again, you choose to believe in what you call self. It's waiting on that center of consciousness. Of course, it is. But the more you rise up, the weaker it gets, because, you see, it only, as I spoke to the student, the gentleman over here, the only way it continues on in your consciousness is from your will power, through identification, feeding this life, this substance, this physical substance to it. Does that help with your question?

Thank you.

Yes. You're welcome. The lady here, please.

Where do the soul faculties fit in?

Soul faculties are in the higher four centers of consciousness. There are forty faculties and forty functions. And one power. That help with your question?

Thank you.

And so, you see, when you, you know, you weary of all these sense functions, you see—it's a matter of balance. You see, in order to be in the physical flesh in the physical world you are, there has to be a certain amount of this physical substance directed to limit or form—do you understand that?—through identity. Well, we're trying to show you or to help you to some degree of balance. You see, let it be 50:50, not 90:10. Hmm? And you know, I'm sure, what centers I'm speaking of. You see, it's a matter of balance, don't you see?

You see, the lower centers only offer a release of the physical substance through the fire center. Do you understand that?

Yes.

This is ridiculous. You see, and it is extremely detrimental, you see. All you [have] got to do is look at your life and see, "Now let's see, how many pounds of energy have I released through that fire center, and I'm this many years old? Hmm. Well, I owe these other four centers a great deal." And so, you see, you could at least move and express through an air center with the energy.

Oh, but you've got to have something that will, you know—you see, the form is so strong and so rigid and so solidified. So you [have] got to really make great effort with your cleansing rhythmic breath, you see. And don't expect miracles overnight, for they don't happen (miracles) period. All right? Yes. It'll work fine. You'll see; 40:40 and there's one totality. Yes.

Yes.

The gentleman here, please.

Is it—in order for something to manifest physically in our creation, I mean, in, in the physical sense, in creation—was I—am I correct to understand that it must, the energy must be released through the fire center?

Not unless you only want experiences in the fire center. There are four centers of creation, child. There's [the] earth center, you know.

Right.

And then there's [the] fire center. And there's [the] water center and an air center. Now if you want something to physically manifest, for you to experience in those centers of creation—now those are the functions, the functions. That which you believe you are is a function.

Right.

That which you truly are is a faculty. So if you want the difference between the two, it's that simple. So you, from the thought of I, believe that you are self and, therefore, experience these functions. And for you, that's what you want to create something in that world you believe that you're in. Isn't that correct?

Yes.

Something physical.

Right.

All right. It requires this *prana*, this life force, this Living Light, this physical energy that's in your body. That's the river of life that you are. Do you understand that?

Yes.

Now how does it get released? Well, say that you want a new car. All right?

Yes.

Now what you first do [is], you think about a new car. Is that correct?

Yes.

Well, that's the air center, isn't it?

Right.

All right. And then again, you start getting a feeling, a little emotional about the possibility—isn't that true?—of getting a new car.

Yes.

You haven't got it yet, though, have you? No, no, no. You only got the air center and the water center. Hmm?
Yes.
Ah! Now we have to go into the fire center. Isn't that true?
Yes.
Now there in the fire center, in creation—this is the fires, you see, which you call lust. But they also serve a good purpose, you understand? You see, that's where the drive is. Do you understand that?
Yes.
The drive in consciousness. Now what happens when you have a thought of a new car: go through all the air center. It gets down into the water center, and you start thinking and you get a little emotional, right? And then the water center mixes a little bit with the fire center and you get a little explosive. Right?
Right.
And it still hasn't come yet. Right?
Right.
And so you're going through all of these centers with all those forms and this is where doubt and fear—fear being the control of the mental substance; that's what fear is. And so here are all these forms ready for the new car, but the earth center forms haven't brought it yet.
Right.
Well, I'll tell you, son, if you really want something worthwhile, start at the top, start at the top, start at the source, and then descend. And remember, there's a bottom so you can bounce back up again. Does that help with your question?
I hope so.
It doesn't? Speak on.
No, sir. OK. In, in what centers do the basic animal instinct live in?
Yes. Earth, fire, water, and air.
OK.

Does that help with your question?

Yes. OK—

Why, people are just as animalistic in thought as they are in lust and fire. Yes. Some. Yes.

All right. Do—is there an instinct of survival in the other, other centers?

Why, certainly not, because belief doesn't exist in the higher centers of consciousness. Why, there's no instinct of survival. What is there to survive? There's no belief. There's no limit. You are what you are. Truth, you see, does not require defense. You see, in the lower four centers of consciousness, it's falsehood that requires defense. It's falsehood [and] it [is] lie, that's what requires defense. But what is it defending? It is defending that which is not true! Does that help with your question?

Yes.

Why, certainly. You see, it is not a matter of never again experiencing the lower centers of consciousness because when that happens, you know, you will not be in those realms at all. You will not exist in limit. There won't be any thought of I for there's no belief; and therefore, you can't be cemented to it. That help with your question? I don't think that my students are ready for wings yet. If someone is, please raise your hand. Let's see if they have a pair that could be attached. *[Several students laugh.]* I don't know how well you could fly with them.

Yes. Are there any more questions? The gentleman here hasn't had a turn. Yes, I'll come to you ladies in a moment. Yes, here.

Yes, sir. Last week I heard you speak about uniting your motivation with the spoken word, your spoken word. And my question is, let's say that a person wants to unite his motivation with his spoken word, but he is so grounded that he is confused. He doesn't know what his motivation is. Now it's my understanding that his first step would be to do the cleansing breath to get out of that grounded area so he could move on up the river. Are there other steps after that to unite the spoken word?

Why, certainly. First of all, once you rise up out of the lower four centers of consciousness, you will awaken to who you are. Not only who you are but what you are. There's where you make conscious choice. And then, as you descend, you remind yourself, these different experiences you're going to have, they are not you. You see, I've given it to you so many different ways: separate truth from creation, that which you are from that which you believe you are.

So, you see, a person believes many things. Now in reference to this man's question over there, he said that, in reference to things manifesting physically, there, you see, in the lower centers, that's, of course that's where they manifest. That's the world you believe in. And so that's the only way for you they manifest.

You're in other centers of consciousness with these beautiful angelic forms that are right in the atmosphere, you don't believe in those. How could you believe in them when belief is totally dependent on limit, form, physical substance? Is that not correct?

Yes.

So it is understandable that, for anyone who believes they are the thought of I, you understand—you see, the thought of I is a belief and a bondage of self and limit—they [the angelic forms] do not exist, you understand. They can only exist when you rise in consciousness where they exist, you see? I am well aware of my students that when I speak to you for moments, fleeting moments only then do I exist. You see the form of my channel. You do not even see my form. And if you did, you'd have compassion for him because he's rather small for me to squeeze inside of. All right. *[Many students laugh.]* Now I don't think you'll have any problem there. The lady over there. And I'll be with you in a moment. Yes.

Yes. I have a question similar. With the cleansing breath we rise to the higher levels of consciousness.

Correct.

I want to understand. I thought last week you had said the odic was the higher consciousness in which forms, physical forms, could be created amid the, those forms.

Of course, that's where they should be created in the odic realm of consciousness and descend down into the fires and earth centers. How many births are heavenly? You know, they talk about this, this heavenly thing. How many start there? How many start at the Source that they are? How many start in the celestial realms and move on down into the ethereal, the odic, and the magnetic and electric realms? You just tell me how many births are created in heaven that you see physically manifest in your world? Why, virgin births are very rare. That help with your question?

Yes.

Depends on where they're created. Yes.

I wasn't just talking of physical forms. I'm also talking of the thought forms. Is that the same? You're, you're—

Why, certainly. I'm talking about the same, too. Because, you see, that which is first in thought manifests itself in your physical world.

Thank you.

Sooner or later. Now what is the one thing that it takes—you see, you can go ahead and you can start with your air center and you can think about having an automobile. And then you can go in your water center and get all the feelings and emotions of it. And then you can go in the fire center and get all the thrust and drive and the impatience to get it. And then you can enter the earth center, where it's a physical substance. But now, controlling all of that, what does it take? It's time you students do a little homework. What is the one four-letter word it takes? Pardon?

Will?

Will! It takes the lord of your universe, correct? *[After a short pause, the teacher continues.]* Pardon?

Yes.

And how could you bring about the manifestation much more harmoniously? What five-letter word could you use and bring it about much more harmoniously? Yes.

Faith?

That is correct. That which you are, you see. You see, faith goes beyond all of that. You don't have to believe. You know, there's no such thing as belief; when you experience faith, belief doesn't exist. Belief is the king of the lower centers of consciousness. Ah, but faith is the servant of freedom of the Light of eternal truth from the higher consciousness. Any other question? The lady there had a question. Yes.

Yes. Earlier you said that disharmony or illness comes from the earth center—

Well, I didn't say it came from the earth center. It is involved with the earth, fire, water, and air center[s], definitely.

OK. So, so then an illness could be related to another center rather than the earth center, although—

Why, it most certainly could be related to the air center and to the water center. It could also be easily related to the fire center, where one is totally frustrated by not having the experiences of what they believe they desire that they should have.

And if they work on those beliefs and desires, does that create wellness?

What creates wellness is to rise in consciousness out of those realms because it takes energy to battle those forms. And the more you battle them, the more feeding you give them. A wise man does not battle the forms. A wise man rises out of the realm where they are and armors himself with the Light of truth and, once prepared, descends into the realms, those lower centers, and does battle. But one does not do battle with forms that they believe that they are. Do you understand that?

Yes.

You see, they say a lot of people have a suicide tendency. Well, of course, there are forms who will do that when they don't get their way. But, you see, it is a rare person that'll say, "Now let's see, how can I cut off my foot?" Correct? So as long as you believe you're the forms, don't tempt yourself to battle with them. Wait until you rise into celestial realms of consciousness and armor yourself with the truth that will not fail. Then you descend with the proper armor to do so.

Thank you.

But you cannot know what that armor is until you reach those realms of consciousness. Hmm? You're welcome. Let's see, the lady here hasn't had a chance yet. Yes.

What's happening when, when a person is hearing everything, but is only half there?

Well, yes, of course, that shows a house divided that cannot stand. That shows that there is a battle between the higher realms of Light within a person and the lower realms of darkness. And that the battle is not yet won. And that reveals that greater homework has to be done with the student, more effort has to be done with their rhythmic cleansing breath. Does that help with your question? Because that reveals that division in consciousness, the battle raging back and forth, you see. Yes, go ahead.

And does—every seventy-two hours, when the, the river is released, is it individual, when it's released? And can you, would you—

Oh, certainly. It certainly is individual. A lot of people don't even release the river in their seventy-two-hour period. They do not release it sufficiently and it floods the banks and they have all kinds of problems. You see, releasing of a river, when you're doing something that, you see, you're totally absorbed in what you are doing and you feel very good about it—do you understand that? Then the river's being released right into that.

That's what's happening. And when you finish, you say, "Oh, I feel real good." Is that not correct?

Yes, it is.

You might be a little tired, but you feel good. But then again, it's something that you can control and you have not cast your pearls before the swine. Is that not true? Pardon?

That's true.

Yes. Did you have another question?

So when you, when you get done with a job, say that you've totally put all your energy into—

Well, you can't put all in or you couldn't be speaking to me right now.

I mean—

Yes, go right ahead.

Well, until it's complete.

Yes.

Do you wait seventy-two more hours before you start creating like that again or—

No, certainly not. You see, that is something that is a balance within one's own consciousness. If you find yourself all up, what you call all uptight and all upset and in everything like that, then you can be rest assured that the river is not being balanced; and it's dammed up there in the water center and probably drowning all those forms along the shore that are waving to you on the ship. *[Many students laugh.]* Do you understand that?

Yeah.

Yes, go ahead.

So then, with, within every seventy-two-hour period what you're—are you saying you need to really release—no?

No. It happens when you live intelligently. When you live intelligently, the intelligence that's within you, you don't have to be concerned about any schedules or charts.

Right.

It is a natural flow, you see. Then you find yourself, every day doing something that is worthwhile, something that you enjoy and you don't find yourself all frustrated and ready to explode. You see, my friends, I told you before about these forms: how, you see, without this so-called sleep, a certain amount of it, you see, these forms don't get the energy. And so you [have] got to look at the good part of the whole thing: they do siphon off some of that so that you don't blow your brains out from frustration. Do you understand that?

Yes.

You see, you see, you can tell right away whether a person is dammed up or not: just turn them loose and see what they do. Hmm? That help with your question? Yes, well, I'm not turning my students loose as long as they're around me. *[Many students laugh.]* The gentleman here has been waiting.

Yes. Would you speak on the expression of forms consciously versus the expression of forms in sleep?

Well, the expression of forms consciously, because a person believes in the thought of I, one could not say that's very conscious. You see, a person so believes they are the self that they're doing all kinds of things, and they believe that that is them. And therefore, one could not really call that conscious. That's more like an unconscious state. I think your world calls that a, well, a robotical state of consciousness or more like a zombie, don't you see. They're physically present, but they really don't know what they're doing. Hmm? So that's what I find that most of this conscious business is.

Now in reference to sleep, you see, it's quite similar. A person walks around and they believe that that emotional upset is them. That's just the same as being asleep. Do you understand? Because, you see, it has just as much control over them whether their eyes are open or closed. Now many people, they'll say, "Now just a minute, this upset here, this is not me." Now that's, that's being conscious. Do you understand? But when their eyes are closed and they're asleep, why, those things come in and they upset them. Did you ever watch a person while they sleep?

Yes.

Did you ever see the jerks and jumps and numbers that they go through while they're supposed to be resting? There's no rest there at all. You see, all the parts of their body are moving. And what I find most interesting are the centers which represent the body, those are the ones that are most active. That tells me plenty. What does it tell you?

Yes, sir.

Did that help with your question?

OK.

Yes, and that also tells me they're not balanced. Yes, thank you. The lady there, please.

Yes, is it my understanding that the four lower centers are located in the base of the spine? And—

Not the base. They're distributed through the lower portion of the physical anatomy of the spine. Yes, that's correct.

OK. Where are the higher centers located from the . . .

Higher up.

From the, from this, from the . . .

Yes.

I see.

Uh-huh. That's where you leave when you leave that flesh.

Right. From that . . .

You leave right out of here. *[The teacher gently taps the top of his head.]* You did know that, didn't you?

Yes.

Yes! You don't leave through your toes, you know. Yes, the lady here, please.

Yes. Last week when you were making reference to the head to the north and facing—

Yes.

—east at a 45-degree angle.
Yes?
Am I correct in understanding that you said many things leave through the north or through the head? And, and if so, what would those be other than at the point of transition?
All the things that you have created. They're yours.
Is that where the forms come out?
Well, they don't only come out there, my friend.
Oh.
They come out at any opening of your physical anatomy. They also come out that place in the head. And they come out at other areas, too. That's a physical substance that leaves your body. Yes. Best it be out the north pole than the south, though, I can assure you of that. *[Many students laugh.]* Let our God stay above. That's the only one that'll free us, is that which is above. Does that help with your question? Yes.
I'd also like to ask—
Well, you see, I see your point. You want to know what things. Well, the things that you have created and believe that you are. And so when you leave the physical body, you can only go that high in consciousness. You can only go to the plane that you're able to, to gravitate to. If you believe you are those things, then you have to take all that baggage with you. And if you don't believe you are those things and you know better and you demonstrate that, then you'll be able to sail right on up. Yes. That help with your question? Go ahead.
Thank you. I'd also like to ask, Which center, if any, is located at the base of the neck, considering so many of us put out our atlas and axis?
I've given you nine centers of consciousness, haven't I?
Yes.
I have also, as a private student of many years ago, given you the different parts of the anatomy, haven't I?

Yes.

You know or should through your own effort. And when you make the effort, having received all of that as a private student over a period of many years, you might use a little bit of discernment when you ask the question.

Thank you.

You're welcome.

I'm sorry.

You're welcome. The lady here, please.

Do we replace the fluid that we give out?

Yes. Yes. It's just like, you know, this fluid, which is being released all the time—but what are you releasing it to is the big question. Because it is yours, you see. This is the great problem people have when they really believe and they're attached to their thought form, because, you see, it is created out of their own very being. You understand that, don't you? See, they've created it. And so it's understandable they have struggle in the sense of believing that that's them.

It is constantly being replaced. Yes, that is the law of nature. Constantly. And the problem is, you see, it is constantly being replaced, but it is not constantly being used in balance. The river, you see, is overflooding the banks at times. Not all the time. Sometimes the river looks like a little, dinky stream, you know, because the water's so low, you see. And so there's a balance there. Under all circumstances, of course, one should keep balance, balance in consciousness. Hmm?

Yes, the lady there, please. Thank you.

[The student clears her throat.] *Excuse me. Do the acupuncturists in the earth realm serve the purpose of trying to release the flow to the people who don't understand the philosophy?*

Well, what you call acupuncturists, they actually do—through a manipulation of certain nerve centers that they are aware of, the energy or the river goes into different parts of the physical and mental anatomy. However, pressure is the wiser path and a very ancient system. I hope that's helped with your question. Thank you. The lady there, please.

In the air center, is it my understanding, all the chemicals exist within the air center—

That is correct.

—of consciousness?

That is correct. For physical manifestation, are you speaking? I was speaking of physical manifestation; all the chemicals exist in the air center. Yes.

OK. Why is it the air center where these are able to exist in the . . .

Why? *[After a short pause, the teacher continues.]* Does anything on your planet exist without air?

No.

Does anyone have anything that exists without air on your planet? Because that's where the full warehouse is! It's in the air center! You see, all your provisions are in the air center. For your lower centers, all your provisions are available to you in the air center. Now the other centers don't have all the provisions the air center does. Why, there's never a moment, there's never a moment you're not taking some provisions off the shelf. Do you ever have a moment when you're not thinking of something? Well, you're in the warehouse, the air center, in a warehouse picking stuff off, constantly picking stuff, picking stuff off. *[Again, many students laugh.]* My, my.

Yes. Now we have time just for one more question, then we—as time has passed. Yes, the gentleman there, please.

How do doubt and fear enter into our consciousness? Are they associated with one of the lower levels or all four?

They are defense mechanisms of the forms. So if you believe that you are one of the forms on the fire center or earth center—you understand that?

Yes.

And believing that you are that form and that form is determined to have its way but it's having a problem in manipulating and controlling you, it will use other forms, its buddies, known as doubt and fear, to get its way. Do you understand that?

Yes.

And so when it senses, within your consciousness, because it's composed of your consciousness, plus the physical substance, and it senses that, "Uh-oh! Now he is just about to do that. Oh, I can't afford that because then I won't get my feeding. I won't— we won't have anywheres near as much." And then he convinces his buddies to instill in your consciousness doubt and fear and what it's going to cost you, you see. Do you understand?

Yes.

I hope that's helped with your question. Thank you very much. I see that our time is up. Thank you. And good day.

JULY 21, 1985

A/V Class Private 7

Good morning, class. A good morning it is.

Now today I know that you're all well prepared and have done your homework. So we'll begin today's class with the questions; so that you can see for yourself how well you have done this past week. And so I will call you by name with the questions on the philosophy that you have spent so much time and so much energy studying. So we'll begin today and I will speak here to [Student S]. You'll kindly name for us the nine centers or planes of consciousness in the human body.

Celestial, the ethereal, the odic, the magnetic, the electric, the air, the water, fire, earth.

Very good. Sometimes it is, of course, we know, beneficial to descend rather than to ascend. And so we have the earth, fire, water, air, electric, magnetic, odic, ethereal, and celestial.

Now where is the location—*[A student's dog experiences difficulty breathing.]* It's all right. It's all right. Open his arms, please. Open his arms. Open his arms. He's all right. No, just open his arms. *[A student spreads the two front legs of the small dog.]* Ah, there. *[The dog's breathing difficulty passes.]* Now, [Student H]—

Yes.

What is the location of the will power in the centers of consciousness or planes of consciousness?

The will power [is in] the, the fire center.

No. Thank you. [Student P].

It's between the air center and before the electric.

Very good. Very good. [Student R], what is the frequency or numerical value of will power?

I don't know.

[Student B]. Thank you.

All I know is that it's electric. I don't know the number.

The will power is located, as [Student P] said, between the air and electric centers or planes of consciousness. [Student M].

Five.

No. [Student U].

I don't know.

[Student H].

Six.

No. [Student J].

Would it be one in the earth center?

No. Now we want to stop and think and do our studies and our homework. And it is very important. You know the location of the will power: located between the electric center [and] the air center. Well, you know that there are nine centers of consciousness. And pause and think. What would be its numerical value or frequency range? [Student R], through what element is electricity conducted?

It'll be conducted through air.

Why?

Or water.

What happens when it's conducted through water?

Under what condition?

Under the conditions of the human being on the planet Earth.

It's a tremendous shock.

In what center?

In the water center.

And what happens in the air center?

It's—I think what it does is clean things out in the air center.

And what would make that possible?

It, it burns whatever, whatever it contacts.

And what is, what is the effect of something that burns?

It's purified.

It is purified. Fine. Now what is the frequency of will power?

Five and a half.

Why is it five and a half? *[After a short pause, the teacher continues.]* Is it totally purified?

Yes, it would be.

And would return to the source from whence it is composed?

Yes.

And if it is totally purified and returns to the source from whence it is composed, what then would be its numerical value?

One.

Thank you. [Student U].

Nine.

Nine. And why would it be nine?

Nine represents the totality.

Nine *is* the totality. Now I have already given you—and we had [better] do a little more homework here—I've already given you what nine represents: a perfect circle and a line of infinity. For there is no such thing in truth as a straight line, for all lines are circles. It is only your perspective that make[s] them lines. So all things return unto itself; therefore, all things are circular. They are not straight; they are not crooked. You perceive them as a straight line. They are in truth a circle. And you all should have known that considering the years of the classwork that has already been given you. More homework, obviously, is required.

Now we understand that will power, whose frequency is nine, total, is, like anything, a perfect circle that returns unto its source or origin. Therefore, what are the functions that are controlled by belief and why so? Yes, [Student S].

The functions controlled by belief are money, ego, and sex.

Yes.

Is that what you're looking for?

No, let's put it in another way. What centers are controlled by belief?

The lower four.

Name them.

Earth, fire, water, and air.

And what centers are controlled by faith?
The next four.
Name them.
Electric, magnetic, odic, ethereal.

Fine. Now why are earth, fire, water, and air centers or planes of consciousness controlled and dependent upon belief? Why is that so? Yes, [Student S].

Because that's representative of creation, dependent on limit.

What is the cause of limit?

Denial and need.

Denial of what?

God.

The denial of truth guarantees the dependence of limit or falsehood. Therefore, you cannot see clearly, hear clearly, or experience clearly what you are. Now why does a person choose belief over faith? Yes.

They choose it because they've denied their truth and registered the need.

I see. Well, the effect of directing the will power through the water center guarantees, beyond a shadow of any doubt, dependence, bondage, and limit. Why is the water center essential to your existence on the planet Earth? [Student S].

Because it's a part of the creation; it must descend through that to manifest in the physical.

Yes. Without the water center, life as you presently know it does not exist on your planet. Therefore, when you, by conscious choice, direct the power of your will to the water center of consciousness, you experience the limits of all your desires, for the water center of consciousness, your form, your limit is dependent upon, on your planet Earth.

Now you have, and have always had, free will. It is free, and you are aware of the freedom of it when you direct it to the higher centers of consciousness. For when you direct this power that you are to the faculties of being within you, beyond this earth, fire, water, and air center—for this power of the will stands patiently between the air and the electric center. And that is why it is stated to "Keep faith with reason; she will transfigure thee." Now "she" is representative, of course, of reproduction, for you are in the process of constantly reproducing your unfulfilled desires. Now you reproduce them with that which you are, the Living Light, that fluid that goes out into the universe. You are in a constant process in creation of reproducing them. Their reproduction[s] return unto you as what you call experiences. And then you'll go along in life, one moment believing how wonderful creation or limit is, only to experience the next moment of how distasteful and what a struggle it is for you in creation.

Now you are doing these things, of course, to yourself. Because you consciously make a choice. Moment by moment you make a choice. You choose to deny the Principle of Good and your right to it. Now we've spoken before on how you deny the Principle of Good and good experiences in your own life. The Principle of Good is activated in your consciousness only by the power of will. Now the power of will directed to the Principle of Good is known as what? [Student H].

Total acceptance.

Total acceptance. So, you see, when you express in your consciousness total acceptance, you free yourself from the control of the lower centers of consciousness, where dependence or limit is the Law of Creation.

Now the first thing that happens in your mind when you think about total acceptance, depending on which of the lower four centers of consciousness that you are in, the moment that you think of total acceptance, the will and the movement of the power of good in your lives, the moment you think of that, you immediately believe you are the forms that rise up to defend themselves for they fear that other forms are going to be created and deprive them of the sustenance that they are used to experiencing from you. And so you permit what is known as shadows to rise up in your consciousness and to convince you of how horrible it is to experience total acceptance, the power and the will and the movement of goodness.

The sadness is that you believe, in those moments, that those things in your mind are you. You do not pause to consider that they are forms that you have created who have made the judgment that they are threatened and will not receive as much sustenance for their livelihood as they are used to.

So when you make the effort to pause and to consider what you are permitting to happen to you, then you will no longer fear the principle of goodness, known as total acceptance.

Now I have spoken to you, some of you, before on accepting the possibility, the possibility. And when you accept the possibility, you have to put that acceptance into motion within your consciousness, for everything that is happening in your life is repeatedly telling you who is in control of your life. And time and again you do not appreciate nor do you like the experiences that you are having. So when you say to yourself, "I don't like these experiences," and do not make changes within your consciousness so those experiences do not repeat themselves, then you must accept the demonstrable truth that what is using your mind are other forms that are not happy with what the other forms are doing. You are vacillating and fluctuating between levels of consciousness in the lower planes of awareness.

Now you can do everything about that. And you can do everything about it this moment and every moment by doing your homework. You see, you cannot be expected to apply this demonstrable truth when you are not doing your homework because you do not have anything intelligent to apply. So it is understandable: the first thing you start doing is your homework, because I have many, many, many questions to ask you on studies that you have already received for many, many, many years. And for me to come here to be with you and permit you not to do your homework is not only a waste of my time, it is a waste of yours.

We're going to pause at this moment. Go turn on our music, please. Pause the camera.

[The class and the recording pauses. During the pause, the location of the class is moved from the back garden of the temple to the front of the temple on the driveway.]

Well, good morning once again, students. I think we can start off and resume our class now. And one of the things that, perhaps, would be helpful to you is that "OK" doesn't mean all is right.

We were discussing the use of this power of will that is available to all of you, and we had a little experience, for whenever we permit our self to identify with the four centers of consciousness of creation, the only way that we will allow our self to accept any changes in our life is through experience, which is the return of the forms that at times we believe we are. So whenever you believe that you are your form, then change in your life is only possible for you through experience, which, as I stated, is the return of the forms that you believe at any time that you are.

Now today was scheduled for a little refresher course, a little of your sharing of your understanding in keeping with the great effort that some of you have been making in studying this philosophy and your homework. And so we were at the point of discussing will power and its location, the understanding of belief, for you can only experience belief when you identify with the first four centers and planes of consciousness.

You do not experience what you know as belief in the higher planes of consciousness. Once you pass from the air center into the electric center, that is where you move from belief and bondage to faith and freedom. Faith offers to us freedom for faith is not dependent. Faith does not contain dependence for faith does not contain denial. And that which does not contain denial does not offer comparison, judgment, and need. So our efforts

[are] to help you to help yourself to move intelligently into the higher planes of consciousness where your freedom and your life is filled with abundant good.

When you look out at life, what you call life, forms, creations, trees, people, animals, and little critters there, when you look out and see them, you see them in keeping, of course, with your belief. Therefore, you see them in keeping with your bondage of need. And, of course, your need is ever subject to the degree of denial of the divine Law of Total Acceptance. Therefore, we look and we see, with these forms, what they have to offer to us. That is based, of course, upon the experiences in our life and our belief that we are those forms or what you call experiences. Change can only come for you, as long as you believe that you are limit, change can only come through what you know as experiences.

However, that which is beneficial to your life is what is, in truth, taking place in your life. For when we slowly but surely awaken to the truth that limit or form or creation does not and cannot offer to us the joy that we are seeking, [we find] that it offers very limited, very limited, temporary satisfaction. And as we grow in the Light within us, our early experiences are a desire to escape from creation. That is not the pathway up. It is, however, the path down for it is born from a function deeply seated in the consciousness, known as denial. It is a denial of the law, the Law of Evolution. It is a denial of the right of the Law of Evolution. It's like when we go to school, and we don't like the test and the lessons that we receive. Then we must pause and ask our self, "Why am I in school?"

So we must ask ourselves why, why are we in creation? We've entered creation in keeping with the Law of Evolution, our evolution. We alone, we alone establish the law. Our time and duration as beings identified with creation is entirely dependent upon the law that we alone establish. It doesn't matter that you may think that you can desire to stay a long time on the earth plane and end up having stayed a very short time. It takes much more than a simple, little, temporal desire.

You have entered creation with a great responsibility: the responsibility of awakening, awakening that which has denied the Light, to once again serve the Light. That is your responsibility. You have that responsibility.

Your hand is creation. You are responsible to tell it what to do and to see that it does it. You have entered creation with that responsibility. Not only with that responsibility but with the opportunity to do the job that you have entered the physical world and the physical flesh to do. However, you cannot do your job and do your job well unless you first understand what your job is and how to do your job.

To deny creation is to destine your life to further bondage to it. If there is anything that you find distasteful, all you have to do to experience the continuity of it is to deny its right of existence and to deny your right of evolution of being in it.

Creation is not good and creation is not bad. Creation is. You are responsible to move it in a direction that you, as the source of its very livelihood, will move it in, [which is an] intelligent direction for the greater good of your being while identified with creation. To do otherwise is to deny your responsibility, and whoever denies their responsibility is destined to serve it for eons yet to come.

You will not escape creation by leaving a physical world, for what you believe creation is, is what you take with you. For in keeping with the Law of Belief are you bound to the judgment. So if you think for any moment that by leaving your physical world you will leave creation because you are no longer happy with creation or because creation doesn't do what you tell it to do, be rest assured you will leave your physical body and you will find yourself without a physical body, but with all the images and limits and forms that creation has to offer.

You cannot escape that which you believe that you are. You can, however, evolve beyond bondage and belief and enter the realms of freedom. It takes will power. It takes the faculty of reason to move from the fourth to the fifth center of consciousness. It takes a conscious act of the power of your will.

Everyone wishes to experience days of harmony, days of peace, and days of joy. That is, of course, your birthright. You cannot experience your birthright as long as you insist on depending on those forms that are a mental world, a world designed to serve you, and you have forgotten the purpose of its design.

Of what benefit is the form created by your mind in a mental world, of what benefit and what good is it, if it does not, as it leaves your universe and attracts unto itself like kind, return to you as an instrument of good and joy and happiness to your mental world? Then it is of no good.

To control one's mind is not to deny its existence. To control one's emotions and one's desires is not to deny their existence, for when you tempt to deny the existence of the right of any form, you only guarantee its wrath. For you alone created it, and you alone will pay for it as long as you permit yourself, through laziness in consciousness, you permit yourself to be controlled by a child that you alone have created.

Everything, *everything* is where you are. The question must then again, once again, be asked, Where are you? Ask yourself the question, Where are you? Don't look outside for good that is inside. And if you will only stop looking outside for the good that is inside of you, you won't be tempted to blame outside when the good you do not experience. It is a laziness in consciousness, the effect of a weakness known as temptation. Temptation: distracted from that which you want to do. Many times a person says, "Well, I want to do better, but . . ." I said long ago the "buts" are all the problems; there are too many "buts" in the way.

How beautiful it is and so peaceful, because, you see, we are moving on. The price is very high, but then the truth, no one can buy. The price is high only to your beliefs, which are in a constant process of changing. You believe that you are unhappy because [of] what something was done beyond your control. And yet you have the truth to keep you free from those disasters.

If it matters to you what someone else thinks, then be rest assured your need to control them has reached phenomenal proportions. What should matter to you is what you think. What should matter to you is what you feel. What should matter to you is finding a better way. That's what should matter. To find a better way to enjoy the beauty that surrounds you.

But you must understand when you look around and you see the beauty of the flowers and the sky and the trees and the water and the hills, when you look around and see those things, life-giving energy is going to those forms. Therefore, you must be alert, very alert, and very awake and aware to what it is that doesn't want you to look and see the beauty that surrounds you. For there is something working within your mind telling you, you don't have time, it's really not that beautiful, or you think that you're totally ignoring it.

And while we're speaking on ignoring it, let us understand, a bit, about some minds who have taken this principle, to ignore, and used it for a device in the temptation to control another. For like anything that is done from the motivations and promptings of limit, the Law of Limit returns unto the sender.

[If] you want to create forms that return to you and you have what you call experiences of a beautiful day, then you alone, through your proper exercises, must rise on this river of life, your identity, your little ship, beyond the fourth center of consciousness. For standing there, between the fourth and fifth center or plane of consciousness, is where your test is. It is where it has always been. It is where it will always be. For between the fourth and the fifth is this great power of action, known as will power, that you have available to you. It only exists between the fourth and fifth plane of consciousness. Between the air and the electric. It is there that you have at your disposal the power of the universe. It is there that you move with this great electric power upward or you move downward. This takes place whenever you make a choice.

Now ofttimes you say to yourself, "Well, I didn't think. I didn't think about that," or "I didn't pause to consider that." Now try to understand, established patterns of mind are created forms. They exist on the plane of consciousness where they were created. When you, standing between the fourth and fifth plane, with the great power and the movement of that power, known as will, will power, you may tell yourself that you didn't think. And you are telling yourself the truth. How are you telling yourself the truth? It's demonstrable, my children. Something else thought for you. Something that you *believe* that you are: a form created in your mind. And therefore, this great will power is taken by the form and expressed on that particular center in which the form was created originally.

So a person goes through their life and says, "I forgot that. I meant to do that, but I didn't. Something distracted me." Understand that something is a child that you alone created. Now the only way that it got control and the use of you is by not being on guard and aware of which plane of consciousness you were on at that moment. Now in order to be aware of "Where am I at this moment," you must pause and be still inside, for only in perfect stillness do you stand between the fourth and fifth center of consciousness. That's where you have at your disposal this great power of will. There you have, in front of you, the faculty of reason through which you must pass to rise to the higher realms of consciousness. That is available to you.

Now if you turn your back and you look backwards, which is down—that which is in back of you, that which is behind you is below you. Whatever is behind or in back of you is below you. This is why you say, "The past event, it's behind me," because in consciousness it is behind you; it is below you. It has been created, it has been formed, and it only exists in those four centers down there. So if you turn your back, as you have at your disposal within you this great power, and you choose not to pass through the faculty of reason and you turn your back on the faculties, which now are behind you, then you can only service the opposite of the faculties. And what is that, [Student S]?

It would be the functions.

The functions. So what takes place at that point, between the fourth and fifth center, what is actually taking place, you have chosen bondage through belief over freedom through faith. And this is the homework that you as students should be working on.

You see, people say, oh, they have difficulty with faith. They have faith: they have faith in this, but don't have faith in that, etc. Faith *is*. You make the conscious choice for faith or belief. And you do it moment by moment.

What, when you're standing between those centers and planes of consciousness, what could you possibly think about to turn your back on freedom and all the goodness it offers to believe in bondage and suffering and the phenomenal cost? What is it that prompts you to turn your back on what you are and experience what you are not? Yes, [Student S]. What is it that tempts the mind to turn its back on what it is?

From the temptation is to self-orientation . . . the lowest . . . [An airplane flying overhead makes it difficult to accurately transcribe the student's response.]

Over-identification with the thought of I is the greatest temptress you will ever, ever know. And it offers to everyone the suffering, the struggle, and a seeming horror of creation. And so I've taught you over the years that selfless [service], service absent the self, is the path of illumination. It is an over-identification with the limit of the I, the form of the I, that is the temptress that calls you below. So do not be tempted by the temptress.

Now why is it a temptress instead of a tempter? Yes, [Student S]. Why is it a temptress and not a tempter? Why is it feminine instead of masculine?

Because it's ruled by the emotions, which are feminine.

Anything else?

Feminine was the first that fell from the grace in the split with man.

Well now, let's ask someone else here. Yes, [Student R].

Because it's magnetic.

Because it's magnetic. Now how does a magnet—how does magnetic separate from electric? What causes the separation?

Well, magnetic is an attraction, and the electric is an emanation.

Well, I think we all understand that. What causes it to separate?

The level of consciousness that one is expressing through.

Well, I'm interested in what causes—I'm interested in your explaining what causes the separation between the electromagnetic forces. What causes the electromagnet, what causes it to divide, to separate?

[For] an electromagnet to separate, would be the removal of the electric.

Now you can discuss it, yes. When you remove the electric, the magnet falls, correct?

That is correct.

Well, that law applies to your experiences and your life. When you, standing there with the power of your will, and you're looking through the faculty of reason that will transform you and you're feeling the emotions of what has been, you divide in consciousness. You know better, but you do it anyway. You separated the electromagnetic within your own consciousness. And then you tell yourself, well, you just couldn't help yourself. You just couldn't help yourself. This is why I have given to you, "In mind as it is in heart." *[This quote is from "The Laws Be" affirmation, which may be found in the appendix.]* Not in mind one thing and in heart something else, for that is a house divided. To know better and to do it anyway can only reveal, to students of Light, that they looked at the Light above in their consciousness and perhaps made a few humble steps towards the door of reason and, having done so, looked below and took the nosedive. And then return from the depths to say, well, they're trying to do better, but they could not help themselves.

You must understand what you're doing to yourself, you see? You see, it is better not to know better than to know better and do it anyway. Though ignorance is no escape from just law, it is temporarily, as some of my students have said to my channel, indeed, most blissful. How long can you thrill over bliss? I can assure you not very long. For some it lasts minutes, for others, hours. But you can't stay in a state of what you call bliss. Now what most of my students call bliss is really satisfaction at its peak. So when you know better, you're telling yourself and the world the truth: you see the door; you know what's right. In your heart you know what's right, but your head, you believe it.

The greatest difficulty in any school of Light is this phenomenal belief in the head at the sacrifice of the goodness and the beauty of the heart. You can do without a head. You cannot do without a heart. And only a fool would choose their head over their heart.

Now a person—you see, I think it's perhaps because some of you have a little confusion about the heart. So many people believe it is an instrument of pointed hearts. That's not the heart I'm speaking about. I'm not speaking about a pointed heart, for, speaking very clearly, pointed hearts piss all over people. I'm speaking about round hearts, not pointed hearts. So who would choose a pointed heart, when a round heart is what you really are? It's a matter of choice. You choose to service forms that are below.

That which is past is that which is gone, that which is below. Try to understand, below is something that has happened. It is not something that is. It isn't even something that's going to be, until you go to serve it. Now when you look behind, as Lot's wife looked behind her—the light of reason spoke and told her not to turn, but she turned around for she was tempted in her belief in that which had passed, and she was turned into a pillar of salt that she may purify the forms that she temporarily believed, in that moment, that she was.

You not only have a responsibility, you have a great opportunity, a great opportunity to experience in creation the beauty and goodness that is there. How is it there? It is there by you're not believing that you are it. You do not experience a good feeling when you step into your automobile, if you believe you are your automobile, for you never know what it might do from your lack of care for it. And if you think that that is not true, then look to the shadows and see the times when it wouldn't start or it stalled or it didn't do what you told it to do. Depending on how much you believed that you are the automobile were the experiences in the water center and the fire center that you had.

Now that's what takes place when you look at the path you know is right for you and turn around and service that which has gone.

You cannot afford the luxury of discouragement. You cannot afford the luxury of forgetting. You can only afford the reason, the pure, beautiful reason of forgiving and freeing. When you free yourself, you are servants of the Light of Goodness. When you free your judgments, when you free your thought forms that are not serving you, when you free them from your consciousness—for only you can free them. Someone else cannot free them for you. Someone else can only open up their home and let them all in, and you temporarily experience a relief from their bombardment in your consciousness. But that doesn't go on forever. That's very temporary, and that's in keeping with divine laws in evolution.

Look at people. When you believe that you are that limit, that thought of I, and you have what you call a honeymoon relationship, and everything is so beautiful and so good. And you smell the fresh air, and you see the beauty of the flowers and all of those things. And it's just wonderful for a time. Then what happens? Disaster. Which only reveals your temporary dependence upon your mind for the goodness of life.

The goodness of life is the effect of what you do with your mind. And what you do with your mind is to see that it does what you want it to do. And you want it to do what is necessary so you can have the abundant good and joy and happiness of life. It doesn't only owe that to you, that's its purpose of design. You're responsible to see that it does that for you. That's your responsibility. And when it doesn't do what you tell it to do, then it's your responsibility to sit down with it and straighten it out in no uncertain terms, and to tell it what it's going to do, when it is going to do it, and not to give you any of those lower lips. That's your responsibility.

It's not your responsibility to say, "Well, I'm trying." Forget about trying. Just totally forget that foolishness. That was long ago stolen by the darkness. Forget about that. That's simply a defense mechanism of a judgment whose telling you, "I'm not about to make any changes." No, no, no. Forget about this business, you know and these—what do you call them?—these weather reports. Forget the weather reports. They're not dependable. They're not even reliable. So forget the weather reports and speak the truth.

It's your mind and you start telling it what to do. And stop telling yourself that you're trying because the more you tell yourself that you're trying, the weaker you get. Stop doing that foolishness. That's not the way to grow. That's not the way to experience the goodness of life. Stop telling yourself you're trying. You're just—that's justifying a hidden judgment that's really speaking and saying, "I'm not about to make any changes! I love my judgments and I'm not changing!" That's another judgment that tells you how it loves its judgments.

So how can you possibly expect, how could you possibly expect the goodness of life when you let those things tell you what they're going to do and then turn around and con you and tell you that you're trying? No. That's like going to the toilet and being constipated for a month and telling your wife each day that you're trying. Now that's kind of ridiculous! I think some of you call that the cosmic toilet. *[Many students laugh.]* Well, get yourself out of the cosmic toilet, and let's get on with the business of living and enjoying the beauty that is ever present and never absent or away.

You don't need anything or anyone to enjoy life. Now if you allow yourself to say, "Well, I'm lonely," how could anyone in any degree of reason, how could they possibly deceive themselves that they're lonely? You have the flowers to keep company. You have the little critters to keep company. You have the trees and the clouds and the sky. You have all—I speak only of the physical things of creation—you have all of that available to you. How could you possibly permit yourself to be conned by a judgment that's trying to have its own way and telling you that you're lonely? No. What it's really telling you is, "That is what I want and if I don't have that, then I'm going to feel sorry for myself by telling myself how lonely I am."

Now let's get to the truth of the matter and let's see where it really is. And with so many little critters to be cared for and so many beautiful little forms and the plants, the physical things that you can see, and the trees and the flowers—no, you cannot, you *cannot* convince any intelligent person that you're lonely. You may convince them that you're lazy. Oh, yes. *[A few students laugh.]* Lazy, yes. Lonely, no!

Now, [Student U], I think we'll speak to you here for a moment on just exactly, in your understanding, do you use the power that you are to bring everything into your life that you believe that you need for the goodness of living. *[After a short pause, the teacher continues.]* Yes?

On how?

Why, certainly. Isn't that why you're in school?

Yes, sir.

To learn how and then the next step to apply that. *[After another short pause, the teacher again continues.]* Yes, we're all waiting for you.

The demonstration that has been most effective for me, in my own experience—

Yes?

—is by stopping the need or the denial, which is the need, and by expressing—

Well, the need's the effect of the denial, yes.

Thank you.

Yes.

And by expressing in gratitude.

Well, I say we'll get a little bit more specific here. I think it's a little too general, don't you? First of all, you're telling all of us that you enjoy denying?

No.

Why do you do it? Do you often do things you don't enjoy?

I try not to.

Well, go ahead.

Well, I—

I want you to stop trying and start doing. Yes, go ahead. *[After a pause, the teacher continues.]* What do you receive out of denying?

The denial—

Do you deny the rights of others?

I have in the past.

Does past mean the last few minutes or years?

Years. Years.

Oh, you haven't denied the rights of others for years.

No, no, no. In the past few years, I have. In the past few minutes, I don't—

Oh, I see. Oh, in the past few years you have denied the rights of others.

Yes, sir.

Oh, all right. Now can you deny the rights of others without denying the rights of yourself?

I must first deny the rights of myself before I can deny the rights of others.

All right. Now this is very important to understand. There is no way possible that you can deny the rights of others until you first deny the rights of yourself. All right?

Correct.

Now, so you say you've had experiences in denying your rights.

Yes.

And the effect of those experiences of denying your rights is your belief in need or needs.

Yes.

Is that correct? Now what do you feel that you experience and what kind of thrill do you think you get or what do you get in insisting on believing that you're in need? This is important. You know you're supposed to be doing your homework.

It seems, to my understanding, that it's a temporary escape from the Law of Personal Responsibility. It's a way, a mental manipulation to seemingly avoid making that payment.

All right. So you're telling me that you choose, I won't say intelligently, but you choose to believe you're in need in order to escape responsibility for your experiences. Is that correct?

That is correct.

Hmm. Do you enjoy that?

No.

Then why do you think you do it?

Ignorance. Habit.

Well now, let's, let's get right down to specifics here. This is very important in doing your homework, you students. I cannot accept, I will not accept that it's ignorance because you know better.

Yes, sir.

And I'm not one to accept this grand cop-out that says, "Oh, it's a habit of mine." Hmm. No.

Now, let's get down here to business, the business of living here. You must pause and think what you are receiving from denial, which you know, from experiences in life, guarantees the feelings of need. You must weigh that out in your mind to see why you insist upon serving that. Do you all understand that?

You see, the human mind is like a sponge. It absorbs everything. It's constantly getting, getting, getting. Gathering and getting. The basic nature of the human mind. It's quite a computer, you know. So it gathers and it gets anything and everything. Therefore, understanding the basic nature of the human mind, you must be honest with yourself and look in there so that you can see what you are getting out of what you call the experience of need, the effect of denying. Because you're getting something or the mind would never allow it in, because the mind only gets and takes, constantly absorbing what it can get out of something. It's the nature of the mind.

The mind doesn't permit the foot to move until it's passed the censorship it's going to get something it wants. The hand does not move without the mind working, "I'm getting something from this." Do you understand that about the nature of the human mind?

Yes.

Pardon?

Yes.

All right. So that's the nature of *all* human minds. So face, first of all, the nature of the human mind and then be honest with yourself: you're getting something out of denying and experiencing need. All right? And then I'm sure we can move on after you are honest with yourself about that.

Now it's—we have a few minutes here for questions in this beautiful light and sun. Lovely day. Just a beautiful day. *[After another short pause, the teacher continues.]* No questions? Well, I thought there would be a few. But I shouldn't think, should I? Yes, the lady there, please. [Student N], yes, please.

On disassociation, is that—are you in the celestial or any of the upper four and still being able to watch everything that's going on in the lower four without being attached or . . .

That is correct. Through the laws of disassociation, you can look and see what your form believes it is. You can separate truth from creation. That's your job. That's a responsibility that you have. You take a look and say, "Oh, my, there goes that mind again that I sometimes believe that I am. There goes," like I've said to my channel many, many times, "Oh, my, Richard, there goes your temper again. There it goes." And then he'll call it back, you see. So you [have] got to take a look at it. You say, "All right. I'm responsible for that wild one down there that sometimes I believe is me. But I am grateful to the Light of eternal truth to know the difference. It's not me. And I've got to get it together. And I [have] got to get it together right now." You see?

Yes.

Yes. Does that help with your question?

Very much. Thank you.

Why, certainly. You see, no one could convince you that you're only your toe, could they?

No.

Now if someone came up and said, "Oh, [Student N]. Oh, you're just a toe." Why, you wouldn't be happy about that at all, would you? *[Student N laughs.]* Well now, you stop and think. You cannot be happy when you permit yourself to believe you're just a pound of flesh. You understand that? So there's no way to be happy when you permit yourself to believe all of those things that you are not; however, you are still responsible for. You're responsible for your car, but you know you're not your car.

Right.

You're responsible for your nose, but you know you're more than your nose. Otherwise, you couldn't be speaking, could you? Yes, I hope that's helped with your question. Do you have another question? Go ahead.

How—what causes a person to believe what other people are telling them they are feeling?

Yes.

Or that they are.

Oh, certainly! Absolutely. It is from a person's own denial. They experience the need and they thrive on that. They just thrive on that. They get emotional thrills out of that. Yes. Does that help with your question?

The person that, that's believing what the other person is—

Why, certainly! Absolutely. The person that is believing has made sure the bridge between them is nice and solid, you see. And they get to have all of those thrills and sensations of disaster. They thrive on that. You see, the functions just thrive on disaster. Doesn't your news media show you how your world thrives on sensation?

Yes.

You get that thrill, you see. Yes. Yes. People who believe they are those limited forms there, they believe that they are the thought of I, they absolutely thrive on any kind of disaster because it gives their senses a thrill. The sense forms get very, very excited that way. Yes, [does] that help with your question?

[After a short pause, the student responds.] *I, I guess.*

Well, no. It isn't what you wanted to hear.

Well, if you're feeling—if you don't like what you're hearing, you know, if, if you know that it's not the truth and yet you don't have the guts to, to say that that's not the truth and be firm, what causes that weakness?

The weakness?

To not, to not say, "No, this is really the way it is it for me."

Oh, no, no, no. That's because you want something out of the person, my dear. You want something out of the person, and you don't want to offend them because your mind has already judged, "Oh, if I offend this person, then I won't get what I want out of them, and they don't know what I want out of them yet. And I'm just about ready to make my move to get what I want out of them."

Ah.

Oh, certainly. Absolutely. Oh, yes, people do that all the time, you see. That's the grand sellout. You know, there's no greater salesperson than the one who believes beyond a shadow of any doubt that they are the perfect thought of I. That's the best salesman you're ever going to find, or saleslady. Yes. Does that help with your question?

Thank you very much.

Why, certainly. First, you know, to be a good salesperson, you must first believe yourself, what you believe you are. You must absolutely convince yourself in your perfection. Definitely. And then, when you go to open your mouth, you have nothing but conviction to offer. And someone's always waiting and ready to get something for nothing. And if you have really convinced yourself what a good deal you are and you're going to give them something, you know, for a good price or perhaps for nothing, why, you have no problem at all: best salesperson in the world. Did that help you?

I need to think about what I really want to ask more.

No, no, no, no, no. I'm trying to help you. Can't you see, [Student N], can't you see that when a person doesn't feel strong enough to say that's not the way that it is, that that person, in honesty, in facing themselves, has to take another look and say, "I don't want to offend them." Is that correct? Do you agree with that?

Right.

"Well, if I don't want to offend that person, what is it I want out of that person?" Because people we want something out of we don't offend. Would you not agree?

OK. Yes.

Well, it's not good salesmanship.

OK.

Do you understand that?

Yes, I do.

So, you see, if you must want, want from God, the Principle of Good. Forget about people. Do you understand that? You see—yes, I know. *[The teacher addresses the recording technician.]* You cannot feel good inside and live constantly manipulating, "Oh, I can't offend this one. Oh, I won't get that if I offend her. Oh, I won't get that if I offend him." Well, that is a terrible way to live, wouldn't you agree?

Yes.

Stand up for what you in your heart know is right for you. You understand that? Inside of you. And remember, your goodness comes from God. And you're not depending on whether you offend them or don't offend them. Do you understand that?

Thank you.

Isn't that a better way to live?

Much.

Why, certainly. Well, you don't see my channel concerned and worried about offending anyone, do you? *[The student laughs.]* I'm not particularly concerned myself in any sense of the word.

My purpose is not here to be a diplomat. My purpose here is to share with you the Light that will free your soul.

And we have just time for one more question. But this—[Student M] was waiting first.

I—

Time passes so quickly. Yes.

Excuse me. I wanted to understand that the will, it originates between the fourth . . .

Yes.

. . . and the fifth. OK, we direct our will in that center at the edge of the air and the electric.

Yes.

What is the—I hate to use the word function, but of the magnetic? Since it attracts and you're directing your will up.

Yes. Because, you see, first of all, is the electric. Do you understand that?

Yes.

You see, all, all religions and philosophies teach you that. They teach you a father God and a mother Nature. That doesn't put women below, you know. *[The teacher laughs.]* I wish you'd stop thinking that way. I'm not interested in whether it's a man or a woman. I'm interested in the Law of the Electric and the Magnetic. So, you see, here you have this great power of will—and we just got a few moments left on this class tape here, he tells me—and you use that and what do you come up to? You come up to the magnet, don't you?

Right.

All right. That power of the will—you understand?—utilizing the air center, because that's where it stands, you see. You must realize that: you do have mental substance. The realm of mental substance is the element air, you hear? And so you must use that because of identity. Otherwise, you don't have identity. So here you have this air, element air. Here you have this great power of will. Moving through that air, the electric amalgamates with the magnetic; that's where the marriage takes place, you see. Now from that marriage is the celestial birth into the odic, the ethereal, and the celestial or heavenly realms of consciousness.

And I'll say good day because our time is up until next week. Thank you.

JULY 28, 1985

A/V Class Private 8

Good morning, class.

And so we will begin our class this morning with the homework that I know that you've been making such great effort to do. And so the first question that I have for you this morning, for [Student R], is, What is an electric thought form and why is it in one's best interest to create them?

Well, an electric thought form is one that is sent out to do a specific thing. It is a positive form; one created above the first four centers. And so it's created in the faculties rather than in the functions.

What, then, is the difference between an electric thought form and a magnetic thought form?

I believe that a magnetic thought form is one created in the lower four centers.

What does an electric thought form contain that a magnetic thought form does not contain?

Reason.

What else?

Total consideration.

Yes. What is an electric thought form freed from?

Duality.

Yes. How is it freed from duality?

It's created in unity, in the, in the light of reason and total consideration. And it has no opposites. It is singular in its creation and purpose.

Therefore, then, what is a magnetic thought form containing and does a magnetic thought form offer freedom?

To my understanding, it does not.

Why doesn't it?

For it has—it's created in duality and in need and, being created in need, has limitation, denial, and offers the pairs of opposites.

Very well. We understand that an electric thought form is created freed from dependence. Why is it free from dependence? How is it free from dependence?

It has no denial.

That which has no denial, therefore, has total acceptance.

That's right.

I see. Therefore, it has no belief.

Correct.

What does it have if it doesn't have belief?

Faith.

I see. Now you were taught some time ago, students, to put God in any thought or to forget it. Now God is the Principle of Good. You have two types of thought forms that you experience. You experience electric thought forms and you experience magnetic thought forms. You create, frequently, of course, magnetic thought forms, which are controlled and governed by the water center of consciousness. They are depending upon things beyond your right of control for their fulfillment, [which is] contrary to an electric thought form, which has no dependence for it has no belief; it contains the will of Goodness, the power of God. It is possible for you, without the use of anything or anyone beyond your power of control and divine right of control, to experience the fulfillment of an electric thought form.

Now when you create an electric thought form in the fifth center of consciousness, that is where it is. It rises through, up to the odic center of consciousness. There it is made manifest. There it returns on the river with you, your ship, to the experiences of what is known as the creation centers of consciousness or the earth centers of consciousness, what you commonly know as the lower centers of consciousness. So when you put good or God into any thought, you are not only free from the dependence upon something or someone you have no right, no right of the divine will of God to control, when you do that, you experience the fulfillment of the form that you alone have created. There, an electric thought form, containing the necessary ingredient of total acceptance, the great power of God expressed through what is known as faith, fulfills itself without your dependence on what you cannot control.

Now any other thought form is not only a great waste of the vital energy, that which you are, it disturbs and robs you of the harmony and the health and the goodness that you are, for it is ever under the control of the water center of consciousness.

Now let us explain, perhaps a little more clearly, for some of your benefits, in reference to electric forms and magnetic forms. When you create an electric thought form, because it contains total acceptance and because the power of faith is being expressed in the thought form—ingredients that it contains by your own creation in that center—you will experience an acceptance within your being that it is happening beyond a shadow of any doubt. You will not have the frustrations of waiting and wanting and needing, for electric thought forms do not contain that. An electric thought form knows, within its own formation, that it shall be fulfilled for it is within your right. It is within your own control. Therefore, you can quickly tell whether your thoughts are from the electric center of consciousness or whether your thoughts are from magnetic centers of consciousness.

Whether they are—if you will understand how a thought must ascend and descend in order for you to have the experience of it. For example, you have a thought that you need something. That is the effect of creating the form in one of the four lower centers of consciousness. Now that center of consciousness in which that is being created is a water center of consciousness. It is magnetic. It will attract unto its kind. Its ingredients contain need. Its ingredients contain dependence. It contains belief. And you are the victim of what someone, somewhere, will do to help you to fulfill it. That is not what life really is. That is what experience is, but it is not what life is. There is a vast difference between life, which *is*, and experience, which is dependent.

And so you find yourselves in life, when you have, you think you have a need, the effect of a denial that you make in your consciousness—try to understand that earth, fire, water, and air centers of consciousness all contain denial. They deny what is and offer what seems to be. In those centers of consciousness, we see differences for in those centers of consciousness we have the function of comparison.

Now as one of my students was told just the other day: What good is there to work for when you know what you have and don't know what you may be getting? Now I instructed my channel the other day, in reference to truth in that matter, that all of you may share in that understanding that what you are used to in life is what you say that you know. And you are used to it for it is the effect of what you call temptation. A person who does not believe in limit cannot experience denial. And a person who cannot and does not experience denial cannot possibly experience need, the effects of denial. They cannot experience judgment. They cannot experience the frustrations of need. They cannot experience judgment. Therefore, a person who does not experience the denial of what they are cannot possibly be tempted, for temptation is only a piecrust promise that easily crumbles, that permits us, for a time, to believe that what we think is need is going to be fulfilled.

Belief offers to everyone temptation, for belief is the bondage and, therefore, the effect of denying what we are. So Truth, the Light, cannot, by its very being, tempt you. It is not a tempter. It is not a temptress. It does not offer to you the fulfillment of your denials. It does not offer to you freedom from your needs. The Light offers to you the process of evolving, the path upon which you may walk to higher realms of consciousness. There, in higher realms of consciousness within you, there are no needs. There are no denials. There are no wants. There are no desires.

To promise you that you may have what you are used to and add to what you believe that you are something even greater is absolutely contrary to demonstrable law. You cannot add to what you have and experience freedom. You may give what you have, and in the giving free yourself from the burden of weight that keeps you in the lower centers of consciousness where you experience denial and need.

When you are ready, at any moment, to give up what you believe that you are, which contains so much need, so much unhappiness, so much struggle, and so much suffering, when you are ready to give up that package, then you will begin to sprout those wings that you may fly from the cage and the concentration camp of creation.

We are only tempted because we deny what we are. And it is through the denial of what we are that we experience the weakness known as temptation.

The creating of electric thought form is the only path of reason or wisdom: to create what you personally, consciously choose to create. There's nothing outside of you to fulfill it; it is nonexistent. You are freed from that delusion and deception. You can do that in any moment, any moment of your choice. Choosing to do that and to sustain that and experiencing the wisdom of patience as it works within your universe to fulfill itself is the wisest path, for there you have forms created of light and reason. For they contain (electric thought forms), they contain the faculties of your true being. It is not a denial of creation. It is a wise use of creation.

The state of consciousness known as heaven is not dependent. That which is in your own good takes place; as you create electric thought forms in your consciousness, you free yourself from the frustration and the temptation of getting it now. We always get what we really want. So let's change what we really want by making a change to what we are instead of what we believe that we are.

Now, [Student S], I would like you to tell me how it is possible for you, for anyone, to experience heaven when there is no thing and nothing outside of you.

By merely moving to that state of consciousness inside the higher centers.

And how do you do that?

By moving the river up through the eighth into the ninth center.

And how do you move the ship on the river? The river is there.

Right.

It's your ship or identity that does the moving. The river is there.

With our will we can use the cleansing breath that's been given to direct it upward.

Now, that's fine. When you experience a thought form, the return of something that you have created, and it does not bring you the experience of goodness inside, from what center of consciousness would you say that it is coming? From what center was it created?

It's from the lower four and usually through the water center.

And what do you do with a thought form when it returns and demands that you service it?

Speak to it. Know that it is not you. But that you have the responsibility that you formed it and must pay the price. But by identifying with that part that is really you, during those times [you] can be freed from the service to that form.

And so what is the very first thing you do when you first are aware of the form or the feeling? What is the first step?

To be aware that it is not you.

Correct. Before you react the first thing you do is awaken, number one, "This feeling, this thought is not me." Is that correct?

Right. Correct.

And then after you have had that awakening, then you act. If you speak to those forms prior to the awakening that they are not you, by the very process of releasing your vital energy, that part of you that is you, to it, you have a very great struggle. So the very first thing to do is to awaken in the moment, as you are aware of it speaking or entering your consciousness, through feeling or sensation, is to declare the truth inside of yourself: "I am not that." After you have done that, you immediately do your rhythmic cleansing breath. That helps you to move your ship along the river to a higher center of consciousness. For a thought form created in the water center of consciousness can only be experienced in the water center of consciousness. You cannot experience a form created and limited by the four lower centers of consciousness until you permit yourself to identify with that center of consciousness.

Now, for example, should you create an electric form which contains all the center[s] of consciousness—not just four centers, all centers of consciousness—then you can experience those forms (created electric forms) in any center of consciousness. However, in the experiencing of them you will be aware that they are not you, that they are something you are responsible for. You will not have to tell them, "Just a moment, you are not me," because, created as an electric form, containing all the centers of consciousness, when you experience them, you know and you know beyond a shadow of all doubt. There is nothing to battle. There is nothing to fight. You know that for that's how you have created them. They contain the all. Therefore, that which is all has no need. You cannot have totality and experience need. You can only experience need in the lower four centers of consciousness for that tells you clearly that the thought form was created in a magnetic center of consciousness.

Now, of all the centers of consciousness, which center, [Student S], contains the fulfillment of need? And by the, the wording *fulfillment of need* I am stating the fullness of need. Of all of the centers of consciousness, which center contains the fullness of need?

In my understanding you can't—if need is being registered, you can't fill it.

You can only be tempted to fill it.

Right.

But I am asking the question of you: Of all of the centers, which center has the greatest need?

The water.

The water center. Why does the water center have the greatest need?

Because it's so magnetic; it pulls.

And what does it pull? Which center services the self the best in creation? Of all the centers, which ones service creation the best, the most?

One in particular or—

Yes, which particular—we're talking of creation, yes, of the centers of consciousness. Which one?

I would say the water.

Why?

I feel because in it contains self-pity, the most destructive force in the universe.

And? What does water reveal?

Emotion.

And the forms that move, what are they dependent on? Is the tree dependent on water for survival?

Yes. [The student speaks very quietly.]

Pardon?

Yes.

Are the forms of your planet dependent on water for survival?

Yes. It's the primary element that all things are dependent upon in form.

So you've answered your question. When you have the greatest dependence, you are servicing the self. So the more one thinks of self, the greater shall their dependence increase, the more they shall express emotionally through a water center of consciousness, for their need shall be ever unfulfilled.

A person who does not deny the truth does not experience need and cannot be tempted. Only people who deny the truth can be tempted for only people who deny the truth experience the effect of the denial, known as need. So if a person feels that they have a great deal of need, what they are telling themselves in truth is, "I am filled with denial in service to what I call myself, which is my throne of judgment." Do we all understand that? So if you have a great deal of need, then you must understand you have a great deal of denial. And if you have a great deal of need and a great deal of denial, then your mind is filled with judgments and ever active in comparison, ever dependent on something that you shall never control, for it is contrary to the Law of Personal Responsibility and the individualization of the soul and its entrance into form.

Now I'd like some questions from you students here this morning before I, like some of you have said into the atmosphere, interrogate you. *[A few students laugh.]* I haven't come to interrogate you; so I'll give you an opportunity to ask a few questions. And I haven't come to embarrass you because I would first have to offer that to myself in order to offer it to you, and I have no need to offer that to myself, that is, embarrassment. So let's see your hands or face interrogation. Yes, the gentleman over here, please.

If the word force *is identified with the lower force, lower four centers of consciousness—*

Correct.

—why do we call [it] a[n] odic force?

Yes. That's a wonderful question. Because the odic is called force for it contains power and force in equal balance. You see, when you create an electric form, it goes up into the odic center of consciousness. Now there in the odic center, it is formed. It is brought or sent down into the lower centers where force is the governor. And so an electric form, that is where it is created, in the odic center of consciousness, and because it contains, there in the odic, the force of creation at its disposal, it is known as odic force. You see, you cannot experience in a mental world anything that does not contain force. You can experience power in a spiritual realm of consciousness; that's what you truly are. But without force, the senses have no sensation or registration.

And so this is why it is so beneficial for the creation of electric forms. For electric forms, created in the odic center containing the force, odic and the force, the power of God, you see, they are the eleven: the power above and the force below, you see. Try to understand that a mental world, which is governed and ruled by force, under the throne and control of belief, is not a bad world. It is a seeming bad world of struggle and suffering when we permit our self to believe that we are it, instead of remembering, "This is not me. This is something I've created. This is something that I've created. Therefore, it is something that *I* shall continue to control. I'm tired of it controlling me."

But in reference to your question, you cannot experience anything in the lower centers of consciousness, known as the senses, that take place in the limit of your world, without force. Force is the ruler of the mental world of sensation.

Now force is not a bad thing. Force is not a good thing. Force *is*. It depends on what you do with it for you. You can force yourself not to eat, for example, but you must pay the price of it. You can force yourself to do many things, but they will always cost you. Now that is what the mental world or duality is all about. It ever has a payment and an attainment.

You see, the loss of anything, when we register a loss in our consciousness, it is ever dependent upon what our attachment is. You see, the greater the attachment, the greater the suffering from the loss. So if we permit our self to overly attach to anything or anyone, we guarantee the payment for that attachment. And that we call a loss. What has happened, you see, when you attach to anything, you depend on it for your survival. So the more you permit yourself to attach to anything or anyone, the greater is your bondage from your own dependence. Now that dependence grows as you deny what you are, and you become and you believe what you are not.

For example, a person [is] attracted to someone; their senses register satisfaction. And unless they're very careful, they will begin to strengthen their belief of experiencing good or God from the person. You understand that. Well, as they strengthen that bondage of belief, they guarantee the ending of it or the loss of it. Now the loss of something is—the loss of one thing is ever the freedom of something else. You've surely had those experiences in life. So each loss and the experience of what the senses call suffering and pain should be looked at by creating, at those times, an electric thought form. As you create an electric thought form, you free yourself not only from the dependence, the suffering, and the struggle, you don't create another magnetic form. Does that help with your question?

Yes, sir.

See, you cannot, you cannot experience with the mind, the mental world, and with creation anything that does not contain force. You see, the creation of a thought is something the mind does constantly. I simply want to show you a way, in the creating of thought forms, that you may create those forms, experience the effects or the goodness therefrom, for that really is your duty in life, and not pay the terrible price of the denial of what you are.

When you create an electric form, a thought form, you can live with it or without it. You see, it doesn't have dependence. It's all inside your universe. It will do what you tell it to do. There's nothing to tempt it or to distract it. It has no dependence out there. You alone are its creator. It will do what you tell it to do. It will do that because you are the creator of it.

Now when you create a magnetic thought form, for a time it'll do what you tell it to do and then another person over here has a created, magnetic thought form and that's where the problem begins, is that dependence. Do you understand that?

Yes, sir.

Yes, certainly.

Thank you very much.

You're welcome. Now the lady there, please.

Yes. In The Living Light *book, it's spoken of the plane of ozone, and I'm wondering how that fits into what we're learning now.*

Well, without the—ozone is a filter. I'm sure you all understand that. Without that plane of consciousness, life, as you know life on your planet, does not exist. It's a barren desert. There'd be nothing. It would finally return to the gasses from whence it is composed. The plane of ozone is physically indispensable to the life you experience on your planet.

Now that's that plane of ozone. Then we have the plane of ozone that is the filter for you, for your mind, that if the light is too bright 'tis best you see it not now. For, you see, a light blinds or shows the way. Therefore, in reference to your question and from the level that is asking it, it is in your best interest to have a filter. In other words, to absorb not too much too quickly for by so doing you would be tempted (the mind), in those realms of consciousness, to discouragement. You see, we can always tell whether or not we are ready for something by how patient we are when we're waiting for it. I hope that's helped with your question. The lady here, please.

Yes. I would like a little more clarification on why the magnetic realm of consciousness is in the upper four realms. [Student M asks.]

Why, certainly. Absolutely. And that's a nice question for you to ask. As above, so below. So you have earth, fire, water, and air that you're aware of, correct?

Correct.

And what's the next ones you're aware of?

Electric, magnetic, odic, ethereal, celestial.

Correct. So there's five above, correct?

Correct.

All right. Or let's more likely say there's one in between the eight, all right? There's four there and there's four up there. As above, so below. So you want to know why the magnetic center is in the upper centers of consciousness along with the electric, is that correct?

Yes.

Well, now what would those two centers correspond to in the lower four? *[After short pause, the teacher continues.]* Don't you see? As above, so below. Yes. What would—

Water.

What would correspond to water?

The magnetic. And air, electric.

Electric? What happened to the fire center?

The fire and the earth would be electric . . . [The student continues to speak but it is difficult to transcribe her words.]

Well, let's see. Let's, let's take these four centers over here and let's put these four centers over here. Now what's the center that's in between the two four. Yes, [Student A].

The center that's between the two four?

Yes. There's four lower centers here, and there's four higher centers here. What's that center in between? What is that center? Did we not discuss the power of will? Yes, [Student S]. What is the center in between these four? Four below and four above.

Oh, when you're talking about the power of will, now I've got it. I thought you meant like celestial to put—

Yes, yes, yes. What is the center between the lower four and the higher four?

Celestial!

Celestial? No.

Well, if you—

Earth, fire, water—

It'd be the electric.

—air. Right? That's four centers there. And then there's [the] electric center. And then what do you have? Magnetic?

Magnetic—

Yes.

Odic, ethereal, and celestial.

And celestial. So we find that the electric center is the balancing center between the higher four centers and the lower four centers. We don't find it to be the water center, do we? And we don't find it to be the magnetic center, do we? And have we, did we not discuss just at our last class about the power of will and where it is located? Did we not discuss that at our last class?

Well, now we have come to the lady's question here. To [Student M]'s question. Here is the electric center of consciousness. It stands between—now think—it stands between the four centers below and the four centers above. Now if you were to take the four centers, the higher centers, and you were to superimpose them over the lower four centers, what would they correspond to? Yes. *[After another short pause, the teacher again continues.]* Yes, I am asking you.

OK. *The thing is that the magnetic would correspond to the water.* [Student S responds.]

All right. Now the magnetic corresponds to the water.

Is that correct?

That seems reasonable. And it is correct!

OK.

We shall not go by seeming and presumption. It is correct. That's what is. The electric?
Well, the electric—
I want you to do your homework and start thinking.
OK. So the magnetic corresponds to the water.
Correct.
Then the odic would correspond to the—
Let's go to the electric.
Well, I thought the electric's in the middle.
It *is* in the middle.
So what—
It is always in the middle. The will power is always in the middle.
So what am I going to use with the—
The fire center.
Oh, OK.
You see, I can see that you have much more homework to do. Much more homework. Because, you see, you know, it's like looking at something in—what do you call [it]?—three dimension[s]. You're looking at it flat. You have four centers below and four centers above. All right? How does heaven come on earth? Would you call celestial the heavenly realms?
Uh-huh.
You wouldn't call them ethereal, would you? Fine. So they're celestial. Well, I want you people, in this coming week, to do your homework, to really do your homework. Because, you see, you have it flat instead of round. And everything is round and nothing in truth is flat. Not even your planet is flat, and you proved that to yourself, I think, a few, just a few centuries ago. Finally. *[Many students laugh.]* Everything is round. Nothing is flat.

Now didn't I discuss with you, here, just the other class that there is no such thing as a straight line? It doesn't exist. Is it supposed to be the fault of the Divine because you cannot see that it returns unto itself? You look at the table and you say it's flat. It is not flat! It is your perspective that's flat. The floor is not flat. Your planet is not flat. The universe is not flat. And your thought forms are not flat. And your mind is not flat. There is nothing that is a straight line. Everything is round. Everything, being round, comes back home.

So when you have a thought and when you have a feeling and when you are trying to apply and to study, try to understand even your understanding is round. Everything is round, and goes around, as one of my students once said there some time ago.

So everything being round, you have here this electric center of consciousness. There's the will. You also have, when you're in the realms of belief, a fire center. And don't tell me you don't have will there, for you all have will there and plenty of it. So let's stop and let's pause and let's begin to think.

What do you do—what takes place when you mix the electric with the magnetic? *[After a short pause, the teacher continues.]* Yes, yes, you. You're interested in that. I'm sure you all are. Yes.

There would be a . . . [The rest of the Student B's response is difficult to transcribe.]

It connects. What is the effect of the connection?

A circuit, which would be circular.

Well, there's a manifestation, usually, of some type.

Right.

Now that's duality. So I'm talking about an electric center, electric thought forms moving upward from the electric to the magnetic, *upward*. I'm not speaking of a fire center and a water center moving downward. First go up, you see. Move upward. We're already very familiar with the descent. Let's become a bit more familiar with the ascent. Now we're all very familiar with the descent, you see.

You see, it's like a person, you know, you decide that you need to eat. You make that, that judgment. If you have made that from the lower four centers of consciousness, it contains limit; it contains dependence; it contains all the things that the lower centers have to offer. It even contains the time in which you've got to go eat. That it can't be two hours from now. It cannot be five hours from now. It's got to be ever in keeping with the denial that has taken place within your consciousness in the water center.

Now in order for a magnetic form, a water center form, to fulfill itself in the lower four centers, not having moved from the electric, magnetic, and odic, ethereal, etc., and celestial, having gone at this point with your will—all right?—and moving downward, that is a magnetic thought form. It will plague you. It will cause you all kinds of frustration and upset, until it has what it was created to get. It contains all the limits. It isn't just the principle of eating. You have to eat a certain thing. You have to eat at a certain time. You have to eat at a certain place. And you have to eat with someone. Now that's what that offers you.

So tell me, in the light of reason, that a person decides—let's make decisions instead of judgments. If you permit yourself—you see, the difference between a decision and a judgment [is] a decision, containing total consideration, in principle moves on up through the centers. Now a judgment moves down. It descends and has all of the struggle and duality that goes with it.

So here, you say that, "I've got to eat. I have this sensation that I have to eat." Well, contained with that sensation comes all of the other restrictions, limits, and censorships based upon what the lower centers have offered you in the past. And if you don't have someone to eat with, you're not as hungry as you thought you were, but you'll eat anyway. And then you, well, you want to eat this or you want to eat that because these other thought forms created in the lower centers of consciousness are not going to get their way because you have to eat by yourself. And therefore, if you have to eat by yourself, you're just going to splurge and you're going to do this and you're going to do that and all of that. And then it turns around and justifies itself,

"Well, I deserve it. I worked real hard this week. I deserve to do that." And then you go on a binge. Do you understand that?

Well, there's a vast difference. Now what does that have to do with an intelligent decision? Moving by the electric power, through this great will power that you are, saying, "I have a sensation to eat." Moving on up, the faculty of reason and all of the faculties, and saying, "Now let's see, well now, this is what I would like to eat. That's fine. However, if that isn't available, I have other choices. It really doesn't matter because what's important is that I have this registration in my consciousness to eat. So it doesn't matter." You understand? You see, an electric thought form, which moves upward, contains total consideration because it contains total acceptance, the divine will of God. That's where you put God into something or forget it.

So the registration is that you're to eat. You have all of these choices that you look at. [And] you say, "Fine. However, well, if it's not that, then it'll be that. If it's not that, it'll be that. And if it isn't there, it'll be someplace else." You don't have any need to be with someone, to eat at a certain time, to eat at a certain place. You're in the light of reason: eating is eating and food is food. Does that help with your question? There's a vast difference between an electric thought form and one that becomes a magnetic thought form by moving downward.

All right. Now there were some other hands here, prior to interrogation. *[The teacher and many students laugh.]* Yes, go ahead, please.

What do hope and possibility have—how are they related to the upper—

Hope and possibility?

Yes.

Well, first of all, let's put it the other way around, shall we? Let's put possibility and hope, for possibility offers hope. Let's take a look at it in a different way. All things are possible. Well, one might even say at some time in their life that all things are hopeful. But anyway, let's say that all things are possible. Now if you permit your mind to consider something that, number one, you've already told yourself that you need—so we're already working with centers of consciousness of denial, correct?

Correct.

First of all, you've told yourself you need it, which denies that you have it. Therefore, we must work with the realms of denial. And so we have to work with the human uneducated ego.

You see, whenever you experience need, you must not forget it is the effect of denial. And the effect of denial is when you rose greater than the Principle of Good, which is known as God, and declared you don't have something. All right. So we now understand that we're working with an uneducated ego who believes that they have a need. Do you understand that?

Yes.

All right. So you look and say, "I have this need. Well, to God all things are possible." Right?

Correct.

Sounds beautiful. Just beautiful. It is great and it sounds beautiful, the very thought. When you experience denial, the denial of God, you see, what happens within the consciousness when you, rising in the error of ignorance, known as an uneducated ego, experience need and you tell the need, "To God all things are possible," you immediately recognize the very thing that you have denied. This is why I say, "Put God in it or forget it." You see, you instantly, in that statement, recognize what you have denied. Now through your recognition—we're speaking of God, the Principle of Good. First of all, you're experiencing the need because you denied God, the Principle of Good; you denied what you are to believe what you are not. So when [you are] in that, now you're paying the price of the denial. Do you understand that?

Yes.

You denied God and experience need. Do you understand?

Yes.

So when the experience, you see, when the payment of your denial is sufficient, you cannot bear this experience of need anymore. Do you understand?

Yes.

Which is only the payment of your own transgression, your own choice. However, so you say, "Need? To God all things are possible." You, in that instant, recognize what you have previously denied. You understand that?

Yes.

By the recognition of what you have denied is the possibility of a greater acceptance. Now it is through this greater acceptance, the will power or the movement of the Principle of God or Goodness that you start on the path to experience fulfillment of what you previously experienced as need. Now that all takes place within your own consciousness. And you can't go out in the universe and grab someone and stick them in your consciousness and tell the divine Power of Goodness that they will fill your need because you're back into denial again. So you must get yourself through that constant roller-coaster ride of acceptance and denial. Do you understand?

Yes.

All right. So we start with: To God all things are possible. Even a beautiful class is possible. So you tell that to yourself, you see. You do that and you have a momentary experience or good feeling. Would you not agree?

Yes.

Would anyone deny that? When they have and are in the process, from having denied good, and they are now paying the price, which is known as need, the effect of their denial, and they tell themselves, "This need is driving me crazy." And they tell themselves, "Ah! To God all things are possible." Do you not, for a moment, feel good? Pardon? *[The teacher asks a different student.]*

Yes.

Do you not? *[The teacher returns to the student who asked about hope and possibility.]*

Yes.

I assure you everyone does. Now it's a fleeting moment for most people, because they go right back to denial. So what really takes place? How can God, good, bring you what you believe you need, which is the effect of your denying of what you are, if you insist on the continuity within your consciousness of denying it? It's not possible. It is not possible. That's one thing that's not possible. You can't have your cake and eat it too.

Now, so you say to yourself, "To God all things are possible." Every time the thought form, that magnetic form, rises in your consciousness, you say, "To God all things are possible. That's it." And you're free for another maybe three seconds. Sometimes even five. *[Several students laugh.]* And each time you keep doing that and you keep doing that. "God, it's in your hands. To you all things are possible." And you live to experience the day when indeed, for you, all things are possible. Perhaps not the way you judged you wanted it, but you may be rest assured the way that is good for you, for you stopped denying good in your life. Does that help with your question?

Yes, sir. Thank you.

Yes. Now I know it takes moment-by-moment effort. I know that a person who denies what they are and then says, "O God, everything is possible," and accepts God for just a fleeting moment—it is indeed a fleeting moment. Why is it a fleeting moment? Because, you see, the denial is created in magnetic centers of consciousness not having risen, you understand, to the higher centers of consciousness, which contain the soul faculties. So there's where all the problem exists for people. Yes, the lady there, please.

So in creating a thought form, is it best to create it in the fifth center and move it up?

All thought forms to anyone with reason are created in the electric center of consciousness [and] moved on up. You understand?

Yes.

You see, I've taught you that in so many different ways: Put God in it or forget it; take the desire you have stolen from the divine principle of desire and return it to it. So for all of these many years you have been receiving that truth. We're now getting right down to the point where the actual centers—you see, you've always had the forty faculties. And you've always had forty functions. And now you are receiving those various centers of consciousness where they express. You see, the functions, when they are balanced with the corresponding faculty grant unto you the joy of living without the terrible payments of denial. The only thing is that you accept the Principle of Good, and it comes in keeping with the law of the Principle of Good. You can't tell it [the Principle of Good], because the moment you tell it, you have denied its authority. And when you deny its authority, the Principle of Good, then you must pay the price of the transgression, which is the experience of what you call bad. Yes.

So you take that thought form and you move it up and then you bring it back down—

Oh, no, no, no! You have nothing to do with the descent. You just make the effort for the ascent. The descent is in keeping with the laws, and that's when it comes into manifestation. And I'm glad you asked that question. So often a person has, you know, a thought and, you see, here's a thought form. And you believe that you are it; so you're constantly waiting 'til when it's going to activate and bring you what it's supposed to bring you. No, no, no, no, no. You just make the effort to get it all the way up there. The divine laws will do all the rest. It takes no time at all for it to return. It takes time for you to get it up there. *[Many students laugh.]* Don't you see? There's nothing for it to return. No, no, no, no, no. No, the descent is automatic. I think you call it in your world just plain old automatic. Comes with the wisdom of age, I think. Yes. Does that help with your question?

Yes, it does. Thank you.

Someone else? Yes, please. The lady in the back group.

What is the—in the emotional center, what is the cause being afraid of what people think, or what they're going, of how they treat you, of reacting to how people treat you? What is the—

It only reveals our dependence upon them, which is an effect of our denying what we are. You see, those who are concerned about what someone else thinks about them are totally dependent upon themselves for their goodness, upon the limit of what they believe is the self, instead of upon the acceptance of what they truly are. You see, to live for another is in truth to live for oneself. *[The teacher's youngest student, a child, coughs and continues to do so for a time.]* So often a person says, oh, how much they love another person. Well, what they are telling you in truth is how much they love themselves.

[As the youngest student continues to cough, the teacher addresses the parent.] Raise his little arms, please, and open up his diaphragm. That's it. That's it.

Does that help with your question? *[The teacher addresses the questioner.]*

You mean, living for the self, the lower centers—

Well, living for the belief of what we are, not for what we are.

I get it.

You see. And that, of course, is an effect of denying what we are. Accept the possibility of something better. Accept, moment by moment, the possibility of something greater, and you guarantee the experience of it. For when you accept the possibility of something better, then you, in that acceptance of possibility, you are recognizing something that you haven't yet recognized. And to do that helps to free you from your denials. Does that help with your question?

Thank you.

You see, you never know if you accept the possibility, even though you cannot guarantee what the experience is going to be, you don't have to worry about guaranteeing what the experience is going to be. It's not something you've already had.

Right. Right.

Does that help with your question? So it's not like old hash or something.

Oh, good.

What? You see? You see. And you never know, you see, what good may come just because you can't control it. Is that not true?

Yes.

Hmm. In fact, the greatest good in life comes when we're not able to control it.

That's right.

And aren't we fortunate in your world that you can't control the weather? *[Many students laugh.]* You see, you have to make a lot of changes before you enter these other worlds because [in] these other worlds, you see, your days, your nights and all of those things, they are subject to your control. So if you had all of that awakening here and now and considering that it is very rare to get two people to agree on anything, I don't know what your weather would be like. Very strange, I would say. *[Again, many students laugh.]* Yes.

So when you say to helps—God helps those who helps—by helping oth—

God helps those who help themselves by helping others. You see, one cannot help another until one helps themselves, for they cannot be qualified. Now the joy of living is giving what you have to give and care less what they do with it; for if you are interested in what their thought forms are going to do about you, then that only reveals that you are interested in what your thought forms and how successful they are in their manipulation of what they want from someone else's thought forms. And that's not what you want at all, is it?

No.

Well, that's what we—you see, when we're interested in someone else and how they're going to react to our presentation, how they're going to react to our, to our, what we call a smile, which is more likely a grin, you see, how they're going to react to all of that, we're in total bondage inside our self. And we're in such terrible bondage we're dependent on what they do and what they don't do. Can you experience the joy of living when you permit yourself to [be] dependent on how somebody reacts to how you look or how you speak or how you act? Pardon?

No. You're right. It's bondage.

You wouldn't want to live that way, would you? So, you see, know what it is that you want to do in life. Do what you have to do and care less what everyone does with it. Do you understand that?

Yes.

But do what you know in your heart is right for you to do. Because that is the law. That *is* the law. You see, whoever considers themselves considers others. But whoever does not consider themselves—now when I'm speaking of themselves, I'm not speaking of one or two thought forms that are totally dependent on what someone else does, no. Totally consider what you are; then that's all that you can offer to the world. And you won't have the slightest thought about what they think or what they don't think. How could it possibly matter? You have totally considered what you are and that's what you offer to others. Hmm? But you will always know in what area, in your experiences, that you are not considering, really considering, for those are the areas in your experiences you'll find yourself dependent on another.

You see, the purpose of evolving is freedom from this dependence. Dependence on what this one does, dependence on what that one does, dependence on how someone thinks and how someone doesn't think, dependence on what someone else is going to do. And by filling the mind with all of those thought forms of depending upon others, you rob yourself of the joy of living. They don't do it. You do it. See? You see, with so much to consider in one's own life, there's really not that much room, in fact, there in truth is no room to be a bit concerned about what someone else thinks. They won't bring you God. They will only bring you effects of your own denials. That's all they'll ever bring you. They couldn't bring anything else in keeping with the law that like attracts like. Does that help with your question?

Thank you very much.

Now someone else has a question here. Yes, the lady there, please.

Yes. [In] the last class it was stated that change, when you're working with the lower four centers, change could only come through experience. I would like to know using the higher four centers, what is the manifestation of change or—if it's not experience, what is it?

Which experience are you talking about? Are you speaking of experience that is dependent on what someone else does?

No. I'm just trying to understand—

I see.

—exactly—

I see. You will have experience, when you create electric thought forms—you've already created electric thought forms in your life. They were not dependent on what someone else did or didn't do.

Right.

You do recall that, don't you?

Yes.

Fine. So you had experiences from them.
Uh-huh.
But you also had freedom from them, didn't you?
Yes.
I'm speaking of the ones that were electric, not magnetic.
Yes.
You see, you didn't have to worry whether this person did this or that person did that or someone else didn't do or what was going to happen. Isn't that correct?
That's correct.
You created a thought form, an electric thought form. You had the experience of, or the effect of, that electric thought form.
Yes.
Do you not find it beneficial?
Oh, I do.
And so there is no problem. You can still continue to create electric thought forms. You see, being with a person, place, or thing and never a part of a person, place, or thing, that's freedom. The loss of anything reveals the attachment or the effect—that's what attachment is: an effect of denying what is. So the more you deny what is, the more suffering in life you must have.

And someday when you stop denying what is, you will stop suffering. We only suffer from denial. No one ever suffered from acceptance. You see, you cannot suffer from acceptance, for acceptance is the will of the Principle of Good. It is not possible to suffer from acceptance.

Say, you have many experiences in your day. And you judge that you're going to do this or you're going to do that, correct?
Correct.
And someone says, "No, you're not going to do that." Well, if you have total acceptance in consciousness, it doesn't matter. Is that not correct?
That's correct.

If you are filled with denial of what you are, then you are filled with judgments and needs and experiences within your consciousness. And [if] someone says, "You're not doing that now. You're doing that," you have all kinds of problems, which reveal to you, you are dependent on what other people do and that you have this weakness of dependence and must pay the price of it. That dependence being the effect of your denial, denial of what you are. Does that help with your question?

That's good.

You see, a person who is moving in the will of God, what comes, comes; and what goes, goes because they know inside of themselves the law does not fail them. So this time they're told yes, and that time they're told no. And they don't ever know if yes will ever come again; then they can say, "Ofttimes no is God's direction. Something better is already working in my life."

You see, when you talk to yourself, when you speak forth those truths, you create those forms. Those forms go to work to serve you. Did that help with your question?

Thank you very much.

Yes. You're welcome. The lady there, please.

Along with what you were just saying, when you're creating those thoughts, are those electric thoughts?

Thought forms that are filled with total consideration, total acceptance only are thought forms which are electric. They have no dependence on what someone else does or does not do. Therefore, if a person moving in the world comes up against another person who says, "No, you're not going to do that. That's what you're going to do," and it's a constant process of change, why, it doesn't matter. How could it possibly matter when you are in total acceptance? It doesn't matter at all.

Now what the uneducated ego tells a person who thinks that way, what it tells them is that they're, well, they're just a slave. That's what it tells them. It doesn't tell them, "You're going to be free." You are free. It doesn't matter. You do what you have to do, and it doesn't matter to others. You see? Because it doesn't matter to *you*.

Yes.

So, you see, that *is* freedom for that *is* the Light. That *is* Truth. What do you have to give up to gain that? You have to give up the denial of what you are. You have to give up believing that you are the limit and must manipulate everything in life. Those are the things that you have to give up to gain the freedom, you see?

Yes.

You have to give up those effects of denial which are judgments that say, "Well, this person's not doing this. That person's not doing that. Life is such a struggle for me. Things are miserable and getting worse." You only prove how right you are: they are miserable and they do get worse. Does that help with your question? Pardon?

Yes.

Why, certainly. Whenever you believe you are the limit and you are the self, then you be rest assured you will prove how right you are by having every miserable experience and to constantly puffivate your own uneducated ego: "I was right again! Look how miserable I am." Thank you. The lady over there, please.

In one of the recent classes you mentioned that the four lower centers were not all bad and the one that you mentioned—

No center is all bad.

The thing that you—

No center is all good.

—had mentioned—

Thank you.

Thank you. The thing you mentioned in the fire center was drive as being good in the fire center. Could you—

Why, certainly. The only problem with the fire center of drive [is] it goes down and casts pearls before the swine. When it goes up, the gates of heaven open. The gates of heaven open through a control of what you are. God has given and granted everything to man. What man does with it are the experiences of so-called good and bad. What he does with it.

Now when you permit yourself, your mind, to depend upon belief, that is the little package of experiences that you've had on your Earth planet, when you permit yourself to believe you are that, then you have phenomenal dependence. And, you see, when you depend upon yourself, you guarantee your dependence on others, for you can only offer to another what you offer to yourself. If you take great pride in being totally dependent on yourself for life, then that's all you offer to others, and you someday find out you are totally dependent upon them. For you have taken great pride in being dependent upon yourself. Does that help with your question?

You see, you cannot apply demonstrable, eternal laws, demonstrable truth in one area of your consciousness and totally deny it in the other area. If you take great pride in being so independent and you don't have to depend on anyone, you depend totally on yourself, don't you understand that's what you offer to the world? And someone's waiting to fill that bill for you. They're just around the corner, and they'll show you how independent you are and what great pride you will take in being, what you call, a free agent? I think I've heard some of you students tell my channel you're free agents. You'll see how free you are. Does that help with your question?

Yes.

We grant to others only what we grant to our self. We can grant them nothing else. So if we grant to our self total dependence on our mind, that's all that we're going to experience with others, is our dependence on their mind. Does that help?

Yes.

Yes. You see, should the day for your world ever come that all of these little creatures, these little critters out there, the birds and the animals and all of them should disappear, man would not survive. He would not survive. And I'm not just speaking about food, for there's all kinds of food that grows. There's vegetables and trees and berries. Man would not survive, for there is an interdependence in realms of consciousness you are yet to be aware of. That all of these creatures and all of these animals and all of these trees and plants, they are interdependent upon each other for their own continuity. And that's what it really is.

And so when you rise in pride and you separate yourself from all humanity and from all these creatures, you're only dying yourself. You're dying inside. You may survive for a time, but live? No. You're dying inside. I spoke to you long ago: Love all life and know the Light. Without love, there is no Light. Without Light, there is no love. Without Light and love, there is no life. And so when you rise and free yourselves from those limits and you love all life, you will know the Light for you will *be* the Light without the shadows. Did that help with your question?

Thank you.

Yes. Now this gentleman, here, had a question, please. Yes, [Student U].

When we pause and are perfectly still, does that automatically take us to the edge of the air center and the edge of electric center?

When you pause and are perfectly still, you have cleansed your universe with the rhythmic breathing exercise, is that what you're saying to me?

What my initial question was, Does pausing necessarily mean we go up to that—

No, it does not. No, no, no, no, no, no, no. No, you cannot move your ship just by pausing. Pausing is certainly beneficial. No, no, no, no. You pause. You do not move, and you do your rhythmic cleansing breath. That's what moves your little ship, your identity on the river of life. Yes, that's what moves it, is your effort.

Thank you.

Yes, now try to understand that you cannot move your physical form without a form to move it. *[The teacher gestures with his hand.]* Something must activate my hand, you see, and those are forms. So when you're doing your meditation or you're doing the cleansing breath, you do not move. No, you do not move at all, for then you are servicing forms. Do you understand that?

Yes.

Well, if you're going to service forms, at least be aware of which forms you're servicing, you know. Yes, the lady there, please.

Does it take great effort to move the new forms you're creating to the higher four—the higher centers? Does that take—is it simple or does it take a great—

It's very simple. It's like climbing—what is your mountain?—Mt. Everest. I think that's the mountain. Does that help with your question?

Yes, it does.

Yes. There are none of those helicopters waiting for you. *[Many students laugh.]* Are there any other questions? We have a little time left. The gentleman—yes, yes, [Student J].

Could you elaborate a bit, sir, on, you mentioned in a prior class about how a release of this vital bod—a partial release of this vital bodily fluid is equivalent to $100,000 in loss in our—

Yes, yes. Absolutely. Absolutely. You see, for example, just an ounce of it—or are we talking about a pound of it? We're talking about an ounce, I suppose.

Well, you, you tell me.

No, I'll let you tell me because you're recalling the class. I'm not—but I can check it. I'll check it.

Just a small amount, small—

A small amount. Yes. Very small. Very, very small. All right. Now, you see, that vital energy, that vital energy is used to create anything. Now whether you create a glass or a vase or you create anything else, it takes that energy. Now a small amount of that energy creates many, many thousands of forms. Those forms go out into the universe from your universe and bring you back experiences. By your effort to control those forms, to create them (electric forms) that same amount of energy can bring you back into your experiences thousands of dollars, *thousands* of dollars. Because, you see, it's an equal amount of energy. Now one doesn't say, "Now let's see, this is this much energy that I am wasting. I choose to have this rather in my bank account. And I want that to take place"—All I can tell you is—and it's very important and you've touched on a very important question—is that you don't want money. You want the forms that you are creating to do their job that you may experience the effects of money. Isn't that correct?

Yes, sir.

Well, there are ways of doing that. And you continue on. *[The teacher removes his microphone.]* Oh, I'm taking this off, am I? You continue on with your loyalty to your rhythmic cleansing breath, and you will not have to be concerned. Five is a very short time, isn't it? Thank you. I see our class time is up.

AUGUST 4, 1985

A/V Class Private 9

Good afternoon, students.

Perhaps now we will continue on with our class. *[These classes were scheduled to be held in the morning.]*

Now we were discussing at our last class the superimposing of these four centers of consciousness upon the lower centers of consciousness. And I had discussed with you at that time that you should consider thinking not in flat dimensions but to consider thinking in what you would say round. Now I know it's going to be difficult for minds that are used to seeing things in the illusion of flat. It's going to be difficult with minds that see straight lines and do not perceive they're part of one complete circle. However, the earth center corresponds to the odic center of consciousness. The fire center corresponds to the electric center of consciousness. The water center corresponds to the magnetic center of consciousness. And the air center corresponds to the ethereal center of consciousness.

When you let go of what you believe, you experience what is. But you cannot experience what is in life until you let go of what you believe.

Now each day, for example, this day, when you come to class, you have within your mind, based upon past experiences, that class will begin at a certain time. Therefore, depending on how much you believe you are your beliefs, you have difficulty in adjustment and in making those changes within your consciousness.

To encourage oneself in life moves your little ship along the river of life. When, in all of these experiences that you have, when you face paying for something that has been and will not be again, it is understandable that your minds would be upset. No mind wants to pay for anything that it purchases, uses, and then judges that it loses. When you go to the store, you make a purchase of your desire. You use what you have purchased, and then, according to your mind, it is stolen or disappears, and you're left with the debt. Well, it is indeed understandable that the human mind would be upset paying for something that it had and was taken away from them. Of course, you would have to deny the Law of Personal Responsibility. It is your insistence on denying the Law of Personal Responsibility that you find yourself upset and disturbed and frustrated in paying a debt for something that you judge you no longer have.

And when you accept the truth, that all experiences in life you are the cause of—no matter what anyone does or does not do, you alone are the cause of it. You alone have to pay the price. It is better to pay a debt when you are aware of the debt, for to know that you have a debt [and] to postpone the payment of the debt only increases the debt by the Law of Interest in your world of creation. So the longer that you take to accept personal responsibility and to pay the just debt in life that you owe, the more interest is accumulated, the greater is the debt.

So no matter what your debts are, face them in personal responsibility: that they are debts that you alone have incurred. Pay them off as quickly as possible, and you will not have this mounting interest. For I know that the interest rates in your world today are indeed very high. So if you owe $5 today and you wait three years to pay it, you'll end up paying at least [$]50. A wise person doesn't want to pay a five-dollar bill by paying [$]50, when by paying it quickly they would only have to pay [$]5.

Now I'm going to take a few moments this morning here with you and see how you are doing in reference to your studies and your homework. Our class is what you would consider a bit late today. But what is early or late when it comes to truth? It's only dependent on the judgments that your mind has already made. You're not here for those things. You don't need any help in making judgments. Why, you don't even need a bit of assistance. Because, you know, there's no problem being so well qualified in that area of consciousness.

Where do you go when you leave here? Where do you go when you leave this physical world? For you're going there, sometimes, when you're sleeping. You're going to many realms of consciousness even when you're awake. You know it not, for one does not know what they do not identify with. You look at the wall, and by looking at the wall, you identify with the wall. So all that you see and all that you hear, all that you smell, all that you sense, and all that you feel, you identify with. That's the nature of the human mind. The thing is not to over-identify with any of it. The problem lies in over-identification.

To walk along a path, to view the flowers, the trees, and the sky, to view the water, to identify with it, to register it within your consciousness, can indeed be most beneficial. To believe that you are, through over-identification, the tree or the flower is indeed detrimental, for to over-identify with anything is always at the cost and the sacrifice of what you are. And that indeed is a very, very expensive way to try to live.

The question may rise within your minds, What am I, as a teacher, to do with what you want me to do? You see, you do not consciously say to me, "I want you to do this or that so I can feel good and be freed of all of these things." That I do not have to offer you. I have to offer you the teachings of centuries that free, and has already freed, millions, millions of souls from the years of believing in the bondage of what you call limit or creation. Those teachings I have to offer you, as I offer them to all my students in many dimensions of consciousness. I offer those same teachings to you. I do understand that when you permit yourselves, like any mind, to think of yourselves, then you have great difficulty, number one, in understanding the teachings and, number two, in applying those teachings. So the real question must remain for you, as students: How to be freed from over-identifying and believing in what is known as self?

It is not difficult to see, as a teacher, whether or not you are applying the teaching for it is, of course, demonstrable. When you are doing your rhythmic breath, when you are doing your rhythmic cleansing breath, there's no problem for you. When you do that, you free yourself for a time from the disturbing realms of creation. But you, *you* must do that. That is something that cannot be done for you. That is something that you must do. And some of you are doing it. And for some of you it's becoming more difficult.

Try to understand, when you receive a teaching, any teaching, to free yourselves and experience abundant good in your life and you begin to apply that teaching, you will find that your effort is short-lived. Now it varies for each student. It is short-lived when the realms of consciousness that have bound you through belief begin to face the freedom of your true being. For they see, being created of mental substance, that, number one, they're not getting as much of your attention or energy. You, your soul, is rising on the river of life. When that happens, they use temptation. They appeal to your weakness that you may go back, that they may feed and become even stronger.

And so it is especially true with the rhythmic cleansing breath that you have received. Some of you have applied it for a very short time. Some apply it very, very little. There are others who are working diligently at it and paying the price. Now what is the price? The price is the forms that you have served over a time rising up and, in so doing, creating a great disturbance within your mind. That is when you do your rhythmic cleansing breath even more. Because, you see, [in] not making that effort, the Light of truth that is your soul that shines in these moments of your classes and that wonderful vibration is a great temptation, a great temptation for creation, that you can only experience when you over-identify with and believe that you are it. And so the brighter the Light shines, that you may rise up from those realms and be free, the brighter that Light shines, the greater is the call of creation, the greater is the call of the forms from below that you spent time in service to.

Now everything in evolution represents a change. So you evolve at the cost and the expense of making changes within your consciousness. The human mind does not want to make any effort to move from what it judges it has to something it is not sure that it wants. Now try to understand that. We find security in the things in life with which we are familiar. We become familiar with things in keeping with our service to them. Our security, our emotional security therefore is dependent upon what has been. And because it is, by its very nature, dependence [dependent] for its feeling of security on what has been, it is a great disturbance within the water center of consciousness for a person to let go of what has been and to move ahead, not knowing for sure, inside of their mind, that it's going to be better.

The reason that the mind doesn't know it's going to be better is because the mind is not controlling it. And because the mind is not controlling it, a person believing they are the self is upset and immediately goes back to serving that which they are familiar with.

Now this little day here today, with all of these wonderful experiences—wonderful, good experiences if you look at the alternatives. The alternatives being very clear. This is what that has to offer, and this is what *that* has to offer. "I'm here to make a choice. Shall I remain weak and tempted to what has been? Or have I had enough of what has been?" That's the question, of course, we must all ask our self.

Like I said to my channel so many years ago, "If the good old days were so good, then why did we ever leave them?" Now we all know that the good old days weren't as good as we like to remember them. You see, temptation tells us how great the good old days were. That's how it weakens us to serve them. That's what speaks in our mind and uses our mouth at times.

Today, this day, my channel was a bit upset in the sense—of course, it doesn't last—but in the sense that he knows he's responsible for any disturbance that is allowed here in the school. He is reminded of his responsibility. And so he is responsible to see that it stops. The method is legal if the motive is pure. So let us remain with a pure motive that the legality of method may be the instrument for an awakening to something of greater value in life.

What is of greater value in life? Freedom from the debts of our belief that we are creation. Creation has a phenomenal debt to whoever believes that they are creation. We do not, you see, appreciate the debts in life. We don't appreciate them, especially when we judge we're paying for something that is gone and we're still paying for it.

These debts in life, however, on a positive side we look at these things, these debts in life are an instrument through which we have the opportunity to make intelligent decisions. I tell you once again, when you do your breathing properly and when you do your breathing regularly, you will not have the disturbance and the experiences within your life that are so discouraging and distasteful.

And so I'm going to take a few moments now for your answers in reference to your homework. And I'm going to start here today with my student here, [Student H]. And I know it's difficult—you know what superimposing is, don't you, [Student H]?

Yes, I do.

Well now, we've gone through the centers and we had the earth, fire, water, air, electric, magnetic, odic, ethereal, and celestial. Now how would you, for you have a little artistic background and talent there, how would you superimpose those in order that they may correspond in the way that I have spoken to you that they do correspond? Yes.

Well, I envision the shape of a globe.

The shape of a globe. Yes.

And if I were to label the centers . . .

Yes.

. . . I would put them on radii that would depict the shape of the globe.

Yes.

Probably.

Yes.

And for me that's how I could relate to it.

Now I want to know, for your benefit and my students, how you get the earth center to correspond with the odic center by moving beyond the flat dimension.

Because if, if I were to take a radius of that globe, just—

Yes?

—isolate one radius, then I would position the label earth, earth center at one point of the radius.

Yes?

And position the odic center at, at a point corresponding to that on the same radius but just on the other side of it.

Yes? And the fire center? You see, you would not have a problem, would you, with the fire and water centers? Correct?

Yes.

For in a flat dimension your mind tells you that the reversal is with the odic and the ethereal centers. Is that not correct?

Right. In the flat.

Is that not correct?

Correct.

Yet when you study, you see that that is not true at all.

That's right.

So this is how your mind works. This is how all minds work in a flat dimension. You see, in a flat dimension you take earth, fire, water, and air—now this is very important. I'm spending this time here with you specifically on this superimposing. Then you take your electric, magnetic, your odic, and your ethereal. Now in your flat world, when I speak to you to superimpose them, they do not correspond, do they?

No.

They will, however, correspond in reference to your explanation. You understand that, don't you?

Yes.

All right. As an artistic background. Now, [Student R], how will it work for you? This has a great deal to do with your thinking and how you think, you see. If you want to evolve and you want to move into those higher centers, then you must understand how to perceive and superimpose. Do you understand that, [Student H]?

Yes, yes.

Go ahead, [Student R].

Well, I think perhaps I would envision it as one inside the other.

Yes? And when you envision it one of inside the other, do you get corresponding the higher center[s] with the other centers in keeping with the teaching that's just been given?

Yes.

And explain to my students how you're able to do it that way.

Well, I just, I just see one large globe and then within that are the others, each one inside the other.

Yes?

And, so it's, it's a little difficult to explain.

All right. Now I will help you just a step farther, for there's some work that you can do. You write yourself, you write on your little papers here in your homework; you make a circle. You all understand that? A circle. Now you place upon that circle earth, fire, water, and air. You place that at what you consider to be the bottom of the circle. All right? Now you place on the top of that circle electric, magnetic, odic, and ethereal. You trace a line in your flat world from the earth center, where you've marked it, to the odic. And you also trace a line from the fire to the electric, the water to the magnetic, and the air to the ethereal. Now after you have made what you consider a straight line, you take a look at the pattern that you have created on the flat piece of paper that you have made that drawing [on].

Now I'll speak to my artist over here, [Student H]. And what type of a pattern do you perceive, for you don't need paper and pencil, being an artist. What do you perceive?

The, the lines have crossed.

Yes. And what pattern are they revealing?

Like a star. Like, like—there's a center of a star and then the arms just radiate outwards.

All right. [Student R]?

Yes. And in that explanation, I would see the same thing.

All right. Well, I'm not going to take a piece of paper and do it for you, but does anyone there have a—[Student S], why don't you go out and get a piece of paper and a pencil and give it to [Student H].

It is so important that you understand how the functions and faculties work. They must follow the line in the center of truth. They do that within your own consciousness, and they create a certain pattern. And because anyone who over-identifies and believes they are that which they identify with are bound by patterns.

Draw your circle. And try to place your earth, fire, water, air equally. Use the [lower] half of the circle for those four centers. Use the upper half of the circle for the other four centers, and then draw your lines. All right?

You see, when we teach the functions of money, ego, and sex and we teach you the corresponding faculties of faith, poise, and humility, for that to be successful in your life, it must go along the pattern that your mind works by.

Now all minds work by a pattern, for they are created [as] a pattern or design. And so what you are going to look at, in a very simple and humble way, is the beginning of the design. You're looking at the first stage of the pattern of the human mind. And not limited to the human mind, for the mind or mental substance in an animal works on the same principle. So you will have to look for yourself at how this is working in your mind; then you will have a better understanding of when you make an effort to do your cleansing breath, when you make an effort to do that rhythmic and that healing inside of you for the greater good, you, in identity moving along these patterns, move your little ship on the river of life.

Yes. Now hand it to [Student R] there, please. *[The teacher refers to the diagram just drawn by Student H.]*

OK. [Student H responds.]

And what do you find for a pattern, [Student H]?

Oh, I, I didn't draw the lines. I just—

Oh no, no, no. I'm sorry. You go right back and put your lines in. Without the lines, you cannot understand what you're passing through whenever you make any effort inside of yourself. Seemingly straight lines.

Right.

[After a short pause, the teacher continues.] What do you have?

OK. I've, I've forgotten all of the connections. I've got magnetic with water.

Oh—No, no, no. I think we ought to start where we are, don't you? We should start from earth.

OK.

To odic.

Right.

Did I not explain to you that that which is created in the odic center brings you the benefit of light? Hmm? You see—you go ahead. Odic to earth.

Yes.

Fire to electric. Water to magnetic.

Yes.

Air to ethereal. Now what do you have as a pattern?

Ah. Well, it's—there are lines that cross the earth to the odic. But the ethereal and the air, it's like a separate line. It's not—

All right. You show it to my student, [Student R]. And then I want it shown to all of my students. Now remember, you will have to, in making your circle, you will have to make them even, of course. There's earth, fire, water, air. And you—no, I can see it fine. Yes. Now that's quite close. Now you explain what happened. What does it look like to you, as it's being passed around? You may pass it to the other students to look at.

Now, [Student S], perhaps you would like to explain what that diagram reveals, what that pattern reveals. What does it show to you as a pattern?

What it shows to me [is] that some of these intersect each other.

Which ones?

The magnetic-water line crosses the earth-odic line.

Yes. The magnetic-water line crosses the earth-odic line. Yes. And what others intersect?

And the earth-odic line crosses the fire-electric line at a low point.

Yes.

And then the ethereal-air line doesn't intersect anybody.

Now why doesn't the ethereal-air line intersect? You see, you see, you must do your homework and understand how these things work in your consciousness. Now we'll start with [Student H]. What do you think is the reason that the ethereal-air center—and pass that behind you, [Student S]. Pass it [Student H's drawing] to my student [Student J]. Do you have it? Is everybody passing it on? That's fine. Why do you think they do not cross, [Student H]?

The ethereal and the air. Well, first of all, we understand that, that the will exists between the air and the electric. And along with that is the faculty of reason, in that area. And reason is the very thing to, to lift you away from those, from the emotions, those centers in which you be grounded. And for me, that's how I can describe it as being apart from the intersecting centers.

All right. Thank you. [Student S]?

Well, it seems with the higher centers, it doesn't take shape, if I understand correctly, until like the odic.

That is correct.

And with the lower centers the first three are concerned with the manifestation of the lower. And it's entering the fourth that gets you beyond it. Just as the ethereal—

You may pause at that point. You are aware of two dimensions. Some are aware of three dimensions. Now it's time in your evolution to be aware and apply the laws of the fourth dimension. Go ahead.

So in my understanding, the air and the ethereal, in each of the perspective areas, are representing getting out of it or not concerned with the manifestation of it.

Correct. Yes, anything else? *[After a short pause, the teacher continues.]* All right. [Student R]?

When, when I envision that diagram crossing, I saw them crossing equally all in the center, rather than having them put down as [Student H] put them down. I saw them to be opposed to each other or opposite of each other. I saw that all lines would intersect at one central point.

What point?

The center point.

I see.

The center point would be the celestial.

You are correct on the center point, yes.

From the celestial you have the Divinity, which is the, the one, which is the, where everything stems from; that would be the center point. And if they were arranged in a manner on the circle so they were opposite, then all intersecting lines would intersect at the center and that center would be the one or the Divinity, which is the source of all.

All right. Thank you. You are all familiar with the rays of the sun. They go in all directions. Would you not agree? Is there anyone who disagrees with that? You just raise your hand. *[After a short pause, the teacher continues.]*

You are all aware of the rainbow in the sky [that] you perceive only as part of a complete circle. Is there anyone who is not aware that a rainbow is a complete circle? Pardon? If you are, then raise your hand, if you have any contrary belief. Do I see a hand? No, I don't.

Now you are this center of consciousness. From this center of consciousness, the Light, the sun, that which you are, you radiate these rays of light out into the universe. When you believe that you are a certain ray, then those are the centers of consciousness that you must service. Now in those emanations from your consciousness, if you take with you the corresponding center, then you will serve those centers of consciousness by a conscious choice, which is the faculty of reason; and in so doing, you will not have the experiences and the debt that you have to pay, for having created it in a higher center of consciousness, it must follow a certain pattern, a certain frequency, a certain ray of light.

And so speaking in other ways of moving your ship on the river of life, it is the same truth. You are the Light. You emanate these rays, these rays of consciousness. And if you do not take with you the higher center that corresponds to the lower center that you are destined for, then you must experience the debts, what your mind calls debts, and the payments thereof.

Now we're going to take a few moments for a few questions. We won't enter those realms of interrogation just yet. We'll take a few moments for your questions. You may raise your hands. *[After a short pause, the teacher continues.]* Do my students prefer interrogation? Yes, [Student B], please.

On that globe, then, where is the river of life?

The river of life is the globe. That is the river of life. You see, you think of a river of life and you think of water, and rightly so. And you think of its flowing, and rightly so. But the water itself is composed of atoms, electrons, and molecules. You do understand that, don't you, [Student B]? Without those atoms, electrons, and molecules, there is no river. It does not exist. And so the river in truth is this globe of which we are discussing. The atoms, electrons, and molecules are round. You know that, don't you? They are round. And so what we are speaking of—and we're speaking of this diagram here and the river of life. You are this round consciousness. You understand that? All things return unto you for you are the consciousness.

That which *is* can only be not in the moment of denial. So that which you are can only not exist in the sense of your own denial of it. It doesn't change it. It changes you in the sense you believe. It does not change that river and that globe, that which you are.

Because a globe—and all things are round. Try to perceive this. All rivers return unto their source for all rivers are round. Everything that is life is round. Everything returns unto its source of origin. Only that which is round could accomplish that. Do you follow me on that, [Student B]?

Yes.

Therefore, you see, all your thoughts and all your feelings are governed by that which *is*. So all of your experiences are round. They all return unto you. All needs return to you. All denials return to you. All goodness returns to you. Everything in life returns to you, for you are that which is.

Now when you permit yourself to see the round consciousness that you are—when you permit yourself from limit of your mind to see only a straight line—in other words, you see a beginning and you see an ending. A person who sees flat sees beginnings and endings. A person who perceives round sees the eternity that they are. For example, you say that, "I had something once, and it was taken from me." That is a flat-minded person. Very flat. Not sharp. Flat. For they see a line and deny the truth that it's a circle, you see?

You see, an experience, you say, comes into your life. You are aware of it on the circle of consciousness; that is what you are. And you look and you think you're happy because you see a straight line. You do not see that it is moving around, passing through your life, and returning unto you again and again and again. Therefore, each thought that you think, each belief that you support, each judgment that you stand firmly upon is on the circle, that which you are. Therefore, if you work with the judgment of the moment, when you return to that position on the circle, the judgment will not be as strong or it will dissipate completely through your own effort. Do you understand that, [Student B]?

Yes.

So, you see, when you have a judgment and you say, "I've always had this judgment. I don't recall any other time," that shows you how much it is able, through your belief, to deceive you. It exists on this circle that you are constantly moving on. And so you're at this point and you move there and there. And you go around. And you say to yourself, "My experiences are repeating themselves."

Now several times some of you students have asked, How long does it take for a law to return to a person? And I have stated the more awakened you are, the sooner returns the experience from the transgression. And I've tried to explain to you how that works. You are moving on a circle of that which you are. That is, the identity is moving on this circle. Do you understand that, [Student B]? The identity, the indentation is moving there.

[It is difficult to transcribe the student's response.]

Now when you believe you are the identity, the indent, then you place yourself on this line, this circle, see? And you move. That's the river of life. Do you understand that?

Yes.

The identification is this little ship, you see. And the destiny. Now this river is like the circle, you see. And so you pass along this river and you have that experience. You move on and you make that transgression of the law. How soon will you experience the effect of that transgression is dependent upon your spiritual awakening, for those who make the effort to awaken within move more rapidly along the circle of life. Does that help with your question there, [Student B]? You see, the more awakened you become, the more you are able to accomplish because you move at a higher rate of vibration and much faster on the circle of life. Do you understand?

Now, the faster you move along this circle of consciousness, this river of life, the faster you move, the less energy you expend. How does that happen? Does anyone know? Yes, [Student B].

Momentum.

Momentum is increased. And therefore, these so-called weaknesses and temptations, you pass over them quickly. They don't get as much of your energy. Do you understand that? So, you see, here you are in this world you call experience; here you are this little boat on this river of life, which is a perfect circle, a globe, and you're moving along the river. Now [if] you move along the river slowly, then you are easily tempted; and you release more energy and then you don't have it for what you want to have it for. Now like one of my students spoke to my channel, and I heard, the other week, and he takes a look at that fire center and he says he'd rather have the cash. Well, there's no problem at all. Keep saying it to yourself and you'll move faster, past those particular forms that you—try to understand [the forms] are at a certain point on this circle of life. Do you hear?

Oh, now let's put it—perhaps they can relate it a little bit better for you. You see, you come to earth and you enter a little form there, an embryo. And you are at a point on this circle, all right? Now you start to, so-called—what you think, you grow. And you move a little farther along on this circle of experiences. Well, what is actually happening [is] you don't move slowly from there to there according to your years; you are moving at a slower frequency, you hear?

Now you have these experiences that you encounter on this circle, and you slow down and you become tempted. As you become tempted, you pause and tarry there, and you service that. And then you move along slowly, and you find another and another and another.

Now what you want to do and what is wise to do is to move at a very high rate of vibration. Therefore, what happens when you're moving at a very high rate of vibration, you rise on this river of life, this perfect circle here—do you understand? By moving at a higher rate of vibration, you start to enter the higher centers of consciousness. When you enter the higher centers of consciousness, you make intelligent choices, guided by the light of reason. And then you slow down your frequency in order to identify back here with the particular area on this circle of life, this river of life that you wish to service. Do you understand that, students? [Student B]?

Yes. Thank you.

So, what is very important, of course, is that you move in consciousness at an ever-increasing rate of speed. Because the higher the rapidity in your consciousness, the higher centers of life you will experience and make intelligent decisions. Now that's revealed to you by how long it takes for a law to return unto you, the effect of the transgression. Do you understand that? You see? So the faster that you are moving and the more momentum in consciousness there is, the quicker is the return, for your identity has moved at such a rapid speed it's instantaneous (its return). You don't have to wait a day, a month, a week, or years for it. It's comes right then. And the benefit of that, of course, is the inner awakening.

If you put your hand on a stove and it burns you, you learn right away if it burns you immediately. If it takes several minutes to burn you, well, then it's going to take longer. Is that not correct?

So what we're here in these classes to understand, to perceive, and to apply is an increased rapidity in the consciousness, an increase in the frequency.

Now you have the rhythmic cleansing breath that moves you on the river of life. The more you use it, the more it moves you to the higher centers of consciousness. And it does that on this perfect circle, that which you are, this consciousness.

Now, did that help with the question there, [Student B] and the other students? Someone else had a question back there. [Student S] had a question here.

Oh, yes. I'd like to—

I'm identifying you personally for this is a private class. Yes.

OK. I'd like to inquire, Is there any tie-in with our teachings with the Living Light river with the turning of the spiral in other understandings?

Yes, well, do you mean by—

There is a spiral turn to it.

Well, let me see. Let me—I want to try to get a clear, a clear light across that. A spiral, what you would call a spiral, I suppose, evolution or whatever they call it, implies that, it has an implication of a dependence on something outside to move. Would you not agree? If you understand some of the teachings that are offering what you call a spiral understanding, then I'm sure if you have investigated to any degree or extent that understanding, you will find that it depends on something outside of you. Yes, go ahead, [Student S].

Also, to me it would imply a beginning and an end; that the two weren't tied together.

Indeed, it does. So, you see, in reference to your question, it is not the teachings of the Living Light. See, everything that you are, you already are. You are not going to become something that you are not already. The only thing you're going to do, and that you are doing, is awaken. You're not going to be something; it isn't something that you've got to work towards. It's something you already have, and the work is simply the awakening to what is.

Now you awaken to what is and what you really are by removing the obstructions that are in the way. And how does a person remove an obstruction? Now a person removes an obstruction by, first, refraining from believing that they are the experience. That's the first step. You see? And so that takes a little effort. Then the next step: you refrain from believing what you have identified with. The next step is to lessen the identification with it. As you do that, you begin to move faster in frequency. As you do that, you rise into consciousness to what you are. There you make an intelligent decision. You bring with you that light of reason through a balance of the soul faculty with the sense function. Because it's the same thing that is happening through these centers of consciousness. Your four lower centers, govern[ed] and control[led] by belief, have to deal exclusively with creation and the senses. Your higher four centers are the servants of this power known as faith. And they serve you in realms of peace and harmony. And so the effort to be made is the balancing between the two.

You don't give up creation. That's not possible and still use it. You awaken through an effort within you to the truth that you are. It is not you. You are using it and are responsible for that which you use. And [you] can only use that which is rightfully yours to use, and that's the temple of goodness that you are inside of. Does that help with your question?

Yes. Thank you.

You see? You see, as I've said before, you can do everything inside of you. There are no obstructions in your way, outside of your over-identification and belief, which creates a dependence on something you can't control. So all of this goodness is inside of you, and it only waits for you to experience it. But you cannot experience it until you stop tarrying along the way, you see, staying along the shore here and not moving at a higher rate of vibration.

You see, a person says that they want something. First of all, we know they've denied that they have it. So we're dealing with centers of creation. We're dealing with, usually, the water center, very frequently the fire center. Now when you mix fire and water, you have what you call steam. That's just the way that it is. So when a person says that they want, need, or desire something, they best check very carefully if in any way it's dependent on the fire or water center. Now if it's dependent on the fire or water center of consciousness in order for them to fulfill it, then you may be rest assured it's dependent on something they can't control.

Because, you see, it is dependent—you see, first of all, if a person says, "I want this and I need this and I desire this," they first must tell themselves they don't have it. And if they tell themselves they don't have it, then the only alternative is someone else has got it. And so because someone else has got it, they must work outside to get what that other person has, which they judge that they need by denying that they have it. Consequently, they're controlled by the fire and water center and must pay the price. Do you understand that, [Student S]?

Yes.

You see? And so everyone is waiting for someone to tell them that they cannot live without them. It is a wonderful challenge and thrill to the uneducated ego. And if you want to puff up a person, all you [have] got to do is to tell them or to imply that you cannot survive, you cannot even exist, let alone live, without them. It's a great puffivation process. All right?

Now someone else back there had a question. And is that my student, [Student U]?

Are there boundaries—

I can see you. Yes, I can see you. And I can see [Student L] very clearly. And who else can I see? Oh, [Student N], I can see her very, very clearly. Right there behind [Student B] there. Yes, go ahead, [Student U].

Are there boundaries to the temptations on that circle? Are there certain areas where certain groups of temptations exist?

Yes, they're all over the circle. *[A few students laugh.]* I don't see any place there that I do not find them. They're just everywhere, [Student U]. Does that help with your question?

Well—

So you should go at a faster rate of vibration, increase the frequency, and run like you know what they say, so that you're not trapped there. Yes, go ahead.

They're not—previously we spoke of the boundaries of judgments and judgments or temptations battling one another.

Indeed, they do. Because you have judgments here and you [have] got judgments there. And when you stop here and those things decide you haven't stopped long enough—and you haven't increased your rapidity or speed—and you find yourself stopping over here in this woods of those judgments, then these judgments that judged that they didn't get enough, they look over there and see that you're over there, and the battle goes on. Does that help with your question?

Yes, sir.

You see, I mean, this is what creation offers to everyone when they do not make the effort to rise in consciousness. And when you rise in consciousness, you make an intelligent decision. You say, "All right. I'm going down there and I'm going to serve what I have spent so much of my life serving. I'm going to serve it for 5 minutes or 10 or even 20 minutes." You make the intelligent choice. You must learn to make the intelligent choice when you're not controlled by it. Because if you think for a moment when you're controlled by the desire that you are making an intelligent choice—that's ridiculous. That's totally contrary to demonstrable law. If you think that you are making an intelligent choice while you are down here at a lower rate of vibration, experiencing the desire, the effect of the judgment, of the needs, and the denials, if you think you can make an intelligent decision there, let the years pass and see how much it will cost you. The debt's very high. That's not where you make an intelligent decision.

When you experience what you know as the fire center or the water center or the earth center or [the] air center, when you have that first awakening, you say, "Oh, well now, let me see, when did I last serve that? Oh, I can't even think about that! I must make the effort with my cleansing rhythmic breath." And you'll rise right up to higher realms of consciousness. You will still have some awakening that there's a thing down there in the fire center that is crying for you to service it, but you're up there in consciousness. *You* decide what day it's going to be. *You* decide intelligently in the light of reason how much energy you're going to give it. *You* decide. That's where you make decision. You don't even think of making decision while you're controlled by it, because if you do, you've got a terrible debt in life to pay. Does anyone have any problem with that simple truth? Hmm?

Someone else had a question back there. You just raise your hand. Now I see [Student L]. I can see you very clearly. You look very nice today.

Is it my, my turn? [Student L asks.]

Yes, indeed it is.

I had the impression—

Is [Student L] still your name?

I beg pardon?

[Student L] is your name, isn't it?

Yes.

Can you hear me all right out there?

Yes, I can hear you.

Oh good.

I had the impression of a centrifuge when you were speaking in terms of how it spins faster and faster and rises. Is, is there—

What happens to it?

It, it's as if it were lifting off the ground. And then, when the energy reaches its peak, it starts to come down again slowly.

Well, I would think perhaps we could better relate to the teachings of what we've been discussing, I think you call it in your world—is it a gyroscope, [Student R]?

Yes. [Student R responds.]

Oh, that's what I— [Student L clarifies herself.]

It's something that spins and doesn't leave the earth center at all? Hmm? *[A few students laugh.]* Look, I'm not teaching you to deny creation. I wouldn't teach you such foolishness. I'm teaching you the rising in consciousness by the increased speed of the rate of vibration.

Now what is actually increasing? You are coming into harmony with that which you are. That's what it's all about. Now that which you are moves very quickly in the universe. Don't you understand that which you are moves faster than what you call the speed of light? That is what you are. Now what you believe you are doesn't even come close to reaching the speed of light. *[Again, a few students laugh.]* There's a vast difference.

So let's be a gyroscope. Let's be in creation and not a part of it. Now you cannot free yourself from creation by the temptation to get out of it. You don't get out of creation by removing its cover. There's no way you get out of creation that way. That's not how you get out of creation. You have a responsibility, my students, to creation. You have a responsibility to creation.

You're not going to escape creation. You cannot escape your personal responsibility of your eternal, evolving being. No, no, no, no, no. You have a responsibility to guide creation in your service to creation.

Now when you permit yourself to forget that you are not creation, that it is a limit, designed as a vehicle that you may direct energy through to activate it and to motivate it, when you forget that simple truth, you have very serious problems. For anyone to deny creation is to destine them[selves] to the continuing bondage of creation. You do not deny creation and be freed from the debts and the transgressions that you insist on establishing by believing that you are creation. You cannot escape the debt by the denial of it. The law does not work that way. I have stated for many years there is no credit in the spiritual realms of Light and truth. It doesn't exist. You cannot escape the debt of the transgressing of the law by denying the realm of consciousness in which the payment comes to. There's no way possible.

You can get a temporary reprieve by rising in consciousness to another realm, but you can't stay up there. And you never know when you're going to descend to where the debt's waiting for you. Does that help with your question?

Thank you.

Let's be a round ball that we can roll up hill as well as down. Let's be a gyroscope so we can keep our feet on this Earth planet for which we have a great responsibility for. You see, you have a great responsibility for this Earth planet and the vehicles upon it; starting with your own. Everyone has that responsibility. Don't try to escape what you consider a great debt by shirking your responsibility because your debt only becomes greater. Hmm?

True.

Yes. Anyone else there have a question here this morning? Yes. Yes, [Student J].

What is the relationship between the 45-degree angle in the north-easterly position while we meditate and the 45-degree angle at the time that we rest?

Very, very important. What is the relationship? When you place yourself in a 45-degree angle—and I'll demonstrate that for you. I think I'll demonstrate it for you. If there's something here—let me see here. *[The teacher examines the chair in which he is sitting to determine if it reclines.]* What's the matter with this thing? Yes. All right now. Here. I will spend some time, a few moments perhaps, *[The teacher adjusts his chair to a reclining position.]* because it would be terrible if, if I experienced that my channel's form was becoming too relaxed. Well, it won't get too relaxed, this won't go—there's approximately, approximately, for me I would like to have it a little farther back, but that won't permit it at this time. Just a little bit farther back.

Now when you're in this type of a position and perhaps just a tiny bit farther back, but not too much. You want a 45-basic-degree angle, see. Now what part of you do you want at a 45-degree angle? What part of me is at the 45?

The upper torso.

Yes, indeed. Has nothing to do with that god below, does it?

No, sir.

Well, I mean that just kind of looks like a straight line, wouldn't you say?

Yes, sir.

So this is what we're talking about, aren't we?

Yes, sir.

We are talking about what this part of the human anatomy is rising and represents. *[The teacher points with both hands toward his waist and then moves his hands upward until they are above his head.]* That's what we're talking about for the best possible rest and the best possible meditation. Do you hear?

Should we meditate in that position as well?

Ah, yes. Now the time has come for you to understand. The spine can be and is—a little bit farther back. Now it's very important because I don't want to demonstrate something and not have exact position. Now don't any of you get tempted. It's been many years before that was able to be revealed to you. Don't any of you get tempted to meditate in a chair and then go and lie down in bed and call that a meditation, do you hear? *[The teacher gets up out of his chair.]* Or I will not continue on with—leave it on. Leave it on. *[The teacher instructs the technician to continue to record.]* Move this, move this out a bit. *[The teacher instructs a student to move the chair a bit farther away from the wall in order to permit the chair to recline to the proper position.]* Oh! Careful there. Now let me see if that'll go back there. Move that table up there.

Don't worry about your film. Take another look if you need to refocus or whatever you call it. This is certainly much more important. I don't think it's going to affect our sales that much. Do you? Are you concerned about sales? I'm not. Hmm?

No, sir.

Well. Are you finished on that thing there?

Yes, go right ahead.

Just a minute. *[The teacher takes a sip of water.]* I will warn those of you who are tempted to lie flat and do a meditation of exactly what'll happen to you: you'll think the dogs have the best life if you're tempted to something like that. What is the matter with this thing? *[Even after the chair is pulled away from the wall, the chair does not recline to the proper position.]* Is there something behind me?

I don't see anything.

Well, take a look and see what's the matter that I hit an obstruction. What obstruction am I—

It's not touching anything.

Are you sure?

The limit of the . . .

No, no, no, there. That can't be the limit of this chair, can it? Well, I am a little bit, a little larger than my channel here. All right. Now when you're in this position, you should be aware of an experience around your whole head. You should have an experience like—I don't know how it would best register; how you would take it as—it's, well, an experience like just as you're drifting off to sleep. Would you understand that?

Yes, sir.

That is the experience that you want to maintain and to sustain. That feeling, that registration in the head. Do you understand that?

Yes, sir.

All right. Now the spine is in the proper position for the finest possible benefit from the rhythmic cleansing breath. Do you understand?

Yes, sir.

The great danger is that the forms which have been created in the prone position will take control. For now you stand between the four lower centers and the four higher centers. Do you understand that?

Yes, sir.

So there is great danger. And this is why I have not revealed it until this day only for a point of resting. For you must—you are now at the very borderline between the darkness and the Light. You are standing right at the border in this position. Do you understand that? So the tendency to a person who does not exercise the power of their will, the forms that take them out to other realms will take them. They're much more susceptible. Do you understand that?

Yes, sir.

All right. So I will spend just a moment here in this position, and then I'm going to sit back up because, you know, our time is running along there. Aren't you aware of that? *[The teacher questions the recording technician.]*

Oh, yes.

I see. So when you're in this position, you do your rhythmic breath. Now this is very important that you're completely relaxed like this. It is extremely important that you have no obstruction to your heels. Do you understand that?

Yes, sir.

You see here?

Yes.

Don't have this. *[With the heel of his foot, the teacher taps the elevated foot rest of the chair, which is so large that his heels rest upon it.]* All right. Now you notice that—of course, this could go back a little bit more for me. However, for my channel, it is fine. He's much smaller. All right. Now so, your heels have no obstruction. The heels are very, very important. More important than any of you students yet know. The heels, they're very, very important.

Now you do a rhythmic cleansing breath. I'll just demonstrate one here in this position. And it is very important: there's one thing that you can have is a little bit of support to your neck. A small, little, just a little—little small [pillow], just this little area. *[The teacher points to the nape of his neck.]* And in fact, there's one of those little pillows running loose around here somewhere because time is running on us. Isn't there one around here someplace? There should be one around here. Is it over there? Well, isn't there one of those little pillows—what's that right in front of you? Right in front of you. My child, my friend, look. Look there in front of—

Ah! OK.

Yes. Now, you see, something of this nature which his good doctor designed and brought through. *[The teacher places a small u-shaped pillow on the chair to support the nape of his neck. The dimensions of the small, roughly-rectangular pillow are 7.5 inches long, 3 inches wide, and 3 inches tall, with a u-shaped area removed to accommodate the neck.]* You see, now, there, you see. All right. Now you're in a perfect position to rise in consciousness; yet it is very dangerous for most people will descend. Do you understand?

Yes, sir.

So you must exercise phenomenal power of your will, which is available to you, if you're going to move in evolution to this next step, you see. Now. *[The teacher demonstrates a single rhythmic cleansing breath. His inhale, holding of his breath, and his exhale each take up one-third of the forty-two seconds that he took to demonstrate the exercise.]* You should experience—I did just a short little rhythmic breath there for you—you should experience a sensation from your toes throughout your entire body, your fingertips, etc.

Now as you make that effort and you gain absolute control through the power of your will and you do not allow yourself to descend, that means while going through that you go to sleep after or during especially—you understand that? For to lose conscious awareness at such a critical time is to become the servant of all of that creation below, you understand. Then you will experience an ever-increasing separation from the weight of and the burden of your physical body. That's the first experience that you'll start to have. It's not something that you can—yes, I understand. Is the timing getting close? I see. And that means— tell me how many minutes that means.

Ten.

Well, that's close. That's close. So you will begin to have those experiences and you'll begin, in time, the separation process. Now the benefit—what is the benefit of that separation process? Not just to fly around the universe, but the absolute conviction your mind will have to register that you are not the body. You see?

You see, when you leave the physical body through your evolution right here in this world here, and you look down upon it, you stand out and you look at it, and you still have *you* and you experience the freedom of the phenomenal weight that the body offers—it is, I cannot describe to you how, it's such a heavy weight of lead, the physical body. It is the experience that the spirit has in the physical body, this phenomenal weight. Well, the weight is the weight of the absolute belief and conviction that all the thoughts and the mental substance is the person. That's the weight that you will free yourself from.

And as that effort in your evolution is made and you look back at that phenomenal weight, the first tendency, which is, of course, another danger, is that you will not desire to return to it. Yet you have a responsibility and you must return to it.

So as time passes in your evolution and you have more and more experiences of being freed from that weight of that, you will, slowly but surely, free yourself from the belief that you are the weight, for it's such an unpleasant sensation, once you've freed yourself from it. Does that help with your question? Yes, you go right ahead.

Should we face our chair in a, in a north-easterly position?
Correct.
The head, the head in a north, north-easterly position?
Absolutely. Absolutely. I can only say this in recommendation: if in your world I had a choice, and I could only have two things, a bed or a recliner for [the] 45-degree angle, the bed would go. If there were only two things that I could have, the bed would go, for the position of the 45-degree angle is in my best interest. So that's all I can say to you, if I had to make a choice to that. Fortunately, my students don't have to make that choice. They can have a bed and they can have a chair. Hmm?

Now its benefits are phenomenal. Its dangers are very great. But anything that is worthwhile certainly has its dangers or chance, as you would say. Would you not agree?

Yes, sir.

You will find a greater benefit, you'll find a relaxation in this particular position to those of you who will exercise the power of your will, which you all have, and not permit yourself to go asleep while [you conduct this exercise], you understand? Now, you see, when you're doing meditation, you must never allow yourself to go asleep. Now you can come into a chair and put it into that position and the thing is to remain perfectly still. Perfectly still. There you will totally recover and rejuvenate, no matter how much disturbance there is. You get your spine, you see, here up *[The teacher points to his waist and then moves his hand upward towards his head.]* into that type of a position, that 45-degree angle, because, you see—perhaps you could understand it if I tell you this much before we conclude today's class—how quickly time in your world passes—if you would understand that your soul entered creation on a pattern of a 45-degree angle, then, you see, the way out of anything in life is the way you came into it. And so because you entered creation on that angle, that's the way to get out of it. Did that help with your question?

Yes. Thank you, sir.

You see? And you will know there is, there is no person, once having experienced the relaxation of a 45-degree angle resting position, that would ever choose anything else. For, you see, inside you know how you got into the body. And inside you really do know how to get back out. Hmm?

And so when the world—we'll be finished in a minute. You still have, I think, two minutes, don't you? *[The teacher addresses the recording technician.]*

Yes.

When the world of creation seems so heavy for you, you see, and you put yourself in this position for say, oh, fifteen [or] twenty minutes, you'll be amazed at the rejuvenation. Did that help you with your question?

Thank you very much.

And I see now that time has passed here. And I've been asked not to talk here after I take off this little bug here. *[The teacher refers to his microphone. In some of the previous classes, he removed his microphone before he stopped speaking.]* And so I will say good day. And now I'll take it off.

AUGUST 11, 1985

A/V Class Private 10

Good morning, class.

Today for our discussion we will discuss what we are, a spiritual being, what we have, a mental limit.

Now in keeping with that topic of discussion, we've already had the understanding of our earth, fire, water, and air centers. And I would like you to pause for a moment in consciousness to understand that a teacher teaches in principle. An uninitiated student receives in personality. That is the difference between spiritual realms of consciousness and mental worlds of belief.

As you progress along the path of Light and you awaken, as you enter the electric center of consciousness and, in so doing, believe that you are the limit of form, you experience, by the attachment to limit, what is known as the fires of purification. As you move through the electric center of consciousness into the magnetic centers of consciousness, from belief you are limit, from belief that you are form, you experience the water center of consciousness. And so it is from the electric to the magnetic on to the odic, you experience the seeming needs and limits of the earth center of consciousness. Moving on into the ethereal realms, you experience the air center of consciousness.

And so it is when you leave your physical body, and so it is as you are here in these classes.

From the belief of the thought of I, when you leave your physical flesh, the same thing, the same experiences take place in these other realms of consciousness only from your bondage of belief in the form of thought instead of the principle. It is the belief that traps you in the personality and the lower centers of consciousness.

Now I have heard stated many times, by some of my students present, that communication, from the understanding of this Light to the understanding of the student, appears, to some of my students, to have a gigantic generation gap. The generation gap that some of you believe exists is only an effect of an unwillingness of your mind to let go of you. That is what you think you are; that is not what you are.

And so the steps that you are making now are not only benefiting you in the here and the now—and the experience of that benefit, of course, is dependent on what you are doing, believing, or expressing that which you are, the expression thereof, known as your absolute, whole, and complete faith.

Because no one can be what they are not, we can only believe for a time that we are what we are not. And therefore, it is only for a time that we can experience these discords and disturbances.

When the rhythmic cleansing breath has a greater value in your consciousness, when you make even greater effort to apply it, these seeming generation gaps between what you are learning and your effort to apply, the gap will soon disintegrate into the nothingness of belief.

This movement that you are always going through, this movement in consciousness, you find moments in your daily life when you are not aware of it. You are not aware of the disturbance. You are not aware of the temptations, the trials, the payments of what you call the concentration camp of creation. I say what you call the concentration camp of experience, of creation for it is what you do with creation that makes creation a concentration camp for you. For through that identification to creation, you find a constant struggle and a constant battle to chase what you believe is a rainbow of fulfillment. Fulfillment, that is the rainbow thereof, is not available in limit; therefore, it does not exist in that sense in creation. To look for fulfillment and the joy of living while believing in its opposite is foolhardy to say the least. You may, for moments, be temporarily deceived by belief that that is where it is; however, the expectations, as one of my students has said, far exceeds the experience.

And so we look around at the world of creation, tempted that this thing or that thing will fulfill us, and we find, after the experience, we are filled, not fulfilled. We are indeed filled: filled with experiences and so-called memories that we judge we never chose to be filled with.

Well, now we see what creation has to offer for those who refuse to accept the power that they are that sustains creation. Creation is beautiful in the limit of its design. That's what creation is: beautiful in the limit of its design. To those who feel they need the continuity of limits to the divine expression known as desire, for them, of course, it serves its purpose. A child can bang its head against the wall many times before it finally makes an intelligent decision that the sensation of banging its head against a wall repeatedly is rather detrimental, at least to his head.

And so you have your homework. I do not expect that you've done your homework. Your co-students will soon make that judgment. I have given you the teachings for you to study, for no one can possibly expect you to apply what you make little or no effort to study and to understand.

Over these past weeks in conducting these private classes for you, it has indeed been interesting to me to note that as you, that which you are, is moving through these higher centers of consciousness, you, from belief in the limit of your flesh, believe that you are suffering with disturbance and discord, with unfulfilled desires. And indeed, it is most understandable, for as that which you are is moving through the electric and magnetic higher centers of consciousness and you insist on believing you are the lower centers of consciousness and, therefore, identifying with them, of course it is understandable that, for you, the experience would be emotionally heart-wrenching to say the least, that desires of your flesh would be indeed a great struggle for you to gain control of. It is indeed most understandable. And this is why I stated in the beginning here this day, teachings given in principle are received by the uninitiated in personality, for personality is limit.

So as you move into these higher centers of consciousness, centers of consciousness that your minds cannot control, by the very Law of Presence you are soliciting the Light of eternal truth. And by that very law, you, that which you are, is experiencing these higher centers of consciousness. That is the Law of Presence, the Law of Solicitation. That is what is taking place with that which you are.

If you have problems, it is because you are not aware, in limit, of the Limitless, for to be aware while in limit of the Limitless would establish an inevitable law of the possibility of controlling that which you cannot control, for believing you are mental substance, you are limited to the control of that which you believe that you are. For you can only control that which you believe that you are. You cannot control that which you truly are, for Truth is what you are and Light is the expression thereof. That cannot be controlled by belief. That cannot be controlled by mental substance.

You are evolving in spite of what you're doing, for you have established the law necessary, the Law of Solicitation. The difference is, for you, from lack of study you experience a lack of understanding. From a lack of understanding, you cannot cope intelligently with the experiences that you believe that you are having. And so the great step and benefit for you is a study of what you receive, which your minds absorb, which your minds therefore, slowly but surely, begin to adjust. And when you believe you are experiencing the lower centers, then you be rest assured, you are experiencing the lower centers for you believe that you are the limit and the lower centers of consciousness.

When you, that which you are is moving through the higher centers of the electric and the magnetic and the odic and the ethereal on your way to celestial realms—a return to home, your home, the home of Light, the home of Truth, that which you are. Therefore, I say to you once again all of these disturbances revealing your belief in the water center of consciousness, all of these great needs and limits of desire, the divine expression, is because you, from lack of application of what you receive, continue at times to believe that you are the limit, the form of the I of eternity.

Now we're going to take these few moments now for some of your questions. And I see my little student over here is receiving just beautifully. However, he has four legs; so don't get any strange thoughts. Kindly raise your hands for your questions. *[After a pause, the teacher continues.]* Well, it looks this morning as though class will be very short or I'll have to go, as I have said before, I have promised you, if there is such a lack of energy in the student body that they cannot raise their hands or that they already know everything that is about to be offered, then we will go into an interrogation. Do I see any hands? Yes, [Student M], please.

Yes. I'd like a little more understanding of, when we had the—what was it called? Transpose the two, the upper and the lower centers of consciousness.

Yes?

I would like a little more understanding. I believe it was said when you're in one of the lower centers, you bring them with you to the higher centers or—I'm not sure how that works, the transposition, the two over the two or why you would—

Well—

—need both.

Yes. I feel that I understand, perhaps, your question in reference to this superimposing. You see, you have, in that which you have received—if you would do your homework and place it on a round globe or a ball or something and equally done, which has not been done by my students, as yet. You have from your belief a fire center. You can only experience that lower center through your own belief and through your belief that you are the form of the I of eternity that you are. From that belief you experience what you know as a fire center. While you are experiencing what you know as a fire center, that which you are is moving through an electric center of consciousness. Do you understand that?

Yes, I think so.

Well, the thing is that you identify with limit, and from the identification, you experience the fire center of consciousness and what it has to offer.

Right.

That which you are is moving on its eternal journey through the electric center of consciousness. You see, throughout these years we've taught you faculties are undeveloped, uneducated functions. *[It is possible that the teacher intended to say "Functions are undeveloped, uneducated faculties, for in CC 226, he stated, "Let us not forget that a function is nothing more nor less than an undeveloped soul faculty." However, it is also possible he did not misspeak.]* You've received that teaching, haven't you?

Yes.

Well, they are only uneducated from your lack of effort and identifying with the limit, through belief, when what you are is moving spiritually in consciousness. Now when you leave the physical body, if you still believe and are therefore attached—for you cannot attach to anything that you do not believe in consciousness. It is not possible. Therefore, you see, when you leave your physical body and you still believe, you continue to experience the purification of what you call the fire center.

Now I think that all of you have had sufficient experiences with the fire center or water center or an earth center that when you are moving in consciousness, identified with it from your belief in your own limit, that it is indeed a distasteful experience to say the least. Would you not?

I agree.

You see, for example, if you believe you are the limit and you, your soul, is moving through an electric center of consciousness, you therefore are experiencing, from believing in limit, that you are in the fire center. Now while you are in the fire center, you move in one of two directions: you move from the fire center down to the earth center and you say that you have money problems; or you move from the fire center on up to the water center and you are all emotional and everything is wrong outside and you are blameless and you are a helpless victim of what someone else has done that they shouldn't have done. Is that not true?

True.

So, you see, you are moving through the electric, magnetic, odic, and ethereal centers of consciousness. Now when you bring those into balance—when you look at your world of limit and you accept personal responsibility that you are in it, you are not a part of it; you are using your body, you are not your body; you are using your mind, you are not your mind—when you evolve through effort, understanding, and application of the teaching, then you bring those faculties into balance with those functions. You are in the world of creation. You are not a part of the world of creation. When that day comes, you have what you call heaven on earth. Do you understand that?

Yes. Thank you.

Yes. Now [Student L] had a question.

Yes. It was stated that the soul enters at the time of conception. Does it enter through the mother's cranium?

The soul enters at the moment of conception. Are you—yes, you're talking of the soul now. You're not talking of the flesh, is that correct?

The soul. The soul of the fetus.

That is correct. Your understanding is—yes, indeed, it is correct. And that's how the soul leaves. Yes, [Student O] has a question, please.

Yes. In, in our efforts to try to create something on this physical plane and we are doing our cleansing rhythmic breath and we're, we're affirming this in consciousness, what we're trying to create, is it correct for us to use words that infer limit?

When creating, as I have discussed with you, that which is beneficial to you and is not the effect of your belief in need, which is the effect of denial, you create it in the odic center of consciousness. Now how can a person experience the odic center of consciousness and still create? Well, try to understand that the odic center of consciousness and the earth center of consciousness are one and the same. They are separated only by the division of the indent or identification, which follows by the belief in limit. Now that which you are, which you are, while in the odic center of consciousness, all things, all designs exist, everything that has ever been, that is, that shall ever be, for it is a realm of Light and Truth. So in a realm of Light and Truth everything *is*. So it is a process, as I have explained to you, of what you understand as creating or forming. You select, in this realm of odic center, you select a design. You bring it with you into the earth center of consciousness, which is taking place within you. Do you understand?

Yes.

So the problem exists in the questioning of the mind: Is it or isn't it happening? when it *is* already. You see, everything there, in that realm of design, manifested in a physical Earth planet, known as creation, already is. There is nothing new under the Light. All things exist by the grace of the Light. No thing, no form, no limit exists that is not sustained by the Light. The darkness is a lesser degree of Light. All things are Light. Do you understand that?

Yes.

And because demonstrably all things are Light, only the Light should be spoken to in reference to creation. Do you understand that?

Yes, sir.

No? Well, I think perhaps you would like a little different answer. The thing is, the mind conceives. It is the nature of the mind. That which you are perceives. It is the nature of the soul. So the experiences in your life are effects. They are effects of conception. They are effects. And so when you talk to your mind, you must learn to educate it. You must learn to work with the mind with the tools of the mind and what the mind is receptive to. Now you can look over your record of life and you can say, "I convinced myself of this. And I have convinced myself of that. At the present time I have convinced myself of a situation. I know I have convinced myself, for I am the one who is having the experience, the effects of my own conviction." Do you understand that?

Yes, sir.

All right. Now, so the first step is to say to oneself the truth: "It's not because something outside happened. It is simply a revelation of my own convictions, my own beliefs. These experiences are revealing to me my own ability to prove to myself how right I am when I convince myself of anything." Now a person ofttimes convinces themselves of how poor they are. Would you not agree?

Yes.

Financially or health or mental balance or happiness, we convince our self in these realms of creation. Now, then a person has the demonstrable proof to the satisfaction of their mind how right they are. They have proven to themselves that they are absolutely right. For once the mind makes a conviction, once it judges that it must have such and such, once it judges and justifies the right of the Divinity to have it, then you have what you believe is you at stake. And because you have convinced yourself, and because through that conviction and your belief that you are what you think, you have those experiences.

I am trying to share with you a better way. To experience that better way, you have to give to gain. So you must learn the difference between what you believe and what you are. And if a student is only inspired to learn and to apply there's a difference between what they are and what they believe when what they believe that they are offers to them suffering, strife, struggle, lack, and limitation, then any student has a way to go. When you are feeling good, that's the time to inspire oneself to make greater effort to free oneself from the belief in the limit that they insist on believing that they are.

Now when you want to bring a change into your life and you want different experiences, that requires a change within one's thinking. It requires a change within one's thinking because one does not make great effort to free themselves from believing that they are the limit of the form. Does that help you, [Student O]?

Yes.

Yes, go ahead with your next question.

Well, am I correct in understanding that to affirm something using words that infer limit is identifying, is identifying or believing?

Absolutely. Absolutely. You see, it's like a person that says, "I need $1,000." Well, if they say to themselves, "I must have $1,000," and the mind goes to work, it will, in keeping with their own beliefs and their own limits, it will bring them the $1,000, but by the time they have received it, it may be the worst thing that could possibly happen to them. For, you see, the human mind does not see the price that comes along with it. Do you understand?

So, however, the wiser path is to awaken by letting go of what you believe you are, you will experience what you are.

However, this is how the human mind works: it says, "Now just a moment. I don't think I want to experience what I am for I will have to give up what I believe I am. Therefore, I want to know what I am so I can make a comparison to see if that is what I want." Well, now think of that type of a statement that some of my students have made to my channel. Think of that. Think of what you're really doing. Think of what you are serving. You say to yourself, "I must first see and experience what I am before I will choose to let go of the falsehood of my belief in what I am." What you are saying to yourself [is], "If what I believe that I am judges that what I see that I am I can control in my realm and world of limit, I will make what some students call the switch." Hmm! My friends, that is totally ridiculous. That is childish, immature, and selfish thinking. How can you move from bondage to freedom, how can you move from belief to faith, when you insist that belief and bondage take a look at faith and freedom and make a judgment, which will be based entirely on its own limits of whether or not it can control it?

You cannot control the Light that you are. That which you believe you are can never ever in all eternity control what you are. It can only control your falsehood. It cannot control Truth. For Truth to be controlled, Truth would not be. For freedom to have something that controls it or has the possibility of controlling it, then freedom does not exist.

So it is very immature and childish thinking to make a judgment that, "When I see what I really am, then I will compare and make my choice."

I do hope that's helped some of you with that type of thinking. Anyone else have a question this morning? I see we don't care for interrogation today. Is that [Student Y]?

Yes.

Yes, please speak up.

You speak of the I of eternity. Is that how one perceives anything?

Perception is only possible through the I of eternity. And the I of eternity is that which you are and not what you believe you are. *[After a short pause, the teacher continues.]* Did you have a further question?

Yes, I did. Thank you.

Go right ahead. Go right ahead.

The—are the upper centers, are they in another dimension or is this all, this, the lower and upper . . .

Are you talking about the temple of God which you are inside of?

Yes.

Yes. As far as location in what your mental world would be able to conceive as location, the lower centers are from the lower part of your body. That is true.

So the, the higher centers are also present with, with us at— I'm trying to understand if it happens in different dimensions simultaneously or if it's all—

No. It happens in different dimensions simultaneously. Indeed, it does. Yes. You see, your movement through the ethereal realms of consciousness is happening at this moment. Because of your belief in the flesh and the limits thereof you are experiencing the opposite end of that higher center of consciousness. Does that help you?

Yes.

You see, for example, at this moment as your soul is moving through the ethereal realms, you are experiencing the mental realms of consciousness. Do you understand that?

Yes.

So, you see, we can't look outside and blame someone else. You see, it's not a point. It isn't and [hasn't] ever been something to add to your mind. It is the removal of what is in there. And so all of these classes are designed to help you remove that which is in there. There's too much in there. And because there's so much in there you get confused in these massive mountains of belief. Do you understand that?

Yes.

So clear out the mind so you can get free from it. You see, it is extremely difficult to get freed from a realm of consciousness that is so filled with so many things. You have to apply the teachings that you have received. You must, through understanding and application, increase the spin of the consciousness that it may move through those centers of consciousness and that you may experience, from bondage, freedom, that you may, through this increased frequency, become aware as you move through ethereal realms of consciousness, become aware as you move through electric, magnetic, and earth realms of consciousness. And it is through your own understanding and the application of what you have received that you will become aware that you are moving in these higher centers of consciousness. It isn't something you're going to. It is something you are becoming aware of.

You see, heaven—I've stated to you for years—heaven is not a place you're going to. It never was a place that you are going to. I have stated it many times. It is a state of consciousness that you are growing to. Well, the growing process is letting go of your over-identification with limit. And as you let go of your over-identification with limit, you become more aware of the heaven that is inside of you. You will not experience heaven when you leave the flesh, unless through your effort to let go of what is not, you are experiencing what is and that you take with you. Now does that help you, [Student Y], with your understanding?

Yes. Thank you.

Yes. And your cleansing rhythmic breath is designed to help you increase your rate of vibration, your frequency, so that you will become aware of what you really are. However, if you do not make the effort to apply what you have been given, that which works, then you must experience this disturbance of a mental world as your soul is moving on through an ethereal world. Yes, the lady there, [Student L], please.

Is the ethereal world and the spiritual world one and the same?

Yes. Yes.

Thank you.

Yes, it is. A lady has her hand up. And I think that that is [Student N].

Yes. I was wondering if the first two soul faculties belong to the, to the first two, ah, magnetic and electric.

Which soul faculties are you speaking of?

Duty, gratitude—

Duty, gratitude, and tolerance. Duty, gratitude, and tolerance is, for a function, an earth center of consciousness. Now tell me what it is for a faculty.

Electric. Oh, no. Wait. Odic?

Indeed, it is. Indeed, it is. Now, [Student O] asked a question, just shortly ago. And you have brought up the question in reference to faith, poise, and humility; duty, gratitude, and tolerance. Though you mentioned only, of course, duty, gratitude, and tolerance. Now you understand that is a soul faculty?

Yes.

It is in the odic realm of consciousness.

Yes.

All right? Now, [Student N], you have permission to move to your right just a little bit. Somehow your chair's a bit off. Move a little more. Ah, now that's better. We'll have your chair adjusted there because I see here everyone. You're the only one that I was missing.

Now, duty, gratitude, and tolerance, a soul faculty, effective, of course, when you believe you are limit on the earth realm of consciousness. So what have I taught you over these years in reference to that which is the right of the earth realm of consciousness? You have problems, usually, with what you call money. Where is the solution? Duty, gratitude, and tolerance. For how many years have I taught you gratitude for the crumb guarantees the loaf? Gratitude is the door through which you must pass into abundant good.

Now it's up to you to make the effort to enter the odic realms of consciousness, there have those faculties (duty, gratitude, and tolerance) [and] to return to an earth realm and there bring about balance in your financial world. Do you understand that, [Student N]?

Yes.

But only you can do it. You see, when you are grateful for what you believe that you have, you establish the Law of Increasing Supply. Now if you experience a decrease in what you believe that you have, then you may be rest assured you are establishing the Law of Ingratitude. Now a person will say, oh, ofttimes in money matters and in relationships, especially in relationships, they will say, "Well, I'm so grateful for this relationship. I never had any ingratitude in this relationship that I had."

But we are not thinking.

Ingratitude expresses itself in many ways. Ingratitude is an expression of greed. Whenever a person tempts to control another individualized soul, they are expressing greed. They are demonstrably expressing ingratitude. They guarantee to lose that which they believe that they have. Now when a person has $5 and they complain that it's only $5, they establish the Law of Greed, an expression of ingratitude, the direct opposite of the soul faculty of duty, gratitude, and tolerance, and that which they have, they soon experience losing. Your philosophers in your world have taught you for eons: "To those who have, even more shall I add. To those who have not, even that shall I take away." "To those who have not," to those who do not have gratitude, "Even that shall I take away."

You see, my friends, ingratitude is expressed in so many different ways. Now does that help with your question, [Student N]?

Yes. Thank you.

So [if] you want an increase of abundant good in your life, then you alone must apply those faculties. You see, greed is a function. Ingratitude is a function; all servants of denial. Duty, gratitude, and tolerance are the angelic servants of the Light of abundant good. Yes, [Student N].

So faith, poise, and humility are in the earth, I mean, in the lower centers, the fire and then—

Now you should study your Living Light Philosophy that you have already received. And talk to some of the students who have been with me for years, for it has been given to you many, many times. You have the functions that bind your soul, known as money, ego, and sex. You have duty, gratitude, and tolerance. You have faith, poise, and humility. Hmm? So you study. A little more study, [Student N], you hear?

Uh-huh.

Because with that, then that question would not be necessary for you. Do you understand? So you study. It has been given and it is available and you already have it. Faith, poise, and humility. Hmm?

Now [Student L] has a question here, please.

Well, mine is the other way. I mean, faith, poise, and humility, is that located in the electric center in the, in the faculties?

You must perceive. And if you don't perceive in the coming six months, then ask the question again.

All right. Thank you.

The homework must be done.

Yes.

Hmm? *[After a pause, the teacher continues.]* It's a nice pause, but none of you like pauses on your videotapes. I am aware of that. That's why we don't want them to last too long. Yes, [Student J], let's have a question here.

Are we ready to learn where the location of the anatomy where the centers of consciousness are represented?

Well, well, excuse me. I know you could only speak for yourself. And I know that you are moving along nicely there. You have to be to even have been inspired to think, when you're tempted, you'd rather have the cash. *[The student and the teacher laugh.]* Therefore, I know that you're coming along. However, I also know that you would not be so foolhardy to speak for everyone else present.

No, sir.

Well. Yes. And so I think you will find it in your best interest with that question that you ask me privately after you have done your resting and meditation seven weeks from this day, in the proper position.

Yes, sir.

Did that help—

I understand.

Yes.

Thank you.

Yes, you're more than welcome. And [Student Y] has a question, please.

Is there any correlation between the astrological placement and the earth, fire, water, and air?

Oh, yes, indeed there are. Yes, indeed. Indeed. You see, don't look out there to the heavens, when the heavens, heaven is within you. And so all the planets move throughout what you call your temple of God. That's what it is. Your body. They're all moving. All you're doing is looking out there and you're looking at a mirror of what the microcosm of the planets inside of you are doing. Yes?

So is there, is there a tool—not a tool, is . . .

The problem is there're too many tools and people believe they're all those tools. That's the problem. We're still having class. Yes, go right ahead. Hmm?

... I'm trying to say. [It is difficult to transcribe a few of her words.]

You got too many tools in your world, you see. And, yes. Some abused, overused, and some are worthless. Yes, go ahead, please, with the question. *[Many students laugh.]* When you get to be my age, they'll long be gone. Yes, thank you. Go ahead.

Is it useful to—is there—

Useful? The tool? It does serve a purpose. Certainly, it does. *[Again, some students laugh.]*

Maybe I should just forget it.

No, I don't—of course, it's human to forget. It's divine—I mean, it's human, it's human to forgive. It's divine to forget. And I don't think any—I haven't reached that divinity yet. And if someone has, would they please show me the way? Hmm? Yes, now I think [Student L] has a question here. No, it wasn't [Student L]. It was [Student N]. Thank you. *[After a short pause, the teacher continues.]* Do you have a question, [Student N]?

I did about the, in The Living Light white book it says, it speaks about the, the odor that you, that you smell—

That's right.

And—

That is correct. Indeed, it does speak about it.

And I've experienced that. And does that come from the, the, which, which center does it—does it matter where it comes from in the four upper . . .

Well—

I guess what I'm trying to say is I'd like to understand that.

I think it's very clearly stated. Do you find yourself aware of a smell or scent?

Yes.

While you're in the fire center burning up? Or the water center drowning?

No.

Or would you say it's more like the earth center? *[After another pause, the teacher continues.]* I think you have your answer there. Yes, [Student U] has a question here this morning. Now I'm not going to use all my energy to lift your hand when you didn't even bother to raise your hand.

Yes, sir. Why is, why is it that water has such properties of breaking vibrations, when it is so associated with one of the, when it is one of the lower realms of consciousness? How is it that it has those properties?

Oh, yes. That's a wonderful question. Well, let's perhaps answer that in [this way]: some time ago in our discussions we discussed some of the properties of one of the most favorite things to most of you people on earth, known as chocolate. It seems that most everyone—well, I wouldn't say most everyone. Everyone has a desire for chocolate. Not for chocolate as it is. No, no, no, no. For the chemicals that are contained within chocolate or cocoa.

Now some people say, "Oh, I don't like cocoa at all. I don't like chocolate at all." However, they, their body receives the ingredient, the chemical, from other foods that contain this same chemical.

I spoke long ago on the detriments to the water center of the overuse or consumption of what you call chocolate, for it contains a certain chemical that the water center reacts to. Do you hear?

Yes, sir.

Now you want to know why water is used to help balance out a water center, was that your question?

Why it is used to break vibrations and how is it particularly that it—

Oh, ah, why, how is it used to break a vibration?

Yes.

Yes, well it's used for descent, not for ascent. Ah, I see what your question is. For example, when I complete your classes, I drink a glass of water. Is that correct?

Yes.

And you have that experience of—you, [Student R], come over here and remove that spot on the carpet, please, while I'm answering this question. Now unless my eyes are getting old, which I don't feel that they are, I'm using his—it is a spot. Yes, kindly see that it is clean when we have class, please. *[The temple was always kept very clean.]*

Water, when a person is in higher realms of consciousness, it is required at times for them to return to lower realms of consciousness or to reidentify with limit. Would you not agree with that?

Yes.

All right. The best way to reidentify with limit, to return to the world of limit and a conscious awareness of limit is through the water center, which governs emotions. Do you understand that?

Yes.

Now there are other centers that could pull a person back, you hear, but they would not be in the best interest of a class of this nature. *[Some students laugh.]* You understand that?

Yes.

Does that help with your question, [Student U]? Pardon?

Yes, that does. But—

I'm so happy to hear that. It's quite all right there, my friend. *[The teacher now addresses and gently pets the church's dog, who is by the teacher's side.]* It's quite all right. You're not going to burn up. No. Just relax. Yes, [Student S] is waiting. Yes.

As chocolate or cocoa helps us identify with the lower center, due to the chemical—

I didn't say it helped us identify with the lower center. I said it is a chemical that is absolutely necessary and an overabundance of it is detrimental to a lower center, known as the water center. That's what I said.

Oh. Thank you for clarifying—

Yes, I think you'll find that, I think you'll find that evidence on this little magnetic tape there when you play it back. However, if I said something else, I will be sure and check it out with my assistants to see if that was true. I said a chemical that is contained within cocoa or chocolate helps a person in identification and is extremely detrimental [in] abuse or overuse of it. Yes. It has a detrimental effect upon the water center. Yes.

Are there any foods that are recommended that we should consider—

Celery.

—to make us go the other way?

Celery.

Thank you.

Celery. Especially people who are nervous and are overactivated by one of the, what we call the lower centers of consciousness. Celery. Celery has a great healing and a great soothing and a relaxation. It contains a chemical that, in small amounts, it contains a chemical that helps a person to rest, to relax, to calm down the mind. And it is especially beneficial to people who are overactive in the water center.

Onions are extremely—contain iodine and contain other chemicals which are extremely beneficial to people who are having over-identification in the fire center.

Any other question? [Student U] has a question here.

Back to the, the water, sir.

Yes.

The Living Light *says the water is not used—well, [it is used] as a neutralizer of vibrations.*

Indeed, it is.

Not a breaker of vibrations. So by the same token, if a person is wallowing in the lower centers in a negative vibration and very heavy, couldn't they, by the same token, use water to, to neutralize that negative vibration to help them rise to higher levels?

Well, may I say one thing in that respect—and it's very important. It is stated and it is true, it is a neutralization, not just a break of vibration. Now what happens, you see, my channel must return from the world he is experiencing into a form for which he is responsible. You understand that, don't you?

Yes, sir.

So for his form, he receives water which acts as an identifier with a water center. Do you understand that?

Yes, sir.

Because, you see, in respect to a balance of the faculties and the functions, he's off over there. You understand that?

Yes.

So he must return to the form for which he is responsible. I, however, leave. So the water helps in the chemicals within the body and pulls him back as I am leaving. Do you understand that?

Yes, sir.

Now water helps us to identify with the limit. It doesn't help us to be free from the limit. You see, it's a magnet. You don't want a magnet. You want electric power, if you want to move, you see. Now follow on your centers—earth, fire, water, air, electric! Electric is what you want to use. Electric. If you want to rise to the higher centers, then use [the] electric. [If] you want to return to the limit centers, use that which is the magnet. Do you understand?

Yes, sir.

So, you see, now when you're going off—you see, here stands this power of your will. There it firmly stands. As I have explained before, you have earth, fire, water, air. Here is the air center. Here is the electric center. You want to use this power

to move from the air, which is a mental world, into the electric center of consciousness. The great danger is for a person who believes they are the form, the electric center of consciousness is experienced as the lust of the flesh. Do you understand that?
Yes.
So this is the great detriment with all spiritual paths. Unless people are in a controlled environment and they are kept under a controlled environment, as their soul is experiencing these higher centers of consciousness, *they* are experiencing the depths of the lower centers.

So that first center, you see, the first center to move them through is the electric center. These are the warnings that I gave in the proper recline position, as the soul is leaving. Because you cannot afford the luxury of believing you are the limit, for to do so you will burn out in the fire center of consciousness.

So you want to use fire to rise and water to descend. Does that help with your question? Yes.

Since water is a mechanical means of doing it, what mechanical means could we use in conjunction with our—

Fire. Fire. You light a little fire. You light a little candle. That's fire. You see, fire is the center of consciousness you must pass through to enter the higher realms. You must pass through the fire center. Now, you see, you will experience—you say, "Well, I'm not consuming fire." You don't need to consume fire, except you consume through your eyes. Do you understand that?

Yes, sir.

You consume through ears. You see, you consume through your senses. So it is fire that moves you through and up to those other realms. You must pass through the fire center. Yes. It's the first center you must, you must—the electric center, you see, which to those in the realm of belief is the fire center, it's the electric center that you must move through. Yes.

During meditation, then, would it be advisable to light a candle while we meditate?

Definitely. Definitely. Definitely.

What about other times besides meditation, sir?

At any time that you wish to consciously move from this limit world of belief, you use fire. The electric center, which to your world is fire, you see? Now, the real fire—you see, you look out there and you see a flame burning. That's fire. The real fire is the fire within. See, there is a flame that flickers inside your being. There is a flame that never goes out. If you believe you are limit, you call that the desire of the flesh. If you free yourself from that bondage, you will experience the illumination, for, you see, that is the illumined center from which you move into the celestial realms of consciousness. You must pass through the electric center which, to belief, is the fire center.

It's only fire to a world of limit. It is Light to a world of truth. What is fire to a world of limit is Light to a world of truth. Hmm? Does that help you, [Student J]?

Thank you, sir, very much.

And so, you see, what happens with the mind in a world of limit, if you see a flame burning—you understand?—a live flame, not an imitation one, a live flame burning, your mind starts relating to fire, you see? And as that—but it's critically important that it become the fire within of illumination; because otherwise, one is trapped in ever-increasing unfulfilled desires of the flesh. That's the thing you don't want. That's the great danger of awakening: you see, that one would mistake those fires, through belief and bondage, you understand?

Yes, sir.

Yes, certainly, [Student J].

Would it also be advisable to light a candle while we're sleeping at night, since we're in a receptive state?

Yes, but not for the full, full night. Because, you see, candles should be contained, like you should have a globe over it or something to protect it, you know. You know you don't want just open flames in the world you live now, unless you're out there in the country somewhere where you can do that.

It is, yes, indeed, it is, for it will attract—now try to understand what a flame, a fire attracts: two things. It attracts the angels of light and it attracts the forms of the deep. So that's the—you see, you see, a person will look at a fire and feel romantic. Shall we say romantic? I think that's a nice word for entering that realm, wouldn't you say? *[A few students laugh.]*

Yes, sir.

So what you must understand, in getting into these higher teachings and the questions you are asking, what you must understand, if you have a flame burning fire and you leave it burning all night, then you want to be very sure of your mind, for you will wake up with, let's say, romantic impulses. And you may find them more than impulses. I think you will probably experience compulsion. You don't want that, I don't think. So you want to do it a little bit at a time. Do you understand that, [Student J]?

Yes, sir.

That's very, very, very important. You see, I said to you people long ago: the greater the sinner, greater is the potential of sainthood. It is only a matter of identification. The difference between a saint and a sinner is identification. The sinner believes and is bound. You hear? The saint expresses faith and is freed. That's the difference between saint and sinner, you see: identification. You see, the sinner denies God and believes in need, the effect of denial. The saint doesn't do those foolish things, for the saint has paid the path of the sinner. You under— you follow me there, [Student J]?

Yes, sir.

So use the electric center, fire, wisely. For fire consumes and purifies. And whatever it touches, it consumes and transforms into the finer substance that it really is. Now, for example, it's like that which you are and the frequency and the spin and etc. You see, the higher the frequency, the faster the spin of a mass, the more solid is the mass. And so you must use this understanding where it will do some good and the only place it's designed to do any good: in the consciousness.

So, for example, if you want to levitate, you see, to levitate, to literally move up from the chair without making any physical move, then you must increase the rapidity of the vibration of the consciousness that what you call mass is so solidified that it moves and levitates. So the greater the spin of the mass, the more solid is the mass. So if you want something solid and secure in your life, then remember that that is to be done must be done quickly on the highest possible frequency.

And you know, for example, you've had that simple teaching, I'm sure, of physics, in many, many ways in your experiences: when you wanted to do something and you just did it and you didn't ask everybody and his brother's advice, in fact, you didn't tell anyone, usually it worked out better. Would you not agree?

Yes, sir.

Because, you see, what happens is that you have an inspiration, you have an idea, and you take that idea and you move with it in consciousness. And you find a momentum. It starts moving within your consciousness. And the next thing you know, it happens. You haven't given it all out to the universe and slowed down the initial spin of the idea. You see, ideas coming from the Godhead, the Principle of Good, come at a very high frequency. This is why there are moments when a person has an idea, for there are only moments when he enters that rapid speed in consciousness. However, when he enters that rapid speed in consciousness, he is solidified and moved to the higher realms, that is, an awakening of the higher realms.

To awaken to the higher realms—you know, I've taught you for years concentration is the key to all power. Concentration is placing the mind pointedly and fixedly upon the object of your choice until only the essence remains. Well, the essence of a thing is the actual speed of a thing. And so people who walk on water or walk on fire or do all of those things have simply learned to increase the speed, its movement, of the consciousness. You see?

Yes.

And the cleansing and rhythmic breath is designed by its very being, by the Light itself, to help you to achieve that. Yes.

Thank you.

You're welcome. Now, yes, [Student D] has a question. I'll come back to you, [Student S], certainly. [Student D], go right ahead.

Is the cleansing rhythmic breath the same as the cleansing breath? Or are those two separate—

They're two separate breaths. Yes, they are two separate ones.

Is the cleansing rhythmic breath the one that we do with the tones?

It absolutely and positively is. That's the one you do with the tone. Yes.

Should we do the cleansing breath before we do the cleansing rhythmic breath or afterwards?

The cleansing rhythmic breath contains both, and it wouldn't be necessary just to do the cleansing one. The cleansing rhythmic breath contains both.

Thank you very much.

You're welcome. [Student S], here, please.

I'd like to know where the location of that candle should be placed in relationship to our angle.

It should be placed up on some type of a shelf so that when you are in a re—are you speaking of a reclining position?

Yes.

When you're at an exact 45-degree angle, then your eyes should not have to move. They should be at a direct angle to the light, to the flame. Yes.

And I would like to ask if it makes a difference what fuels the flame, be it a wax candle or a kerosene lamp.

Preferably beeswax.

Thank you.

Others contain petroleum. And you're working with a mineral element. You have enough problem working with the other elements, let alone a mineral one.

Thank you.

Yes. You don't want a volcano now. Just a flame. Yes, [Student L], please. *[Many students laugh.]* [Student L].

Thank you.

Time is moving quickly. [Student L].

It occurred to me, when we started speaking of candles, that the churches, the orthodox churches and the Hebrew churches have been using candles in their . . .

Yes?

They've been using candles in their services and in their, well, in their services. They have them in church. Is that the purpose originally?

Well, they don't know that that is the purpose, but that is the purpose, yes, originally.

Thank you.

You're welcome. Someone else had a question? [Student M], please.

Yes. Thank you. We use our will to get to the electric center through the fire center. The next—

You don't have to worry about the fire center. It's there waiting for you.

Thank you.

We hope that you're using the flame to move through the electric center. However, go ahead with your question.

To the next center, being the magnetic, I believe I've asked that question before and I'm not sure what exactly the magnetic center does. After, OK, the electric, I know, you're, you're pushing forward up to the higher realms of consciousness and the—

The magnet attracts them as you move through the electric. You are a mother, aren't you?

Yes.

You should understand the principle, my dear. Yes. Now someone else had a question here? Yes, [Student B], please.

Why, why are we doing this?

Why are we doing it?

Yes.

The reason that we are doing it is to awaken to what we are and stop being bound by what we believe that we are. That is a responsibility that we have to what we are: the awakening. Yes. Does that help with the question, [Student B]? You are responsible for the temple of God in which you are. You understand that, [Student B]?

Right.

You are responsible. Part of your responsibility is to awaken that you are not that flesh and that mind. That's your responsibility to that which you are. Do you understand that, [Student B]?

Yes.

So the reason that you are doing these things, if you are doing them, is so that you can awaken and free yourself from the bondage of believing that you are the thought of the mind or the mind. The awakening that you are using your mind, but you are not your mind. The awakening that you are using your flesh, but you are not your flesh. For, you see, not to awaken to demonstrable truth is not only a disservice to that which you have, by the Law of Evolution, earned to use, it is an absolute abuse of the temple of God. Does that help with your question?

Thanks.

Our body, what we think is our body and what we think is our mind, we use and abuse constantly because we are not awakened that it is not us. We are responsible not only for being in it, we are responsible for creating it. Do you understand that, [Student B]? *You* are responsible for creating the house in which you live. Do you understand that, [Student B]?

[After a pause, the student responds.] *Well, that's the problem.*

You establish laws in evolution. You establish laws in evolution.

Yes.

You earned certain color eyes. You understand that?

Yes.

You earned a house which you know as a female house. You earned a house that has a certain complexion. You earned a house that was to be built in a certain area of your country. Do you understand that?

Yes.

You earned the parents through which your house was made possible for your soul to enter. Do you understand that?

Yes.

Because you earned it in evolution and the laws that you established, you are responsible for the particular form that you are in, known as the temple of God. You see? You are not that temple. You are responsible for that temple. The laws of creation—you, by your own evolving soul, have earned certain laws which bring you the form that you now believe you are, and that is the bondage. Do you understand that, [Student B]?

Yes.

All right. Now was that helpful in your question?

Well, it just sort of makes me wonder, like, there's enough to take care of in creation.

Yes, the reason that there's enough to take care of in creation is because my own students still believe that they are creation.

That's the reason there's too much to take care of in creation. Do you understand, [Student B]? There will always be too much in creation—and by too much, not enough of what you believe that you need—because you still insist on believing that you are creation.

And these teachings are designed to help you free yourself, that which you are, from the absolute tenacity, the tenacity of the human mind that you believe that you are creation. Does that help with your question, [Student B]?

I, I guess I just have this feeling that, of leaving a messy house and going to another house, when I've not cleaned up my own house.

I see, because you misunderstand the teachings that have been given, I see. You see, the reason that you feel that way is because you have yet to awaken, as all other students present have [yet] to awaken, that you are not that house, and therefore you cannot clean that house until you accept that you are not that house.

Now how can you free yourself from that absolute bondage and believing that you are the thought of your mind instead of the power that is using your mind? How is that possible for you in that tenacious belief in creation unless you free yourself from it—you understand that?—and then return to it? And when you free yourself from it and then return to it, you will know beyond a shadow of any doubt what you are and the fallacy of what you believe you are. Does that help with your question?

Yes.

You see, you cannot clean a filthy house until you have the awakening that it is filthy. Is that not true?

Yes.

No person is going to clean up the mess of their life until they have an awakening that it is a mess! Does that help with your question, [Student B]?

Would that happen?

Yes, it will happen for that's the Law of Evolution. You see, it won't happen the way one of my students said that it would happen in the sense that, "I'm not giving up creation until I have a comparison." That is not what's going to happen because you have no comparison for the mind to control. All that you have is a recall of being someplace beautiful. Do you understand that?

Yes.

Now that's your return. That comes—heaven comes back with you and lasts for a time. You understand?

Yes.

Until you once again believe you are that messy house. Do you understand that? And then as you descend and believe you are that messy house, you become the mess. Do you understand?

Thank you.

And so as that effort is made to free yourself from that filthy, messy house and more and more times you ascend and have a conscious awareness of that wonderful feeling of ascending and you return with a little recall of returning from that beautiful realm of consciousness that you are, in those fleeting moments you will awaken and have less and less desire to be the messy house that you've made of old creation. Do you understand that, [Student B]?

Yes. So it rubs off? [The student speaks very quietly.]

So—pardon?

You're saying that it rubs off?

Indeed, it does. There is no way possible, there is no possible way to expose yourself—you hear me?—

Yes.

—to anything without having some of it rub off. How much will rub off? Well, that depends on your ability to rub, doesn't it? *[Many students laugh.]* Yes, who else has—time is running out, I know. Thank you. I'm sure that will help you. You know, there are some who are better rubbers than others. That's what creation reveals to me and always has over these many eons. Yes, [Student O], there, please.

Yes. Would you speak on—

And some are better duds. Yes, speak up, please. Thank you.

Yes. Would you speak on the subconscious versus our memory par excellence?

Our subconscious. Oh, yes, yes. I think—that's very important to you, [Student O], I know. Well, let us look here quickly at the so-called subconscious or the unconscious; I would say that's perhaps even more applicable to most of my students, known as the unconscious, because they're so unaware of it. Look, the minute that you believe that you are this limit, in that minute everything that has existed in your earth experiences rises up as now. Say, for example, you were in love ten years ago. [If] you permit yourself to enter deeply into self, [then] that experience rises right up in your consciousness, your emotions and your feelings, as a present experience.

You see, the forms that you put down into the basement of the deep sub- and unconscious realms, they don't grow old. They don't age with you. They don't change. All of those things are just as they were when you put them down there. They don't change at all. And so an experience of thirty years ago is just as fresh and just as real as the very day you put it down there. Do you understand that? *[After a short pause, the teacher continues.]* Pardon?

Yes, sir.

And I was going to speak today, but I see that our time—we've only a couple of minutes left; an hour and a half here goes so quickly—I was going to speak to you on the true cause of advanced senility, but I think we will have to reserve that for another day.

And have a very nice day. It's a lovely morning. And I know that you will. And remember that if we want to look deeply enough, everyone's got a dirty closet somewhere, and we'll all get to clean them up someday. And indeed, that is encouraging. Good day.

AUGUST 18, 1985

A/V Class Private 11

Good morning, class.

This morning for our topic of discussion we will speak on under contract. I have refrained from discussing that topic with you over these past years for the tendency of the human mind is to justify in order to defend its judgments of the denial of personal responsibility. In other words, to blame circumstances beyond its ability to control for the plight one might experience in their life.

However, today I feel that you, as a student body, have grown sufficiently spiritually in accepting personal responsibility, the path of truth, that we may now discuss this matter. And so pause for a moment in consciousness and come with me into the heavenly gardens, past the waterfalls of life and the rivers of eternal truth, as we enter the Great Rotunda of divine justice.

Each person in keeping with divine law entering limit or form must first enter the Great Rotunda before entering the expression that you believe that you are. Contracts are familiar to all of you, for contracts are merely a signed commitment. And so we all are very familiar with commitments. And so we are indeed familiar with contracts.

A contract offers to you an alternative, once you have signed it, an alternative if you do not fulfill it: the alternative of an obstruction to a desire that you believe you must have in order to fulfill the needs you believe at times that you are.

And so a contract signed in the Great Rotunda prior to your entrance to your earth plane must be fulfilled. Without the fulfillment of the contract, you must experience what you call penalty, the payment of your lack of fulfillment.

Now you have entered this Earth planet under contract. You will leave the Earth planet under contract. There is no, what you might call, escape from your contract. However, there is no justification for the belief in predestination. You voluntarily chose to sign your contracts. You voluntarily choose to fulfill part of them or not to fulfill them.

In the Great Rotunda stands the representative of the Prince of Light. In the Great Rotunda stands the representative of the prince of darkness. One representing the freedom and the full expression of joy of what you are; the other offering to you the temptation and satisfaction of how to get what you believe that you need.

And so as you enter the Rotunda and you pause and you think, and in your thinking you believe that you need, you have, in that moment, chosen the contractual agreement with the prince of darkness. You therefore enter your earth plane. You enter it with need. You enter it with unfulfilled desires. You enter it with the denial of truth. You enter with the lack of personal responsibility. You therefore seek happiness, for inside of you, you know that happiness is what you are. You seek wealth for you know that wealth, you also are. You seek the abundant good that you know that you are. But having signed a contractual agreement with the prince of darkness, who promises an easy path to the attainment of all the things you have denied and in denial believe that you need, you pay the price of the contract that you have signed.

However, a contractual agreement is not only signed with the representative of limit; there is the contractual agreement that is signed with what it is you have to accomplish with the Light that you are.

And so you find yourself each moment, each day tempted and not tempted, experiencing penalties, obstructions to your desires, from believing that you are in need from denial of your contractual agreement with the representative of Light.

Now it is the basic nature of that which is limited—and by its very being of existence dependent upon the Limitless for its own being—it is within the nature of limit to control that which it is dependent upon. And so we find that the human mind, controlled by the prince of darkness, knows intuitively that its sustenance is beyond its control. And so it is the eternal search of the limit ever to control that which it is dependent upon for its own existence.

I've spoken to you, some time ago, in reference to the fall of the angel Lucifer. For Lucifer desired to control that which sustained him. And in that desire was the expression of the denial of what he is. All of your religions and philosophies have taught you: there is the Light and there is the dark. Without the darkness of limit, you cannot experience the value of the Limitless, for in a realm and a world of identity, known as limit, you must have what you understand as comparison. For without comparison, you do not have choice, for then there are no opposites. There is nothing to tempt you. There is nothing for you to desire. Therefore, in order that you may experience choice, which is the right of your divinity, you must have the opposite, for the opposite reveals to your mind what you believe you do not have; therefore, from that belief, you must experience desire and awaken.

There are many paths to one truth. There are many ways to reach the one truth that you are.

And now the time has come to understand the contracts that you alone have signed and what your responsibility is to them. Whenever you permit yourself to believe that you need, the effect of denying what you are, you are then, in that moment, in service to the contractual agreement that you have signed with the prince of darkness, known as the limit of being. Now each day you are under contract: the contract to the Light of what you are; the contract to the limit, the darkness that you are not.

And the purpose of these teachings is not only to share with you the truth but to clearly reveal to you that limit has a purpose to serve to the wise man who uses it and is not used by it; that man is fulfilling the contract of Light, truth, and freedom.

It is the very nature of our being to express joy and happiness. It is also the nature of the prince of darkness to convince us that we do not have it, for by that conviction he is able to tempt us to seek it, and in so doing, do we fulfill the contract that we have signed with him.

You have come to the Earth planet with a job to accomplish. When you return to the Great Rotunda, after your record has been read of your thoughts, your acts, and your deeds during your stay on the planet Earth, you will be asked one question: What have you accomplished? That question you should prepare yourself for today. For in the agreements, the contracts, and accords that have been signed, your mind does not have access to the job you really have to do for the Light, for it is not within the domain of the prince of darkness to dictate nor to control that which sustains him. And so prepare yourself with a joyous heart for an answer to the question, the one and only question you will be asked: What have you accomplished in your stay on the planet Earth?

Your answer will be checked by what you know as the conscience, for the judge that you go before, that magistrate is the representative of your true being. He knows beyond a shadow of all doubt what your motives have been on Earth, what your thoughts, your acts, and deeds truly are.

And so when you awaken in the morning on Earth, be more aware, awake, and alert of your thoughts and your feelings. And when you close your eyes and go to sleep in your planet, remember, when sleep comes, satisfaction rules. And so I have shared with you over these many years the sleep of satisfaction, for that's what sleep is. That's when the prince of darkness does his greatest work. While you sleep and your faculty of reason is numbed, satisfaction, the servant of temptation, comes to whisper in your ear.

You know the way to rest. You know, some of you, the benefit of rest. And so you awaken in the morning and find yourself in what you call varied moods. You find yourself feeling good or not good. You find yourself plagued with unfulfilled desires. You find yourself in confusion, a lack of guidance and understanding, for you have not done your part when you entered his realm, known as the sleep of satisfaction.

We sleep at times with eyes open or eyes closed. Sleep is not controlled by the opening or closing of the eyes. Sleep is controlled by a conscious choice. Whoever fills their consciousness with need, the effect of denial, requires a great deal of sleep, for satisfaction, the need for it, is so great that it requires far more than eight and ten hours for its own fulfillment.

Satisfaction, sleep, the lack of the faculty of reason is not why you are allowed here in these private classes. You are here in order to fulfill your contractual agreement and accords with the Light that you are. You are not here to fulfill contractual agreements with the prince of darkness, the very thing that you are not.

And so, my good students, think more often and think more deeply. "From whence cometh this thought that soon shall rise and be a judgment, demanding its very existence of survival from my very vital body of energy?"

Now you are the round, perfect round, perfect Light, perfect unadulterated Energy. That is what you are. That is all that you are. You are not a hand nor a foot. That is what you believe that you are for you have entered and signed a contractual agreement with the prince who controls what you know as the senses of limit or form.

And so when you permit yourself to think of self, you can only offer to yourself the illusion that you believe that you are. Only in illusion, my good students, do you experience need. You cannot experience need when you are freed from illusion. It's up to you to not only discern the difference between illusion and truth, it is up to you to make the step moment by moment on the path that you are by consciously refraining from the temptation of believing, for belief only offers to you bondage of illusion. A person believes they feel good, and if they believe it sufficiently and they over-identify with self, for a time they will feel good. At what cost, when you *are* good? And therefore, being good, you do not have a need to feel good. You *are* good. It is when you believe you are what you are not—that's what belief offers to you.

You say, "I have such a good day. Everything's going my way." But in the very statement you do not even know what your way is, for if you knew what your way is, you would not believe it's going your way for that implies moments when you believe that it is not going your way. Don't you understand that is the illusion and the trap of all traps of old creation?

And so believe, and enter the concentration camp of creation. It's easy to get in the camp. It's indeed difficult to get out. It is always easier to get into something than ever to get out of it. The reason that it is easier to get into creation than it is to get out of the concentration camp of creation is very simple: it reveals to you who controls it. The prince of darkness makes the path so easy, so peaceful, you don't have to move a finger to follow him. That's called temptation. You have to make little or no effort to enter the concentration camps of creation, for once you're behind the barbed wire, all you will ever do is work in the salt mines, for there's much salt they have to mine for the realms below.

And now, perhaps, in speaking on that matter of salt, perhaps you might review within your consciousness Lot's wife. Of all things to be turned into, she had to be turned into a pillar of salt. Perhaps you might ask yourself and your little Light within, of all of the minerals available on your planet, why, of all of them, would she be turned into a pillar of salt? Why not a pillar of sand? Why not a pillar of gold? There are so many pillars of things she could have been turned into. But no, my friends, she was turned into a pillar of salt. Oh, I would be happy to tell you why, but you already know when you do your homework why she was turned into a pillar of salt.

And now, my friends, I think we've perhaps spoken enough here this morning on your entrance and your exit in the Great Rotunda of Eternal Truth. It is nothing to be sad about for that only reveals who is in control. You see, my friends, when you go to face that which you truly are, you could only be joyous if you are freed from belief in what you are not. If you are sad and discouraged in entering the Great Rotunda of Eternal Truth, then it reveals who is entering the Rotunda, and it also reveals which contract has been fulfilled.

And so I can assure you, believe in self and cry all the way to the Rotunda, or free yourself from the illusion and the belief in limit and in self and enter the Great Rotunda through the glorious gardens of heaven with a joyous heart and a strong upright awakening that you have accomplished what you have entered the illusion of creation to accomplish. For whoever accomplishes and fulfills their contractual agreement with the Light that they are is freed from want, is freed from need, is freed from desire, is freed from discord, is freed from disease, is freed from the trials and tribulations of what the prince of darkness really has to offer.

You cannot fulfill the job that you earn in a contractual agreement with the prince of darkness. He's a terrible taskmaster. He offers you everything for little or no effort.

Now you live in a world of creation. You sign contracts all the time. You sign the contracts of commitment. How many of you read the fine print? Or do you stop at the reading of the contract of all that it's going to offer you for little or no effort? If you only read the part that you are tempted to read and you never bother to read the fine print, be rest assured who is offering you the contract, for they are promising you something for nothing. That's contrary to the law that like attracts like. If you are seeking something for nothing, then you will sign the contracts, the agreements, and accords with the prince of darkness. If you really do believe that it is possible for you with the cunningness of your mind to manipulate other minds, then I can assure you, you will meet the prince of princes. He is beautiful at the con game.

And so remember, no one outside cons us. We do con our self. But for every temptation that he offers you in the contracts you have signed, for every single temptation, he extracts from you in payment 90 percent of a 100 percent of your effort. And if at any time you awaken and in that awakening you go to make effort to fulfill the contract of Light you have also signed, when he gets you back, he makes sure the price is ten times greater than it was before.

Now you can relate these contractual agreements that you have signed in your effort to make a change in your life. You make an intelligent decision, for example, and you decide, "Now I have done that long enough. I now decide that it is not bringing great benefit into my life. Therefore, I hereby refrain from doing that again." Well, he might let you go for even a year, possibly two. Sometimes even longer. But when he gets you back, you work ten times harder than you ever worked before and the expectation, as one of my students has said so often, is always greater than the experience itself. Because, you see, it has to be greater. The expectation must be greater; otherwise, he could not get you into his concentration camp to work in his salt mines.

You see, darkness must have its salt. Without its salt, it does not exist. And so, my friends, if you must be salt, be salt of the sea that ever moves and washes the thirsty shore. Do not be the salt of earth.

And now it's time for your questions. So if you'll kindly raise your hands. Of course, you do have a little different seating arrangement today. I don't expect my channel to experience any complaints, for I personally shall see that students who are not happy with what they have earned in keeping with personal responsibility are excused from any future private classes. Now you may raise your hands if you have any questions. Or shall I go into interrogation this morning? Yes, my friend here, [Student J].

In this Great Rotunda, sir, do we sign both contracts or just one or the other?

Both. Both contracts are signed in the Great Rotunda of Eternal Truth before you enter the Earth planet and after you leave the Earth planet, for, you see, you are only in what you would call the limitless expression for the time of the Great Rotunda. Then, you see, you enter limit and you carry with you two contracts. Yes.

If we're so aware of the limit during the course of our trip through this earth plane, why aren't we equally or at least partially aware of what our spiritual responsibility is?

Because of the contractual agreements that were signed before you entered form. You see, the soul is evolving through many forms and many planets. Now the lessons that were not perceived, that is, in the contractual agreement from the prior expression in limit—you understand?—the lessons get stronger. For example, let me say [it] in this way: that a person [who] is over-identified with limit, that reveals they have yet to have sufficient experience in limit in order to sign a new contract for their next expression. You see, by an over-identification with limit, one gradually, slowly but surely awakens to what one might say, "That's not where it is." In other words, "I'd rather have the cash." Does that help with your question, [Student J]?

Yes, sir.

You see, sooner or later that does happen. Now there are many ways of teaching and helping the eternal soul. And one of the ways—and I do feel that you should be well aware of it as students. You see, by offering the, what you would call, the fulfillment of limit or the blatant promiscuity of the form, many teachers have felt in ages past, and still do, that when they've had enough, they'll be finished with it and move on to their spiritual work in life. Do you understand that? However, that does not and has not proven over eons of time to be the wisest path, for usually what has happened, they end up in the final analysis with a condition of addiction that takes centuries to overcome. And so our school does not offer the over-identification with creation and the promiscuity of its expression in order that a person may finally get enough and free themselves from it. Because we have found, after they leave the physical body, from an over fulfillment in the contract with the prince of darkness, that it takes many centuries to free them from it.

You see, it's like a person, say they want a piece of chocolate cake. And perhaps chocolate cake and ice cream. And they have it on a regular basis, you see. And they enjoy it very much and believe that they must have it. You take and offer that person for, say, a three-week period five large cakes and five gallons of ice cream every single day. Well, the theory is that they'll soon get so sick of it, they'll never want it again. But that is not true, you see. So that's not the path that we, our school is founded on or expresses.

Although that philosophy, that type of philosophy is increasing in your world on the earth plane. It's increasing at a very rapid speed. Yes. Does that help with your question? Yes, go ahead.

I'm still—how can we become aware of our spiritual responsibilities?

You are doing that through the exercises and through your meditation and through your cleansing and rhythmic breath. You see, as you do that, you're going to find that—why a person has great difficulty in sticking consistently, daily with a spiritual effort is because of the contractual agreement with the prince of darkness. If you want to know how beneficial something is to you spiritually, for what you really are, if you want to know, all you have to do is to listen to the hullabaloo they put up in your mind when you're about to do it or stick with it. You've had those experiences, haven't you, [Student J]?

Yes.

Pardon?

Indeed, yes.

Yes, yes. Well, you see, what they—that tells you in truth, what that is telling you is that the contract of darkness and its representatives are furious that you are being tempted to fulfill your contract of Light. Do you understand? And so in keeping with that, what really happens, in keeping with that we teach you and have taught you: The darker the night, the brighter the light. You see? Or the brighter the light, the darker the night. Because you have two contracts that you have to fulfill in life.

To be more aware of your contractual agreement for the Light is happening for you. It's happening for you right in this school. When you go to make a step in the fulfillment of your contract with the Light, that which you are, you have all kinds of experience taking place in your water center and fire center, would you not agree?

Yes, sir.

Yes. But, you see, the benefit is, you see, students, is that at least you know. You know there's something going on. That's number one. You know that you don't appreciate it. And many of you have got to the point that you really are aware that that isn't you, and you don't like it because it isn't you. Do you understand that?

Yes, sir.

Now one of the first things is, you know, you have an experience, say with a young lady, you know. And everything's fine there for a short time. And then one day, perhaps you go to breakfast or something with her. Vibrations, vibrations are just terrible, are just terrible. Well, that's wonderful because you're beginning to wake up, you see. *[Student J laughs.]* It's most encouraging. Because then you soon find that she's not around very long. Is that not true?

Yes, sir.

Well, it means you made a change. Because if you didn't make a change, she'd still be around, don't you see, because like attracts like.

Yes.

So it's so wonderful to have those experiences because a person can say, "Well, yes. Why, isn't that strange. I really thought I was having a good time there. How foolish I was for a time."

Yes.

Isn't that right? So, you see, the whole thing is taking place inside. So you don't have to worry. Those are times and fleeting moments, you say, "Oh, yes, I have this contract over here. I'm fulfilling this one." It might last a short time, but at least it's a little bit; and a little bit is better than none at all, isn't it?

Yes, it is.

Does that help you on the contracts?

Yes, it does.

If it doesn't, I can be more specific.

Well, be as specific as you like.

Well, yes, I, I think that's sufficient, don't you? You know, when a person's having a nice time or they believe they're having a nice time, and then the next time it's just the direct opposite, something has to be wrong, right?

Yes, sir.

You fell out of grace with the level! *[The teacher laughs joyfully.]* Do you understand how that works?

Yes, sir.

So you say, "That's enough payment! I'd rather have the cash." Yes, now this, my friend here, [Student U]—

Thank you.

—yes, has a question to ask.

Is that why—

I'd rather have the cash. Yes, go ahead.

Is that why, then, that when our struggle is the greatest, our light is brightest? Because—

Why, of course! When your struggle is the greatest, victory is at hand. You see, I teach that when the struggle is the greatest, victory is at hand. I teach the brighter the light, the darker the night. Now we want to get them in the proper perspective. When the struggle is the greatest, victory is at hand. Does that help with your question? You are about to enter your contractual agreement with the Light, [Student U]. Do you understand that?

Yes.

Now, you see, something else goes to work on you when you're about to accomplish that. Is that not true?

Yes, sir.

And what do you usually say? You say, "Oh my, all hell's breaking loose." Is that correct?

That is correct!

Isn't that how you feel? Isn't that how you think there?

Yes, sir.

Yes. Yes. I expect maybe some of you have noted I have a new chair. It's not really new at all. It's the one that I prefer. My channel is not particularly fond of it. He says his feet won't touch the floor. Well, of course, I suppose, if, you know, you sit properly, he's worried about that. But there's no problem. Anyway. Can you see me all right?

Yes.

Does that help with your question?

Yes, sir.

Yes, I prefer this chair. I have my reasons since—and not just because it films better, either, you know. I just happen to like this chair for other reasons. Yes. Now is that [Student Y] back there?

No. [Student L]. [The student speaks quietly.]

Pardon?

[Student L].

Oh! [Student L]! Isn't that nice, you see. You couldn't see me, and now I can't see you. *[Many students laugh.]* Isn't that nice? Well, that's divine justice for you. Yes, [Student L].

I'm wondering—

Yes, you just speak right up there. Don't be afraid of me this morning.

When, when we go back to the other side, is it a balance between the, the fulfillment of the two contracts that we're seeking or do you—I guess what I'm saying is—

That's all right. I get exactly what you're saying. There's nothing balanced about a contract with what you are not and a contract with what you are. A contract with what you are is the only one you want to fulfill. Wouldn't you agree, [Student J]?

Yes, sir. [Student J responds.]

You have contracts. All kinds of them.

Yes, sir.

I mean, at times in your life.

Yes, sir.

So you want to fulfill—you see, to fulfill a contract with what you are, you can't be playing around with the contract with what you are not.

I see. [Student L responds.]

So there's no balance between Light—you see, the moment you think of self, then, you see, you have, if you serve 50 percent of the contract of darkness, which is limit, and 50 percent of the contract of Light, you're in very good condition. Do you understand that?

Yes.

While you're identified with limit. Because, you see, if, in the identification with limit, if you don't serve some part of the contract with one who controls limit, well, you're not going to find yourself in limit very long. In other words, you won't have no little piece of flesh to move around. Do you understand that?

Yes.

So, you see, we must understand that while man is identified with limit, he is expressing through limit. Now he has a responsibility in expressing through it to be in it, but not to be a part of it. That's the difference! You see, you must respect creation for what it has to offer. Creation offers you a vehicle of the planet on which you find yourself expressing at any given time. Now at this time you're on the planet Earth, and you have what you call a vehicle of form of flesh and bone. You understand that?

Yes.

Now, you have a responsibility to it: to be in it and not be a part of it. Does that help with your balance question?

Yes. Thank you.

You see, for example, if you say to yourself, "I'd like to have an ice cream," you have a responsibility to make an intelligent choice. "Yes, my mind, which is programmed by my experiences and my belief in limit, is telling me that I want to have an ice cream. Now I know that that's not me. I will now choose to permit this vehicle to have an ice cream to satisfy itself. But it better not tell me how much. It better not tell me when. It better not tell me where. For if it does, I am now trapped by believing that this programming of limit, from my experiences in limit, is now telling *me* what I have to do. So I, the Light, am now serving that which I am not. And I have done so, so dutifully and so religiously that I am now addicted to it because I am firmly convinced that I am it." Does that help with your question?

Yes. Just—

That is not balance. It's the direct opposite of it. Yes, [Student L].

Well, in, in recognizing and—no—in fulfilling the contract with the Light, is the, the continued recognition that we are the Light the fulfillment of it?

Well, it takes more than that to fulfill a contract. It first takes—of course, by recognizing that you are the Light, you have done so at the glorious awakening of accepting that you are not the limited form. Yes, in that respect, yes. Does that help with your question?

Well, I, I think I . . .

Yes?

I can't form the question.

That's all right. We'll give you time to reform it. I thought you formed it quite well. It was just as tight as could be. Thank you. Now if someone else had a question here. Yes, now I'm going to get to recognize you soon. I'll use my other vision. And I am going first speak to [Student Y]. That is you, isn't it?

Yes, it is. Thank you.

You see, and that other lady there, I know that she's a Scorpio because I want to tell you why: her hand rose higher than anyone else. You had a question, did you, [Student N]?

No.

That was not you?

No.

Oh, my! I best get back down here to your realm. Now let me speak to [Student Y]. That was not you raising your hand back there?

No, it was the person in front of me. [Student L responds.]

Never mind the person in front of you. I'm interested in your question. But I'll come back to you. Yes, [Student Y], I'll speak to.

When—

Isn't it nice to show that working through my channel (and I won't blame him), nothing's infallible. Yes, go ahead. *[The teacher laughs joyfully.]* Yes, go ahead with your question, [Student Y].

OK. Ah—

Interesting.

So, will you, through the cleansing breath, can one discover what it is one's to accomplish?

One is awakened to what they have come to earth to accomplish when they enter the Great Rotunda of Eternal Truth.

Not before that?

Not before. And just remember this: whoever frees themselves from the contract to the prince of darkness is therefore freed and may enter the Rotunda at any time that they are fully in the Light. Hmm? But that is at the cost of freeing oneself, through the Law of Disassociation, from identification with limit, bondage, and belief. Did that help with your question?

Yes. Thank you.

So you don't have to leave a physical body at transition, permanently, to enter the Rotunda and awaken, because you are awake in that respect when you get to enter the Rotunda. Do you understand that?

Yes.

All right. Fine. Now, is that [Student M] back there?

Yes.

Was that your hand?

Earlier, yes, it was.

That's fine. Then you just speak right up. I have several people—I'm going to get you readjusted here. Yes.

OK. It was just said that the prince of darkness . . .

He serves a good purpose. Without him, you wouldn't have any flesh to move in. Yes, go ahead.

It was just said about he has to take more or something like 90 percent. He takes more once you've—I'm not real clear about that.

Well, I'll help you, if you would like there. For example, say that you make a dollar an hour. Well, I know that you make much more, but let's say you make a dollar an hour.

Uh-huh.

All right?

Yes.

He gets ninety cents. Does that help you? Does that help you?

Yes, but why?

What do you mean, why? *[A few students laugh.]* Now listen. Just try to understand something very basic. Power moves an obstruction with 10 percent use. Force takes 100 percent. Do you understand that?

Yes.

Now if you understand that, then you understand the prince of darkness controls mental substance. He is the epitome of it. Mental substance, the only thing it can move an obstruction with is force. Do you follow me now, [Student M]?

I do.

So it takes for every movement that it would take the Light—you understand?—

Yes.

—10 percent of energy—

OK.

—it takes the prince of darkness—you understand?—

Yes.

—to accomplish the same [moving] of the obstruction 90 percent. So he's only taking what is justly his when you service him, known as temptation. He's only taking what is justly his. He has many obstructions to move. Do you know what those obstructions are?

No.

When you make a decision to follow the Light of what you truly are, you create, by that choice, an obstruction for the prince of darkness. Now he has to take 90 percent energy of force to instill in your consciousness that there's an easier way, and that's called temptation.

Thank you.

Does that help you?

Yes, it does.

All right. Now did someone else back there, that [Student N], have a question in the back?

Oh, the Rotunda—[Student I speaks.]

Are you [Student N]?

I thought you said other than [Student N].

Oh. No. I'll come to you. You're [Student I], aren't you?

Yes. [Student I responds.]

No, I wanted to speak to [Student N] at this moment. Now we must have no identity crises while we're in class, please, children. Now [Student N], speak up, please.

Yes.

All right, [Student I]? I'll come back to you. All right?

That's all right. [Student I responds.]

That's fine. I don't want any identity crisis. My channel has enough to go through without adding that burden to him. Thank you. [Student N], please.

I was wondering about contracts on, not just with the, the spiritual spheres, but the contracts on, on the earth plane. How could they relate?

They are manifestations of contracts you signed before you ever got to Earth.

So they've already been presigned.

Well, now they are presigned and you are never left without choice. So don't you ever fall into that pit of predestination. You are never left without choice. You see, you're constantly, already, in the process of reneging on certain contracts, either the Light or the darkness. And you're—if it's the darkness, you're always paying the price. It's called obstructions. Right?

Right.

Well, does that help with your question? Now young man— *[The teacher now addresses the church's dog.]*

But—what—How do you know when, when the, at the final, when you go to sign that everything is all right?

In the reading of the contract be sure and read the small print, which, you see, even the prince of darkness must put on the last page—sometimes he tucks it off into some corner some place under a staple—he must put in small print, no matter how small it is, the full wording of the contract. So if you read all the small print, even that part that's under the staple, you will find—that's the best I can relate to your world—you will find that it is clearly stated, no matter how small the print is—because that is the law, you understand—it is clearly stated that you will service and work for him for everything that is promised in that contract. And that he will receive, as his just share, 90 percent of every one of your 100 percent efforts. Do you understand that?

Ah...

You see, if you don't read the fine print and you don't make effort to understand it, that's not his fault because you signed the contract.

Right. So if you understand the whole contract—

You won't sign it. *[A few students laugh.]*

You won't sign it.

Not if you understand it, you won't. Because, you see, when you weigh it out intelligently, you find that he is, from what you call temptation, he is promising you to have this and to have that by doing such and such through mental manipulation. Now if you continue on through the pages—and usually there's anywheres from 600 to 800 pages when it's the contract for the prince of darkness, compared to three pages for the representative of Light. So you have to spend much more time in reading his contract because there are so many exceptions, you understand. Kind of like signing an insurance contract or something. And so it takes much longer to read and to understand his contract.

And so how do you know for sure you're going to get your money's worth? Well, it's really quite simple: when you read all the small print you say, "Now let's see, he promises that I can have this in 3 months. The contract of the Light tells me it's going to take me 3 years." Now, you see, you look at 3 years and you look at 3 months and you say, "Oh, no, no. Three years is way too long." And especially if it's something real important and the contract with the Light says it's going to take you 30 years, and the contract with the prince of darkness says, "Well, you can have it in 3 years, not 30, on my contract." When you weigh it out and you see that he's taking 90 percent of your energy over that period, you understand, of 3 years, that he'll give it to you in 3 years, when you weigh out how much you're going to spend for his contract compared to the 30 years of effort with the contract of the Light, you're farther ahead from the wisdom of patience. Do you understand that?

Yes.

Because you're not paying anywheres near that kind of cost. Yes. Now that's what it's all about. Now [Student I], you may speak now.

I'd like to end the contract of the—

You'd like to end it?

Yes.

I think it's a wonderful idea. You want to know what you [have] got to do to end it?

Yes.

No problem at all. You no longer exist in form. That's the end of the contract, and you're now in the Rotunda. Is that what you want?

That was not the contract that I was thinking of ending.

What contract are you thinking of? That's the contract. The prince of darkness controls limit, flesh, and form. Pardon? *[After a short pause, the teacher continues.]* God expresses through creation. God is not creation. God never was creation. God cannot be creation. It's contrary to the very law. God expresses through creation. You are not creation. Which contract did you want to, ah, end?

A, a verbal contract.

The verbal contract that you made with who?

With another individual.

Have you fulfilled the contract?

Yes.

Then it has ended.

He, he feels it hasn't.

That has nothing to do with the contract. If you have fulfilled the contract, the contract is ended. Doesn't matter how he feels. A lot of people—why do you think there's such a high divorce rate in your country today? Hmm?

Disagreements.

Well, one is absolutely convinced that the contract is not fulfilled, and the other one is convinced they have fulfilled it. And that's the end of it. So for one, it's the end, and for the other, it's a never-ending story. Does that help you with your question?

Yes.

You see, if you really had accepted that you had fulfilled the contract and it had ended for you—do you understand that?

Yes.

If you had truly accepted that, then you would not be plagued with the thought of ending the contract which you have already ended. Do you understand?

Yes.

By entertaining it in consciousness is an expression of your belief of the possibility that you really didn't end the contract to your satisfaction. Do you understand?

I—

Because your satisfaction doesn't agree with their satisfaction. Do you understand that, [Student I]?

Yes.

Fine. Then you have no problem in reference that you have ended the contract. All you have to do, if you've ended the contract, is stop listening to someone else who says the contract isn't ended. As long as you feel honest inside yourself that you've ended the contract, yes. [Student O], do you have a question this morning?

Yes, sir. Is—

It's very important to have light. And it's most interesting to have it directly in your eyes, you know. Well, it's no problem because we have lovely filters there. Go ahead, please. *[The teacher refers to the spotlights that are directed toward him to aid in videotaping.]*

Is, is the earth plane the only realm or, or plane that we enter that we sign a contract?

Oh, no. There's no way possible that you can enter form, which is controlled by the prince of darkness—stop looking at darkness as such a horrible thing. It's only an expression of denial. *[The teacher laughs joyously.]* I mean, let's stop—you know, here we are servicing the prince of darkness constantly, and we seem to suddenly shudder that, oh, such a terrible thing! Well, what is so terrible about it when you're serving it all the time? Why, no, no, no, no, no, no, no, it's not terrible. It's just he's the prince of denial; [in his belief,] he's greater than God, that which he truly is; [he believes] he is greater than that which he is. Does that help with your question, [Student O]?

One more.

Yes.

In other words—OK—if we don't pass the lessons here on this earth plane—

Don't worry, you got them waiting for you on the next time.

Yes.

No problem. You're not going to be—you're not going to lose a thing. Each one you don't pass here, you get double shot next time.

OK. That's—

Oh, yes. You see, you're already getting triple shot, some of you, and many of you quadruple shot on this round. Do you understand? Those are the ones you didn't pass four times before.

See, you get the test and you get the lesson each time through each expression. Now if you don't pass it in that incarnation, the next time you got two. [If] you don't pass it in the next one, then you got three of the same lesson, you understand. You just get compounded three times worth, you see. I say, I think they call it hitting you over the head with a sledgehammer. *[A few students laugh.]* Some of you have already merited those because there's been so many times you say, "Oh, well, I'll wait 'til the next time." And each time you say "Well, now I'm going to wait 'til the next time," each time you do that, the next time does come and then it's added that much more. Then there's five. Then there's ten. Ten times the weight you get, you see.

And sometimes I look at my students and see how they're so weighted down it's difficult, sometimes, for them to move. This is why I can understand this need to collapse, you know, like a lizard basking in the sunset, you see. Yes. Did that help with your question, [Student O]?

Yes, it did. Thank you.

The workers win. Because, you see, whatever you have to do, do it quickly and get it over with. Because the longer you wait, next thing you know you've postponed it to the next incarnation. Do you understand that?

Yes, sir.

And then, going with that kind of feeling, "Well, I'll just wait, you know, no rush. I don't want to rush into anything." And the next time, you know, it's the one after that. And it's the one after that. And each time, you see, it becomes more difficult for you to accomplish.

You know, it's like a person, you see, they start to decide they're a little on the heavy side and they start to slim down. And they become very successful, right?

Right.

And then time passes on and they permit themselves to think of themselves. And when they think of themselves, the old prince comes up and he offers them, "Oh, well, that won't hurt. You deserve that. You work so hard. Have three or four of those desserts. Don't worry about that. Just have some more. And some more. And some more." And the next thing you know, here they are again. Oh, and then they're unhappy, and they're back down on the treadmill again, saying, "I got to start all over again." It's much more difficult the second time. And the third time it's even more difficult. The fourth time it's almost impossible, but it's never totally impossible.

It's like a man, you know, he works for a while and he says, "Well, I deserve to lie around." Well, he lies around for a month, maybe two months, and then he says, "Not bad lying around." Lies around for four months! "Not bad at all." And then time comes he has to go to work. He's got to survive. Oh, my gosh, it's difficult. Wouldn't you agree, [Student O]?

Yes, sir.

And so then he works for a while and then he decides, well, he's got to rest. He deserves a rest. Lies around again. The next thing you know he's got to find someone to look after him to take care of him. Wouldn't you agree, [Student O]?

He does.

But, you see, that's the way it is. You see, once you give in—this is what—try to understand, you see, once you give in, you see, it's 90 percent. Lucifer takes 90 percent of your efforts. Ninety percent of the energy!

And so once you have broken contract with him and you've decided to make a change, when you slip back down to his temptation, back into his contract, he takes plenty! And it's much more difficult. Do you understand that?

Yes.

Well, that's very important. Very, very important there. Yes. Any other questions here? Yes, now let's get—oh, yes,

[Student S], right here in front. And I'm going to get to [Student Y] and everyone there in the back. And if you can't see me, well, you have permission to move your head just a little bit because I can see you. Yes. [Student S], right up here, please. Yes.

Yes. You mentioned entering the Rotunda . . .

Yes?

As far as our efforts in fulfilling our contract with the Light, is it possible to reenter the Rotunda for guidance and help in fulfilling that contract?

No, I just covered that. The only way you're going to enter the Rotunda is when you are freed from the limit of form.

May I ask for a clarification?

Yes.

Earlier you said something to the point that it, it didn't matter about passing on—

It doesn't.

—as long as we ended the belief.

It most certainly does not. You see, my channel daily visits in our world from a freedom of identification with form. He's done it most of his life. So it's possible for anyone. And many other souls from your world of limit leave their form of limit; they enter our world. And, of course, they look into the Rotunda, in keeping with the law established, so that when they return, they are more inspired and strengthened to make the changes that are necessary for them.

If you want to—the closest thing you can come to, in reference to that, if you are not at the point of evolution or feel that you are [unable] in leaving and entering the Rotunda in that way, is for you to sit down quietly and pray to the divine Light within you. And the conscience will rise up, and it will speak to you, as it does to everyone. Does that help with your question? Yes, go right ahead.

Thank you. I'd like to ask, then, since it's, it's not known to our conscious mind about the contract with the Light, is the—

Only through your conscience, that spiritual ability within you, yes.

Is the best way to work on it, then, by trying to end our contract with the darkness?

Yes, because, you see, that's one thing that we're all very familiar with. And each time that you renege on any part of the contract with the darkness, you must pay the price, and he extracts 90 percent. But each time you do that, you cannot renege on any of the agreements with the contract of darkness without fulfilling, at the same time, a part of the contract of Light, you see. You see, you just don't go into limbo. There is no just a limbo situation or state there that you would enter with your energies or effort, you see. So for whatever you choose to renege because you find that he is very greedy and very selfish, he always promises you more than he ever fulfills and because that's the way that it is and always has been, then each time that you renege on any of the agreements you have in the contract with him, you are at that moment, you see, from that reneging, your energies go over to serve the contract of Light.

Thank you.

You're welcome. Now, you speak right up. Is that [Student Y]?

Yes.

All right. Fine.

If you are in a contract and—

You *are* in a contract. There are no ifs about contracts, except with the prince of darkness. Now the prince of darkness is filled with buts and ifs. Go right ahead, [Student Y].

OK.

Especially buts. *[A few students laugh.]* Yes.

In a, in a contract and you are—

You are in a contract.

You are in a contract.

Yes.

And you know it has not been fulfilled—

Yes?

Yet difficulties arise. What does one do in that?

Well, difficulties always arise. It's part of—I explained earlier—the payments that are made with the contract of darkness. Now you cannot be in a contract to the Light and say that you are having difficulties, for the difficulties are merely the expression of the contract of darkness. So you have to move in consciousness out of self so that you can continue graciously with the fulfillment of the contract of Light. Does that help with your question?

Yes. Thank you.

You see, I spoke earlier that just before the victory come the hissing hounds of hell, don't you see? And the struggle is the greatest just before the victory. Well, of course, the struggle is the greatest because you've got a contract. And a person who you've signed that with is furious that you are reneging on the contract you have with them. Do you understand how people get that way?

Yes.

Well, the one that controls the mind is the same old way. Did that help, [Student Y]?

Yes. Thank you.

Anyone else back there have a question now? That's [Student B], isn't it?

Yes.

Yes. You'll have to bear with me, you know, because I [have] got to work through these vibrations. I will adapt. And I will adjust. It'll take just a little while. But you go right ahead, [Student B].

How—

Because I must use his form and his sight for this physical world here. Yes.

How does that, the spiritual bank account come into play in regard to the contract?

Yes, indeed, in fact, because, as I said when opening this class today, I have refrained from discussing the Rotunda of Eternal Truth and have refrained from discussing the contracts that everyone has to sign in order to enter limit. I spoke to you in a way of your spiritual bank account and your spiritual deposits. Try to understand, [Student B], it's one and the same thing, but we could not—it was not in your best interest to discuss the Rotunda and the contractual agreement with the prince of darkness. Do you understand?

Yes.

But it's the same thing of which we have spoken. You hear?

Yes.

And now we're just putting it to you as private, advanced students of what it really is.

Thank you.

Before we spoke to you of divine grace and the spiritual bank account, the deposits, and etc. Well, it's the contract and that's how it works. And if you look at your notes, you see, we're discussing the same thing only we're making it much more clear to you as advanced students. Because if you will recall at that time, those students, several are not with us today, are they, in private class?

Right.

Pardon?

No.

Yes. So it's the same principle, the same law that we're dealing with. All right? Yes. All right. Now that's [Student L]. [Student L], I can see you so clearly. Are you happy with your new position there?

Yes, I am.

Oh, yes, because you see so nicely now.

Yes. Thank you.

Go ahead.

Are the Akashic records kept in the, in the Rotunda of Truth?
That's the only place they exist.
Thank you.
Yes. You're welcome. Yes, [Student U].
Ofttimes it seems when I face struggle, that I do not succeed in overcoming the struggle.
Well, you see, you tell me ofttimes when you face struggle, you do not succeed. Tell me something, when you make the effort to stop thinking about yourself, do you always succeed?
Not always.
Not always. Well, it's understandable then, you see? Then, when you face struggle, which is only possible for you to experience when you think of self—otherwise, it does not exist, for it does not exist in truth. It is an illusion that you have created by your mind in your service to a contractual agreement with the prince who controls the mental world. Then you don't experience it. Is that not true?
That is true, sir.
All right. Be in the world and not a part of the world. Thank you. And [Student H], please.
My question is in reference to a person choosing to make effort to fulfill his spiritual contract. On our planet certain financial institutions try to discourage the prepayment of a loan.
Of course.
And they have a prepayment penalty.
That is correct.
Now—
Same thing works in the contract you signed with the prince.
That is my question. What, what—
The only one that has a penalty is the prince of darkness contract. That's why it's so long. Do you understand? Go ahead.
Ah—
First of all, it's based on all your temptations of your previous expressions in other forms. You understand that? So his

contract is basically based upon all of your temptations. All right, go ahead.

My question is, then—

And there's quite a list.

Does his—what form does his prepayment penalty take?

The prepayment penalty?

Yes.

Yes, it takes a beautiful form. How well do you like salt mines? Did that help with your question?

Thank you.

You know, there is no escape. But if a person has to serve in the salt mine, well, let's get it over, shall we? Maybe we could work out something to go down there at the wintertime. When it's cold up above, it's awfully hot down there, you know. It is warm. Yes. Yes. Did that help with your question?

Thank you.

Yes, oh, yes, you must pay the penalties. Oh, definitely. Hmm. Now don't think that you're going to wait and when you leave the physical body to go work in the salt mine. That's foolishness. You serve in the salt mines and many days you already served them. Would you not agree you feel terrible sometimes and totally exhausted?

I agree.

Well, if you'd only see what your other bodies down there [are] having to work out. They're very costly. You know, you ought to tell yourself what my good student, [Student J], said: "I'd rather have the cash." *[The teacher laughs joyously.]* Someone else have a question? Yes, it's expensive. Try to understand they turned Lot's wife into a pillar of salt. My goodness, children, why don't you study some of your—yes, who had that question there? [Student B]?

Yes.

You go right ahead.

What percentage of mankind fulfills their contract with the Prince of the Light?

The Prince of Light? Yes. In your world of creation on the specific planet—the Earth planet? Because other planets, they have—are governed by various laws.

On Earth.

On Earth, 5 percent. Five percent, [Student B].

Thank you.

You're welcome. [Student L], please.

Will those of us in this class be able to, to fulfill it?

Pardon?

Will those of us in this class be able to fulfill the contract with the Light?

You have the opportunity.

OK.

You have the opportunity. What you do with that opportunity, of course, is up to you. You know, you are fulfilling part of your contractual agreement with the Light by your presence. But it takes more than your presence, you understand? It takes doing your homework, and it takes applying what you're receiving for your own benefit. You see, what is at stake—you're wrenching yourself free from that. That doesn't mean you're not continuing to experience it, but as you stop believing that you are that stuff, you see, the limit, as you stop believing that, you do so [with] a struggle inside of you. Because he's not going to let you go very, very easily when you've got all of that that he judges, in keeping with the contract signed, that you owe him. You understand?

Yes.

Yes.

Thank you.

You're welcome. You see, many times when you think you're sleeping—ah, the realms of satisfaction, if you only knew when you wake up so exhausted. You know, when you sleep and you wake up so exhausted, where do you think you [have] been?

Mostly down there in the salt mines working like a little beaver to pay for the temptations that you were granted during the course of the day or the ones possible down the road. Yes. Oh my, it's a heavy contract. Who do I have back there? Is that [Student Y]?

It's [Student D].

Oh, now we know where [Student D] is! Good for you. Speak right up, [Student D]. Lovely day.

I have—

It's a nice day for [Student D]. Yes.

Yes, it is. Thank you. I have—

I wouldn't call it a daisy day, but it's a light and beautiful day. Go ahead, [Student D]. *[The teacher laughs joyfully.]* Yes?

I have been having great difficulty with sleep, taking over—

Yes.

—my realm. And my will is weaker. What can I do—

No, no, no, my dear. We must stop at that point. Excuse me for stopping you at that point. Your will is stronger than ever before, if anything. The will doesn't weaken. It only gets stronger. It's where we're directing it. [Student D]?

Yes.

Your will is stronger than ever before. It's being directed someplace else.

Well, where can I direct it to eliminate some of the sleep taking over?

All right now, let me tell you something. You have within your consciousness a desire that has been plaguing you. Do you hear me? You have not educated it. You have forced it into what you call the basement of the unconscious. You hear?

OK.

Down there it enters the salt mines. Down there you are experiencing the possibility of its fulfillment. Do you understand me?

Yes.

Therefore, your energy, which flows through your will, is going down below: 90 percent of it to the salt mine work and 10 percent in the dreaming it may happen someday. Do you understand that, [Student D]?

Yes.

Now this is very important that all of you students understand that principle. I have taught you for years you do not suppress desire. Desire is an expression of a judgment, which is the expression of need, which is the expression of your denying what you are. Now you suppress that, and you enter those salt mines. You awaken exhausted. You find almost like a condition of self-hypnosis. Do you understand that, [Student D]?

Yes, I do.

Now the reason that you find that—and you will find [you have] less and less energy—is because you go down there [and] you are tempted like a rabbit is to a carrot of the possibility of getting that, as your vitality is siphoned off in the salt mines for the work at 90 percent of it. Now does that help with your question?

Yes.

Communicate with yourself in the faculty of reason. To God all things are possible. The way that the mind is going about it—because the mind is controlled by the prince of darkness—will not bring you any good. Do you understand?

Yes.

That's not the way that God fulfills it. You hear?

Yes, I do.

It's the way that temptation and the lack of the wisdom of patience fills it. Do you understand?

Yes.

All right. Does that help with your question?

Thank you very much.

You're welcome. *[After a pause, the teacher continues.]* We're moving on, but I know you people that like the videos don't like long pauses; so do we have—is it interrogation time this morning, [Student A]? *[After another short pause, the teacher again continues.]* Is [Student A] with us? Isn't that [Student A]'s little face?

Yes.

Yes, is it interrogation time or do you have a question?

Well, I had several but—

Well, now we'll only take one at a time, [Student A]. So you just speak out that question. Just the one now. Adjust it in your priorities. And I will get to as many of those lovely questions as I can this morning. All right, [Student A]?

OK. What is your responsibility to the Light if you have, say, a child that you're responsible for? And how can you help that child, if that child is not, say, in the Light like you are?

Yes, I understand. How can you help that child? You can help them with never saying a word. The living demonstration, [Student A]. You see, the law clearly reveals to us that like attracts like. That that is around us grows or goes with us. Right? Isn't that the law, [Student A], that you accept?

That's right.

So, as [Student A] grows in the Light, that that is around her is benefited, as long as it remains around her. Do you understand that?

Yes, I do.

Now that help you with your child?

Yes. Thank you.

Now you can go on with your next question. Lovely day today.

Uhm—

Yes.

Since we're on the planet of faith and you said earlier that 5 percent make it into the Light.

That is correct.

Does that have, correlate with the fact that we're on the planet of, that is the number of faith?

That is correct.

Thank you.

We choose here, from our contractual agreements, what we consider to be the short way to something. There are no short ways. There are no shortcuts. Do you understand, [Student A]?

Yes.

There aren't any. The masses of the planet Earth choose what they believe—for they must first believe it—the shortcut. Hmm? You see, everything is accelerated. They want everything done now. They have a thought, a desire; they want it now. Not tomorrow. Not next year. Not twenty years. Not thirty years. Now. Do you understand?

Yes.

Well, he promises them *now* for all your desires. Now.

And you continue to pay 90 percent.

Yes, 90 percent. Say that you have a desire for something that costs you $100. Well, he promises to fill that desire; the only thing is, he takes 90 and you've only made a $10 down payment. Hmm?

Now [Student R], if you'd concentrate on your left foot, you wouldn't have the problem.

Thank you. [Student R responds.]

All you have to do is send the energy down there, and it won't get numb like that.

Yes, does that help with your question, [Student A]?

Yes.

Good. Any other—[Student H], you had a question? *[After a short pause, the teacher continues.]* Oh, is that a daydream I'm looking at? I do hope it's not. *[The teacher laughs.]* Yes?

Well, I'm interested in, in making effort to, here on earth, to fulfill the spiritual contract and I'd like to— [Student H begins to speak.]

I would like to clarify that. The spiritual contract, of course, is the contract with what you are. I think we'd feel better if we clarified the words. That's the contract with what you really are, you see? Not what you believe you are. And you know what you believe you are is in a constant process of change.

Right.

Now some things you believe you are you've had quite a while. But when you were 2 years old, you didn't have them. You acquired them along about 12 or was it 14 for you?

Twelve.

Well, I didn't want to reveal too much. Go right ahead, [Student H].

Ah—

But for twelve years you didn't have it, isn't that correct?

That's right.

So therefore, it's something that you acquired.

That's correct.

It's not something that you are.

That's right.

But it's something you acquired through belief. Because, after all, you still had that part of your anatomy when you were twelve years old and ten years old, didn't you?

Right.

But you used it for other things then, exclusively. Is that correct?

Correct.

I think so, yes. *[The teacher laughs.]* Well, when, you know, as my good student, Isa, said to her son, "When you can no longer laugh, life's not worth living." *[Isa Goodwin is Mr. Goodwin's mother. She would regularly instruct, guide, and correct the students through Mr. Goodwin's mediumship.]* So I am firmly convinced that life is worth living; so let's laugh and go ahead with your little question. Were we at twelve or how old are we talking about now?

Moving beyond that. [Some students laugh.]

Oh, we've moved above that, have we? Good for you! I'm happy to hear that. Better the heart than the head. It won't offer you so many problems, a little heart, you see. Go ahead. And besides, you don't need your head to express your heart, you know. That's not required. Oh, no, no, no, no, no, no, that's such a foolish delusion that you require your head in order to express your heart. That's totally ridiculous. Yes. Go ahead with that question.

Well, my, my question is . . .

Your heart or your head?

The head, really.

Oh, the head. Oh, dear. Well, let's stick to the head, then, for a time.

Because—

I see a lot of them nailed on the pole there. *[Many students laugh.]*

Because it's a, it's a disappointment—

Totem pole. Yes. Go ahead. What did you say?

It's the disappointment that comes each time you make effort. We know where the disappointment comes from. And it's coming from the head. It's coming from the realms below. And—

Well, you [have] got to pay 90 percent.

Yeah. That I—

You're trying to renege on the contract.

Yeah.

Go ahead.

You've, you've answered my question. That, that explains it.

Well, you knew you can't sign a contract and then think you're going to get off scot-free. You must pay.

Right. And so—

You know—

—that disappointment is the payment.

Why, certainly. And the expectation is always greater than the actual experience, one of my students said. Yes, I like that.

Because it's so true, you see. Oh, yes, yes, I know. *[The teacher acknowledges a signal from the recording technician that the videotape is about to end.]* Yes. Does that help you?

Yes. Thank you very much.

Well, you know, you see, when you no longer have the need to be twelve years old, you will be free from that. Won't that be wonderful? Don't you understand? You see, when you have an experience in life and you say, "Well, that experience was twenty-some years ago," you have to understand in order for you to continue with that experience, you must return to the timing within your consciousness, whether you're aware of it or not, to when you first had the experience. You see, the cause of anything—the cure of anything is ever in the cause. So each time you think you have a need to, to have that—you know what I'm talking about—you understand—anybody—each time, you have to say, "Now when did this first happen to me?" For that is the state of consciousness that you have entered in the unconscious.

Now understand something about the unconscious: experiences enter the unconscious [and] they do not change. They're absolutely solidified. They don't grow old. They don't recognize time. They have no recognition of change. They just exist. They exist as they were initially placed into the unconscious. Do you understand that?

Yes.

That is very important. So whenever you think you have that need, what is in control is a form that was created at that time in your life that you have opened the door to.

And I must say good day. Time has certainly passed quickly. Thank you so very much. Have a fine day. I know that you will.

AUGUST 25, 1985

A/V Class Private 12

Good morning, students.

Today's class will begin with the three most important questions the human mind has to ask itself. They are: "What am I? Who am I? Where am I?"

Now, as part of your homework, it is your responsibility, from this moment on, to ask yourself those three most important questions of your mental world. "What am I? Who am I? Where am I?"

Now, for example, we ask ourselves that question, "What am I?" and our mind begins to think, based upon its past experiences, and it says, "I am a form. I am different than all other forms. I experience pain. I experience satisfaction. And my pain and my satisfaction is dependent upon what I believe that I need." And so our mind immediately tells us what we are. Unfortunately, it tells us very little. For the very little that it has to offer is dependent upon the limited experiences of its own identification.

And it moves on to ask itself, "Who am I?" "I am that, I believe, whichever seeks to find something that I know is my right to have." And it moves on into deeper waters for mental substance and asks itself, "Where am I?" One moment it says it is one place in the universe; another moment it says it is someplace else.

So we find on those three most important questions that the human mind can ask itself, we find a confusion, a confusion of thoughts. We find a constant changing, dependent upon the fulfillment of the needs that it has at any given moment. The mind tells us how beautiful a certain experience for us was; and yet the very same mind that tells us that is the same mind that moved us from the experience. So we find in truth that the human mind is in a constant state of mass confusion, and that confusion is the effect and the result of a lack of guidance, a lack of responsibility to the being that is responsible to teach it, to train it, to guide it, and to discipline it. Therefore, whenever we permit our self to believe what the human mind offers, we find our self not enjoying, not experiencing the happiness, the goodness, the well-being that we are.

And yet we also find ourselves, repeatedly, believing that we are that which is unguided, undisciplined, uncontrolled. Now we must ask our self the question, viewing a world, a mental world that from one moment to the next is not reliable, from one moment to the next is contradictory, we must ask our self, Why? Why do we not make greater effort to refrain from serving an instrument that has far exceeded, from our lack of guidance of it, an instrument that has far exceeded the true purpose of its design?

And so this morning I'm going to speak to those of you—all of you I'm going to speak [with], as many as time will permit. And I expect an answer from what you think you are and who you think you are and where you think you are. And so we'll begin this morning with [Student H]. What are you, [Student H]?

[The student clears his throat.] *Excuse me. I'm a member of a species known as human race here on this planet. And as far as who am I—*

Then let us pause at that and ask, Who are they? If it is true that you believe that you are a member of a species known as a human race, then one must have some understanding of who they are, considering one believes they are that. Go ahead.

Yes.

Then who are they?

Well, they are, at least at this point in evolution, in charge of the other species on the planet. They have taken that position. They bear a great responsibility for the welfare of the planet.

And you believe you are a member of those who have taken over that responsibility, is that what you're telling me?

Yes.

I see. Go ahead.

Then therefore, it behooves me, being a member, to really understand who, who I am, who am I. That it's more than just the form that I'm inhabiting.

I see. Then let us ask our self the next question: Where are we? *[After a short pause, the teacher continues.]* When one asks themselves the question of "Where am I?" does the answer come that "I am, my physical being, that's where I am."

That's part of it.

And the other part?

The other part is, Where am I in consciousness? Am I joined with my physical being at this moment, right now? Or am I somewhere else? Is my attention on what I'm doing or is it somewhere else?

Do you understand that you are wherever your attention is?

Yes.

Do you accept that as a demonstrable truth?

I do.

Therefore, if you are where your attention is and your attention is not where your physical body is, then who or what is caring for your physical body?

Yes. That's a good question because it demonstrates that, that . . .

If you are not in your physical body to take care of the various needs of the limited form, then who is present taking care of that responsibility?

Well, the problem is the door is left open for almost anyone or anything to come into that responsibility.

And when you return how do you feel?

Not too good.

Now this is very important for all of us to understand when you are not present some *thing* or someone *is* present.

Therefore, the question must rise in your consciousness, "Who or what is the thing that is using my body when I am not present?" Then one must ask the question, once they investigate and understand that some *thing* or someone else is caring for their body, they must ask the question, "Who is that someone? Who is that some *thing*? And how well am I informed on their true motive and their true purpose for using the body which I alone am responsible for?"

Now when you, through a lack of awareness of your form by an over-identification somewhere else, when at those times—and you have just stated you don't feel well when you return. Did you feel well when you left?

No.

And so you returned as you left.

Yes, if not worse.

If not worse. Now why do you think that happens and how do you think that's happening?

Because I did not demonstrate the care and consideration for my body when I left, and therefore I merited someone or something who demonstrates the very same thing. Because the demonstration is evident upon my return that I had messed up and made mistakes. By being away, I demonstrated a lack of responsibility. And I may have to account for actions for which I don't really enjoy taking the responsibility for, but I have to upon my return.

Thank you. Now in these contracts that we have discussed at our last class and in these experiences, as students, that you have daily, whoever is easily tempted is one who easily leaves their body to whatever chooses to enter it. For temptation, being a weakness of the direction of the power of will, a weakness in respect to one's not using the faculty of reason and guiding the power of the will accordingly, then one is easily tempted and, therefore, loses control over that which they are responsible for.

No one, of course, is lacking in the power of what you understand as will. The problem lies in the direction of the power, for the power is what you are; the energy is what you are. It is what you have always been. It is what you will always be. The direction of that is, of course, in keeping with your evolution, and what you have already done affects what you are doing, as what you are doing is already affecting of what you are yet to do.

And so whenever the effort is not made daily to ask those most important questions—as an opening to the light of reason, so that the form that you are responsible for does as you guide and tell it to do, so that you may have more beneficial experiences in life. For example, when that which you have the greatest responsibility for does not respond according to your guidance, there is no possible way for anyone to expect that experiences, successes, happiness, and good will respond to their wishes or their dictates. It is not possible for that which they have, in evolution, earned as their greatest responsibility, the form in which they presently reside, when that does not respond, there is no way to expect that forms created are going to respond. Do you understand that?

Yes.

Now. Encouragement, as I've spoken many times, is something to identify with. For whoever makes the effort to encourage themselves establishes the necessary laws of the good that they are seeking. For all of your life, each moment reveals what you're doing with the mental world that you believe that you are. We spend so much time on a mental world for so much time is spent by people, by students on your planet identified with the mental world.

Obstructions in life cast their shadows. That's all that a shadow is. A shadow is only an obstruction to what you are. And so when you permit that which you are to believe in the flesh and the bone, when you permit this power and this energy that you are to be directed by your will to believing that you are the obstruction, you are the limit, when you permit yourself to believe that, you become it. You become the shadow that it casts. And so one shadow becomes two, and they multiply by the moment. And then a person, one day, awakens and finds that their life is a mist; that it's difficult to see the way; that it is such a struggle to enjoy life; that life is filled with so much discord and so many trials and tribulations. For you have identified and believed that you are the obstruction and, therefore, must experience what the obstruction has to offer: the shadows of life. The shadowland, the world of mist, where it's difficult to see a foot, let alone to see a mile.

Now we've spoken many times that fools quit before the victory. Fools are fools for they believe they are the obstruction and cannot see beyond a foot in the land of mist; they cannot see the mile for they believe they are the obstruction and can only experience the shadows.

Now let us have some questions on that truth: "What am I? Who am I? And where am I?"

You have a desire to accomplish something, and you find, through all of your efforts, it seems to begin to appear, then it disappears. You seem to be getting close to your goal only the next moment to believe that you're farther from your goal, for you believe you are the obstruction. And so an obstruction to that which you are, the Light, an obstruction casts its shadow ever in keeping with the Light as it moves in its perfect circle. And so you take the light of the sun, for that, too, is the Light that you are, and as you view the sun move in its perfect circle, obstructions to its movement cast their shadows in many different ways. But they all cast their shadows. Sometimes a shadow is very short. Sometimes a shadow is very long. The shadow is still cast in keeping with the obstruction that is between what you are and what you believe that you are.

And so with your day-to-day moments and activities, as that which you are, the moving Light on the perfect circle of eternal life, all of these obstructions are in the way of your light. And that is where the student trips and falls, for he believes he is the obstruction and experiences the ever-changing, fleeting shadows that the obstruction he believes that he is casts at various times of your so-called day.

Now you have many, many laws, spiritual laws, that have been revealed to you to free yourself from these so-called traps along your path as you move through creation. They all serve their purpose when you serve them. When you serve your affirmations, your affirmations serve you. And when you don't, they don't serve you at all.

Now at any time during your day, your experiences—you see, you say that [at] night, there is no light. That is not true. Night is a lesser light. Night is when you, the Light, in its movement on its perfect circle, enters the area of density of the obstructions known as creation, and that density is so great that there's little light to be aware of. And so you call that night. Some people have their nights at 10 a.m. Some at 3 a.m. Some at midnight. Some at 4 in the afternoon. For obstructions without number, people permit themselves to identify with at any time in a 24-hour period. And so at the time when you look and you see, "Oh, it's now nighttime," yes, the light has moved; and in respect to creation and the mass of limit or forms, you now say you are experiencing night. Yet you experience the same night in consciousness irrespective of the time of day of your physical, material world. You experience the night of your soul or the night, the obstructions to the Light that you are, when you fill your mind with many things. And each time you fill your mind with more things, you only increase the so-called darkness of the night. Therefore, a cleansing process is necessary to cleanse out what's in there so that the laws that reveal the path of the Light may enter.

Each time you receive a new law that's revealed to you, it tries to enter into your consciousness through all of these forms that you believe that you are. Yet you have been given the very things, so many of them, the very laws to free yourself from that, for you're constantly moving on this great circle.

One of the most important affirmations given to free you from identification with an obstruction in your consciousness [was given] some time ago:

All that has been cannot be
That's not Good and I'm not free
Until I give then I be
The joy of life that sets me free.

[For a variation of this affirmation, please see the appendix.]
And yet, you see, why we have difficulty with that is, first of all, it sounds very nice. Then the forms that we believe we are say, "Well, that's not really going to work." Never given it a chance anyway. It says that (those forms of your mind) because it already knows that for its cousins it's worked beautifully, and it doesn't want to go that route, to put it bluntly. This is why it tells you, "Well, that really won't work anyway." And you don't even give it half a chance. Well, you don't even give it a quarter of a chance. It works. Those things work for those are laws. Those are laws. And the Light is far greater than the shadows and the obstructions, for the Light sustains them. And that which sustains anything in life is greater than that which is sustained. So no matter how many obstructions you believe you are and, therefore, live in experiences of the shadow world, don't ever forget that that which you are is the very power that sustains them so that they may exist at all.

This is why to look at obstructions, which are creations to what you are, and, by looking at obstructions, establish the law in believing that you are them and, therefore, experience the shadows that they cast to that which you are, to look at it in an adverse way is only a guarantee to become more attached to it. One does not escape anything by becoming adverse to it. To think that it's possible to escape something because you don't like it only guarantees the day that you will love it. So that's obviously not the way, for you direct energy to it and, therefore, make it even greater for you.

Therefore, one looks at obstruction, recognizes it for what it is, knows beyond a shadow of any doubt it is something they have, in ignorance, created and accept[s] responsibility for their own creation and, therefore, move[s] on to the next step. And that's through the soul faculty and the path of encouragement. For each time you permit yourself to identify with dissatisfaction, to identify with sorrow, to identify with pity, each time you permit yourself to identify with discouragement, you only have more experiences of like kind in order to prove to you beyond a shadow of any doubt how right that you are.

So when you want to be right—and everyone wants to be right for everyone has their own judgment of what right is. You see, we desire to be right for, through the Law of Association in our mental world, we associate right with superior. And therefore, we associate superior with feeling good. And because we—that is, a person who believes they are limit and in order to feel better than limit, one must therefore believe that they are superior. So one views all out there and says, "Oh, look at those poor, pathetic souls." And therefore, one feels superior, supposedly believing at their expense when it's at their own expense. Now I hope that's helped there along that.

And we're going to take time now here for some of your questions. *[After a short pause, the teacher continues.]* No questions? Then—I don't like to use that word, but I will because some of you relate to it—[it's] interrogation time. I don't expect to do all the work myself. And who do I have back here this morning? Is that—you know, there's a light greater than those spotlights on me. I can tell you that right now. *[To aid in the video recording, the teacher had spotlights directed at him, which may have interfered with his ability to physically see his students.]* Yes, speak up, please.

Ah—

That's [Student U]. Thank you.

Thank you. How is it that salt purifies the forms we temporarily believe we are?

Well, what does the mineral salt offer to your world of salt?

It's used as a preservative.

Yes. What does it preserve?

Form.

What form?

Meats. Fish.

Meats and fish?

Yes, sir.

Well, isn't that what most people believe they are, a combination of meat and fish? *[A few students laugh.]*

Yes, sir.

I mean, in your world on the earth realm, isn't that what you refer to your people as?

Yes.

Either meat or fish? Or am I incorrect in my investigation of your planet?

No, sir.

And the species on it. Well, go ahead with your discussion. Hmm? *[After a pause, the teacher continues.]* You were talking about preserving meat and fish. Is that correct?

That's correct.

And what do you use for that preservation of meat and fish?

Salt.

And now what was your question that you had? I prefer my students to answer their own questions when they start thinking.

Yes, sir. I—

Yes.

The, the question was, How is it that salt is used to purify the forms that we temporarily believe we are?

Well, didn't you just get through answering your question?

Yes, sir.

Well, tell me what your answer was.

My answer was that it preserves meat and fish.

Well, are you meat or fish? You have meat and fish, don't you?

Yes.

You know, if I—really, here, I think we ought to have a clear understanding. I'm looking out there at my students and in your terminology, I see fish and I see meat. Are we relating? *[A few students laugh.]*

Yes.

And then you want to know in what way salt preserves it? When you know very well that salt preserves it. Now stop and think. Let's take that a little step farther; perhaps help you there. You believe you are meat. And you believe that lady in front of you, I think it's [Student M] here, is fish. Right?

Right.

I mean, isn't that what you believe?

Right.

She's of, she's of the same human race, but she's the female species and you're the male. Right?

Right.

And in your world, you call that meat and fish. Is that correct?

That's correct.

Terrible combination. Did you ever smell it when it's combined? *[Some students laugh.]* But anyway, and so we're talking about preservation there, aren't we?

Yes.

All right. Fine. Life is just beautiful in your world. It really is, when you understand it. Now you ask the question, How does salt preserve the forms that humans create? Is that correct?

That's correct.

Well, it does it the way it always does it. You have a thought. You release from your being—you're meat, right?—all right, you release from your being a part of your being in the creating of the form. Do you understand?

Yes.

And so you want to preserve that, is that correct?

Yes.

Well, give it a little salt of your life and then you'll understand you've totally answered your question. Anyone else have a question? Is there any further question about that? *[After another short pause, the teacher again continues.]* [Student U]?

Not at this time.

Not publicly or not at this time. A little heavy there. Any other questions? Yes, [Student S], please.

We've been told and I'd like to know if it's correct if you take an object and bury it in salt it helps neutralize the vibrations. Is that correct and how would that work?

Well, let us say this—because here's one question dealing with forms and creation, and here's another question dealing with forms protected from creation. So we have two basic different questions here. Now you're speaking to me about a form that has been what you call buried or taken away from association with other forms of like kind. Is that what you're talking to me about?

Yes.

Well, the removal of it, of course, is the salt of preserving it. You see, for example, if there is not an interchange between the forms of like kind, then there is a preservation of the form that is removed from it.

Thank you.

In other words, you know, our contamination is ever dependent upon our exposure. Would that help with your question? As exposure frees the soul, it contaminates the form. Does that help with your question?

Yes, it does. Thank you.

Yes, is that [Student Y], this morning?

Yes.

It's interesting how the path opened up, and this [is] not so blinding here now. [Student Y], you speak right up.

Yes.

A little change in the light, in the atmosphere. Yes, go ahead.

I would like to know when you put the four lower centers and the four higher centers on a round sphere, do they—is it, is the concept that they're circular in connection?

All lines are circular. All connect. And they pass through, as well as around. Did that help with that question?

Somewhat.

Well, what's, what's the rest of it?

Oh. I wanted to know—so they, so in their, in their circular, they return to one another. Right?

That is correct.

OK.

That is correct. Now think round. Don't think flat. Because when you think flat, you have confusion there, you see. You must learn to think in a dimensional [way], not flat.

OK.

Hmm?

Yes. Thank you.

You're welcome. Is that [Student U] this morning?

Yes, it is.

I thought I was going to get a call on cars here, but go right ahead. Now where's my student that's all thinking about their automobile this morning? Where are you [Student N]? Yes, now you give it to God there. Your automobile.

OK. [Student N responds.]

And you'll feel a lot better, and you'll get much more out of the class because we haven't got to the point of classes on automobiles yet. Do you understand? I don't think the other students would care for that. There's so many different models nowadays in your world. Where's this [Student U] here? Now you, you talk to God about that. All right now let's go on. What is it?

What—why is truth at the equator?

Truth?

Yes.

Well, what is the equator?

The balance.

You define the equator on your planet to me and then I'll explain to you how it is.

It's the line that separates the northern hemisphere from the southern hemisphere.

And what does it do?

Bal—

What does the equator do? *[After a short pause, the teacher continues.]* Does it equate?

I, I don't know.

Well, who knows? Does the equator equate or doesn't the equator equate? *[After another pause, the teacher again continues.]* Is that [Student O]?

Yes, sir.

What does the equator do?

I think the equator divides or separate[s].

Thank you. [Student R].

The equator, being in the center, would be the equal point or the equal portion of whatever it is. Being, being the equal point, would be the neutral point.

Does it equate?

Yes.

What does it equate?

It equates all parts.

Now that which equates all parts, wouldn't you consider that, [Student U], to be truth?

Yes, sir.

It leaves out nothing. Now what was your question?

It's been answered, sir.

Well, ask your question again. You see, my student, it's time you start doing a little homework.

Why is truth at the equator?

Well, you just got through explaining. The equator equates. It equates everything. Correct?

Correct.

Well, let's get to the equator of your consciousness where only truth can reside, for nothing is left out. That which leaves out no thing is all thing; therefore, there's nothing to discuss. That's truth. That help, [Student U]?

Yes, sir. Thank you.

All right. Any other questions this morning? *[After a short pause, the teacher continues.]* Didn't you people have any breakfast today? *[A few students laugh.]* You people had no breakfast today? I think we're going to have to serve steak and eggs or something like that. There's no energy down here. All right. I'll just take a little nap here if there's no energy. *[A few more students laugh.]* Yes, [Student M].

Yes. I have a question. In removing the obstructions which we believe we are . . .

Yes?

. . . we've been given various steps. [The student clears her throat.] *Excuse me. And those are mental beliefs. Where does the heart come in? You know, when we believe something that's, like,*

that seems very powerful in our heart, that's the, that's the, the same thing as our mind and it goes to our heart.

Most interesting statement. Thank you, [Student M]. We desire with our mind. We care with our heart. So in reference to your statement, when you believe you love in your heart, try to understand, you're talking about desire of your mind. Heart has nothing to do with it.

The heart is a vehicle through which the soul expresses itself. Now you show me one soul in all of the universes that has within it the denial of goodness or God. Only the mind could do such a thing. No, that does not exist in the soul. The soul is. And the soul knows that it is, beyond a shadow of any doubt. The soul expresses through the heart. One cares for many things in creation. And if it is care, true care, it's from the heart. It doesn't dictate how little care, how much care; it doesn't have to dictate. And so if we will understand and separate truth from creation and demonstrate—desire is of the mind; care is of the heart, an expression of the soul. Does that help with your question?

Thank you.

So, you see, it's like a person says, "Well, I really do care for my son. However, reason reveals he would be better off and have a much better life if I gave him to this other lady over here who could do much more for him." Now if a person really cared, as an expression of their little soul, then they would take their little, little son and they'd give them to the lady over there because they really cared for their little son. Now if they say, "Well, I love my son. There's no way possible I can do that," they're talking to me about the mind: desire and need and the denial of God and goodness. Does that help with your question?

Yes.

I hope so.

Thank you.

Thank you. Yes, who do we have here back there this morning?

It's [Student D].

Well, [Student D]. Now these chairs, I think what we'll have to do, [Student D], next Sunday here—they're not properly arranged. We'll move them more to right, which will be to your left. And I want the directors to be aware of that, please. Now we'll make room, because I can see that my student [Student J] could move over a little, not right now, though. And [Student S] and on down the line. We kind of spread it so that we can see out thataway, see? All right, you go right ahead, [Student D].

If a person has taken desire and focused it, taken it from God and focused it on something, say, to spend time with someone, is need in that desire at that point?

[During] the time that they desire to be with someone, is there any need? Is that what you're asking me, [Student D]?

Need and desire.

Oh, there's nothing but need. It's so filled with need that one even believes it's love, at times, you know. You see, if you fill your consciousness with enough need, you will convince yourself that you're in love. Do you understand that?

Ah...

Not yet.

No.

Well, first of all, you must flood your consciousness with denial in order to experience the insatiable drive of desire to the point that you call it love. Pardon?

Yes, I understand.

I mean, you know, when a person says—I hear many people say, "Well, I just love that person there." But I never once hear them say, "Oh, I love that cloud that's passing by. How beautiful it is. I love that little flower there. I love that little ant crawling over there." I never hear them convince themselves of how much they love the cloud that's passing by. Have you?

Well, sometimes I find myself in that situation.

Freed from need?

Well, loving—

What happens when the cloud goes by? What happens when the cloud passes you?

Then it's gone.

But what happens to your need?

Well, if it hasn't been given up, I guess it follows the car.

Doesn't leave you feeling very good, does it?

No.

What if a storm comes up and blows the cloud away real fast while you're sitting there enjoying filling your need for it? What happens then? Are you angry at the storm that did it?

I don't know.

Well, now that's very important that we discuss these things because they apply in principle to all of our experiences in life. Yes. Anyone else have a question here this morning? *[After a short pause, the teacher continues.]* Well, I'm almost convinced it's time for my nap here. [Student Y].

Is the fourth dimension, is that the out reaching of the circle? Would that be the fourth dimension, that plane that . . .

No, [Student Y], go in. Don't go out.

OK.

You're correct. The direction is wrong.

Thank you.

All right? The most difficult things to find are the most valuable. And the reason they're so difficult to find is because they're inside. Yes, [Student J].

In relation to the circle, when we draw the lines, they don't seem to intersect, unless it's beyond our vision or beyond the paper that we're using. And yet you told a student that the intersection is the celestial. At what point do they intersect?

They intersect at the point of your consciousness. Now, for example, the finest way: one of my students did take a recommendation from that class and [got] a little ball. Now I want you to talk to that student after class. And I did guide them and help them at their request, and you will find that it not only intersects perfectly, when it's done correctly, and hers is done very close to correctly. Although in your world you cannot, unless you use your imaging, your imagination, pass the lines through the sphere or the ball as well as on the surface because you're looking at a flat dimension. And in order to experience the other dimension, you're going to have to move in consciousness and visualize it. But you will see that they do interconnect, [Student J].

Thank you, sir.

Yes. And my student has permission to show that to you.

Thank you.

Yes. Privately. And because, you see, once you've got it on a ball, then you can see it all around. But the step from that point is to visualize it passing through, because that's what it does. I know it is difficult to perceive because we're used to thinking flat. And we're used to going step-by-step and not seeing the whole thing from a different perspective. I would say the best perspective to have is—what do they call it?—you need an airplane view. You know. You like to look down anyway.

Yes, sir.

And out. Not just down. I'm happy to say that you like to look out, too. A lot of people like to look down. A few like to look out. You do like to look down and out and up. Because, you know, down and out isn't the best vibration to be looking, wouldn't you say, [Student J]?

Yes, sir.

So let's look—you know, we know we're already thinking flat. You know what thinking flat is? Down and out. That's a flat dimension. Up is a next dimension. So whenever you're tempted to look down, remember, you're going to be out, down and out. And so don't forget to go up. All right? *[Several students laugh.]*

Yes, sir. Thank you.

Yes. Let's forget this duality business of down and out. And let's move down, out, and up. All right? Good. Someone else have a question there? What happened to my student [Student I] there? Is that [Student A] speaking to me this morning?

Oh, yes, I have a question. [Student A responds.]

Good for you. You did have a question. You see, I know, [Student A]. Now here, my chair's in the same spot. Yes, my chair's fine. You're moved too far over that way. Someone tried to move you out the door. I want you moved back over this way. We'll get this corrected. I can't even see your face there this morning here. Hmm? And I could last week. So I know the chair's [moved] for sure. All right, you speak up, [Student A].

Yes.

Yes.

I was wondering about the questions that we're supposed to be asking ourselves.

Yes?

What we are? Where we are? And who we are?

Well, I think the question was, What are you? Who are you? and Where are you? You want to be sure and figure out what you are to know who you are before you understand where you are. Thank you. Go ahead, [Student A].

Excuse me. So it's very important to ask those questions in that sequence.

Oh, indeed. It's like down and out and up.

OK.

Did that help you?

Yes, it does.

You see, I find students who think flat are down and out. And I find students who think round are down, out, and up. There is a difference. So I have many flat-heads and a few round ones. *[The teacher and several students laugh.]*

I would like to know, Should we pause to be at peace before we ask this question of our self?

Well, certainly. And in that pause, say that wonderful affirmation "All that has been cannot be, / That's not Good and I'm not free." *[For the complete text of this affirmation, please see the appendix.]* You see, first of all, you're aware that you're not free, so why not declare the truth and get free?

Right.

Wouldn't you agree, [Student A]?

Yes.

Yes, it seems to me that would be a practical thing. And it's like my good student, Isa, my channel's mother, she said, "Oh, yes," she says, "Down and out seems to do about everybody. But there are a few who have decided to move up." Hmm? *[Isa Goodwin is Mr. Goodwin's mother. She would regularly instruct, guide, and correct the students through Mr. Goodwin's mediumship.]*

Now I'm going to remind my channel when he's speaking to a flat-head and when he's speaking to a round-head. And so if he doesn't spend much time with you, you know that your flat-headed, at least at that time. Hmm?

Now I'm quite serious now. Let's get these vibrations up. There's plenty of down-and-outers. You would think there was a depression. In fact, there is a depression. It's a depression in consciousness. It's almost got to the point of a compression. Forget the depression. *[The teacher and many students laugh.]* I don't like being compressed. I like to expand. I have a lot to expand.

So when you're round, you're expanding.

When you're round-headed, you're expanding. I didn't say expanded. Hopefully I wouldn't be that foolhardy. No. You are in the process of expanding. Hmm? With so much interest in expansion, wouldn't you think a person would start with their consciousness? I mean, especially in your country where everybody wants everything bigger and better—and that's expansion, you see. Everyone wants everything bigger and better. Wouldn't you think they would start in their own consciousness and get it bigger and better? Hmm?

That's right.

Yes. All right?

Uh-huh.

Do you know why the mind desires things bigger? And judges it's better? Do you know why? *[After a short pause, the teacher continues.]* Would you like to know why, [Student A]?

Yes, I would.

Well, because in the consciousness it is associated with luxury and laziness. Hmm?

Ah.

That's why the mind wants things bigger and better. It means they can just not have to move a finger or do anything, just kind of lie back and relax, like a—

But when we're doing that, we're—

Not like a lizard, they're very active. Like a toad. Yes?

When we're doing that, we're not working for the Light.

Oh, we're working for something.

That's right. We're working for the prince—

It takes energy to sleep and feed all those forms, [Student A]. Didn't you know that?

Yes.

Well, it takes energy. Certainly. Working like little beavers. I find people sleep and snore away. And I find them wake up totally exhausted, you see. Hmm? Slow awakeners [are] totally exhausted because they've worked so hard all the time they've been unconscious. Now did [Student B] have a question there? *[After a short pause, the teacher continues.]* I saw a hand up back there.

I didn't put up my hand. Maybe somebody—

All right. Whoever has their hand up, speak up. Yes, who is that? [Student D]?

Yes, it is.

Yes, it is. All right.

Is the fourth dimension within us the expanding consciousness? And is it reflected in the outer world by the expanding universe?

Yes, of course. You see, it, it exists within us. We are the microcosm of the macrocosm. Whatever happens to the universe of which you are aware, you can be rest assured you're responsible for. Because it reacts to you. You see, as your body, which is limit, reacts to a thought that you entertain within your mind, so the planets in your universe react accordingly. Do you understand that?

Yes.

And so man's responsibility isn't limited to the limit that he believes that he is. His responsibility in the entering of form—when man entered form, man's responsibility is basically the form of which he is aware, but his responsibility, also, is for all of the forms that surround him, for he is a part of the whole in that responsibility. Do you understand that?

Yes.

All right. [Student H], you have a question, please.

Yes. Thank you. When we ultimately have to ask ourselves the question, "What have I accomplished?" can we answer that question by asking the three questions that were given today?

Well, you cannot honestly answer the latter question—the first question until you've answered the other three. You cannot answer what you have accomplished when you are asked, and you *are* asked, "What have I accomplished?" because, you see, you have a record. And you've got to carry back with you your accomplishments. You have contracts that you are committed to. You have contracts.

And so when you're in the Great Rotunda and the question is asked you, "What have you accomplished in your journey on earth?" you have to answer. You have to answer. But how are you going to know what you have accomplished if you don't know who you are? If you don't know what you are, you don't know who you are, and you don't know where you are, how are you going to be prepared to answer that question? You will not be prepared. This is why I'm spending the time and following our class of last week: under contract. You can prepare yourself. You see, you see, it isn't a matter of, "Well, when I get there I'll prepare myself." No, when you get there, you'll spend centuries in trying to waken up to find out what you must prepare yourself for. You prepare yourself now. Then you don't—you have no interest or concern about tomorrow, for you know what tomorrow is. You know what tomorrow is.

You see, it's just like my student, [Student N], back there. If she'd stop worrying about a car, she'd feel good. Do you understand that, [Student N]?

Yes.

But, you see, as long as you insist on putting mental substance in the way, you're going to experience nothing but obstructions. Do you understand that?

Yes.

Now try to understand, anything you bring into your life through the concentration camp of creation and there's nothing but obstructions in bringing it through, you can be rest assured you've got a problem. You've got a real problem. Because, you see, God, good, isn't in it; concern is in it. And be rest assured of what you're going to get back from it. Now all of you have had experiences, rather with people or things: in putting concern over something, you establish the law and guarantee to prove how right you are that you were concerned in the first place. Yes. Now you had a question, [Student H]. [Student L] has a question.

Yes. In, in speaking forth what I have accomplished, would that refer only to spiritual growth? [Student L asks her question.]

Why, what do you mean by that, would only refer to spiritual—

Where I was when I left and what I have learned while I'm here or—

What you have learned—spiritual growth—creation is an instrument through which you awaken. You see, you see, creation serves a wonderful purpose to an awakened soul. It constantly says, "Come follow me and believe that you are me and you will have everything." So creation offers you a constant reminder so that you may continue to spiritually grow. How do you suppose a person feels, you know, right in the midst of a satisfaction, [who] says, "Oh, this isn't me. This is something else." Well, that takes spiritual awakening, you see. *[The teacher laughs joyfully.]* It kind of puts a damper on the satisfaction of the senses, wouldn't you think?

It sure does.

You know, well, in the midst of it you step aside, you see, and pet the dog or something. [You] say, "That's interesting over there. And I really thought that was me. My, isn't that interesting how those forms are getting satisfied?" Well, you know, how many of you are making that effort? I don't find you making that effort, midstream. Well, that's the only time that it's really effective. When you really want something, which is an expression of your blatant and absolute denial that you have it, stop [and] say no. Yes, [do so]. Or step aside and say, "Well, aren't you interesting doing that strange number over there? Why, I never even saw dogs act like that." Yes, step aside and tell the form that, and see how you grow.

And I see our time is moving. So you best be quickly with your questions. Are you not aware there, [Student R], that time is passing? Yes. Any questions before I take my rest? Yes, [Student S].

Could you please relate for us this expanding consciousness and the concept about going, the idea about going within to the center of what we really are to increase the spin to go within?

Well, the only way that that's going to be possible—and this is our last question I can answer—the only way that's going to be possible is when the mind is controlled to such an extent it totally refrains—he doesn't like me taking off this microphone *[The teacher refers to the technician recording the class.]*—totally refrains from the belief in all those things.

Thank you and have a very nice day. I see our time is passed.

SEPTEMBER 1, 1985

A/V Class Private 13

Good morning, students.

For our discussion today, to question what we believe we are is to accept the possibility of being something better than what we have been. It is a traumatic and necessary step in our evolution. And so to help us and guide us in making that step, you have received many exercises and affirmations.

What is it that is really taking place? Well, let us go to one of the exercises you were given so many years ago: to look at a cloud. And what do you see when you look at the cloud? The cloud takes the form of the strongest desire in the deeper consciousness.

And so it is when you speak a word, the word is power when the form that rises in the mind is equal to the word that is spoken. For example, you speak the word *happy*. Everyone believes that they desire to be happy. Everyone believes they have a right to be happy. And so you speak the word *happy* and many different things come up into your mind.

A necessary exercise is to look at the cloud, for you'll have no problem finding one. You don't necessarily need to look to the sky to find a cloud. We all seem to have a special talent in finding the clouds on any day regardless of the weather. So you look at the cloud in your mind and you speak forth the word *happy*. And you will find that cloud transformed into what you believe has already made you happy. You will also find, in that exercise, that what you believe has made you happy is dependent upon someone outside of you. You will find in those many visions that rise in your mind's eye that first it was this experience and then it was that. And each and every one of those experiences ended up contrary to the way that they started.

Now that would, of course, seem to be contrary to the very teachings that you are studying. For you have these experiences, you have these visions of what made you happy, but you also have associated with those experiences that that which you believed made you happy left you, finally, in a state that you believe is unhappy. Therefore, you will find from this daily exercise that when you speak the word *happy*, you are unhappy when you speak the word. Therefore, in keeping with the law that like attracts like, your final experience is one of being unhappy. Therefore, when you permit yourself to think and to speak the word that you need to be happy, what you are actually doing is declaring the Law of Unhappiness that will not fail you. So we find in our experiences, we say, "I only want to be happy," only to end up with a temporary deception.

Man, then, understanding how clear and infallible the law is, declares the truth: "I am happy. At moments I am tempted to believe that I am not happy for I am tempted by denial of what I am." You will soon realize beyond a shadow of all doubt that whenever you permit your mind to declare that you are unhappy or that you are in need of anything, you will establish by that very law that which is necessary for you to grow, to evolve, and be what you are: free, happy, and the joy of living.

These many exercises given to you, at times, I am aware, that some of you believe what a thought in your mind declares: that for you they do not work; they absolutely do not work. I assure you that in your world of creation whatever you convince yourself of, whatever you believe in, in a world of creation, works for you. For all of your experiences are revealing to you whatever you believe is what is working for you. So when you believe that a particular affirmation or a cleansing breath or any of the various spiritual exercises given to you, when you permit yourself to declare for you they do not work, you may be rest assured *for you* they cannot work. For you are the obstruction standing in your own Light.

Now a house divided cannot stand. A house divided cannot even be successful, unless, in keeping with the law, you understand that failure is success. Many, many people, in fact, all people are successful. Some say they are a failure; they reveal to themselves and to the world how successful they are in believing that something for them will not work. And so in that sense they are indeed a successful failure. Some people are more successful failures than other people. Then there are those who are successful successes.

And so I am interested here, today, as I have always been, in success, the success of living, the success of joy and happiness and abundant good. To speak that life is as you take it, of course, is truth. To apply that life is as you take it is entirely something else. For none of us want to pause and to think that this day, such a beautiful day—it is beautiful to some levels of consciousness, and it is miserable to other levels of consciousness. So, of course, it is dependent on what level we wish to identify [with] at any moment. Now it is not possible for anyone to believe until they identify, for identification and belief are inseparable.

Many of you over the years have been interested in, "Where am I going?" Well, "Who am I? What am I? and Where am I?" is a question that we should all be asking our self. "What have I accomplished?" is a question that we should be asking our self. When we tell our self, "I'll never do this," or "I'll never do that," we only guarantee the experience. A wise man does not say never. A wise man does not say, "I will not do this; I will not do that," for he only lives to experience the day when he does it with a joyous heart. For, you see, my friends, the separation of truth from creation—what you are and not what you believe that you are—that's what's important.

You have experiences that you consider are so miserable. And you look and see that things are so discouraging. You say, at times, you cannot help yourself. Well, what is using your mouth cannot help itself. I assure you of that, for it's totally dependent on what you give to it. It cannot help itself. No thought of its mind can—of your mind can help itself. It's dependent on what you give to it. The more you give to it, the more it can help itself.

If you give nothing to it, through the Law of Identification, it cannot do anything.

So if you speak forth that this doesn't work for you and that doesn't work for you, you guarantee that it cannot work for you. There's no way possible that it can, for it is contrary to the very law of the divine right of choice. When you choose an obstruction, no one, not even God, can move it for you. You see, my friends, that would be contrary to the Law of Personal Responsibility. You must understand and realize your right to choose the obstructions in your life. You must also realize and accept the divine law that no one can do it for you. It is your obstruction that you choose. There's no one [who] can remove it for you. They may guide you to the path of wisdom where you may accept personal responsibility for your life and accept, "Yes, indeed, I have placed this obstruction in my path in life. I alone have placed it there. I alone can and shall remove it someday. Let that someday be today."

Whatever you want in life is a realization of your denial of it. Whatever you say that you need and desire is an awakening for you to grow and say, "Yes, I have denied this. Therefore, I have a need for it by believing I don't have it." We believe so many things, for we identify with so many things. But it's *we* who are doing it.

When you leave this little limited form and you see the many forms of the many realms, as long as you identify with yourself, then you can only see realms of forms. Now some of you have expressed a desire to have some classes without forms, without creation. Well, we're all going to pause for a moment and rise to the state of consciousness where everything is a movement of color and vibration. First, we must accept that's what we are in truth. We're not flesh. We're not bone. We're not hair. We're not blood. We are that which is using all of that. So if you want classes and discussions of what you really are, then you must first make the effort to accept the possibility that you are not a finger; you are not a toe; you are not an eyeball; you are not a nostril; and you are not a thumb. And when you accept that, then we can pause in consciousness for a moment and we can realize, slowly but surely, that we are a movement; we are energy itself; we are the golden Light.

And as it moves and as it gains speed and frequency, varying colors begin to appear. Now from those colors, they spin off into the universe. And when they reach another spinning universe of what you call another soul and another person, and those colors come in contact, they either harmonize, and the unity and the power of itself, the realization awakens, or it reaches a soul on a different state of evolution in its spinning expression and those colors do not harmonize and you have an obstruction. Now from the obstruction, you begin to experience varying colors taking shape and form. And this, most of you identify with and believe that you are: that which has met an obstruction. And from the obstruction a form, a vapor, is gradually created, and you believe that you are that. That's the electromagnetic vibration or frequency in its expression.

And so if you want to move to those realms of consciousness, you first must make the effort to accept you are not the thoughts of your mind. And when you move and apply that demonstrable truth, then we can discuss more thoroughly and more fully what you really are and how you come to identify with what you are not.

Because it is the law, the Law of Magnetism, to attract, man finds himself in a constant process of attraction or temptation. What we permit our self to be attracted to reveals, of course, our evolution of our own being. And so the day comes in this great eternity when we say, "I've had enough attraction. I'm going to start doing something. I've had enough reacting in my life. I'm going to start acting. I'm going to give that a chance in my life, to experience consciously what my next moment shall be in keeping with the law of the unity of my own consciousness."

Now I've given you this little exercise for today, for this week, hopefully, for the rest of your earthly experience and on, to speak forth the word, to be aware of what rises in your mind, for that tells you everything about what you believe you are at the moment of the exercise itself. It is a personal experience, for you still believe that you are personal. You still believe and establish the law of what will work for you and what will not work for you. When the law clearly tells us: all things work for him who want them to work for them.

Now it's time for the question time. And so I will speak to you as you raise your hands. *[After a pause, the teacher continues.]* And I always find it so interesting that the hands get so heavy when it comes time for our morning classes. I sometimes question if the work for the hands is too heavy, perhaps we should consider dispensing with breakfast; it seems to weigh the arms down. Yes, my student here, [Student J].

Sir, does this exercise you just gave us relate to the fountain exercise?

Indeed, it does. The fountain exercise. The cloud exercise. And it's a step beyond it. Absolutely. You have practiced that. I am aware of that. You know how it works. Are there any further questions on that, [Student J]?

Not at this moment. Thank you.

Yes, it definitely works. And does someone else have a question here? Who is that?

[Student L].

Yes, please speak up. You can see me so well that you blind me, it seems. Go right ahead and speak up.

It, it seems that when we work the, the spheres around the globe that we are, you know, like from the earth to the odic and so forth . . .

Yes?

The loops are various sizes. And it, it—is it that they spin when they're shorter? If it's a smaller circle, does it spin at a higher vibration in a faster . . .

Yes, indeed it does for when it is at the proper spin, they're all equal.

Oh.

It is your perspective.

I see.

It's not the sphere itself. It is your own perspective of it.

I see.

Does that help with your question, [Student L]?

Yes. Thank you.

Yes, [does] someone else there had a question? Who is it? You just speak right up until I can get all of this lighting adjusted. And before you speak—I think, is that [Student N]?

Yes.

I thought so. Well, you just wait for a moment. I want to share this with you. You know, over these several weeks we've had, in your realm, quite a bit of what you would consider struggle and difficulty in bringing to you quality filming. Quality. And so I want to share a little bit here with you in keeping with spiritual understanding. I had my channel speak to our cameraman here many times that for proper filming or imaging—because what you call filming is a recording of images, is what it is—that it is indispensable to the finest possible quality, the proper lighting; that light is the key to all recorded images. And without light, no image can be recorded. And so it is absolutely necessary for the best, finest quality recording of images or filmmaking to consider the light as the number one key, which it is.

And so because of the seeming struggle that you've been having in reference to recording the images of these classes so that you can relate with your world of image or your mental world, I sent to your world here on earth one of our technicians. He happened to be a student of mine of a long, long time ago.

And we had to send quite a distance for him. And so he came to your world and he reported back to me that, "I don't know," he says, "They don't know anything about image-making or recording." And I said, "Well, that's why I've called on you, for you to go down there and help them."

Well, the number one problem was quite simple: the little movie box there, that picture box, has to be directed, to set it up, to the highest possible source of light. Whether it's an artificial light that you must directly test it at or it is the sunlight itself, in order to get the best possible images. And so that's one of the first things that my student instructed our cameraman here to do. It was a big step. It was a big step because that isn't what was being done.

Light is critical. It's critical not only to what you are, for you are Light, it is critical and indispensable for recording the obstructions to the Light. You see, obstructions to the Light are what you call images. You see, this is why it's so important [with] filming and these things: because it reveals to you, once you pause to study, to apply, to understand, that what you believe you are is an obstruction to what you are. You are Light. Form is what you think you are because you are looking at the obstruction. And as long as you've—as long as you view the obstruction, you will believe that you are the limit.

And so it is in what you call your filmmaking. You direct your little picture box directly to the light itself, the strongest light available. Once you have done that and you set your proper lighting and your different filters create a different type of atmosphere—you see, what you don't seem to understand, and you will someday, is that in the atmosphere which your physical eyes do not see, unless it is recorded, the image is recorded on what you call film, there is the mixing of various colors. So it is critical that you have certain filters directed in certain ways; that you have certain light directed in certain ways if you want the best possible what you call video as the final result. So it reveals to you that by turning to the strongest light, you are freed from the obstruction or the limit that you believe that you are at any given moment.

You see, what is in your world, such as filmmaking, video, etc., has first come from our world. And when you understand the principle of the law that governs it, you will understand more about yourself. You see, you experience frustrations in your life by identifying with the obstructions in your life. And you deceive yourselves by believing that is the way to experience your happiness or the joy of living. So I hope that may have helped, sharing that little bit with you, that there must be light. And the brighter the light, the clearer are the obstructions. And so think of the obstruction and become it; the final result is total frustration.

Now, [Student N], I will come to your question.

Yes, I was wondering if the rhythmic cleansing breath was equal to the twenty-minute meditation.

Your rhythmic cleansing breath does not and should not be done for that long a time. Does that help with your question?

The, the video?

You're—No. You're talking about you're cleansing breath?

The rhythmic—the video sound . . .

Yes. You're able to sustain it for twenty minutes are you, without interruption?

No.

My channel does well to do that and he's been at it for forty-some years. Pardon? No. Your question is that there should—you should relax and experience that. You should do it for the time that is comfortable for you, for a forced growth is not a healthy growth, [Student N]. Do you understand?

Yes.

Is there any other question in reference to that?

Yes. I was asking in place of the twenty-minute meditation that we've had—

Yes?

—at, you know, a certain time each day.

Yes?

Can we do the rhythmic video instead?

It should be in addition, not instead. All right?

Yes. Thank you.

All right. Fine. And so we look at all of these things here this day: nice and peaceful. It's as peaceful and as enjoyable as you will permit it through your own conscious choice. Yes, [Student M], you have a question, please.

Yes. You had said that we're made up of color and sound.

We're not made up of. That's what we are. Everything else is made up of something; yes, that is true. Go right ahead, [Student M].

And we're magnetic and the color and sound—

Just a moment. I say you are magnetic and electric. I never said you were magnetic only.

Electric-mag—electromagnetic.

Well, that's electric and magnetic, yes. Yes, your form is quite magnetic, wouldn't you agree?

Yes.

Well, your mind may be something else. Go right ahead, [Student M].

And the combination—the electro—this is what I'm trying to understand: the electromagnetic—we're putting out things into the atmosphere. You said that we do not see the color in—

That's correct.

—in the atmosphere.

If we saw the color, we'd know the frequency. If we knew the frequency, then we could, with assurance, say, "Yes, this is my experience the next moment from now." Go ahead, [Student M].

OK. And some of which we attract is harmonious, the colors and the sounds.

Yes, that is correct.

Some of it is not. And obstructions are forms.

Correct.

Um...

Let us pause at this moment. Whatever obstructs the Light casts a shadow. Whatever you believe—do you follow that?—

Yes.

—is a shadow. That is known in your world as the world of *maya* or illusion. Do you understand that?

Yes.

Go right ahead with your question.

Now these forms that are created, if it's harmonious, there's forms created. If it is, if it is an obstruction, forms are created. Is that not true? There's always forms, in a sense, being created.

No. No. If it is harmonious, then it amalgamates and is absorbed.

OK. That was what I was trying to understand.

Did that help with your question?

Yes, it does. Thank you.

You see, here you have what you are, and here you have what you believe that you are. Here you have what you call creation, and that's what you believe that you are. But over here, what you are is not what you believe that you are. So, as I said earlier, whoever questions what they believe that they are accepts the possibility of evolving to something greater. And that something greater is what they are. You see, therefore, for that which you are, there is no obstruction; for that which you believe you are, it is known as the concentration camp of creation.

So it isn't a matter of just saying, "Well, I will no longer believe." For when you no longer believe, you no longer have obstruction. When you no longer have obstruction, you no longer have the shadows. [When] you no longer have the shadows, you're out of creation. Does that help with your question?

Yes, that does. Thank you.

You see, when the angel, sitting at the side of the Divine Spirit of Goodness, called God, when the angel made his decision—do you follow me?

Yes.

When he awakened to self and realized he was dependent upon what you call the Father for his very existence, when that happened, you see, he was offered that realm in keeping with the law that he had established. Now that realm was the realm of obstruction or limit, what you call creation. So he governs that realm. He governs it at the cost of believing, which is at the sacrifice of what he is. You see, the angel which fell is still an angel. From his belief, he is the obstruction.

You see, we believe; [then] we are bound. And when we are—when we believe, we are dependent, you see? So we depend from our beliefs upon limit and upon obstructions and, therefore, experience the shadow of the obstruction to what we are, which is the Light. And we have our trials and tribulations; we have our frustrations and the obstructions to what we think that we need in life. We wouldn't even think that we needed until we believe and, by belief, have the obstruction to what we are. We believe that we need because we identify with what we are not. Does that help you?

Very much so. Thank you.

You see. See, if you have experiences that you find distasteful and discordant, and you do not want yourself or your child exposed to them, then you must make the changes within your consciousness. You see, the cause of the experience—you experience the effect of the experience, you see. You have the—you have the effect. Correct?

Correct.

You don't like the effect.

Correct.

You want to change it.

Correct.

Correct?

Yes.

You cannot change another person. Correct?

Right.

You can change yourself. Correct?

Correct.

You know that you are the instrument through which this experience occurs. Correct?

Correct.

Even though it's expressed through another person. Correct?

Correct.

Therefore, it is *you* who can make the change and, therefore, no longer have the experience. That help with your question?

Thank you.

Yes, I do feel that's what your question was about. And who has their hand up there, please?

It's [Student L].

No, the lady in the back here.

It's [Student D].

Is that [Student D]?

Yes, it is.

Oh, [Student D], I'll get you located someday soon.

I'm fine. Thank you.

Yes. Yes. You speak right up, [Student D].

I have the audio rhythmic cleansing breath. Sometimes I feel I wish it was longer. Is it possible to run it back and do it one more time? [The tones used in the rhythmic cleansing breath on the audio cassette tape were about four minutes long, while the rhythmic cleansing breath tones on the videotape were about eighteen minutes long.]

Yes, it is, [Student D].

Thank you.

You are welcome. Now [Student L] spoke up.

Yes. In speaking of color this morning, I recalled that in the very early classes and even in The Living Light *book, that early, they spoke of our aura and the colors it emits.*

Yes?

Is that the same color or is that in addition to?

You can ask that question after our momentary break. We will—pause the camera for a few moment—

[After a break, the recording of the class resumes.]

We've had our little break and our pause here. And before I get to your question, [Student L], I think we should spend a little time today on understanding your experiences while you're in these private classes and your experiences during the week when you are not here in private class. We all, while identified with form, experience at some time in our day what we understand is fear. We also know that fear is the effort of mental substance when it judges that its existence is threatened. And so over these many years there have been many experiences, expressed in different ways, with people. I have heard it stated throughout the ages of people saying that they're losing their identity. Well, it's the greatest blessing they could ever have if one can be blessed. However, the reactions vary with different people in their evolution.

And so as the Light shines brighter, the darkness gets darker. And when it gets dark enough, the obstruction, which created the shadow or darkness in the first place, it moves out of the way. And so that's what's really happening with you private students here. You're looking at the obstructions; as the Light shines brighter, the obstruction gets stronger in your view. And you believe, as the obstruction gets stronger, that your need has reached a point, your denial has reached a point that you can no longer bear it. And the effect of that is known as frustration. Frustration: trying to find a way around the obstruction in your path, which is the one that you have placed there. And so it is in spiritual awakening, evolving, and growing.

Some of you, however, have already found that, well, yes, the obstruction did get to use your mouth and your mind and your little house for a time, but it passed. Now you feel better. You're not frustrated, at least for the moment, until you call it back again. And so that path of personal responsibility, the awakening of what your obstructions are offering to you and where they leave you in the final analysis, is beginning to gain greater strength in your consciousness, that awakening. I want to assure all of you children this morning there are no shortcuts. *There are no shortcuts.*

When you believe that you have an obstruction and you believe it to the point that you keep dodging and trying to get around it, take your obstruction in your consciousness, pull it up by the bootstraps and stick it right in front of the strongest light that you can possibly view. And when you do that, you're going to find it disintegrate before your view. And the strongest light that you have, the very strongest within you, that you can put the obstruction in front of is the light of reason. So you keep faith with reason. You will find the transfiguration, for you will find the disintegration of the obstruction. So take those beliefs of yours, those obstructions, put them in front of the faculty of reason.

Now a person may say, "Well, the faculty of reason, don't know about that." Well, let's take it and put them in front of what you call your self-interest. Lift those up. Let's use self-interest then. If you don't feel that you're ready to or really understand, let alone accept, the faculty of reason, that which is reasonable, take it in front of what you say is the function of self-interest. And see how long that obstruction will be able to hold it together (itself) when you put that in front of self-interest. You're going to find how quickly it's going to disintegrate.

Now, [Student L], we can get to your question. And please state it forth. *[After a short pause, the teacher continues.]* Self-interest can serve a very good purpose, you know, when it's under the guidance of some kind of reason in your life. Hmm?

Did you want me to restate it?

That's what I said, yes. Thank you. Have you forgotten what your question was?

No, I have a clearer image, though, now.

You have a clearer image. Fine. Well, go right ahead and speak forth the clearer image.

The question was—

We're all looking for clarity. I think that's why we've come to class. Isn't it, [Student J]?

Yes, sir. [Student J responds.]

Aren't we looking for clarity? *[The teacher again addresses Student J.]*

Yes, sir.

Yes. Let's have things nice and clear. Hmm?

Well, the question had been, Is the aura that we were taught about early in the Living Light Philosophy that same coloration and light that you spoke of today? And it seems to me that it would have to be, but the different colors that come into the aura would be as a result of the way our own obstructions filter the light. [Student L remarks.]

Yes, yes, indeed. I mean, after all, you see, here's our little being, our soul, that which is, and it has to be sifted through that which is not. And that changes frequency also and changes color, of course, yes.

Then when we shine the light of reason on it, we shine a white light on it and it can blend more harmoniously with those things that don't blend earlier.

Yes, well, I guess the best analogy I could give is to take and pour some red paint down a sewer line and tell me what color it comes out on the other end. Pardon?

I just laughed.

Yes, well, I think perhaps we can get a little better understanding that way. Yes, does someone else have a question here this morning? [Student B].

When we, when we do the cloud exercise, should we be consciously thinking about where we place our ship on the river or do we just do the exercise?

No. We should also think at the same time where our little ship is. Because, you see, what will happen, all of these images will rise up into your mind. Do you understand? Now what you will find from that [is] you will begin to get an inner awakening of the obstructions that are in your path that you've never consciously looked at before. Do you understand that, [Student B]? For these obstructions and judgments are deeply seated within our consciousness. Do you understand?

Yes.

And so one cannot be qualified to remove anything that they are not consciously aware of. Would you not agree?

Yes.

So the whole purpose is to first become consciously aware of them, and through that conscious awareness know exactly which ones to bring up in front of the light of reason. Place [them] there in front of self-interest, survival, you hear? And when that is done, you'll be amazed; they're no longer attractive at all. They just absolutely disintegrate, you see?

Thank you.

So just bring them—but, you see, first we must do the exercises which are required to bring those images on up. Like we say, *happiness* or *happy* and you're going to find all of this rising up. And as I spoke a little earlier, you're also going to find that associated with that word is a dependence on something you cannot control. Do you understand?

Yes.

And so that's where the obstructions are. That's where the effect, the final effect of frustration is, you see. And our purpose is that inner awakening, for it is the Light within us that we must allow to shine more clearly by removing the obstructions that are in its way. You see, here we are, the Light, and it is shining. And we have all of these obstructions that we believe that we are, you see. And by that belief is that bondage, and then we get to look at the shadow that they cast. That's not life and that's not living. Pardon?

True.

So that's what we want to be working on. Was there any other question there, [Student B]?

I was sort of thinking of the obstruction, like for the obstruction to happy, would vary depending on what center I was in.

It does. It will vary moment to moment and because it varies moment to moment reveals to a person, on the frequency of it varying, how much control they have over their mind, [Student B].

Ah.

You see, this is so critical and so important for the awakening. You know, we like to believe that, "I'm in control. I'm in control of my thoughts, my acts, and my deeds." And this daily exercise will reveal to us very clearly—choose any word that you want to choose, you understand. But from moment to moment you will see, "There's different things coming up!" But they're on different levels of consciousness, [Student B].

Thank you.

And that will show to us clearly, "Well, I don't have as much control as I thought. Today I have more control than I had yesterday." Do you understand? And that will tell us a great deal. You see, truth is individually perceived from within one's own being. That's where it is, [Student B]. It is deep within our own being. Our job and our work is to help you to understand what is in the way of your experiencing of it. You hear?

Yes.

And you have all of these wonderful exercises. Like one of my students, in fact, several of my students said, "Well, this cleansing breath, it doesn't work for me *at all*." Well, it's never going to work for them *at all*, you understand, because they're proving to themselves how right they are. The sadness of the whole thing is they are proving to a level of consciousness that they have permitted themselves to believe in how right that level is. But, you see, because we express through eighty-one levels of consciousness, it isn't even reasonable, let alone possible, that we would be all eighty-one of those levels all at one time. Do you understand?

Yes.

And so our job and our work is to be aware. "This is this level, and it tells me that nothing works for me but it works for everyone else." Well, that's a level of the absolute over-identification with self, known as self-pity. You see, if one can walk around the universe and say, "Works for everyone that I know of. Just works for them fine. But when it comes to me, it don't work at all." Well, there's no greater glorification of the self than the pity that it works for everyone but for us. You see, you couldn't feel more sad and pity yourself more than to look at the world and see that everything works and others are successful, but when it comes to you, it doesn't work at all. It absolutely feeds the glory of the self. Do you understand, [Student B]?

Yes.

You see. And so whenever I hear those kinds of statements made, I know that I have to work with the student's glorification of the pity of themselves, that life is so miserable they should put themselves into—what do they call it?—the cosmic bathroom or something. Yes. Yes, now go ahead with your questions. Yes. Hope they have some toothpaste there. Clean up the determination. *[A few students laugh and then the teacher joins them.]* Yes, there's a question there.

Yes.

Is that—oh, that's [Student O] there.

Yes, sir. Is showing any type, is showing any type of emotion about an experience—

Yes?

Is, is that the process by which we add salt to it and preserve it in our consciousness?

Well, yes, it's a wonderful way of preserving it. You see, many times we feel that we are expressing our divine right or we are expressing our individuality by ranting and raving and screaming and beating our fists on the wall or somebody's head; that we're simply expressing our individuality. Now a lot of people—there are certain levels that say, "Well, I'm no dog to crawl on my knees." And we express what that level says is our divine right. Of course, our divine right, because we've decided what is divine, has zero consideration for anyone else's. Do you understand that, [Student O]?

Yes, I understand.

Yes. So what we want to consider here, we want to consider, "Now just a moment. I believe that this is my divine right, and that I can express myself and I can do whatever I want. I can be violent or anything else because this is my free expression. This is my divine right." Do you understand?

OK.

But in that is there an ounce of consideration for the Law of Return? You see, like attracts like. So if violence goes out from our universe, violence shall return in ways we cannot know at the moment. Do you understand?

Right.

And whenever we permit our self to lose control, when we do that, we are the victims of the forms that are created from the loss of controlling them. You understand? And so all of the obstructions come into our pathway, and we do not have peace or happiness or joy or health or wealth or anything else. So we don't want that path, do we, [Student O]?

No, we don't.

All right. So now, what is it in our life that can cause our temper to explode? Do you have an answer for that?

What can?

What is there in our life—there's only one principle involved.

Well—

An attachment in our consciousness is not doing what we want it to do at the moment. And we call that losing our temper. Do you understand that?

Yes, sir.

It is an attachment that we believe that exists within our consciousness that we momentarily believe that we are, and then we experience what we call our loss of temper, our total loss of control. It has to do with believing one of the attachments on one of the levels of our own mind. We are not those levels. And to be attached to them is not only ridiculous, it's an expression of stupidity. Does that help with your question, [Student O]?

Yes.

Pardon?

It does.

You're not very happy about my answer.

Happy?

Yes. *[After a pause, the teacher continues.]* That tells me therefore that that level that has that attachment is not happy with me. You know, you must realize that to some of my students' levels at sometimes I am a direct threat to what they believe that they are. And because of that, you know, ofttimes I have considered my channel, but he pays a great price because you don't seem to be able to reach me. But at times you try to reach my channel, some of you. Do you understand that, [Student O]?

Yes, sir.

You see, it is true that these teachings, to those levels of consciousness that sometimes some of you students believe that you are, it's a great threat. But I'm here, right at this moment. So I want you to be honest with yourselves, and I will be happy, if you consider it doing battle, to do battle with those levels. But please don't pick on my channel. All right?

Oh, for sure.

Yes. Do you feel better now? I'm speaking to all my students in answer to your question, [Student O]. Hmm?

I feel better.

Don't you feel better? You see, it's a matter of levels of consciousness and believing what those levels of consciousness have to offer: whether we believe we are those attachments or we don't believe we are those attachments.

Now I want to speak for my channel for a moment. There are times that he would rather that I not share with you so much Light because he knows, and he is absolutely right, that it is a direct threat to what some of you believe that you are at some times. But, then again, that is not how we operate, and he just gets that much stronger. But if you want to do battle with him, you're doing battle with the wrong person. You should wait 'til class, 'til I come here, and then you speak up like a man and you do battle with me. I'm used to doing battle for eons of time. My channel hasn't had that many eons in battling those realms. I have no problem with them at all for I know what they are, and I know how to end them, as well as to begin them.

So if any of you have any of those things there, at the present moment there, stop and think, and you want to do battle— they tell you that I'm a threat to you—well, I'm here now, but I can't be here every day. I have other work to do. So just raise your hands and say, "Yes, I want to do battle with what you have to say and how you run this place." Speak to me now. Hmm? Otherwise, go on with the questions.

[After a short pause, the teacher continues.] Yes, [Student H].

Yes, sir. In placing the obstruction that we've created in front of the light of reason or—

Or self-interest.

Or self-interest.

Yes. You might choose self-interest at the present states of growth and evolution. Just say, "Self-interest, here you are. Now here's this, this thing that I believe in." And put it in front of it. Go ahead. Yes.

My question is, Would it also be helpful at that time to forgive our self for having created the obstruction?

Well, of course, one must forgive themselves because if one does not forgive, they do not give forth the shadows that they believe that they have been.

Thank you.

You see, try to understand, as I spoke before at one of our other classes, when you permit yourself to believe that you are attached and identified to these things that you believe will bring you what you want and what you need, when you do that, ofttimes you are expressing a level of consciousness, a form created when you were just a child. It has served its purpose for a child at that point in its evolution, but it is not serving well today at all. Now those things should be removed from the consciousness. Do you understand?

Yes.

Well, put them in front of self-interest and take a good look. And self-interest will look at it and say, "This brings me no good at all. This is ridiculous for me to even *think* of the possibility of letting it take energy from me." Does that help you, [Student H]?

Yes. Thank you.

Yes, and who do we have back there? [Student N]?

[Student Y].

[Student Y]. Good morning, [Student Y].

Good morning. What is the best remedy for the attitude of thinking you know everything? Is there—

Thinking that you know everything? Oh, yes, that's critically important, self-importance, you know. People do so many things to feed self-importance, when everyone's important to the Principle of Good, for they are good, and, therefore, important to the principle thereof. Go right ahead with your question on feeling self-important. That's really what you're talking about, isn't it?

Yes.

Yes. Go right ahead.

And expressing it in the attitude of—it seems—so what I want to know is what is the, what is the best remedy to—how does one work on oneself?

With the need to feel self-important.

Yes.

Well, first realizing, number one, that it is a need, which is a denial of what they are. That's the first thing to consider. Then after considering that, say, "All right, it is not what I am, but it is what I believe that I am. And it's a denial of my importance to the Principle of Good, for I am good." Then to realize in order to feed what you call or consider self-importance that you will be dependent on something you can't control. Anyone who permits themselves the belief of a need to feel self-important instantly becomes the victim of something they can't control. They need people to tell them how great they are. They need all of these things to feed back to them in order to sustain their belief in their need to be self-important. Does that help with your question?

Yes.

So anyone who permits themselves to believe in the need to be self-important guarantees themselves to be the victim of circumstances, conditions, and people that they shall not control. Does that help with your question?

Yes. Thank you.

In fact, it does wonders on the belief in the need to be self-important. All you have to do is take a look at the record, and you'll see you're dependent on somebody else or others, and you can't control them. And when they don't do what you believe that they must do in order to feed your self-importance, then you become very upset and very miserable and terribly frustrated. Does that help you, [Student Y]?

Yes. Thank you.

Yes. Well, just accept the demonstrable truth: you *are* important. You are very important. You are good and, therefore, not only important but indispensable to the Principle of Good, which is God. Hmm?

Thank you so much.

You're welcome. *[After a short pause, the teacher remarks on the church's dog, who is lying at his side.]* This student here has no problem at all. Don't think that he's asleep. The slightest thing moves and he'll be right there, yes.

Well, I notice this morning that we seem to be a little bit tired there. I don't see too many questions rising up this morning. Is it because I have all self-important students and they know everything that—yes, who do we have there? Is that [Student D]?

Yes, it is.

Well, now we're getting better, aren't we?

Thank you. If the forms that you have created are feeding on you and they can endanger your physical form, do they exist after your physical form passes on or are they annihilated at that time?

Well, I'll be happy to help with your question. Now first of all, the forms that are created are the children, of course, that we have created. We do understand that. And they have a detrimental effect upon our physical form. We understand that, correct?

Yes.

But we also have to understand the physical form reacts to the mental form; it reacts to the astral form and etc. You understand that, don't you?

Yes.

So in understanding that, when you lose the physical form, you do not lose the forms because they are not in physical substance and still affect the physical body because they're first affecting the other bodies and the physical body is reacting. You do understand that, don't you?

Yes.

Does that answer your question, [Student D]?

Then how can you reason with them? You can't say to them, "If you destroy my physical form, then you're destroyed also."

You cannot reason with that which has been created to serve the self. You can only take that form in [the] face of the light of reason or put it in the face of self-interest. And because it was created in a self-interest that is no longer serving the self of the moment, it will disintegrate in self-interest. Does that help with your question?

Yes, that does.

Yes. So, you see, this is why I've recommended to you if you haven't got to the step of taking it before the light of reason—see, the light of reason doesn't reason with it. The light of reason just shines its light upon it. Just like the light of self-interest, it shines its light upon it, you see? You see, what happens with a form that's created to serve a purpose of the self-interest of a time past and you bring it before the self-interest light of the present day, because you have already created and fed it, and you put it before the self-interest, the self-interest takes a look at it and says, "No, I can't use you now." And just blots it out, you see. Do you understand that, [Student D]?

Can you do that, like as a visualization, when you talk about bringing it before—

Why, certainly. Why, certainly. And you put it right before the light of self-interest. Now, of course, it is in your best interest to move it to the light of reason because the light of self-interest at some times it could use that form and at other times it could not. And when it doesn't want to use it, it'll just get rid of it immediately. You understand that?

Yes.

So the next step and the wisest step is to make, when you evolve to placing it in front of the light of reason—the light of reason, you see, has total consideration of all events past, present, or yet to be. Do you understand?

Yes.

The light of reason considers the whole of your life, not just a part of it. Now the light of self-interest just considers the part of your life at the moment of your identification. So that form may or may not pass through that light of self-interest. So that's why it's better to use the light of reason, but until you can use the light of reason consistently, then it, of course, is in your best interest to at least take it before the light of self-interest. And, you know, when you take a form that you've already experienced before the light of self-interest and unless the light of self-interest at that moment wants to reexperience it, it will just blind it right out immediately. Have no problem with it at all.

Thank you.

You're welcome. No problem at all. Yes, who do we have here?

Good morning. It's [Student U].

Well, good morning, [Student U].

How can we best encourage ourselves? At times when I make an effort to encourage myself, I succeed. And at other times, what I—the result that I get, I'm very suspicious of.

Yes, I would be suspicious, too. Ofttimes certain levels are very cunning in deceiving us, [Student U]. Well, when one makes effort to encourage themselves, one must have support for the effort of encouraging themselves. It doesn't mean you should associate with people who tell you how great that you are, but with people who are honest and will tell you the truth. Then you won't be trapped by those levels of consciousness that are so deceiving and so cunning they want something out of you, and they'll tell you how great you are any time they want something out of you. Does that help with your question?

Yes, sir. Thank you.

And, you know, for a person to feel encouraged and finally awaken, "That's encouragement? Look what it cost me. No, I don't want to be encouraged anymore." So you've got to look at these things. I'm sure you've all had experiences in what you would say, "Oh, I was so encouraged. I felt so good. Life became so beautiful for me. Everything was just rosy on my path." And then something happened. And then you say, "Oh, no, I don't want to be encouraged that way at all." You must be encouraged with discernment. Do you understand, [Student U]?

Yes, sir.

Discernment. A little reason with it, you see. It is much better to have a little encouragement consistently than a hailstorm of it for other interests. You hear?

Yes.

Hmm? It isn't a matter of being negative. It's a matter of the continuity of an effort, and to let time pass to see if there is a slow, stable, but gradual evolution of one's efforts. Hmm? *[After a pause, the teacher continues.]*

Well, I'm going to talk to a few of my assistants and see if I can't get them down here for the purpose of inspiration of my private students. Or perhaps we should move Sunday class to evening where there's perhaps enough rest or something. Do you have a suggestion there, [Student S]?

No. [Student S speaks very softly.]

Pardon?

No, I don't.

Well, then why do you feel that we seem to be pulling teeth from chickens to get participation in these classes? Hmm?

I guess it's getting to the right level where we have the questions.

Oh, I see. Well, that's interesting. Those levels have no questions. Well, that's most interesting. Yes, thank you. Yes, who is this here, please?

[Student Y].

Yes, [Student Y].

When in the question we ask ourselves, What are we? Who are we? and Where are we?, what if you get stuck on one of those and nothing really—

Which one do you feel you're stuck on?

The who.

Who are you?

Yes.

Yes. And what is the problem with the question of Who are you?

Well, my mind goes into confusion. I don't really understand what it means to say "Who are you?"

Who? In other words, your mind is not sure who you are. Is that correct?

That's it.

Yes. Well, there's no way the mind can be sure of who you are because what the mind is, you are not. So, actually, it's a wonderful step that you're making. You are that which uses the mind. You are not the mind. And so when you ask the mind, "Who am I?", and it responds and reacts to you in a state of total confusion, that's a wonderful growth step, [Student Y].

OK. [Student Y speaks very quietly.]

Pardon?

OK. Thank you.

"When of thy mind thou seekest to know the truth, / On the wheel of delusion thou shalt traverse." [Discourse 1] For that's what the mind is. So you should be most encouraged that you asked and your mind says, "I'm totally confused." That's a wonderful step, you see? It's not trying to deceive you anymore. It's telling you the truth. "Who am I?" You are asking inside of you to that which you are, and your mind is reacting in a state of confusion because it knows it is not you. Do you understand that, [Student Y]?

Yes.

That's most encouraging. Most encouraging in a person's evolution and their growth.

Thank you.

You're welcome. *[After another pause, the teacher again continues.]* Well, perhaps we could, in these long pauses, put a little music in, perhaps. Yes, is that [Student D]?

Yes, it is.

Good morning.

You spoke a couple of weeks ago, we were talking about working in the salt mines while we're sleeping. And—

Yes?

You mentioned something about as well as paying for what is happening that you also can be working there paying for future possibilities. Could you speak on that a little more?

Future possibilities? Yes, the daydream state of consciousness?

Ah—

Pardon?

Yes.

Are you relating?

Yes, I am.

That's what they're paying for.

Thank you.

Yes, yes. You see, people who daydream, there's nothing constructive [that] comes out of it. Wouldn't you agree?

Especially if you have to work all night on it.

Yes. So I think you've answered your question quite nicely, [Student D].

Thank you so much.

You're welcome. Yes. Well, I have a solution to our questions here on private class. You'll start preparing your questions so that you have them there handy for you. Starting next Sunday. Yes, is that [Student Y]?

Yes. I would like to know is the place, is the Rotunda, number one, I would like to know, is it in a certain dimension? And is it within us? Is all that contained within us? Is that the—

You are the microcosm of the macrocosm. So it is miniature affirmative in your question. Do you understand?

Yes.

All right.

Thank you.

Yes, [Student B].

A lot of this, in fact, all of this seems to be geared toward bringing us back to the tree of life. My question is, in the Bible the symbol that's used, the guardian at the, at the garden to, to prevent the entry of, I don't know, form into the garden, of the flaming sword and the cherubims—do we have, is that just, are they just symbols from the Bible or are, or is there such a—

Yes, indeed, there is. It's only symbols, but what it is talking to you about is the Light of truth, the faculty of reason, [Student B]. You're speaking of the flaming sword?

Yes.

Yes. The flaming sword *is* the faculty of reason that *is* within you.

Thank you.

And, you see, that is why it is able to transform you. It transforms what you believe that you are. Do you understand?

Yes.

It cannot change or transform that which you are, but it can and it does transform that which you believe that you are.

Thank you.

And this is why I recommend that you bring whatever those obstructions you believe that you are in life, that cause frustration and the struggles in your path, to bring them before the light of reason. And if you have difficulty in that belief, first bring them to self-interest, then move them right up to the light of reason. That's evolution. That *is* the flaming sword, for that is how they are disintegrated by the Light, you see. See, the flaming sword—the flame represents the Light; the sword represents the battle, [Student B].

Oh.

And it has been given in many of your religions. All right?

Yes. Thank you.

And so when the Light does battle with the darkness, with the obstructions, with the forms, it uses the flaming sword or the Light, the sword of the Light, you see.

Yes.

Yes. Time is passing quickly. If you have any questions—[Student Y].

Is, is it beneficial to use color in your meditation, to use that as a technique?

Well, until one is aware of color is frequency, frequency is vibration, and what it represents to their consciousness, it would not be advisable in that respect.

OK.

Pardon?

OK. Thank you.

Yes. Yes, speak right up, [Student D], please.

Is there a specific color that is beneficial for healing or does it depend on the disease within a person what color is healing for them?

Red is healing for everything, including plants.

Oh, thank you.

And animals.

Oh, great.

Yes. You're welcome. Yes, [Student J].

I thought white or gold represented the healing color.

No. No. Red. Red is the action. White is the purity. And gold is the divine wisdom.

Why, in The Living Light, *did you say during the healing process the healer should envision white or gold over the recipient?*

Because they should purify their own vibration with divine wisdom, [Student J]. You see, to offer someone action without the wisdom of purity could create quite a problem. Would you not agree?

Yes, sir. Indeed.

And so a person has a personal responsibility to place themselves in a pure state and only divine wisdom knows what that pure state is before they act. And so now I have given you what was not scheduled at this moment to be given to you. I have given you gold, red, and white, haven't I?

Yes.

And those of you who know anything about color will know what it's all about. All right? And time's passing quickly. Oh, I know how many minutes are left, [Student R]. Nine. *[The teacher addresses the recording technician.]* Yes, is that [Student I] back there I see?

Yes.

Indeed, it is. Well, good morning.

Good morning. How does, how does one look, look at the obstructions with joy, that they're glad they see the obstructions?

How does one look at an obstruction in their life with a joyous attitude?

Yes. To overcome it.

By the ability to even make the effort to recognize that they do have an obstruction that they alone have created; and that by creating it themselves alone, they have the power of creating it, [and] they have the power to disintegrate it. That is a joyous experience, wouldn't you say?

Yes.

Well, then you have no problem looking at your obstructions with a joyous attitude. Is that correct, [Student I]?

Not up to this point.

What do mean, "Not up to this point"?

Well, it's nice to have that attitude that you—

Why, certainly, because that is your divine right. It is your divine right to realize that you alone created the obstruction, and because you alone created it, you alone will disintegrate it. And you now have chosen to disintegrate it. Is that not correct?

Yes.

Therefore, the process of disintegrating the obstruction you have created is to no longer believe in the obstruction you have created and to make the changes necessary within your consciousness. And it will disintegrate before your very view. Does that help with your question?

Yes.

Oh, I'm so happy to see that you're joyous over that. Thank you. We have a few minutes left.

It's going to be so nice. You know, I just told my channel the other day how comfortable it will be in the library with the winter coming on, you see. You only have 2600 watts of heat in here. *[The teacher laughs joyously.]* I do hope some of it passes through the door for your benefit. *[Many students laugh.]* I wouldn't want to sit here so warm and comfortable—think I'm in the tropics—and have you sitting out there shivering. So be sure and dress comfortably for winter. Of course, I don't think you would appreciate me sitting here with a pair of Bermuda shorts on. *[Again, many students laugh, and after another pause, the teacher continues.]*

And so next Sunday we will all come with our little papers with all of the questions that we have during the week on our classes. And I will expect so many questions that we'll just barely fit them in to the time that is allotted. Hmm? And I will expect our secretary, [Student S] to see that everyone has all their questions. They don't have to show their questions to her, but to be sure that they have them written down. Because I know how many of you like to take notes of things. I see during the week you note many things. Now you're going to get a chance to note what goes on Sunday. Hmm? Yes, [Student I].

Are questions obstructions?

Are questions obstructions?

If you don't know the answer.

They're not if you open your mouth and ask and get an answer. It may not be satisfactory to what you decide, but go ahead. *[After a short pause, the teacher continues.]* You mean—oh, yes. I see what you're talking about. Questions, yes. For the mind to allow itself to ask a question, it is an obstruction to the belief that they know everything and are therefore perfect. Yes, in that respect, it is definitely an obstruction, yes. *[A few students laugh.]* That help with your question now, [Student I]?

That was, that was a very good answer. [The student speaks very softly.]

Fancy?

No, it was a very nice answer.

Oh. Thank you. It was very clear. It is, at least to me. If it isn't to anyone else, well, then that's their problem. But I'm sure we all realize for us to permit our self to ask a question, we have an obstruction to our belief in our know-it-all and self-importance. And that takes a little effort, you see. A little bit of effort. I do understand that. I've never claimed to know it all. I don't want that kind of an obstruction in my way. I've had enough in my life, be it in divine order. I don't need to add any more. Hmm? Yes. Yes, [Student B].

Are we allowed to ask advice on how we, on how we're doing with our exercises? Is that—

Yes, yes, you may ask any questions in reference to your exercises, [Student B] and students, that you feel, in reference to how you're doing, in reference to stating your understanding while doing them. Does that help with your question, [Student B]?

Sort of.

Yes. Because, you see, for example, in the classes if you say, "Well, I'm doing exercise such and such and this is my experience," things of that nature, you would all benefit from. Do you understand, [Student B]?

General.

Yes.

Right.

You would all benefit from. Definitely. Because, you see, then others could benefit from a broader understanding of the exercise itself.

Now I want to take this off, *[The teacher refers to his microphone.]* but I want to finish speaking first because I have this complaint registered that I take off this little thing here before I stop speaking. So I'll say good day. Have a wonderful week. And don't forget—I'll wait a minute—to have your questions for next week. Thank you. And good day.

SEPTEMBER 8, 1985

A/V Class Private 14

Good morning, students. Such a lovely day today.

I'm happy to see that you have made the effort to do your part in these private classes and to have your questions ready that you have given considerable thought to. For as I stated before, a part of these classes, your part, is to put your effort in, in order that you may receive the benefits that are available for you. You cannot receive nor experience those benefits unless you do your part in keeping with the law that whatever we put into a thing is what we get out of the thing and not one iota more.

Now we'll get to your questions here in a few moments. I did speak to you last Sunday in reference to any temptations that you may have to do battle should and shall be directed to me at these classes at the time that I am here to speak with you. For I realize that it is only an error of ignorance that sometimes some of you tempt yourselves to do battle and to justify the reasons that you have for such temptations.

Whenever you go against the orders in this temple of Light, you are not only going against the orders of my channel, for he is very faithful and loyal to the orders that he receives in respect to this temple, you are going against the Light that I serve. And when you do that, you are going against the Light, that which you truly are. And your reason for being here is in order for you to study, to apply, to understand what you truly are, not what you have believed that you are. And so that is why you are here.

This is the first time, as I have spoken before, that a temple of this Light has ever been permitted in the midst of creation. And so when you feel tempted to do battle with my servant, you are battling with me and with the Light that you are. And a house divided cannot and shall not stand.

You will note that we have made one change this day in the student body. It is not the only change that we may make. So I tell you this in order that you may inspire yourself that after so much effort in your evolution has already been made that you will be a bit more on guard and not be tempted with the shadows of what you are not in order that you may continue with your efforts in evolution.

Now some of you, over the years, have stated that you have looked through creation; you have turned over every stone there is to turn. I want to assure you this temple is not a stone. It is not a rock. It is not a boulder. This temple is the way you have been seeking for [a] long, long, long, long time. And when you are honest with your true self, you know, deep inside of you, beyond a shadow of any doubt, how many times you have tried and how many times you have failed. And so you are here today to try, once again, to make the effort necessary to free yourselves from these struggles and upsets and emotional trauma that you sometimes believe that you are. And so when you have those temptations, you have those needs, take control for the few days necessary. For I'll be here on Sunday. And I will see that time is reserved and set aside for those of you who feel the need to do battle with my channel, [which] is in truth battle with me and battle with the Light that you are.

And now we'll get to the questions that you have this morning. So you'll be so kind as to raise your hand. Yes, [Student H], please.

Yes, sir. Thank you. When you take a fear before the light of self-interest and that fear just refuses to budge, how do we deal with it at that point? Do we pit it against a greater fear? Or how do we work with that?

Well, first of all, when you take something that you fear before the image of self-interest that you have and the fear refuses in your mind to bow, it reveals to you that you have not created, in your consciousness, a self-image of importance. It reveals that you desire to be an image that you believe that you are not, which is insufficient to stand to the fear that you have. Do you understand that, [Student H]?

Yes, I do.

Well, for example, you will find that a person who in their life desires to be what someone else (they believe) is—they would like to be like that person or that person or that person, for they judge they have everything that they need. That in truth creates a very weak self-image. And that weak self-image is not strong enough to do battle with the fear that one has. So the improvement and the work to be done is to be done on one's own image of themselves. Do you understand that?

Yes, sir.

You see, many people put up a facade of how important they are and how great they are. They have judged in their mind, for their own self-protection, you see, for their own self-interest, that they have that, for underlining that facade is a great inferior attitude of mind, one of sadness, one of disappointment, one of discouragement, one that tells the mind, "Whatever I do, I fail. Whatever I tried, I have flunked," and on down the list. And it definitely is down. Did that help there—

Yes. Thank you.

—with that question, [Student H]? So, you see, you can make the change through honesty. You can speak to yourself; because, you see, the world will grant to you what you first grant to yourself. And so one should not expect from another, one should not expect from the world, until one first expects, and does, from oneself. So you expect the improvement for yourself, freed from any dependence on anyone or anything that you cannot control. You *can* improve. You are improving. It's a matter of making that effort and convincing the mind, for the mind, the level of consciousness from long ago, has already convinced you of the opposite. So you have the same mind to use for convincing you of what it is that you want in a world of creation, as long as you do not permit it to depend on something that is not within your own control.

You're welcome. Someone else have a question? Was that [Student D] back there?

My hand was not up. [Student D responds.]

Oh, it wasn't. Your questions aren't ready yet. Well, we'll come right up here. Someone else have a question? [Student M] has a question, please.

Yes. It was said that to get a clear video picture . . .

Yes?

. . . there was the combination and the mixture of colors.

That is correct.

Now in our consciousness, [does] that hold true where we have to—well, I can't say we have to. But is there a mixture of colors within our consciousness for us to get the clearest image?

Indeed. [If] you want a beautiful self-image, then you must work on rate of vibrations, which are colors. And they must converge together and they must blend into the purity that you desire. What creates the color?

Yes.

Thoughts and attitudes of mind. That's what creates the color. That's what creates the sound.

Right. We, we have been told various colors in the philosophy, in The Living Light *book, that correspond to different soul faculties.*

That is correct.

Those are the colors of which you are speaking.

That is correct. One should not think of the color. One should consider and apply what they mean.

Yes.

For each color is revealing the rate of vibration of a certain attitude of mind, a certain soul faculty, a certain sense function. And balance is what white or purity is. Balance in all things.

Thank you.

You're welcome. Yes, is that [Student N]?

Yes. I was, I was wondering if the ego is a composite of all the judgments that we believe we are.

The uneducated ego is, yes.

And the educated ego?

The educated ego accepts its responsibility of a vehicle of expression for the true being that you are. It does not believe. It is far beyond that. It is—you see, the ego is absolutely necessary. It's part of the divine order and the divine plan. It is a matter of using it intelligently by not believing that you are it. You cannot use something wisely when you believe you are the something that you use. If you believe you are your shoe, then you cannot intelligently use your shoe properly.

Thank you.

Do you understand, [Student N]?

Yes.

Yes. You're welcome. [Student Y] has a question, please.

Yes. Thank you. What is it in the mind that causes someone to be easily used or duped by things outside of themselves?

Yes. What is it in our mind that is the cause of us to have a need to be used by others? Is this what you're talking about, aren't you?

Yes.

Well, first of all, in honesty one will take a look inside of themselves and see what they're getting out of being used. Because we don't do anything with our minds that we don't first judge we're going to get something. So if we find in our life's experiences that we are used and abused and cast aside, then honesty will reveal to us our need for those experiences. Do you understand, [Student Y]?

Yes, I do.

You see, if a person has judged that that's the way they can get what they want, by being used and abused, they will continue on that merry-go-round of being used and abused for they are getting what they believe that they need. Though consciously, when they rise to the conscious mind, to the light of reason, they say, "This is just insane. That I should put myself through such insanity, for what?" Then they start to grow, you see. Does that help you, [Student Y]?

It does. And I have just another addition—

Certainly. Go right ahead.

—to the question. So what would be, since it seems so, that it comes upon one so quickly, what would be the best, what would help the most in . . .

By being honest, that one is an impulsive person; that they do not have to be impulsive. And to take control of their desires and not react to them the moment they strike a blow to the mind, not to permit the body to react, [Student Y].

OK.

You see. I'm sure you will find that people who have those experiences are very impulsive. They quickly react to what someone says, thinks, or does. Is that not correct?

Yes.

Remember that we react to what someone thinks, acts, or does when there's something we want from the person. Do you understand?

Yes.

But let us not forget when they are in our sphere of action within our own domain, we have what is known as personal responsibility to preserve what we, in our understanding, believe is right for us. [Does] that help you, [Student Y]?

Thank you.

You're welcome. And who do I have here this morning?

[Student L].

Oh, good morning, [Student L].

Good morning.

You see me so well. But with all these—you notice that all the lights are blue today. You would understand if you saw all the tests that were tried. Go ahead, [Student L].

Yes. Thank you. Once it was stated—I found it in my notes—when you understand the principle of infrared, you will know the Law of Infinity.

Yes.

Would you please speak to us on that?

What do you understand infinity as? And what do you understand infrared as? Because in order to share with you our understanding, we must first come to some terms on what your understanding already is. Thank you, [Student L]. Go ahead.

Well, infinity to me is, it's like a figure eight. It goes out and returns, in my mind, endlessly. Infrared, I only know it as, about it, as light that's used sometimes in photography, but I'm not familiar with the rest of it.

What do they do?

I think it's a black light; is it?

I don't think my students will agree with you.

I, I, I didn't—I mean for the darkness. I think it penetrates.

Oh, I see. Well, [Student R], what do you think?

I don't agree. [Student R responds.]

Then let's hear your understanding. You see, of what benefit can it be to discuss infrared and infinity and the teaching that has been given, if we don't have some agreement on what infrared is and what infinity is? Go ahead.

What would you like me to discuss?

Infrared.

Really, my understanding of infrared is quite limited.

So, then share your limited—I didn't ask for your unlimited, absolute, infallible sharing of infrared. Please continue.

Ah...

I don't see anything around here that is infallible or not limited. Go ahead.

About the only thing I know about it is that it has to do with the red spectrum of light which is above what we are able to see with the physical eye.

And what do they use it for? In your world. In your world of limit, what is it used for?

It's used in photography.

For what purpose?

For taking film at night.

Why?

Because it picks up the heat radiation from physical form or other forms.

And what is a heat radiation?

It's a light, but it's not in the visible spectrum.

Now, so [Student L], you understand what infrared is used for in your world of creation. It registers emanations from objects that cannot be registered by your other available equipment because it is beyond the rate of vibration or color that you're able to perceive. Do you understand that?

Yes. [Student R responds.]

All right. Now that's what you use it for in your world of limit. Now what do you understand besides an eight ball on infinity? Did you say eight ball, [Student L]? Pardon? Now what do you understand besides an eight ball on infinity? *[A few students laugh.]*

Well, as infrared related to infinity, I haven't been able to— [Student R replies.]

No, I didn't ask you about infrared related to infinity. I asked you about an eight ball in reference to infinity.

Well, the figure eight is the customary symbol for the, for infinity. But infinity we've been taught here is just a circle. [Student R continues to respond.]

Without beginning and ending.

That's right. [Again, Student R responds.]

Thank you. [Student L responds.]

Thank you. Now what do you understand about the teaching that has been given to you years ago in reference to infrared and infinity, as one of my older students here in this world of creation?

I haven't been able to relate the two. [Student R responds.]

Well, then please state what it says in that little book that we gave you.

Well, it said when you understand the principles of infrared, then you will understand infinity.

When you understand the principles of infrared, you will understand infinity. Now you have shared with me your understanding of the principles of infrared in your world of limit. Correct?

Well, I didn't realize it was the principles. I just thought it was just some of the characteristics. [Student R responds.]

What do characteristics reveal on anything? Are they expressions—is a characteristic an expression of principle?

Yes, it's a part of it.

Well, is a character of something an expression of its principle?

Yes.

Are the characteristics of anything the expressions of the principle of the thing?

Yes, but the principle of the thing is the essence of the thing.

Yes. Well, you said that you shared with me some of the characteristics of infrared.

Uh-huh.

And I am telling you, you shared with me an expression of the principle.

Yes. I—yeah.

I see. Now, [Student L]—this is important. You see, this is where all these problems are. I come to speak to you in a language that you believe you are familiar with, and yet the difficulties are communication. You have one understanding of just a very small part of the teachings. [Student R] over here has another understanding. And then he shares his understanding and expresses the characteristics of the principle and then is tempted to believe it has nothing to do with the principle. So, you see—state what it said once more for the benefit of all my students. When you understand—go ahead.

When you understand the principles of infrared, then you will understand infinity. [Student R responds.]

Well, now don't you think that first we should understand, in your world of limit, the characteristics of infrared in order that we may perceive the principles? For the characteristics of anything being the expression of its principle. And after effort of study and application of that, that we can move on to an awakening to infinity. Would you not agree, [Student L]?

Yes, I would. Thank you. [Student L responds.]

So, you see, for me to do it for you is to cripple you. For you to question, to receive, and to do it for yourself is to grow and be free and not dependent. I have not come for anyone to be dependent on me. I had enough in my evolution of all things that I created that were dependent upon me, and it took me eons to get through those realms of dependence. Those forms were after me for untold thousands of years. Thank you. I hope that's helped with your question. Someone else there have a question? [Student S], please.

In the cleansing breath, is the hold count for nine counts or for three counts?

The hold count?

Uh-huh.

And what is your understanding that it's for?

I recall that when it was originally given it was for three. And it appears now with the rhythmic cleansing breath that was given with the tones that it was held for nine.

That's correct.

And is this—

That's correct.

—an update then for us?

Well, I wouldn't consider anything an update, considering the teachings that I'm sharing for the Light are not considered dated by anyone that I've ever been in discussion with. Dates, usually, are reserved to trees in your world, I think. *[Many students laugh.]* Yes.

Is nine the proper one that we should be doing at this time then?

All things proper for those who have evolved to the realm of consciousness of propriety.

Thank you.

I hope that's helped with your question.

Thank you.

Yes. Is that [Student N]? Or [Student D]?

Well, I had my hand up. [Student D responds.]

That's—you are [Student D], aren't you?

Yes, I am.

Well, you speak right up.

I have a question on inspiration. If you have an idea and you feel an excitement with it, I would like to know the difference between inspiration and forms that your ego may have created as an idea.

If you have excitement with anything, you can be rest assured it's perspiration, not inspiration. I hope that's helped you, [Student D].

Thank you.

Perspiration doesn't come from the soul. Perspiration comes from the functions. So that which excites us is expression of our functions. Souls aren't excited. You see, what is excitement? What would you say excitement is? Is excitement an act or a react?

That would be a react.

Is it a stimulation created by an external force?

It would be a stimulation, yes.

I have never known of any form in any universe who was excited who was not the victim of a stimulation from an external force. Now a person may say they have a thought, and they are excited. Well, that thought is dependent on something that is external. Do you understand?

Yes.

Yes. Excitement is a function. It's an expression of the functions, [Student D]. I do hope that's helped you today.

Thank you.

Yes, [Student N], please.

Is there an exercise that can help us understand sound in relation to healing?

In relation to healing?

Yes.

An exercise to understand the healing power?

Of sound.

Well, to understand the, what you call sound, to understand the healing power, one must first demonstrate, in small ways, with themselves. Whenever you find a need for healing, that's the golden opportunity to understand the process. Do you hear, [Student N]?

Yes.

Oh, yes. That's growing up inside, [Student N], and that's what we do. Now you have all of the teachings for application. Now you apply them. You also have the teachings on middle C, don't you?

Yes.

Well, then start applying and then you won't have any problem. And then, when you've done your part, I'll be happy to share with you our understanding on that very question. But first you must do your part, and you haven't been, in reference to sound.

OK.

All right?

Thank you.

You're welcome. Yes, [Student N].

It's [Student Y].

[Student Y]. Well, we'll get you straightened out back there. Someday you will get properly placed here, someday. Go ahead, [Student Y].

Thank you. May I ask a question on mediumship?

Mediumship?

Uh-huh. Or something of that?

Well, certainly.

OK—

Communication, certainly.

All right. I would like to know, Does a medium go to the fourth dimension when higher teachings are coming through them?

What do you understand by a fourth dimension?

I understand it as, to be higher than the third. That's all I understand.

What do you understand the third to be?

The third I understand to be . . . vision.

To be this one?

Yes.

Fine. Then in reference to your question, Do all mediums go to a fourth dimension when they communicate—is that the question?

Well, those who are, those, those mediums who, that the higher teachings are coming through.

Well, they'd have to go to a higher dimension, absolutely, [Student Y]. But that is no guarantee or implication that all people who communicate go to a higher dimension in order to communicate. Do you understand that, [Student Y]?

Yes. Could I ask another?

Certainly. Go right ahead.

Can I, may I be more specific?

You certainly may.

OK. For instance—

I'm always interested in specifics. Yes.

So, your channel, does he go to the fourth dimension?

May I ask you a question at this moment?

Yes.

Are you reading from your prepared text of your questions?

Well, I wrote it down just rather generally.

I see. Then in keeping with the law, I'll give you a general answer. Some do; some don't. Thank you. When you are specific, I'm very happy to be specific. In fact, I enjoy being specific.

I apologize. I have it—

It's quite all right. You see, we must do our homework because I won't do it for you.

So—

I have other gardens to weed (my own) without weeding someone else's. Yes, [Student Y].

So you're saying that I need to give it more thought.

No. I'm saying that you need to make a little effort to prepare it and to consider it and think of it more deeply. And then just simply write your question down. All right?

OK.

Then, you see, next Sunday, perhaps these questions will not have been rushed at the last minute, [Student Y]. Right?

Yes . . .

Yes, and they might even be considered on Sunday evening, Monday morning, Tuesday, Wednesday, Thursday, Friday, or Saturday. All right?

OK. I wrote it last night, but—

Pardon?

I, I have been thinking about it for some time.

Yes, and you wrote it last night?

Yes.

Well, how many hours is that before class?
Eight.
I don't think you would pass in your schools in your world if that's how your tests were done, do you?
No. OK.
All right. Now let's encourage our self and make a little more effort for next Sunday. Yes, [Student P] hasn't had a chance to ask her questions yet.
I was—last week we were discussing vibration and the healing. And I was wondering if you could expound on the colors, like if we want a healing and we want a certain part of our body healed and like, for instance, our hands are the color red, I believe, from the Living Light Philosophy. And in order for us to be, to be able to heal ourselves the Friends in The Living Light *said to visualize white and gold.*
Uh-huh.
And I understand that we should clean ourselves up before we try and visualize something to heal ourselves. And I was wondering if the Friends could help, help me with understanding on that.
Well, the most beneficial thing that could be done at this stage of evolution, the most beneficial thing that could be done is to take control of the mind so it won't identify with the form. Because when the mind is no longer identified with the form, then the Divine Light can flood the form and a healing take place. As long as the mind is identified with the form, the obstructions are in the way, known as self-concern. Do you understand that, [Student P]?
Right.
So, you see, when you want or feel that you need a healing, the best thing you can possibly do is to place your attention on anything but what you want healed. Get it out of the way. You see, it's a matter of getting the obstructions out of the way. So

take off in consciousness and when you return, you'll be amazed how much better you feel in keeping with your own evolution. Does that help you?

Yes. Thank you.

You see, it's like a child. If you say, "Oh, you look so poorly. Oh my, you are getting worse, aren't you?" Well, the child, of course, does get worse. You see, all of these forms and things, you get them out of the way. Think about something that interests you, and you'll be amazed, when you get back home in your house, how much better you feel.

Now I know very well that my students are extremely qualified in leaving their houses. Unfortunately, they leave them unattended. But leave them for a beneficial use, you see, to return to a house that's all cleaned up by putting someone on duty there to do the job. And that's taking place through your own true motivations. All right?

Right.

Yes. You're welcome. Did you have another question, [Student P]?

Well, I was also interested—the universe is made up of numbers and—

It's not made up of numbers. It *is* numbers.

Yeah, it is numbers. And I was wondering if the healing vibration, the number nine—I, I know everything goes back unto itself and it's a circle. And I was wondering, color—sound is the effect of color. And I was wondering how color and numbers correspond. In other words, are there numbers for—or colors for numbers and I'd just like some greater understanding.

Well, color is number. And number is color. And they all are sound. So they're one and the same. But depending upon your own level of consciousness is how you are going to experience them. You see, you hear a sound. You hear the sound of your own voice or the voice of another. Now you hear that along certain frequencies, mathematically. You also experience the color of the sound. Well, you should. You will when, when you no longer have the obstructions to your sight, to your eyes. And so if a person is receiving on a certain level of consciousness, they only receive a portion of that that is being broadcast or sent into the atmosphere. [Do] you follow that?

Right. So—

So, you see, it's a matter of our own receptivity through the totality of our own acceptance. You see, when you accept more, you experience more. When you experience more, you have more at your disposal to do something constructive with. People believe they're in need because they have so many denials. That's why you experience what you call need, is because of denial; and you destine yourself to more and more need, when you have the same divine right of choice to demonstrate the will of goodness and to experience the abundance thereof through acceptance. See, a person [may] say, "Well, I accept." And then they sit around and say, "Hasn't got here yet. Hasn't got here yet." And every second the mind is saying, "Well, I still don't see it. Oh, it doesn't work at all. It's not happening." But they must understand that that is their denials that are telling their mind that. And their own denials are not about to move out. All right?

All right.

Do you have another question, [Student P]?

Well, I was wondering in seeking, you know, to be more at peace and have this acceptance—

Accept that you are.

Right.

Accept that you are, and that acceptance, whether or not you have accepted that you are or just told yourself that you accept that you are, will be revealed to you in your experiences by your own demonstration.

Depending on our judgments, right? That's . . .

Did you ever know of a judgment that did not survive by denial?

No, it can't survive.

It is not possible.

Right.

It is not possible for a judgment to exist without denial.

Right.

Now the only one that I am aware of that denied anything was the one who has the realm below, of creation.

Lucifer, yeah.

You see, when you look at the truth and you say, "Creation, that's fine. That's a world of denial, for it is a world of judgment." That's what it is. In order to judge, you must first deny. You cannot judge until you have denied. And when you deny, you destine yourself to the experience. All right?

Right.

So refrain from denying and experience the abundant good of life.

Now who else—oh, [Student J]! [Student J], you haven't had a chance to ask your questions this morning.

Well, I was wondering about the relationship of salt in relationship to the realms, the higher and the lower realms of consciousness.

Yes. That is very, very important, salt. The use of it in reference to—it is also used as a purifier, you do understand that, don't you?

Yes, sir.

Salt. Now salt is also the sustenance of the realms of denial. It is a preserver, and it preserves. It is non-discriminatory in its preservation. Whatever you put in it, it's going to preserve. So you can put a judgment in it and it'll be well preserved. And you can put in a way or pathway to something greater and it will be well preserved.

Now the salt of the oceans of life and the salts of the earth. Now those workers down there, they work in the salt mines. Those are not the—they do not get their salt from the oceans of life. They get their salt from the deep, deep caverns that they dig out in the mines below, you see, in the earth. And so the salt that is used in our realms of consciousness for its purification benefits is the salt of life or the salt of the waters of life.

Now in your world, you see, that salt is unfortunately, in your world of creation, it is rarely, if ever, used, the salts of the oceans of your planet. It is the best salt. It is the finest salt. And it is the salt that someday your world will be using and not the salt it is using.

So salt is a preservative. Whatever you want to preserve, you salt it. And it shall be preserved. However, use discernment whether you preserve a judgment, which is an obstruction in your path, or you use it to preserve your continuity of your efforts. For example, you see, the judgments of our mind require a chemical from our body in order to preserve themselves. And so if you understand that your body contains a, a high amount of salt—you hear?

Yes, sir.

Your physical body contains salt. And that chemical is used as a preservative in these realms of your consciousness to preserve your judgments or to preserve your efforts in the continuity of moving and growing through them.

So not only does the mind act upon the body but the chemicals of the body act upon the mind. Each thought, each emotion, each attitude uses certain chemicals of the body. And if those chemicals are not kept in some degree of balance, then you experience problems with your physical body and your mental body. Go ahead with your questions, if you have any more, [Student J].

Would it be in our best interests to ingest sea salt?

Because it has not been purified and your body is not used to it, it would have to be taken in very small doses.

Now you have in your world the false belief that salt is very bad for you; that salt creates all kinds of problems for you. So one—I can tell you where you can get the salt which would benefit you: the seaweed.

Seaweed.

Yes, definitely. Don't mention it to my channel. He had to grow up on it, you know. Seaweed instead of candy. *[As a child, Mr. Goodwin would be given seaweed, which had been prescribed by his doctor, and he did not enjoy its flavor.]* However, you know, taken in a small amount. They have them in various stores, the seaweed, you know. It's been dried, dried in the light of the sun. And they do have that. You take it in certain small amounts. It's most beneficial. You will find interesting experiences from it with yourself, yes. I know. Did that help with your question there?

Indeed. Thank you very much.

Yes. But you need a small amount, you see. You know, just a little bit, a little tidbit of something. Once or twice a day, because otherwise, your body will react to it, not being used to it. So for the salt of the waters, I would take it from the plants that grow in the oceans. [A] common one is seaweed. Yes. Very beneficial. Very beneficial.

Now who do we have here? [Student Y]? No. [Student L].

[Student L]. Following what was just said, is that something we can put on our food instead of salt?

You haven't got it processed to that point. And you shouldn't try that until your world gets to the point of processing the salt from the oceans. However, as I just explained there to [Student J], you can have salt [and] get some of its great benefits from dried seaweed. You'll have great difficulty eating it directly from the ocean, I can assure you.

Thank you.

Yes, [Student S], please.

In regard to that—

It's rather chewy. Unless you like chewing gum that continues to chew. Yes.

What's happening with these ponds that they cultivate around here where they allow the seawater to come in and dehydrate it and then cultivate the salt. Is that . . .

Yes, but you haven't reached—it's excellent—but they haven't reached a point of purification of it yet, you see. There are many contaminants still in it. Now, for example—and I'm talking about contaminants in the air, you see. [If] you take seaweed directly from the ocean and you dry it in the heat and light of the sun, you do not get as many of the contaminants that they're getting from this other process that's going on.

Thank you.

You see, they're moving in the right direction, but they still have too many contaminants. You see, ofttimes, you know, a person says they want to sterilize everything. Well, when you sterilize everything, you introduce other contaminants that you're not aware of. Do you understand that?

Uh-huh.

You see, your hospitals have been on this for so many years, haven't they? They sterilize this. You sterilize that; you sterilize that. You sterilize and what you do is introduce other contaminants that they're not aware of, and the health of the person seems to get worse instead of better. Yes.

In regard to that, may I ask, as far as sterilization goes, then, of instruments, is it better to sterilize it under steam heat or alcohol heat?

Oh, no. No, no, no, no, no. Alcohol.

Is better?

Oh, much. Far superior. Yes. Steam introduces something else.

Thank you.

You're welcome. You do have both, don't you?

Yes.

And you do have a choice, don't you?

Yes.

It just takes a little more effort to use the alcohol purification, doesn't it?

They have it almost the same.

Oh, that's nice.

And it doesn't corrode.

It cannot corrode because it doesn't have the contaminants.

Thank you.

You're welcome. Yes, [Student J].

Sir, in keeping with what you just said about steam, would then taking a steam bath be detrimental instead of beneficial to one's health?

No. [A] steam bath could be beneficial if it's done properly. Now if you want to steam bath, they have these places where they have these mudholes; that's the most beneficial of all. You'll get plenty of steam.

Yes, sir.

You see. You see, where you get so much contamination is where you have a room and there are several people all steaming.

And that's, that's detrimental, you say?

That's detrimental. That exhausts a person. You see, because you not only [have] got all these other people, you [have] got all these other vibrations; that's all emanated out chemically into the steam, and you're absorbing that. [It] would be better to have a few little insects from one of the mudholes that they step down into. You do have those places still, yes?

Yes, sir. Thank you.

And then you're out in the air. You understand, let it dissipate out into the atmosphere. Because those other places, you see, it's all contained, you see, and so it's all intermixed, all that vibration. It's not good at all. No.

Thank you.

No, because usually the ones who attend there, you'll find, on an average, you see, they're kind of—I wouldn't call them, what you would say, up.

That's true.

You see? And you wouldn't want to absorb the lows. There's enough of that running loose.

Yes. I see. Thank you very much.

You're more than welcome, [Student J]. Now who do we have there?

It's [Student O].

Oh, my, [Student O], speak right up.

OK. I want to ask you, Is earth, could earth be considered as an avenue of communication? [The chimes of the clock strike as the student asks his question.]

Could what be considered an avenue of communication?

Earth and, and the creation, creation, such as man and animal and plants. Could that be considered as an avenue of communication?

Well, yes, if you would understand that the animal is more highly evolved in reference to communication than man.

OK.

You know, it just is. You see, truth just *is*, [Student O]. It isn't OK or not OK. It just is. Now an animal communicates with their surroundings. Like this animal here. *[The teacher refers to the church's dog.]* He communicates in his own way with the birds. You hear nothing because, you see, we are not evolved to perceive what they are talking about because we are dependent on physical substance. They are evolved where they communicate on what you would call telepathic. They know what you think and when you think it. They know what those other creatures there, what they're thinking and when they think it. They have their own feelings for the trees and all of nature. Now that is certainly more evolved than what man is doing to himself, wouldn't you say?

Yes.

Can you look at this animal down here and understand what he is dreaming? *[The teacher again refers to the church's dog.]*

No, I can't.

He can, when you're dreaming.

Yes, sir.

All of them do. They understand. They know how you really feel. They sometimes look at you, people, you see, and they hear what you say, but that's not what they are—that's not what their higher priority [is]. Their priority is the images coming into their consciousness of what you're really thinking about them. You see?

Right.

They know what you're talking about, but they want to know what you're thinking because they know you will do what you're thinking, not necessarily what you're saying. And that's how they look at the two-legged animals. Did that help with that question there, [Student O]?

Yes.

Yes. You go ahead with the next one.

OK. Is, OK, is sound and sight the highest avenue of communication that man registers?

Sight and sound is the rate of communication that *most* men register—no—that most men are aware of. They do register in their consciousness, but they're not aware of it because they've got so many obstructions there they—it's totally blotted out, [Student O]. You see, all, all forms are telepathic. They all communicate. Man is so filled with so much into his mind he's no longer aware of the communication. Does that help you, [Student O]?

Yes.

Go ahead with your next question.

OK. Well, color is, is an avenue by, from, from my understanding, color is an avenue of the, of the expression of communication.

Yes, it's one of the expressions.

OK. I don't—well, maybe I should get a better understanding of what telepathic is and how it's communicated in the atmosphere or the universe. I don't have a clear understanding.

All right, [Student O], think of an elephant. Are you thinking of it?

OK.

Are you thinking of it?

Of an elephant?

Do you see an elephant?

Yes.

All right. Now describe the elephant to me.

The first thing I see is his tusk.

Yes.

And his nostril.

Uh-huh.

It's in the air.

Uh-huh. Now you just created it, didn't you?

Yes.

Now every other mind receptive to that level of consciousness on which you created it experiences it. Do you understand that?

To that form or creation or creating it?

They experience what you just created.

Right.

All right?

Right.

Now if they are not aware of their experiencing it, that doesn't change that it's registering. It's just their mind is so filled with so many other images that they are no longer aware of the other ones that are in the atmosphere. Does that help you, [Student O]?

Yes. What, what, I'm getting to under—what I'm trying to say is that, the way I see it, man, the, the form of man is somewhat of, it's an expression or an obstruction that's being created out of, out of substance in the universe, that, out of, out of substance that's in the universe. And it's, it's something to, to me, man is an obstruction.

Man has made himself an obstruction. And you are absolutely correct, [Student O]. He has made himself an obstruction, but he doesn't have to be. All right?

Yes.

So if one doesn't have to be something, one doesn't have to be it. Isn't that correct?

Yes, sir.

So you can only look after [Student O]. You can't make every other man stop being an obstruction to the universe. Isn't that true?

That's true.

There you are. However, as you make the effort not to be an obstruction in this divine universe, in this great world in which you live, you will establish a law through which others shall make that same effort. Do you understand?

Yes, sir.

Yes. Thank you. Does someone else have a question? [Student S] has a question here, please.

Yes. Is it advisable to meditate in same place that we sleep if this is where we recline in a 45-degree angle?

If it is used exclusively for that purpose, yes.

Thank you.

You're welcome. Now someone else had a question? Who is that?

[Student U], sir.

Oh, [Student U], speak up, please.

When we accept something in consciousness that we don't like or want, is there the light of reason in that acceptance?

Is there the light of reason, by accepting something we don't want?

Yes.

Well, how do you think you're going to be successful in life, if you don't expand in tolerance?

It's not possible.

You've answered your question, haven't you, [Student U]?

Yes, sir.

You see, we had a discussion here Thursday night on that very thing, didn't we, [Student U]? *[The teacher refers to A/V Seminar 6, which was given on September 12, 1985.]*

Yes.

And one must grow in consciousness to see the benefit therefrom. You see, what will help a person more? To accept what they are and stop being bound by what they believe they are then accepting what they don't want in consciousness, they'll start moving out of that limit that they believe that they are. Would you not agree?

Yes, sir.

Oh, yes. Sooner or later you're moving out anyway. Can't have your house forever, [Student U].

That's very encouraging.

You're going to have to move out of it. And if someone cuts off your foot, are you going to die because you believe you're your foot?

No, sir.

Well, there you are. Yes? [Student L]?

Yes. In, in regards to placing the obstruction before the light of self-interest, I had the impression, prior to what you said to [Student H] earlier, that it was the same as self-preservation. Am I incorrect?

Yes. Well, self-interest is certainly self-preservation. We're certainly interested in preserving what we believe that we are. Wouldn't you say so, [Student S]? *[After a short pause, the teacher continues.]* Well, there are certain things one believes that they are. They're not about to let go of, wouldn't you agree?

Are you speaking to me? [Student S asks.]

Yes, [Student S].

Yes, until it becomes so uncomfortable, we can't believe in it. [A few students laugh.]

That's known as growth. Does that help you, [Student L]?

Yes.

And are we getting some lovely pictures of this beautiful view out here? *[Referring to the view out of the window next to the teacher, he addresses the recording technician.]*

No. [The technician responds.]

You haven't got any at all?

Not yet.

Not yet? Well, do you realize what time it is, young man?

Yes, sir.

Yes, [Student L], did that help with your question?

Yes. Thank you.

Yes. Yes, [Student H].

From one of the previous seminars, it's my understanding, what was said was in eons past mankind used to control his breath and, thereby, his thoughts.

Why, certainly.

And my question is—

He's descended below the evolution of the animals.

Uh-huh.

These little fellows here have no problem at all in communicating telepathically [and] in knowing beyond a shadow of any doubt what your motives are, yes. *[The teacher again refers to the church's dog.]*

Well, my question is, What happened along the way in evolution that mankind gave up controlling his breath?

He became aware of his form, himself, his toes, and his fingers and what he could do with them. You see? You see, when the tool, the physical body, the mental body, no longer serves the worker, the worker begins to serve the tool. And so in his evolution, as he became more self-aware, that which he uses as a tool began to use him. And so he lost the other benefits of what he is, and he became what he is not. And so man now is serving the tool.

Now some men serve the tool of the ear. Just the ear. Some, they serve the finger. And others, they serve just the toe. Well, I'm sure that you cannot help but agree there's some part of your tool that you serve more exclusively than another part. Pardon?

That's right.

And so, you see, that tool, that part of your tool chest—see, you're a tool chest in that respect. It's not serving you at all. You are serving it. Does that help with that question, [Student H]?

Yes. Thank you.

Yes. That's how it works. You know, it's like having a tool chest that has saws and files. And it has hammers and it has cutters and knives and all these different things. And of all the things in the tool chest, you try to do every single job in life with a sledgehammer. It really isn't reasonable. I hope that's helped you, [Student H]. Doesn't pay to over-identify with only one of the tools in this great tool chest that you're inside of. Yes.

Somebody else have a question? *[After a short pause, the teacher continues.]* No questions?! Are you, are you thinking about your tool chest? Yes, [Student S] has a question.

Would you please explain the process of reversing the outward centrifugal spin to inward or centripetal spin in regard to the nine centers as discussed in the previous classes?

Yes, now that's a question that one can do something with in their personal, very personal [lives] in working with that. Now you want to know how to reverse the spin?

Yes.

Each time that you make a change in your consciousness and free yourself from what you believe that you are and accept what you are, you change the spin. Does that help with your question? Yes.

And I'd like to know: Is it necessary to slow it down before that opposite spin? And is there a neutral stopping point of no spin for an instant?

Yes. You have to, you have to increase it until it stops. Do you understand? Just the opposite of what you've been tempting to do. Now that's answered your question.

OK. Thank you.

You're welcome. Any other questions? Yes.

And I'd also like to ask: If they call them centrifugal and centripetal forces, are they correctly forces or is going inward more the power?

Well, of course, the inward is the power. But they are forces because they act upon substance in a world of creation. Yes.

And could you please discuss the origin of the symbol used by Hitler? And were the bend of the arms of the cross due to a spin?

That is correct. That is the original cross. What you have derived your cross from is the North, South, East, and West. It is an ancient symbol, long, long before your planet existed. Yes?

And did they have the, the final crook in the bend or did he apply that or how, how did that come about?

Well, in reference to that, that's something that was added to. But it was very straight, you see.

I see.

You're talking about that little part that comes over, aren't you?

Yes.

That's been added. Doesn't point correctly. Yes.

And could you discuss the level of consciousness that would cause them to do that and how it works, since it was such an important symbol in our history?

It's a spiritual symbol. Whatever the mind takes, it changes.

I see.

It is the nature of the mind in order to make it its own in its belief. For man to believe that it's his, he must change it. Man cannot receive and believe that it is his without a change in it. Do you understand that?

Thank you.

Because otherwise, it cannot be accepted into the realms of bondage. You see? Well, you must consider that belief, a realm of bondage, contains within it, it has a limit. And everything that is in there rises up to take a look at it. And when it rises up, it's got to be satisfied at least 51 percent or it cannot get in. Therefore, that 51 percent of self-interest takes a look and makes at least some slight change. Some changes are very great, and you hardly recognize what it was when it was first received. But the changes must be made as long as a person is the tool—is the worker serving the tool, instead of the tool serving the worker. Now when the tool begins to serve the worker, then the change will not take place, you see, the changing of what is received. But as long as the worker is serving the tool, then that change will take place by 51 percent of the forms that are in the realms of belief or bondage who cannot and will not accept it, except by a fulfillment of their own self-interest. If it represents a threat, it will never get accepted. Does that help you, [Student S]?

Yes, it does. Thank you.

Yes. Time is passing quickly, or haven't you noticed, [Student R]? *[The teacher addresses the recording technician.]*

Yes, sir.

And what does that mean?

That means we have about twenty minutes.

Good. Yes, [Student N] is waiting, please.

I was wondering, Why is it hard to make a decision? And how do you know when you've made the correct one?

One has difficulty in making decisions when one believes more than they have faith. Pardon?

With the mind.

Yes.

Yeah.

When one believes in their mind more than faith in the law, then one has difficulty making decisions. That help you, [Student N]?

Thank you. Yes, a lot.

You're welcome. [Student N] has another question and then [Student U]. Yes.

It, it's [Student Y].

Pardon?

[Student Y]. I—

Oh, [Student Y]. Go right ahead, [Student Y].

At night—

I think I'm going to put some flags out there. *[Many students laugh.]* I've never experienced this except in this room here. Well, perhaps, you can understand. Yes, go right ahead.

OK. At night when, there are times when—what I want to know is sometimes at night it feels like there are forms that are very frightening to me. And I want to know are those, are those real or are those actually just things that I'm creating at the moment?

Well, first, [Student Y]—and it's very important to understand—we only fear what we believe we cannot control. So where we want to go to work on is the fear by accepting, "I have, by the divine law, the right to control anything within my sphere of action. Therefore, that which I am experiencing I have the responsibility for and I can create." Do you understand that, [Student Y]?

Yes.

"And I can control." Do you understand?

Yes.

So, you see, apply that simple truth and you will not experience the fear.

OK.

All right?

Yes.

You're welcome. Now [Student U] has a question, please.

Why is it important that our heels be uncovered during our exercises?

Well, [Student U], you know what the heel represents? Have you done your studies? *[After a pause, the teacher continues.]* Have you done your studies to know what the heel represents?

No, sir.

Well, you do your study first and then you come back with your question.

Yes, sir.

All right? Now just before we get here to [Student O], [Student A] hasn't had an opportunity this morning to ask her questions.

Thank you.

Nor [Student B]. You did have your hand up, didn't you, [Student A]?

Yes, I did.

Yes.

Earlier. When you—

Well, better late than never is what they say in your world.

Yes.

That's true. Thank you.

You're welcome.

When you hear the levels talking back to each other in your head, is that a step towards neutralizing them?

Are they agreeing or fighting?

Well, one was fighting and the other was not agreeing.

So they weren't in accord?

No.

Oh, rejoice! Keep them that way.

OK. So they can go—

Well, they can battle with each other instead of bothering you.

I know. It was really a good feeling.

Yes, isn't it a good feeling?

Yeah. Very good.

Yes, yes. Growing in consciousness, entering the realms of objectivity, [Student A, where] you can take a look at them and say, "OK, well, go to it. And don't drain too much of my energy. I'll be back in a few moments." Do you understand?

Oh, good. Thank you.

Yes, yes. Do you have another question, [Student A]?

Well, could I ask one about understanding?

Certainly. We're all seeking understanding. And we're seeking it because we denied we have it.

Thank you.

Yes, go right ahead, [Student A].

In The Living Light *the foot represents understanding and the heels are supposed to be closed so that it doesn't mix with the understanding of others. Does this also apply—*

Did you talk to [Student U] earlier?

No.

Tell [Student U] where you got that information from.

[In] The Living Light *[textbook].*

Do you have *The Living Light* textbook, [Student U]?

Yes, sir. [Student U responds.]

Now start from the beginning. Perhaps you will be able to help [Student U].

In The Living Light, *the foot represents understanding.* [Student A responds.]

Correct.

And the heels should be closed so that it doesn't mix with the understanding of others.

Correct.

Does this apply to being in one's own environment, as in one's own home and garden?

It does.

Thank you.

You're welcome. Did you have another question, [Student A]?

When you look at a cloud and you don't see images, what does this mean?

What do you see?

Mist.

And what does it look like to you? Just mist, correct?

Yes.

You don't see anything else?

Well, I see, well, the clou—I've been looking at clouds all this week. And some of them are puppies. Some of them are—

But you didn't see any forms?

Yeah.

Did you think of [your son] when you were looking at them?

No, I didn't.

Why don't you try that?

Thank you.

Well, you see, as a mother, you know, that which one is closely attached to, why, one has no problem imaging anyplace, even in a drop of water. Why don't you think of [your son] when you look at the cloud? But don't think of him too much.

Yes, I understand.

Because you must consider [Student A]. All right? *[After a pause, the teacher continues to address Student A.]* Hello?
Yes. Thank you.
Yes. But, you see, select something that has a great meaning to you. You understand, [Student A]?
Yes, I do.
And, you see, the people who say, "Well, I have problems in imagining, in creating in my mind's eye." Choose something that you really want or like or [are] attached to, you'll be amazed. There won't be no problem at all. Pardon?
Well, don't I want to get away from that attachment or—
Why, of course! But while you've worked so hard and paid so much for it, why not use it constructively while you still have it?
Oh.
You haven't freed yourself of it, have you, [Student A]?
No.
Well, why not use it for some constructive good for your own benefit?
All right.
I mean, you see, it's yours in your consciousness, right? It exists in your mind.
Yes.
Well, why not use it for some constructive good? Like opening the doors to imagination, which is the doorway through which you must pass to these other realms, [Student A].
Thank you.
You see, when a person works so hard and pays so dearly for something or someone, why not use it for constructive good? Otherwise, all that energy was totally wasted, right?
That's right.
Yes. One must be practical in life. Hmm? Yes. Thank you.
Thank you.
[Student B].

I was going to ask about that cloud exercise, but I guess I did it all wrong. That's why it didn't work, because I was trying to think of a cloud.

Oh, no. No. Look at the cloud that exists in the sky.

OK.

And then see it transformed to whatever you choose it to transform into. Do you understand? You see, because by doing that, by mastering that, you gain control over your experiences. That's the first step to gaining control. So you create your atmosphere. Consciously you create your experiences. Your experiences, you're creating anyway, but you are not creating them with the conscious mind, [Student B]. Do you understand?

No.

You don't understand.

No.

You are creating all of your experiences. Do you understand that?

Yes.

You want to be aware of what your experiences are going to be. You understand that, [Student B]?

Yes.

Then you must make the conscious effort to control the mind by looking at a cloud and creating whatever image you want out of that cloud. Do you understand that?

Yes.

Because that is the very law and the principle through which all of your experiences in life are being created.

But I thought that was the conscious mind that's doing that creating.

Yes, the conscious mind creates it. That is an electrical vibration, and then you experience the return of it with your emotions, right?

Right.

So once you gain control over your conscious mind to create what you want to create, when you want to create it, how you want to create it, you won't have any problem with the return of those creations.

OK.

You see?

Yes.

So your experiences, of course, are of like kind, like they are for all of us. So if you consciously make the effort to create what you want to create and when you say you want to create a ship there, you instantly see that ship, then, you see, you're gaining control over your mind, and you can do it that quickly. Do you understand, [Student B]?

OK. But it has to be a cloud out there or—

Well, at first you have some object. Now, of course, it's much better to just take a look and create the cloud right in front of you. And then transform it into whatever you want to transform it into, [Student B].

Yes.

However, we must start—you know, we must crawl before we walk. And we must walk before we run. So when the sky offers you the cloud and you look at it and you can change it to whatever you want to change it to, you're on the pathway. All right?

Well, I am not on the path. [Student B speaks very quietly.]

Pardon?

I'm not on the path, then, because I can't even—nothing happens in there.

No. That's, that's true. I understand that. But to some, something happens. Doesn't it, [Student H]?

Yes. Yes, that's right. [Student H responds.]

You see? You see, it isn't—it is a matter of practice; that's what it is. And you use a cloud that is out there. Now what has been your experiences, [Student H]?

Well, following that exercise—
Yes.
When I see the image in the cloud, then following that exercise I see what that image has brought me.
Yes?
You know, because in the exercise they are saying speak forth the word happy.
Correct.
And then you'll find out what's made you unhappy.
That is true!
And—
It's an awakening process.
An awakening, that's right.
You have been finding out, though, haven't you?
Sure have.
And have you looked at the cloud to see how you can change it to what you want to change it to?
Yes, but I need to make more effort in that.
Have you been able to change it a little bit?
A little bit.
That's better than none at all. It takes practice. It takes practice. [Student S], have you been looking at a cloud?
Yes.
And have you been able to create some of the things you want to create in it?
Uh-huh.
You see?
It works.
It works, but you must practice. See, what's important is the laws that you are establishing to take control over your experiences in life. That's what's important. So as I recommended to [Student A], well, choose something that you like very much and that you're attached to. And you look at the cloud; and you

won't have any problem at all because your attachment immediately will go right out there and you'll see it right in the clouds, you see. Hmm.

Choose something that you like to do and then do it well. And don't tell yourself, "Well, it's pretty good. Well, it's so-so." Either it is excellent and very good or just don't even tell yourself anything.

You know, it's a tendency of that realm to see nothing good in anything. You see, a person who cannot see good in others is one who has restricted seeing good only in themselves. It's quite a limited way of thinking, wouldn't you say? Hmm? You see, if a person believes in a perfect, uneducated ego—well, they wouldn't call it uneducated, but that's what it really is—if a person believes they're an uneducated ego or they believe they're a limit there, you see, then everything possible, everything good, they [have] already got. Therefore, they look out and everyone else, they see no good in anything or anyone because they [have] got it all. Now it might be one of the tools or it might be the whole chest. *[Many students laugh.]* But I can assure you, they [have] got it all. So if they [have] got it all, how can anyone else possibly have any? They can't possibly say, "Oh, that was such a good person. They were so kind to do that." That's not possible because they [have] got it all in their chest, you see. And kindness or goodness couldn't possibly take place until they open up their chest—Do you understand?—and service one of their tools. Well, we must understand these things. Don't you agree, [Student J]?

Yes, sir. [Student J responds.]

Well, yes, certainly. Now are there any other questions while we have a few moments left? [Student N] or [Student Y]?

[Student Y].

Yes, [Student Y].

Is it—so if you can use a cloud, can you use other elements, like fire and water to . . .

That is not what we—first, when you become proficient in using the cloud, you come back to me on the question of using something else, all right?

OK.

Our problem is and our difficulty in seeing anything in the cloud is because we've used everything else, and the poor cloud's just been floating on by. *[Many students laugh.]*

OK.

Try to understand, friends, you can be in a thing, you don't have to be part of a thing to understand it. Just be in it. Yes, I know. *[The teacher addresses the recording technician.]* Yes? Who is this? [Student B]?

Yes.

Yes, it is [Student B].

Is it true that the energy, when you're looking at the cloud, is going to the cloud, your ener—the energy from your mind?

That is correct.

So the cloud's actually . . .

Absorbing it.

. . . physically affected.

That is correct. Just like a cloud is affected, so is a flower or plant or tree. And you can imagine how people are affected.

So then the form of the cloud is really changing. You're not just, I mean, according to, I mean, physically it's changing.

It will be physically changed for anyone who is on the rate of vibration or frequency that you're on at that moment. That is correct, [Student B].

Ah.

You see, that's like—and we just have a few moments left—that is just like in Spiritualism with the seances, material seances and everything. Oh, they've claimed that people are hypnotized and this and that and they're out of this and that. That is not true. There is a physical manifestation; to those who are in the frequency of the physical manifestation it is actually physical. You hear?

Yes.

It is physical to the physical sitters. It would not exist to someone who walked in the door at that moment unless they entered that frequency. Does that help you? Yes. You see, it's just like the light, the light in this room. This room was filled with golden light this morning. Isn't that correct, [Student R]? Everything was golden. Everything. And it was so golden that, of course, it was not acceptable for our filming today. And so my assistants helped and brought in all these blue filters, this blue light, in order to counteract so much of the golden light.

And now I do see that our time is up. How quickly it passed. And I know you'll have a very good week. And do, do your questions and consider them and think about them. It's very, very, very important. Thank you and good day.

SEPTEMBER 15, 1985

A/V Class Private 15

Good morning, friends.

Life indeed is a beautiful experience whenever we choose the faculty of responsibility rather than the function of dependence. And we choose ofttimes the function of dependence as we look out at the world in which we are aware of and we see what others have and, in so seeing, establish, of course, the Law of Comparison. We have a tendency, when we look out at the world, to see what others have as something choice and desirable, and then to look at what we think we have and to judge we do not have it. And so it is that as we look at our life, [we do so] based upon the Law of Dependence, for to look at another and then to look at oneself establishes the Law of Dependence. It denies the Law of Responsibility. And so from that error in our evolution we become convinced of our needs. We become convinced of our needs from the denial of responsibility.

Need can only exist in our consciousness through the function of dependence. Looking outside, then looking inside, depending on what we judge, through the Law of Comparison, that another has, we become dependent upon them at the expense not only of denial of what we are and what we have but at the great expense of struggling and suffering, when life, in the faculty of responsibility, is indeed a beautiful experience.

We don't have to be dependent on others. However, through an awakening and an awareness, [we learn] that whenever we look outside first, we establish dependence. Now a wise man in evolution will look inside first. A wise person will take stock of what they have and will accept, through responsibility, what they think they do not have is in truth a denial of it in their own mind. For example, whenever we look out there at others and, through this Law of Comparison, establish the judgment which serves the denial, whenever we do that we look out and we think they have this and they have that; and that is what we would like to have, but we do not have. It reveals to us we are dependent on what they have. We are dependent on what they have by first denying what we have.

Now if we do not use wisely in evolution what we have earned—and we have all earned beautiful assets to serve us very, very well—if we do not look at what we do have, then we are ever dependent, throughout that realm of consciousness, upon what someone else does or does not do. And being dependent upon what they do or do not do is not a life of beauty or of enjoyment or the true, true purpose of being. I know a person, looking outside and seeing what another has or has not, does not think that in that moment they are dependent upon that person. They are dependent upon that person because they are looking at the responsibilities of that person. And by looking at what another has earned or has not earned establishes the Law of Dependence for them upon that person, their rate of vibration, and their evolution.

We've spoken before on picking up another's package. I think my students over the years have referred to it as that or entering into another person's universe or rate of vibration, transgressing our Law of Evolution by stepping upon the path of another through the error of dependence on what we believe that they have.

A person's mind is easily convinced in keeping with a person's own denials. Now this conviction is established by what we understand as need. The more we deny what we are and what we have, the more need we will experience. The more need that we experience, the more dependent we will become upon others, the more we will deny our faculty of responsibility and, in so doing, lose control of our life.

Now we are here to understand these laws. Some of them seemingly subtle to the conscious mind. They work infallible. They just are. Man steps upon them; he does not change the law; he transforms himself. So we pause before we step onto another's path. Pause, before we permit our self, through denial and need, to be convinced and, by that conviction, to make them the Principle of Good in our life. For the Principle of Good is God. And to make anything you cannot control God is not only foolhardy but it does not offer any goodness in life.

You are the Principle of Good. Anything that you make in your thinking that Principle is a false god. So if you permit your mind to become dependent on anything you cannot control, that, then, is not the true God; it is not the Principle of Good. It is the false god. And we all, in our evolution, must pay for making things we cannot control our Principle of Good in life. And it is a very expensive lesson to learn for it comes at such cost to the beautiful experience which life truly is.

Now some of us may think, well, we don't make any people our god; it's just the things that we need. Well, the things that we need are the gods, the false gods, that we have made. And by making those false gods, we must serve whatever we make.

A person works and they study and they apply. And they make for themselves a business of various types. Well, what they have made is what they have created. Now they are responsible to care for their creation, to feed their creation, to help it through its growing pains and through its trials and tribulations, so that the day will come when that which they have made, that which they have created, will begin to serve them. However, that which serves us shall first be served. So if we do not take stock and say, "I choose for this or that or that or something else to serve me," then, if we do not awaken that we first must serve it before it can ever serve us, [then it cannot serve us].

So, you see, my friends, in keeping with the demonstrable truth that God, the divine Principle of Good, is the greatest servant there could ever be, we must first serve that which we choose to have serve us. We first must make that step. So if we, in our denials, are convinced of our needs, the effect thereof, then we must face that what we have convinced our self of is a need and believe therefore that we are; we first shall serve it before it serves us.

And so whatever it is, whatever your work or whatever your job, it does not matter: it will serve you as well as you serve it. And if it is not serving you well, then you can be rest assured that you have not served it well.

Now with that understanding and with the acceptance of that demonstrable truth, you begin to walk upon the path of the beauty of life. For life is beautiful. That's what life is. We make of it many things at various moments in the course of one day. That does not change what life is. It is beautiful; it is the purpose of its design. And it is not dependent upon that which it cannot control.

So when you find yourself tempted to believe that you need something, then pause and think, "This is an effect of a denial in my consciousness. I am completely convinced of this need. Therefore, I am not, at this stage in my evolution, able to just set it on the shelf and say, 'I know exactly what you are. You are nothing but a denial of the truth that I am.' However, I believe that I am this denial in my present stage of evolution. Let me therefore choose wisely and fully accept that in my mind: when I permit it to judge that this or that is going to fill this vacuum or need that I, in my evolution, believe that I am, how much control will I have over it? How long will I permit myself to serve it? And where will I be when I finally decide I have evolved, at least in my thinking, through that particular need at this time?" Will you have as good a feeling in ending it as you had a good feeling in the thought of beginning it? If you do, you are moving on in evolution to the freedom which is the effect of self-control.

And now it's time for these lovely questions that you have prepared this morning. And remember, as strong as we are to feel like drowned little ducklings, we are just as strong and can make ourselves feel like the eagles of the sky. It is only a matter of the moment of your choice. So I'll now respond to your questions, if you'll raise your hands, please. Yes, [Student S].

Do we go to the Great Rotunda directly upon passing over or is there a time of preparation?

We are preparing our self each and every moment of earthly experience for our entrance to the Great Rotunda. Each moment offers to us the opportunity of choice. So we are in that process in the here and now, speaking with you this moment of preparation. Perhaps you'd like to know how well are we preparing ourselves? Well, we are preparing ourselves in keeping with our own willingness to prepare ourselves and to understand that which is inevitable is inevitable. Go ahead with your question.

And I'd like to ask, please, who asks the question, What have we accomplished?

The conscience. That which we truly are in expression: the conscience. Not the educated conscience. The conscience. The conscience which knows the work that you had to do when you entered your particular form in evolution on your particular planet. It knows what you were given as the work and the job to do. And it knows what you have done, like anyone has done, with it. For example, take a person who has permitted their mind to totally convince them of their needs. If they find themselves in one incarnation totally convinced of their needs, they find themselves in their next experience in evolution with more dependence than they did in the last incarnation. For, you see, the Law of Form is the rise and the fall.

A person walking upon the path of being in form or creation and not a part of it does not believe in the rise and, therefore, does not experience the fall. Go ahead with your question.

And I'd also like to ask, Do our guides and teachers accompany us at the time of entering the Rotunda or not?

Indeed, they do, the ones that are able to remain with us throughout the experiences of form or creation. Many guides and teachers who come with us in keeping with their responsibilities when we enter the particular planet on which we are expressing, some are able to remain for a few years. And some are able to remain for the full expression on that particular planet.

Thank you.

You're welcome. Did you have another question there?

Not at this time on that subject.

If you have another subject, you go ahead.

Would you please give us guidelines if we wish to eliminate meat from our diet?

Meat? Well, first of all, if you wish to eliminate something from your experiences, it is in your best interest to understand the motivation for the desire. For, you see, whenever there is a change in a person's experience, if the person experiencing the change has not first made the effort to understand the motivating factor, the motive behind the desire, then they are not as qualified and, therefore, as strong as one should be when the patterns of past experiences rise to demand their sustenance. Yes.

Could this be a gradual change?

Gradual is more advisable for children respond to gradual changes rather than seeming impulsive or instantaneous ones. One in service to a form is not freed from the form by the judgment of the mind. One only becomes more subservient to it. So gradual growth is of course, in anything, the healthy way to approach it.

Thank you.

Yes. You're welcome. Now did [Student M] have some questions this morning?

Yes. Thank you. When the image on our monitor is not visible, how does one begin to shed the light of reason on the many judgments, consciously or subconsciously, that are obstructing our lives?

I see. Are you speaking of a physical object?

Yes.

Now I see.

Well . . .

Are you referring to an experience that you've had in reference to one of my classes?

Yes.

I see. I see. Are you referring specifically to our seminar?

Yes.

I see. Well, am I to understand that your little film box, you are not able to view it, is that correct?

Yes.

And has that not been physically tested to your satisfaction?

Oh, yes. I'm wondering how does one work on it spiritually. Where to begin.

Did you make a judgment prior to receiving it?

Not that I'm aware of.

Did your husband?

Not that I'm aware of.

Is he present?

Yes, he's right here.

[Student O], speak to me.

Yes, sir. Yes, I did make a judgment, prior to.

Share with us the judgment, considering the experience is not something that you desire.

Well, upon receiving the class I made the judgment that, to me, that was, to me and my limited mind, rather, that was the most amount of, of Light that, that had ever been given. And I felt that the Friends had revealed something that I, that, well, I felt that they had revealed something that, a thought that I had been harboring in the back of my mind and that I thought I would never hear.

I see. I see. Now, now it is my understanding you're telling me that your little film of that particular seminar is not viewable?

Yes, sir. It's, it's not viewable, but, also, we had, earlier, before, we—it wasn't a seminar or class tapes but we had encountered beta tapes that would not show on, on our picture box. [Student O responds.]

Oh, you have encountered some others?

Yes, sir. Earlier. They—

I see.

They weren't, they weren't Serenity tapes. They were tapes that we had rented out about, about a year or so back from a club.

Well, I'm interested in the spiritual lesson here to be perceived. However, I have my friends here who tell me that you should make changes within your consciousness and move to the next state of evolution with your little player. Do you understand?

Yes, sir.

Now I know that's not what you want to hear, but that's what you're going to hear because you asked me a question. That's the number one thing for you to do in a physical world. Because it's my understanding you've asked about a physical situation, an experience, right?

Yes.

All right. So first of all, make that change, which will be an instrument through which several tenacious judgments will have to bow. Would you not agree?

Yes, sir.

I see. First you make that [change] to help the judgments go. In reference to making a judgment on the amount of Light available at any time, spiritual Light—that which—without Light, we do not exist, we understand. To convince oneself of something of that nature, it takes a very heavy cloud in order to accomplish that. Hmm? And so it is not in one's best interest as a student to convince themselves of how much Light is available from the Divine Source itself at any given moment.

Now to convince oneself of how receptive one might be at any moment is more in keeping with the freedom of the soul faculty of responsibility. But to permit one's mind to convince themselves of how much actual Light is available, not that they are receptive to, but how much is available at any moment is a function of dependence. And you wouldn't want that.

However, we will move on with our other—your wife has some other questions there. We'll move on with that, but I would advise, in keeping with my assistant who came in to help you, to make a change in your little playback box there. Hmm?

Yes, sir.

Yes. And to do it with a joyous spirit and to accept it from the Divine Source and not be plagued with all that other foolishness. All right?

Yes, sir.

Yes. But you have a combined problem there. You see, first of all, you have a little player, they tell me, that is very temperamental and extremely emotional. And when you have a little playback film and you have a great deal of emotion, conviction, and judgment over it at the time of receiving it, then it reacts. You see, you're working with an electromagnetic piece of equipment. And look at the good that is in it and say, "Thank you. You've served your purpose. The next one I get I'm not going to be so emotional or so judgmental over." You understand? And you'll see how much better that it works.

Now, [Student M], go ahead with the question, please.

Thank you. When doing the cloud exercise, it was said that, it was said—two things, I believe, it was our strongest desires come to light as we're viewing the cloud.

Why, yes, isn't that what we usually see in life is a mirror reflecting our strongest desires?

Yes.

Do not our strongest desires—are they not avenues of expressing the conviction of our greatest denials, which are our needs?

Yes.

Go ahead.

Yes. And, and also our judgments. And it was said, I believe, last week that the cloud exercise, to consciously—to be able to control the mind and consciously choose which form you would like to see in the cloud starting outside with the physical cloud.

Yes. And you have a wonderful opportunity to put a little—what do you call those things—a VCR [video cassette recorder] there. Yes. Why don't you do that?

I have—

Yes, you see, let your faith demonstrate itself instead of being upset over a shadow that has passed. Work with what you have. And you desire that because you have convinced yourself that you need that, isn't that correct? There's a golden opportunity to put a nice little one right there inside of that cloud there. The next thing you know it will manifest itself ever in keeping with your faith. Hmm?

Thank you.

Yes. Because, after all, as long as a person is convinced they are creation, then let it serve them well and stop serving it. Why should you have one of those boxes insist on you serving it when it's designed to serve you? Put one in the cloud and then experience it and move on. Do you have some other question?

It's true.

Yes.

Uhm...

It's true? Truth is demonstrable. I'll wait to see your, the manifestation thereof there. Yes.

Thank you. I have a question about thought. The frequency of thought, the higher the frequency, is that the expression of the soul faculties which brings a lighter color versus the sense functions which are a darker color?

The lighter the color, the brighter the light. Yes?

And the combination of the two colors—the lower the frequencies are, the sense functions, meaning the rate of vibration?

Yes, but let us not get confused in case you have black hair instead of blonde, all right? Hmm? You see, let us not fall into the trap of self-identification, let's see, like my poor channel and I. He has brown eyes and I have light blue. And for me to say, "Well, you got brown eyes; you're not as evolved." That's like someone once telling him that he smokes; and therefore, he could never attain any kind of spiritual heights of any degree. *[The teacher laughs joyfully.]* So let us not get our self into the realms of comparison. When we're talking about frequencies, we're talking about things of a spiritual nature which manifest themselves into a physical, mundane world. Hmm?

So what color VCR are you putting up there? *[A few students laugh.]*

Silver.

Well, that's good character, yes. Silver's hard to get ahold of, though; it has a judgment in front of it. Why don't you have one that's easier to get ahold of? Hmm?

Like—

Like your favorite color.

Mine?

You're the one that's wanting it, aren't you, dear?

Yes.

Hmm?

Yes.

Well, anyone who wants something has a favorite color. I've yet to meet a person who ever wanted something that didn't have a favorite color.

Uh-huh.

Have you?

No.

There you are. *[After a short pause, the teacher continues.]* Did you want me to tell you your color rather than for you to tell me?

I feel that it's red.

Well, I feel that you have great desire for action, and that would be in keeping with your evolution.

Yes.

Yes. Well, perhaps they make some red ones. All right. Now are there any other questions? It's a lovely day. Is that—who do I have back there? [Student N]?

[Student Y].

Oh, [Student Y]. All right, [Student Y].

If you keep telling yourself that you are Light, do you eventually see yourself as Light?

Did you say *liked*?

Yes, Light.

With a *k*?

No. Light: l-i-g-h-t.

Don't tell yourself you're Light. Don't tell yourself what you are. You already are. You don't have to tell yourself. That's something else that wants to be convinced. That's not you. You *are* Light.

OK.

You are joy. You are happiness. You are the abundant good of life. That's what you are. You don't have to tell yourself what you are. You already know what you are. Pardon?

So—

That's something else that insists on you convincing it. Forget that foolishness. You already are the goodness of life.

All right.

And when you're thinking something else, then you are deluding yourself.

But, but the mind does keep—there seems to be within me this battle that goes back and forth.

Why, certainly there's a battle that goes back and forth. Why, certainly. Every time you think—you're [Student Y], aren't you?

Yes.

Well, every time you think of [Student Y], you start battling whether you're good or bad.

Uh-huh.

And end up convincing yourself that you're the latter. Is that not true?

Yes.

Well, do you enjoy it?

No.

Oh, then I'm happy to see that you'll stop doing it.

Is that a thing the mind naturally does?

That is something—

. . . that's specialized . . .

—that what you think is mind, which is form, which is patterns, which is attitudes, which have been created by past experiences. Why, certainly they're not going to just die off because you think of making a change and accepting what you are instead of what you believe you are. Pardon?

OK.

Hmm? So, you see, you are what you are. And all you have to do is make an intelligent decision. And say, "Just a minute. This is alien to me. That's not what I am." Stop thinking about it, you see?

Yes.

The more you think about something, the more you convince yourself. You know, it's like—oh, I know you have had. You've had various—what do you call them? I've never had one, so I [have] got to try—what is—what do they call those things? Well, involvements, you know what I mean. Yes, you see. What does one of my students call it? A meaningful relationship! *[Many students laugh.]* All right. Now I finally got it! A meaningful relationship. Now I know that you've had meaningful relationships in life, in creation already, correct?

Yes.

Because you're not two [years old]. Anyway, so you've had meaningful relationships. Now you convinced yourself of how important it was and it was so beautiful and etc. And then you turned around and convinced yourself it was the direct opposite. And the meaningful relationship became meaningful in ways that you didn't intend it to be meaningful. *[Again, many students laugh.]* Isn't that correct? Pardon?

Yes.

Well, you see, that's all taking place—that's a mental world. Has nothing to do with what you are. Has everything to do with what you're responsible for, but it doesn't have anything to do with what you are. Pardon?

OK. That helps. Thank you.

Doesn't that help?

Yes.

It always helps when we have—you see, some of my students feel that, well, I'm glad they say that I talk over heads, instead of under. But anyway, sometimes they feel that I talk over their head. So I work diligently here with you to try to relate so that I'm not over, under, left, or right—hopefully, dead-on. That did help, didn't it, [Student Y]?

Yes.

Well now, you stop and think. That's what that world offers, you see. That's what it offers to us. All right, someone else has a question. Yes, that must be [Student L] that I'm looking at there today.

Thank you.

You seem to—I seem to be able to identify you better with that green light over there. Yes, [Student L], speak up, please.

Yes.

And the blue one seems to have blotted you out a bit. Yes.

Is the gross weight of an individual related in any way to the rate of vibration in the centers?

Well, if you mean their emotional upset, it most certainly is related. Absolutely. You can't have the water center in a hurricane and a tornado without adding weight. Yes. Did that help with your question?

Thank you.

Yes. So if you want to get yourself in shape, you take corrective measures and stop being so emotional. Hmm? You see, a person, also, to help stop being so emotional, of course, they must work diligently on freeing themselves from dependence. You see. I find that people, as they free themselves from dependence, they don't have all this emotional foolishness. Hmm?

I can see that, yes.

But that's very good. You see, it's so nice to be able to see the path that we're destined for. Isn't that lovely?

Yes.

Yes. Did you have another question?

Yes, I did.

Just lovely.

Do we choose families and friends on the earth realm with whom we shared previous incarnations?

We have a tendency to return rather than to go forward, but in spite of that tendency we go forward anyway. Does that help with your question?

Yes.

Do you have another one?

Yes. Recently when I asked, Where am I? I felt as if I was in the midst of a huge collision of, like, timbers and railroad ties all converging. And I couldn't answer where I am. Would you please discuss this?

Well, isn't that nice to have that experience rather than some of my students who are convinced they're in Dante's Inferno? *[A few students laugh.]* Yes. Thank you. Have a lovely day. Now who is that next to you that has a question? Yes, is that you, [Student N]?

Yes.

All right.

I wanted to know [about] the relationship between goals and desires.

Between what, [Student N]?

Goals, of goals . . .

Oh, goals.

. . . in life and desire.

And desire? Yes. A goal is something that you ever work towards and you never attain.

You never attain a goal?

No. No. It's always a step ahead of you. You're always working towards it.

Uh-huh.

Pardon?

OK.

A desire is something that you judge that you need in order to fill what you judge is a vacuum in your life. You get it; it becomes a meaningful relationship to you; and it ends in—speak to my student [Student Y]. Pardon?

OK.

A wise person does not attain a goal, for whoever attains their goal suffers the payments of desire. Hmm?

Ah.

Do you understand? What do they have to move towards if they [have] got it all? Pardon?

Nothing.

So you wouldn't want to attain your goal, would you?

No.

One continually works towards their goal. Don't ever attain it. Don't ever attain it.

So what would little goals be? Like—or little steps.

Steps to goals are the things to move on to.

Oh.

There must ever be another step to go. Do you understand that, [Student N]?

Yes.

One must never permit themselves to enter the throne and be seated. Pardon? *[Many students laugh.]* Perhaps you can understand it that way.

Thank you.

Does someone else have a question here? Who do I have here? [Student B]?

No. [Student B responds.]

[Student D].

[Student D]. All right, [Student D], speak right up.

I've been told that many problems come from small thinking in consciousness. Could you explain what thinking small in consciousness is and how to think greater?

Yes, certainly. One who is thinking small or a small thinker is one who looks out into the world and sees what everyone else has and judges they don't have it. Well, it's true; there's no way that they can have it because they've already judged someone else has got what they need. And they need it because they have denied it. So, you see, you offer to another, don't you understand, in consciousness what you offer to yourself. You see, so you offer to that person out there the lack of personal responsibility because that's what you offer to yourself. So that's small thinking. Small thinking is a person who is convinced that their thoughts are theirs, and that they have to have someone to service those thoughts; that they're filled with needs and desires.

Now, big thinking, thinking largely, universal thinking in consciousness is accepting the good that you are and the manifestation thereof. You will know when you have accepted the good that you are, for in that moment it shall manifest unto you. Do you understand that, [Student D]?

Yes. Thank you.

You see, but if you insist, or anyone insist, on thinking small—small thinkers are constantly in need. Large thinkers are ever fulfilled. Hmm?

Thank you.

Does that help you?

Yes, it does.

All right. You're welcome. Now did you have a question there, [Student B]?

Yes.

Yes. Go right ahead.

You mentioned to [Student S] that our spirit teachers and guides move on or leave us sometimes.

It depends on what we do with our responsibilities, [Student B].

That's what I wanted to ask: why that is.

Yes, indeed. They have a responsibility in keeping with their evolution. Part of their responsibility is to serve you as you are working and they are working with you in this earthly experience that you have. You hear?

Right.

And if you transgress the law, the original law through which they are destined to be with you for the earth experience, if you transgress basic laws, they go on to someone else in keeping with the laws established of evolution. Do you understand that, [Student B]? There's no personality. It's totally impartial law. In other words, you've come to your planet and to your experiences to accomplish certain things. You understand that, [Student B]?

Yes.

You have come for that purpose. You have a purpose in life, like everything does: purpose of its design. So you have come to this earth down here to accomplish that. Now if you do not accomplish a certain percent of that, 51 or more percent, then

those guides who, in keeping with their law, came to earth with you, they move on to someone else. You understand that?
Yes.
Yes. You see, there's a part of you that already knows how many hours, minutes, days, years you will remain on the planet that you're on. There's a part of you that knows that. And that part of you knows, the deep inner consciousness, it knows whether or not, in the span of time you have left, you can balance the scales. That's the preparation for entering the Great Rotunda, you see. Hmm? You will find people become more inspired as they begin to sense their time left is quite short. Pardon? Hello?
More inspired?
Yes. We seem to have a tendency to get more inspired as we get closer to the end of the race rather than at the beginning, you see. Pardon?
I understand.
Wouldn't you agree?
Right.
Yes. They call that, I think, quite human. Isn't that what they call that? Quite human. Yes. *[The teacher laughs.]* Now I note here that [Student H] has a question here.
Yes.
Yes.
Thank you. My question is on, on the discussion in reference to What am I? Who am I? and Where am I?
Yes, before I answer, before we get into that, though, I would like to know, Did you have your breakfast this morning?
Yes, I did.
Didn't it give your arm any energy?
Ah . . .
Try to raise, try to raise your hands, children, for your questions. Yes, go ahead, [Student H].

Thank you. Anyhow, in reference to that discussion, I noticed in The Living Light *the chapter on leadership and how a leader must know where he's going in order to lead those who've chosen to follow him.*

Yes. And it's amazing how many, how many of those people are following us.

Right.

Yes. It's very difficult to get to be by oneself when there's just thousands of those children following us everywhere, so hungry. Yes, go right ahead, [Student H].

That's pretty much my question, which is, When the leader finds that he is being led by his own thoughts, isn't that chapter referring to the questions that he must ask himself?

Yes, indeed it is.

Thank you.

Absolutely. And to encourage oneself and say, "Thank you, God, for the awakening and the evolution to know the difference between what I am and what I thought I was or what I am tempted to believe I am." You see, a person spends a little time and they say, "All right, I don't feel very good. That can't possibly be me, because I am good. So what I am thinking at this moment, what is using my mind, is not me." Now you tell that [form], "You've used my mind long enough. I'm not going to feel bad anymore because I'm good. And because I am good, therefore I can only feel good. So if I think I am feeling bad, I am directing my energy to a form that I have created in my errors of ignorance in my experiences in life." Hmm?

OK.

You're welcome.

Thank you.

Now do I see another hand here? Is that [Student N]? No, it's [Student Y].

Thank you. What is it in the mind, and I'm including my own, of course, that gets comfort and delights when another falters?

Yes. That feels delighted when another falls along the path, is that correct, [Student Y]?

It is.

Yes. Because then one can say to themselves, "Well, I'm not the only one that stumbles." And one, then, thinks in the moment they feel good. Isn't that correct?

Yes.

Hmm? But it's not good thinking. It doesn't bring good into one's experiences, wouldn't you say, [Student Y]?

Yes, I would say that.

Yes, it doesn't bring any good. You see, for each one that you are instrumental in encouraging and happy that they have risen and are walking along the path of life to the Light, which they truly are, for each one you feel good about, you establish the law, of course, for yourself. And to do otherwise establishes only the direct opposite. Do you understand, [Student Y]?

Yes.

Yes. And I know you wouldn't want to think that way. Now someone else here? Just raise your hand there. [Student O], please. I wonder if [Student A] had her breakfast this morning. I'm beginning to question whether some of you had enough breakfast this morning. Go right ahead, [Student O].

Yes, sir. I wanted to ask, What does—OK, we have been advised first, I believe, that we could, in doing our cleansing, that we could use a candle or—

Yes?

—a lighted candle of pure beeswax.

That is correct.

OK.

But you'll also have to understand if you use that, you're going [to] have to go through the many forms that have been created when the candle was used for something else. Go ahead, [Student O]. *[After a pause during which a few students laugh, the teacher continues.]* Lovely, beautiful experiences in life. Yes, indeed. Yes, yes, please go ahead, [Student O]. Trying to help you.

All right. I want to know, What does the flame represent to the lower centers and what does it represent to the higher centers?

I don't think we have any problem understanding what it represents to the lower centers of our experiences.

Oh—

I don't think that's the problem. You do have a little child, don't you?

I do.

Well, you don't have any problem at all. It's an understanding of what the flame represents: the Light, you see.

If—

You see, it's the purification. You see, fire is the purification. Purifies, [Student O]. Yes.

OK. So in other words, it's—

Yes. Yes, you go right ahead.

In other words, whatever thoughts that we're having, if any, while we're doing the cleansing—[The church's dog, Reddy, begins to bark loudly.]

It's all right. It's all right. It's all right. *[The teacher addresses Reddy.]*

Reddy! [The vice president addresses Reddy as he continues to bark loudly.]

It's all right.

Reddy, stop it! [The vice president continues.]

Just, just give him a moment here. At least they won't, they—someday some of them [will] see, the spiritual students, you know, very well that it wasn't canned or all mechanical. *[Reddy continues to loudly bark.]* Tell him to go over here.

Come here. Come here. Reddy, come here! Reddy.

You know—

Reddy!

I well recall the days when I spoke to some of you, and you had a little clock on the wall that every few minutes went cuckoo! *[The teacher and many students laugh.]* But it did keep the time for you in your world.

Stop that! [Reddy continues to bark.]

He doesn't like the other people. You tell him—here! My friend, here! *[Reddy continues to bark loudly.]* No, no, no. No. You—

[At this point the videotape recorder was shut off and, after a few minutes, class resumed.]

Turn that, you turn that back on there. *[The teacher instructs the recording technician to start recording.]*

Now [Student O], what was your question, please?

I'm saying, I'm asking rather that—

Oh, the fire! Fire! You're interested in the fire.

Right.

Yes, it represents purification. It is a realm through which we all go through. And the thing is so often a person thinks, "Oh well, I'll get purified somewhere down the road." Well, you're being purified all the time. Don't you feel the fire is burning inside of you at times? Sometimes they're lower, and sometimes they're higher.

Yes, I do.

Pardon?

Yes, sir, I do.

Why, certainly! And you have no problem knowing when they're lower, do you?

No, sir.

Does your wife have a problem knowing?

She doesn't.

Well, there you are! So you know what the higher flame is not, by knowing what the lower flame is. Isn't that beautiful? Yes.

Yes, I understand. OK. I understand that. I'm saying, OK, is, is the flame annihilating any form that, that might come to consciousness while we're doing this cleansing breath?

Why, certainly. Absolutely. Absolutely. It's its purpose, [which] is purification of those forms. When you are not experiencing it the way you're used to, then you know that it's purifying that which will be instrumental in you getting free. Hmm? Do you understand it that way, [Student O]?

Yes, sir.

I think so. Thank you. Now who do we have that hasn't had a chance—well now, where's [Student A] this morning? And where is my student [Student J] here? Where are you? Yes, where are you?

Right here.

Yes, speak up here this morning, [Student J].

If—when we get to the Great Rotunda and we're asked what did we accomplish—

Yes?

And most people just grind away trying to exist and survive and they have nothing to report of a positive nature.

Oh, I wouldn't say that at all. They have a great deal to report. You have a great deal to report, though you may sometimes believe you're grinding away at old creation. You're going through phenomenal changes over a period of many years. And would you not agree to that, [Student J]?

Yes.

So that's where the accomplishments are. It's nothing outside. It's everything inside. Those are the accomplishments for which you are responsible, you see, that you have to face at the Rotunda. You have to face: you had this here to accomplish and so many years you were granted [for] that, you see, in keeping to accords and in keeping with agreements and everything that has been signed, before you entered the earth. Do you understand, [Student J]?

Yes, sir.

So when they look—all of those records, you see, they're all spread out there in the Rotunda. And you're asked now what have you accomplished? Because, you see, you signed those agreements and those accords and those contracts before you got to earth. Do you understand?

Yes, sir.

As part of your incarnation process. And so at that time, here is the scales. Here is the Light and here is the darkness. And, you see, all these accords and agreements were made. Therefore, certain people you were destined to meet; certain experiences you were [destined for] along the path; that you already know, that part of you already knows all that. And you have this allotted time to accomplish that, and then your experience on earth, in that school, is over. You have to make your report when you enter the Rotunda. You see?

Yes, sir.

Now, if you have passed 51 percent, then you move on. And if you have not passed 51 percent—of course, that's a low, very low margin, you know, that's just barely making it. I think you'll find yourself more along 79. But anyway, you see, then you come into another expression, and all of those that you didn't pass, like if you believed and let mental substance convince you that you have need and you did not evolve through that in the time allotted you in your experiences, you find your next experience with greater need than you had the time before, you see. Does that help with that, [Student J]?

It helps. Thank you, sir.

Yes, it's inside, you see. You've made several changes. So have all of you students. These changes are taking place inside. And when you look inside, you'll find, "Oh, my, my, you're nowheres near, not even close, to the dependence and bondage you used to have." Now you do know that, don't you?

Yes, sir.

In many areas.

Yes, sir.

But a miracle has yet to happen. *[The teacher and many students laugh.]* You don't want to have those wings get too large before you leave. You still need your feet to move around, right?

Yes, sir.

All right. You go ahead, if you have any other questions there. That's very important, [Student J].

Thank you. That, that was the main question, sir.

Well, yes, because you've accomplished many things inside, and that's the only record that you are responsible for. That's the one you have to—that's the one you have to face. "Did I make changes in my thinking? Did I become less dependent? Did I get myself, slowly but surely, freer along the time that I had allotted?" You see? Those are the things. You see, all of the material things, everything out there, you understand, that doesn't go to the Rotunda. What you did in here, *[The teacher points with both hands to his upper chest.]* that goes to the Rotunda. That's what you have to face.

I wouldn't feel so badly. Sometimes, you know—you see, I think, some minds have a tendency to feel badly of what they could have done and they just didn't do it. Well, that's not the way to—you see, that's a form that likes to think like that. You don't want that. You see, that's not you. That's not you. And it isn't anyone else. Those are forms. And they do that so you won't make certain changes that they see you're about to make. Do you understand? You see, when they look and see, "Uh-oh! Now [Student J] is about to make these changes in his consciousness. Oh, no, no. We better start talking to him about what he could have got done and he never did get done." Do you understand?

Yes, sir.

That's to put a damper, so to speak, on what you are thinking about doing, [Student J]. Don't pay attention to those things. They get a person very discouraged, and then they laugh at you. And they say, "You see how right I was all the time." No, no, no. Don't pay attention to those things. They'll always laugh at you. You know, no one, no one likes to have anyone laughing at them. And I'm sure, you see, when we pause for a few moments and we see these various forms and they think it's so funny that they got their way and they're laughing at us and then we feel bad and then they laugh that much more because they get that much more energy. No, no, no, no. No. You recognize them for what they are and say, "Listen. I got a lot to do right now. And don't bother me. And I'll have a lot to do in the next minute so don't try bothering me then."

Thank you very much.

No. This is the—you see, right now you can do everything with the beauty of life. That's your path and destiny. And when those things get in, say, "Listen. You're not stealing and robbing me of a beautiful life because you're not worth it. I've had so many experiences with you and that is it!" Hmm? Yes. You're welcome, [Student J].

Now does someone else have a question? [Student A], I know you had your breakfast now. That hand almost touched the heavens.

Good morning. When we have passed the different lessons, does this mean we have come full circle in these particular experiences?

Oh, yes. When you've gone full circle, you've gone full circle. They don't repeat themselves.

Good.

Yes.

Are we then prepared and able to assist another soul who is struggling through that?

We are then qualified. Yes. When we go full circle with the experience, you see, we return—it returns unto itself. It consumes itself. Try to understand it perhaps in this way. When you have—through experiences you create a form, a thought form, and you service that thought form. And it grows. And it becomes stronger, and it's able to convince you, and for you to believe it, that you have to do a certain thing at a certain time, right?

Yes.

Have you ever noticed that it's never enough for them? The forms?

That's true.

They never get enough, do they?

No, sir.

Whatever it is they want, they want it all and they want it now and they want it constantly. Wouldn't you agree?

Yes.

For example, say that you make a change in consciousness, and you don't care to eat any more of those Oreo cookies.

Yes.

Is that what they call them?

Yes.

The chocolate ones?

Chocolate chip.

The chocolate ones?

Yes.

They call them Oreos?

Well, they could call them Oreos or they could call them, well, chocolate chip, too.

Oh, I see. Well, we want to have a proper identification here. And one, one says, is good. Two is better. Three is great. And four is fantastic. And the next thing you know it's a whole box. Pardon?

Not anymore it isn't.

No. But have you not had those experiences?
Yes.
Were they ever satisfied?
No.
Now. However, not anymore is correct. Isn't that right?
That's right.
All right. Now I'm trying to help you because, as I say, some of my students have said I don't relate to you. I'm talking over your head or something. I'm not talking over your head, am I?
Not at all.
I'm getting to the principle of what I started with. When you have gone full circle, the form consumes itself. Do you understand that?
Yes, I do.
See, that which you have created, it literally consumes itself, you see. Now that's wisdom, isn't it? Isn't that wisdom? You see, you see, it begins here and goes out on its expression and returns unto itself. It consumes itself, and you are free. So whatever judgments you have, when it consumes itself, as it's destined to do someday, when it has finally consumed itself, you are free from its bondage. Hmm? But you can help it consume itself anytime you want to give it a hand. It won't like it, but it will consume itself.
Good.
Did that help you with your question there, [Student A]?
Yes, it did. Thank you.
All right. You're welcome. And, yes, there's [Student B], please.
Is it possible that we are individual links in a chain of beings from the simplest form of life to the highest grade of formless beings and that any weak link in the chain affects everyone in the chain?
Indeed, it does. From the ant to the angel, there is no separation. Pardon? That help with your question, [Student B]?

Yes.

An inseparable link. My dear, little friend was an ant.

That's always the same, I mean. You're saying, then, that it doesn't change. That—

It cannot change.

The chain is the same chain.

That is correct. That is correct.

So you can't step out of the chain.

You can never ever step off the chain because to tempt to do so is not possible because you're an inseparable part of it, you see. It's the link of life, [Student B]. You may falter and weaken as one of the links, but you are never freed from the chain of life. Pardon? You will experience through many forms on the chain of life, but you're never free from the chain of life because the chain of life is the freedom. That's what it is. But you're—What does the chain of life represent? It represents responsibility, not dependence, [Student B]. Pardon? *[After a pause, the teacher continues.]* Did that help with your question?

Yes.

Yes. So if you have one of the link[s], or more, the chain, as far as expression—remember that the chain is the expression. Do you understand that?

Yes.

It is the expression of the link of life, you see. The links are the expression. And so if you have a few weak links—and remember, they are weak links within the thinking processes, whether it's a little ant or it's an angel. See, everything, *everything*, all form thinks. Trees think. Flowers think. Insects think. Dogs, cats, elephants, people think. Because we are not communicating with them and do not understand how to communicate with them—for we lost that understanding as we became more identified with self. That's how we lost the communication with the rest of the links of the chain, so to speak. They think. They are just as intelligent as any of us. Do you understand that, [Student B]? Pardon?

Then each of us has a different chain—is a, is a link in a different chain?

No.

No?

We're all links on the same chain. There is no difference in the chain this creature here is linked to than the one we are linked to. *[The teacher refers to the church's dog.]* Do you understand that?

Yes.

We're all links on the same chain of life. Now, we take a look at this form and we judge, based upon our over-identification with self and our limited experiences and from that great evolution of our mental substance—we have got that at the sacrifice of the simple laws of communication with the other creatures. This form here, a dog, thinks as intelligently as anyone. It knows things that are happening in the atmosphere that the human mind has long ago denied as it became more identified with what it believes is self. Did that help with your question, [Student B]?

Yes. Thank you.

Yes. And who is that? [Student D]?

Yes.

Yes.

I asked a question a few classes ago on inspiration and I used the word excitement. *I, I would like to know the difference between enthusiasm and excitement.*

A person who is enthused is moving along the path of the Principle of Good, constructive. You understand that, [Student D]?

Yes.

All right. Freed from dependence, for they are now identified with the true being that they are and are not dependent on anything they cannot control. That's an enthused person, you see. To be enthused is to be in God, the Principle of Good. There you have total control and you are enthused.

Now if you are not careful with the wise usage of that enthusiasm—hmm? You become inspired. Now you're expressing and you're enthused. If you are not careful with the expression of that enthusiasm, you will become excited by being dependent on something you cannot control. You see, we are not excited over something we can control, and what we can control is in our own universe. The moment enthusiasm falls to dependence, instead of responsibility, we become excited and only, of course, God can help us. Does that help with your question now?

Yes, it does.

Hmm? So you can know when you are enthused: you are in total control of it; it is happening within your universe. You are expressing an inspiration you have received; you are enthused. It is not dependent on what somebody thinks about it, what they don't think about it, what they do with it, or don't do with it, because you are not dependent upon anything you can't control. All right?

OK. Thank you.

All right. Now [Student Y] has a question. All the hands went up at that time. Yes! I'm happy to see that. [Student Y].

OK. Thank you. When life force is present in form, the life force you spoke of in the seminar—you spoke of a life force. Is it, is it in reality color, vibration, and energy instead of what we call matter?

Well, that's what it is. But, you see, this Light, as it manifests itself, the more dense its manifestation, the more gross is the mass. Does that help you, [Student Y]?

Yes. OK.

You're welcome. Now [Student L] has a question.

Yes. I wondered, in your discussion about the links of life and the animals being a part of it, do they also report to the Rotunda before coming into the earth plane?

Why, certainly! You see, to deny the individualization of the evolving soul, to deny that the life that is flowing through there, the spiritual essence, that which we all are, does not exist in animal or the tree, it's just ridiculous. It's just absolutely ridiculous. It would take a person totally identified with self at the expense of excluding all other forms in the universes. Certainly. Does that help you, [Student L]?

Thank you.

Well. Yes. And now is that [Student O]?

Yes.

Yes.

I'd like to ask, Could the celestial be likened to the axles on a sphere? [The student slightly mispronounced the word *sphere;* it sounded like *spear.*]

The axles on a—

Yes.

Oh, the axis on a sphere.

Of a sphere. Yes, sir. [Again, the student slightly mispronounced the word *sphere.*]

Spear or sphere?

Sp... sp...

Sphere.

Sphere.

Is that what you said, [Student O]?

Yes.

I would, if we must liken it for the mental world, if I were to liken the celestial realms of consciousness to something that the mind can conceive—

Yes, sir.

—you know, because conception means limit—I would liken it to the movement of a ray of light that is perceived as a perfect, harmonious balance of all color which emanates, in keeping with its color, the natural signs which, of course, would be known as the music of the spheres. Hmm? Yes, [Student O].

Yes, sir. [The student speaks very quietly.]

Pardon?

No, sir. Well . . .

You see, to try to make it square, oblong, round, or anything else—it just is. And perhaps if you, mentally, will pause and think about that which you conceive is the most beautiful experience, then that would be the closest for you to the celestial realms. Do you understand that, [Student O]?

Yes, sir. Thank you.

The experience therefore is not dependent on something you can't control. All right? Yes. Now [Student H] has a question.

Yes. My question is, is about color. I thought a few years ago your channel had said that the green foliage out there, the plant life, is really in shades of yellow.

It is.

OK. Now my question is, Is it our intellect which filters it as green to us?

Well, for example, you have noted over these past weeks that the technician that I sent to your world to adjust lighting, just for this room, has made several changes. I think you will—perhaps you've noted today that you have a green and blue [light] in the room. *[Green and blue filters were used on the spotlights for this class.]* Is that correct?

Yes.

I see. Well, the atmosphere, you see, what you would consider to be average or regular, as fall, what you call fall comes into your atmosphere and you're headed towards wintertime, the emanation of light is gold in the fall or the cooler days in the wintertime. It's gold. It's a golden light. Now as you enter the warmer months of spring and summer, the emanations of light in the atmosphere, that your eyes long ago have blocked out, is blue, a shade of blue, a lovely shade of blue. Now that's known in filmmaking as temperature, the temperatures of light, the coloring of light, you see, and the convergence of light, see. And its conversion.

So you take a look in the atmosphere, and you see objects and you see trees and you see this and you see that. But you're looking *through* the atmosphere; you're not looking at the atmosphere. You must learn to look at the atmosphere to see what color the atmosphere is. For example, here, as we've been sitting in our class, the golden light, which the technicians set up to balance out the golden light through the introduction of green and the introduction of certain shades of blue and etc., for the room atmosphere in order that my channel wouldn't look like he was all yellow, which he doesn't appreciate and, of course, is not proper, the lighting has been changing in the atmosphere outside. You see, it has been moving, since we've been sitting here, from a bright golden atmosphere to just to the tinge of a light blue.

Now you look into the atmosphere here, which also affects this room also. It affects it much more if we're out there. *[While the teacher and the recording technician were seated in the library, students were seated just outside of the library.]* The thoughts and the feelings, the beliefs and the bondages are electromagnetic emanations, which are, in your world, known as light, for that's what light is. Light is electromagnetic emanation. That's what it is. And that's what you are: an electromagnetic emanation. That's what you truly are.

Now the conversion of all of these thoughts, judgments, beliefs, and etc. that are emanating out of a student body, all have to be balanced with this light—[and] has an effect [upon]— here in the atmosphere. So when you take a look at your little films and you say, "Oh, that was very good or very clear," you must try, as students, to understand that—you see, we do not have for your world controls and equipment that will register the changing temperature or coloring of lighting moment by moment. And as your thoughts, judgments, and beliefs are in a constant process of changing, even in a class, the coloring is changing tremendously and the temperature, you understand, which is the coloring. And so we don't have equipment where we can just have it automatically adjust because you don't have that in your world yet. You someday will.

And so in reference to color, it's very dependent on the viewer, for example, because you emanate your own coloring over that. Say that you look at a leaf. While you are looking at the leaf, you are casting a coloring over the leaf. Then you see through the coloring that you are casting over the object that you are looking at. Your coloring is ever an effect or an expression of the thoughts, feelings, attitudes, and judgments that you entertain at the moment. So you find yourself looking at one person at a certain time, feeling a certain way from your reflection. You see, what you are seeing is your reflection, for you are the one who is emanating the electromagnetic energy over the object. Then, you are viewing through your own emanation. So you do not see the object as the object's emanation; you only see how it reflects to your emanation. Do you understand that?

Yes. Thank you.

No matter what it is that you see. And so they say that beauty is in the eye of the beholder. Well, of course, beauty is in the eye of the beholder for the beholder is the one who is doing it. For they are casting their emanation, color, sound, light over the object that they are viewing.

Now I want our cameraman here to wake up. He just kind of seems to be going to a realm I'm not really that acquainted with. So just wake right up and check the time there. Let's have a report from you.

All right. It's eighteen minutes after.

Uh-huh. Yes. Now who do we have there? Is that [Student N] there?

Yes.

Yes. Please speak up, [Student N].

If an animal is suffering and he's still hanging on, how do you know what's the best thing to do for it?

You want to know what's the best thing to do for it?

Yes.

If you take a look at the animal, and you say the animal is just hanging on—is the animal eating? How long—if not, how long have they gone? Have they gone past seventy-two hours without eating?

Well, it's been getting fed with a, with a syringe.

That's not the way. When it comes to the time that one must feed an animal or a human through artificial means, it's the time to let the divine laws fulfill themselves. Did that help with your question?

Thank you.

You're welcome. And, you see, no one likes to—you see, in reference to seeing things from our own emanation, they are nothing but reflections. We look at an animal and we see the animal through our own emanation. And they are colored and they are in keeping with whatever judgments [we have] of the moment, you see? So you don't have to see suffering. If you want to look through different eyesight, then you can see the little soul as it's wrenching to get free from all of that. You know, it's like a person who, oh, who walks out, goes out for the evening and suddenly there's a rainstorm comes up and they're sopping wet. And then the sun comes out and dries them out. Well, they'd like to get out of the clothes because, somehow, they seem to have shrunk. Well, it's the same when the little soul's trying to get out. It wants to get out, you see. So don't put your attention upon the form it's trying to get out of. Put your attention upon the beautiful little soul that is working its way on out. Does that help you, [Student N]?

Very much. Thank you.

Yes. You're welcome. Someone else there had a question. [Who] hasn't had a chance yet? Now wait a minute. Who is that there? [Student B]?

Yes.

Just speak right up, please.

Could you explain what happens in déjà vu?

Ahh. Well, there are many, many things that take place in such a state of consciousness, you understand that, [Student B]? Pardon?

Yes.

And you also understand that is not, of course, a part of our understanding or our teaching because it becomes very confused, the expression of that. You hear?

Yes.

And it becomes very limited by the person's evolution and their ability to perceive. You hear, [Student B]?

Yes.

So a person may liken it to the ninth celestial realm of consciousness, and that's the best that I can share with you in these classes about that. You hear?

Thank you.

You're welcome. And now [Student L] has been waiting, please.

Did you say [Student L]? [Student L asks.]

[Student L]? Yes.

Yes. Years ago, you spoke of those who were in charge of us as humans, and I'm wondering if they were the spirit realm or the extraterrestrials, which were part of the missing link.

Depends on the earth person's evolution.

I see. Thank you.

They can be both. They're usually one. And who is that next to you that was ques—I have—

[Student U].

[Student U]. Yes. That's who I want to speak to, is [Student U].

Could you please speak more on the power of prayer and how that affects those who have passed on?

You see, the power of prayer, of course, is—you know, a person in praying, they don't ask; they accept. You see, that's the difference: you accept and stop asking. Because when you ask, you are asking for what you have denied. When you accept, you are freed from that foolishness, and the good and the good work gets done. Do you understand that, [Student U]? Pardon? *[After a short pause, the teacher continues.]* Hello?

I'm not sure that's . . .

You want to help someone through prayer that has passed on?

Yes.

Well, how do you help them? By helping yourself. How can you qualify yourself to help them if you don't first work on yourself?

Thank you.

You see, a person should never pray for a person unless they're feeling good themselves. I wouldn't want anyone ever praying for me that didn't feel good first because I know very well that I can only grant to another what I've granted to myself. And why would I want their prayers from that rate of vibration? [It would] be most detrimental to me. Hmm?

Thank you.

So when you feel good, that's the time to pray. And then you become an instrument through which that goodness goes to that person, you see. Whether or not they are receptive to it, that's in the hands of the Divine Intelligence and the laws established. You understand?

Yes, sir.

So to feel badly and to get on your knees and to pray for someone, I wouldn't. I'm sure that my channel would not merit someone that would be that unkind. No. When you feel good, real happy, and then you think, "Oh, yes, that person there. Well, I'll just send some of that along to them. I [have] got so much of it, I can afford a little of it." That's prayer. Yes. Yes, who do we have here? Now [Student S], please.

I would like to know—

Something good.

Is it advisable to have our feet, especially our heels, covered with, like, a sock or a slipper during meditation? Or are they to be totally not touched by anything?

Well, of course, as we know, that's a weak part of our temple. And it's a part through which things that [are] not too desirable ofttimes enter. However, it's more than a physical thing that is involved. You know what the heels represent, [Student S]?

Yes.

Then speak it forth and see if you can understand what we're talking about.

Well, the heel represents, my understanding, the door to our understanding.

Uh-huh.

And we're to keep it closed.

Uh-huh.

So it doesn't mix with another's.

That's all you [have] got to do is keep it closed. How do you—how does one keep the door of their—I understand. We're short. [We're] ending on time. *[The teacher addresses the cameraman.]* How does one keep the door to their understanding closed?

I think by not casting our pearls before the swine.

Yes, that's one of the ways. And by not experiencing need, which guarantees dependence and experiences in our life of losing control.

Thank you.

Wouldn't you say?

Uh-huh.

So when you don't lose control, you never—you don't open the door to your understanding.

Good.

You see?

Uh-huh.

So stay in control, and you won't have to worry about that. Just stay in control of that that you're responsible for. You see, control and responsibility are inseparable. Without control, one does not express responsibility. Without responsibility, one does not truly express control. So one takes a look in their understanding, with the door closed in their own universe, and say[s], "All right. This here I can control. How can I control it? Quite simple. I'm responsible for it. So whatever I'm responsible for, I can control. Now anything beyond that, I open the door to my understanding and I must pay the price."

OK.

That help with your question, [Student S]?

Thank you.

And my, you see how quickly time passes. Here we are, all up on time today in this world of time. And I look forward to all of you having a very fine week. I know you've had some ups and downs, but I also know they don't last. *[The teacher had removed his microphone and was about to set it down on an end table.]* Oh, my, he's just always after me about not [taking off my microphone.] *[The teacher, holding his microphone, moves it closer to him.]* I [will] keep talking here. I know you've had some ups and downs, but also know they don't last. Thank you. And good day.

SEPTEMBER 22, 1985

APPENDIX

The Divine Healing Prayer

I accept that the Divine Healing Power
Is removing all obstructions
From my mind and body
And is restoring me
To perfect health, wealth, and happiness.
My heart is filled with gratitude
For the Divine Law of Acceptance
That is healing both present and absent ones
Who are in need of help.
Peace, the power that healeth,
Is guiding my thoughts, acts, and deeds
As God and I go hand in hand
Living a life of joyful abundance.

The Total Consideration Affirmation

I am the manifestation of Divine Intelligence. Formless and free. Whole and complete. Peace, Poise, and Power are my birthright.

The Law of Harmony is my thought and guarantees Unity in all my acts and activities, expressing perfect Rhythm and limitless flow throughout my entire being.

Without beginning or ending, eternity is my true awareness and sees the tides of creation, as a captain sees his ship.

As the Light of Truth is sustained by the faculty of Reason, I pause to think and claim my Divine right.

Right Thought. Right Action. Total Consideration.
Amen. Amen. Amen.

Divine Abundance

Thank
(Gratitude)

You
(Principle)

God
(Divine Intelligence)

I'm
(Individualizing)

Moving
(Rhythm)

In
(Unity)

Your
(Realization)

Divine
(Total)

Flow
(Consideration)

The Controlled Spiritual Environment Affirmation

You are in a controlled spiritual environment of truth and freedom
Where peace and harmony reign supreme.
Be awake, be aware, be alert.
Your purpose of being is freedom from what has been.
Thoughts of self are foreign to this environment.
Take control of your mind and experience the joy of living.

The Laws Be

Our being is the consciousness, Truth.
Holy be the identity
The joy of Life
The totality of Acceptance
In mind as it is in heart
Grant us the Light
Our daily sustenance
And forgive us our has-beens
As we forgive those has-beens who tempt to steal our joy
Free us from the romance of self-love
Deliver us from the service to the false king of shadows
For Light is the kingdom
And the power and the glory forever
Peace be, the order of Divinity

The All That Has Been Affirmation
From A/V Class Private 12

All that has been cannot be
That's not Good and I'm not free
Until I give then I be
The joy of life that sets me free.

The All That Has Been Affirmation
From a Recording of Affirmations

All that has been cannot be
That's not God and I'm not free
Until I give then I be
The joy of life that sets me free.

[In Seminar 33, the teacher refers to a pamphlet that was published by Serenity many years earlier. The name published on the cover of the pamphlet is "The Descent of Man," but the title page has two titles, "The Celestial Marriage" and "The Descent of Man." Here is the text of that pamphlet as it was published. An asterisk indicates a page break.]

THE CELESTIAL MARRIAGE
or
THE DESCENT OF MAN

A FABLE
FROM
THE BOOK OF LIFE

*

GIVEN IN HUMILITY
TO ALL
HUMANITY

*

One day in great **ASPIRATION GOD** sent forth from itself **WILL**, and the sons of **WILL** became. Now the sons of **WILL** were of **GOD**, yea, they were **GODS** sent into form, but knew not because of form. The sons of **WILL** roamed the universes for eons and eons of time ever seeking other forms. After much searching they met to consider what they must do. For seven days and seven nights they discussed, and at the seventh hour **ILLUMINATION** fell upon them and said, "Behold, sons of **WILL**, within thyself is **COMPASSION**, know it, and unto thee shall be given." Alas, the sons of **WILL** knew **COMPASSION** and that night the daughters of **DESTINY** became.

In the morning when the daughters of **DESTINY** awoke to the sons of **WILL**, the **GODS** and **GODESSESS** of nature danced in jubilee.

Now the sons of **WILL** married the daughters of **DESTINY** and all nature wept with joy.

One day in **TRUTH** a son was born, his name was **INEVITABLE**, and the sons of **WILL** were greatly pleased. Now the daughters of **DESTINY** were quite unhappy for they **HOPED** for a daughter, and so that night in **DESIRE** a girl was born, her name was **LUST**.

Now **INEVITABLE** grew in the warmth and sunshine of the day. Oh how he loved the sun, for to him all **LIFE** was **LIGHT**.

LUST grew up to be a beautiful and lovely woman with a great fondness for the moon and darkness, for had she not been born in the night of **DESIRE**.

Time passed on, and one day **INEVITABLE** felt he would go into the night to find **LUST**, for he had heard so much about her, and had sent her many messages asking her to come into the **LIGHT** so that they may know more of each other. **INEVITABLE** went down, down into the darkness of night, and as he descended a great **FEAR** overcame him, but he found **LUST**, her face glowing so beautiful by the reflection of the sun. From the shadows where the **LIGHT** of the moon shone not, a voice spoke unto **INEVITABLE** and said, "Behold the beauty and the glory thou hast found, is it not worth the descent into our realms?" But from within, a voice spoke to **INEVITABLE** and said, "Take her to the realms of **LIGHT** that you may see more clearly in a day of **REASON**."

The senses won, and that night in **DESPAIR** a child was born, her name was **GRIEF**. The years passed and **GRIEF** could not be comforted, for she had been born of **LUST**, in the night of **DESIRE**, by the promptings of **PASSION**, and knew not of **TRUTH**.

INEVITABLE wandered on and on with the daughter **GRIEF**, hoping to return to the realms of **LIGHT**, but no, the centuries passed and only **SORROW** did they know.

Then one day a bird from the realms of **LIGHT** landed on his shoulder and sang this song, "In **SORROW** doth thou stay for self-pity knows no way."

INEVITABLE thought and thought of the meaning of those words, then he thought of his homeland **TRUTH** where he had been so very, very happy; and in **CONCENTRATION**, he found himself leaving the realms of darkness, passing through the lands of **IGNORANCE** and **EXPERIENCE** to return to his blessed land.

LOVE ALL LIFE
AND KNOW
THE LIGHT

*

OH MAN THINK HUMBLE
YET WELL OF THYSELF
FOR IN THY THINKING
IS CREATED
THE VEHICLE OF
THE SOUL

www.ingramcontent.com/pod-product-compliance
Lightning Source LLC
Chambersburg PA
CBHW030144100526
44592CB00009B/106